Tracing the Modern:
Selections from the Tel Aviv Museum of Art, 1880–1989

Tracing the Modern

Selections from the Tel Aviv Museum of Art, 1880–1989

Edited by Hillary Reder

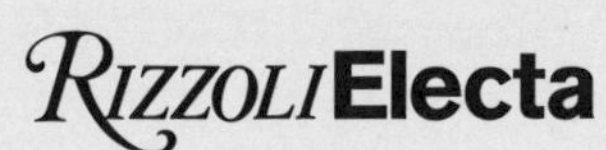

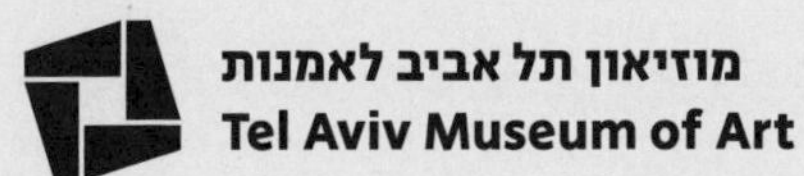

Overleaf
Henry Moore's *Reclining Figure* (1969–70) in the museum plaza, in front of the Main Building, c. 1971. Archive of the Tel Aviv Museum of Art

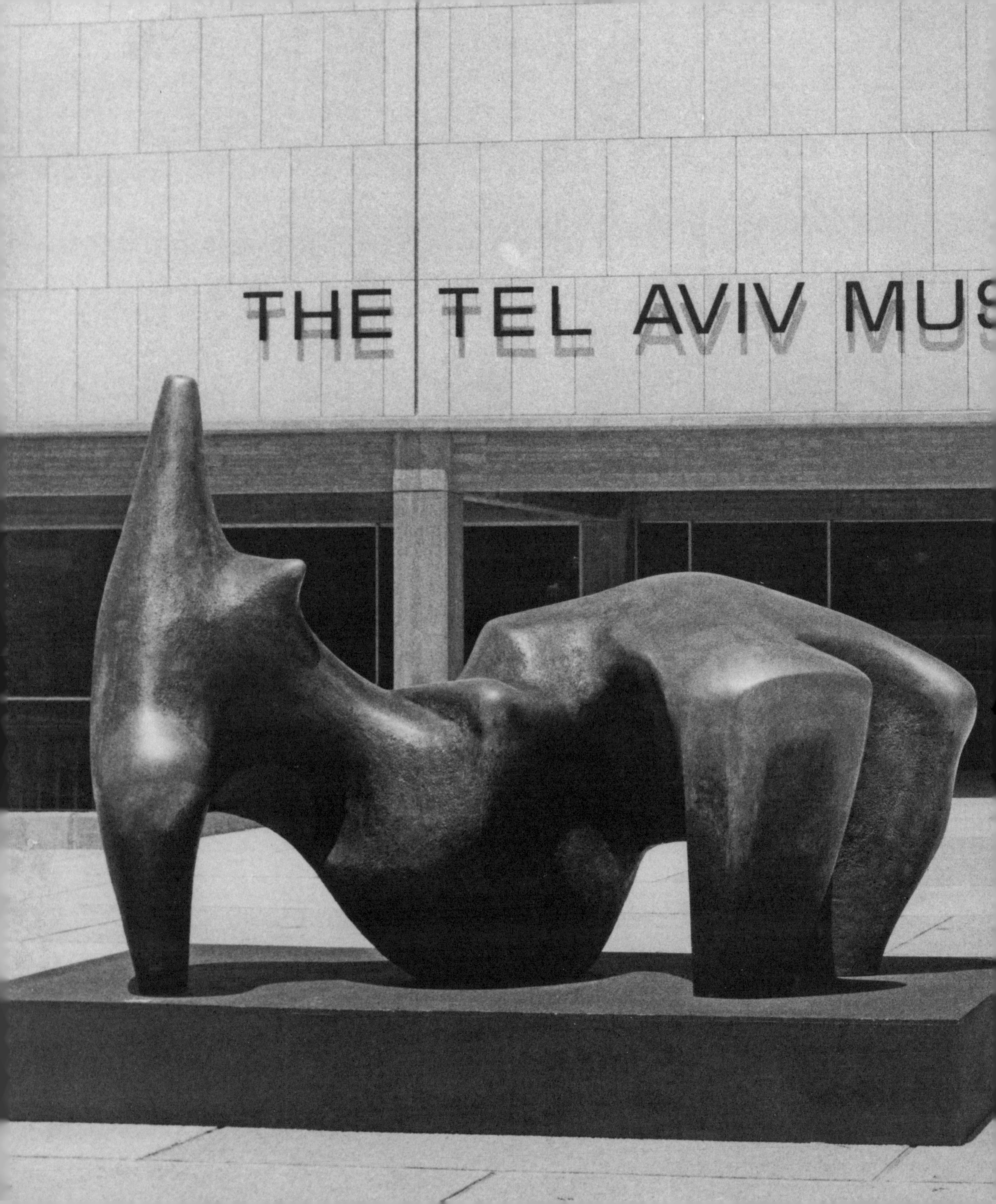

THE TEL AVIV MUS

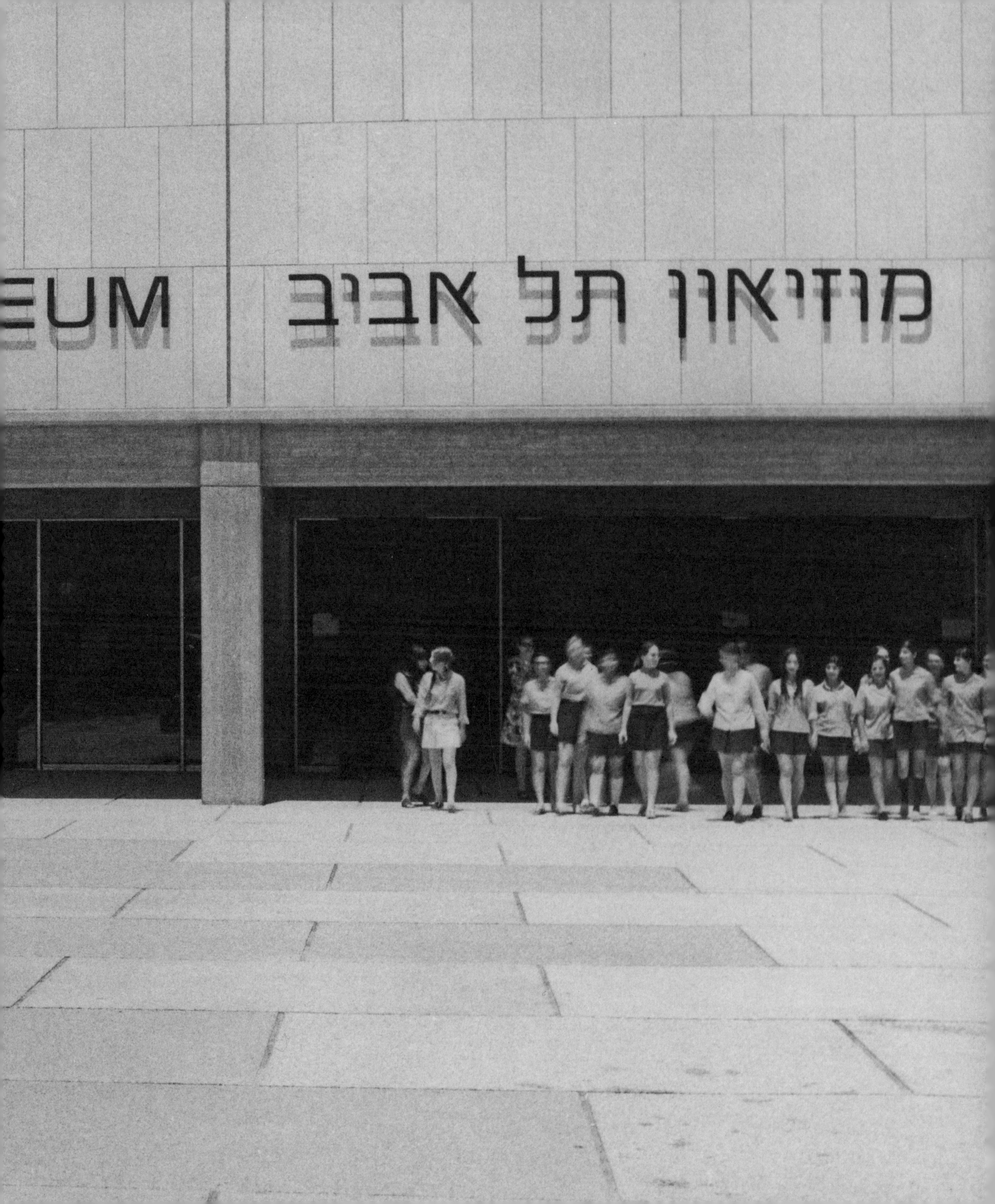

מוזיאון תל אביב

Sponsor's Greeting

John Paulson
President, Paulson Family Foundation

In the center of Tel Aviv stands a beautifully designed museum on spacious grounds, the Tel Aviv Museum of Art. Although I had visited Israel many times since 1968, I had never been to this gem of a museum until 2019. It was upon the insistence of my good friend, art dealer Nathan Bernstein, that I visited for the first time.

The experience was exhilarating. From the monumental Lichtenstein mural greeting you in the foyer, to the continuous unveiling of one masterpiece after another in the upstairs galleries, the Tel Aviv Museum of Art is a treasure trove: Renoir, Cézanne, Van Gogh, Gauguin, Kandinsky, Archipenko, Klimt, Modigliani, Monet, Picasso, Matisse, Chagall, O'Keeffe, Dalí, Ernst, Pollock, Miró, Rothko, Giacometti, Dubuffet, Bacon, Richter, Moore, Calder. They are all here.

The collection was amassed over the past ninety years through the generosity of pioneering artists and collectors—such as Marc Chagall and Peggy Guggenheim—as well as works saved from the Nazis by European collectors and dealers through the efforts of Karl Schwarz, who left Germany in 1933 to serve as the Museum's first director and chief curator. I was so moved by the Museum and its history that after my visit I became a principal benefactor.

If you haven't been to the Tel Aviv Museum of Art, we hope that you will visit one day to see the collection in person. In the meantime, please enjoy the art by perusing these pages. If you are already a visitor, this book will remind you of the wonderful art you have previously seen.

There are many people to thank for making this book possible. First to my curator Abigail Teller, who oversaw the production with Rizzoli, to Tania Coen-Uzzielli for her committed leadership of the Museum, to curators Mira Lapidot, Noa Rosenberg, and Hillary Reder for their stewardship of this project, and to Jenna Schneider from the Tel Aviv Museum of Art American Friends. Lastly to Nathan Bernstein and his dear wife Katharina Otto-Bernstein, for introducing me to this exceptional institution.

Foreword

Tania Coen-Uzzielli
Director, Tel Aviv Museum of Art

The story of any museum's collection is often best told from credit lines. The Tel Aviv Museum of Art is no exception, and yet, when examining the credit lines of its modern art collection—which comprises painting and sculpture spanning the 1860s to the 1980s—one unusual fact arises, given its considerable scope and quality: the word "acquisition" seldom appears. Rather, the collection consists almost exclusively of donations, which in many cases were made as whole collections. In this sense, TAMA's holdings of modern art—to which this book is dedicated—may be characterized as "a collection of collections." Countless donors have made outstanding contributions. In what follows, I will highlight just a few whose gifts have most influenced the character of TAMA's collection.

The first substantial gift came from German-Jewish art historian Karl Schwarz, who immigrated to Mandatory Palestine in 1933 to become the Museum's first director, a year after it was founded by Tel Aviv's first mayor, Meir Dizengoff. Schwarz had been the founding director of Berlin's Jewish Museum, which opened in 1933—yet just six days after its opening, Hitler seized power. Months later, Schwarz left Germany permanently for Tel Aviv, taking Dizengoff up on his invitation to head the new museum. Schwarz brought a collection of 1,300 works on paper by contemporary German artists with him and, deploying his substantial connections in Europe, began to build up a world-class collection of modern art. Much of the work brought to Tel Aviv in these years was likely saved from seizure or destruction during the Nazi purges of "degenerate" art. Most significantly during Schwarz's tenure, Erich Goeritz, a German-Jewish textile manufacturer with an exceptional collection of German and French modern art, sent over 500 of his works to Tel Aviv from Germany for safekeeping during the war. These works entered TAMA's permanent collection in 1955—bestowing the Museum with the most important group of early Alexander Archipenko works in the world.

Schwarz remained director until 1947, just missing the declaration of the State of Israel in 1948, which was held in the Museum's first building on Rothschild Boulevard—the country's first Prime Minister, David Ben-Gurion, signed the declaration surrounded by artworks that Schwarz collected. His vision of the Museum as "a nurturing institution, from which education will emerge [...] a place where new ideas are given impetus" continued to guide the development of the collection over the next several decades.

Between the 1950s and 1970s, several remarkable women donors made important gifts to the Museum. Peggy Guggenheim, among the twentieth century's most influential collectors, dealers, and patrons of modern art, donated thirty-six works between 1954 and 1955, adding major examples of Surrealism and abstraction to the collection, including three Jackson Pollock paintings. This was the largest gift Guggenheim made to any museum besides the Solomon R. Guggenheim Museum in New York, founded by her uncle, and the only one outside the United States. She made the gift after meeting TAMA director Eugen Kolb, in Venice in 1952, when Kolb curated the Israeli pavilion at the Biennale. Kolb asked Guggenheim to lend works to the Museum, but instead, as a testament to their friendship, she sent the works as gifts. Thanking her in a letter, Kolb wrote, "Your gesture shows real understanding for the needs and troubles of our young institution to get our public acquainted with such important trends of this century's art." Also in 1955, New York philanthropist and arts patron Alma Morgenthau made a gift of twenty-four works by leading European modernists, including Giorgio Morandi and Alberto Giacometti. In 1956, art historian Rosa Schapire, a non-artist member of Brücke, donated forty German Expressionist works, including a unique collection of postcards illustrated and mailed to her by the artists of Brücke. Between 1968 and 1978, Manka (Marya) Rubinstein, sister of cosmetics magnate Helena Rubinstein—herself an important supporter of the Museum—donated several masterpieces, including a large-scale Leonora Carrington painting.

In the 1980s and 1990s, several notable collections arrived at TAMA that continue to shape the narrative of modernism in the Museum's galleries today. The Moshe and Sara Mayer Collection, on long-term loan since 1982, contains masterpieces that illustrate key developments of early modernism, from Impressionism to the School of Paris, and includes singular works by Edgar Degas, Berthe Morisot, and Vincent van Gogh. The Mizne-Blumental Collection, on view at the Museum since 1993, before becoming a permanent gift in 2018, is a wonderfully eclectic compilation of twentieth-century art, including iconic works by Wassily Kandinsky, Gustav Klimt, Pablo Picasso, and Kees van Dongen. The Simon and Marie Jaglom Collection, on long-term loan since 1994, focuses on Impressionism, Post-Impressionism, and the School of Paris, including major works by artists such as Claude Monet, Amedeo Modigliani, and Chaim Soutine. The Susan and Anton Roland-Rosenberg Collection, which focuses on postwar European and American Art, entered the collection in 1996, allowing the Museum to present masterpieces by Francis Bacon, Georgia O'Keeffe, and others.

Between the late 1980s and early 2000s, both the Department of Prints and Drawings and the Department of Photography received major gifts, amplifying the Museum's representation of modern art across mediums, and in some cases, creating new areas of strength and excellence. In 1987, Abraham Horodisch, a German print publisher, bequeathed a collection of over 3,000 prints that greatly enhanced the Museum's holdings of German Expressionist works on paper. In 1996, New York collectors Charles and Evelyn Kramer gifted nearly 150 etchings, lithographs, and woodcuts by Edvard Munch, which together offer a nearly complete representation of the artist's print oeuvre. Over the last thirty years, Michael S. Sachs of Westport, Connecticut, gifted a transformative selection of 700 prints that span the history of photography, including those by Eugène Atget, Aleksandr Rodchenko, Edward Weston, and many others.

Together, each of these collections suggests a unique perspective on modernism, bestowing TAMA's galleries with an intimate sense of the personalities that assembled them. The collection's notable strengths in Impressionism, German Expressionism, and the School of Paris artists—many of whom were Jewish immigrants from Eastern Europe, including Marc Chagall, Chana Orloff, Jacques Lipchitz, and Moïse Kisling—reflect the shared taste of the Jewish collectors, primarily from North America, Europe, and Israel, who supported the creation of TAMA's collection over the past century.

My first and deepest thank goes to John Paulson, who not only made it possible to publish this book but planted the earliest seeds for it. Impressed and perhaps surprised after visiting the modern art galleries at TAMA for the first time, he proposed creating a book of the collection. We are humbled by his utmost dedication to the Museum. Thanks also to Abigail Teller, Director of Fine Art, Paulson & Co., and to Katharina Otto-Bernstein and Nathan Bernstein.

Hillary Reder, Assistant Curator of Modern Art, oversaw all aspects of this book since its conception, and I thank her for her dedication and enthusiasm. I would like to acknowledge Mira Lapidot, Chief Curator, for her wisdom and guidance as always, and for her vital role in shaping this publication, and Noa Rosenberg, Head and Curator of Modern Art, for her support of this project. Levi Prombaum stepped in at a critical moment, and I am grateful for his impactful work.

I would like to thank our writers—from TAMA, Israel, and abroad—for their insightful texts that expand our understanding of and reverence for the collection. I am grateful to Orna Yehudaioff for her edits to the Hebrew texts, and to Daria Kassovsky for her sensitive English editing and translation. Sincere thanks to Yaffa Goldfinger for expertly handling image permissions, and to Margarita Perlin, Yigal Pardo, and Elad Sarig for their beautiful photography. Lior Misano, International Relations and Resource Development, helped to move the project forward at key junctures. I am grateful to Jenna Schneider, Executive Director, TAMAF, for her essential support. At Rizzoli, I would like to thank Ellen Cohen, Senior Editor, who made every aspect of putting this book together a pleasure, along with her whole team, particularly copy editors Stephanie Cash and Anya Szykitka. Special thanks to Jesse Kidwell for his beautiful and thoughtful design that brings our collection to life.

Editor's Note

Hillary Reder

From the beginning, forming a collection of modern art was central to the Tel Aviv Museum's program. Meir Dizengoff, Tel Aviv's first mayor and founder of the Museum, envisioned a collection divided into three categories: modern art, with works by Jewish artists made between the eighteenth and twentieth centuries; casts and reproductions of major works throughout art history related to the Hebrew Bible; and ethnographic artifacts gathered from Jewish groups around the world.[1] In the early 1930s, he approached several artists for guidance in developing the nascent institution's mission, including Marc Chagall, who sailed to Tel Aviv to meet with Dizengoff in 1931. Chagall disapproved of the didactic aspect of Dizengoff's plan, and instead advocated for a collection that would focus on recent art by Jewish artists, believing that "a new Hebrew city should exhibit new Hebrew art."[2]

After the Museum opened in 1932, founding director Karl Schwarz began assembling a collection that not only fulfilled Chagall's call for collecting modern Jewish art—a topic in which he was an expert—but also included modern art more broadly, as well as works by local artists. Arriving from the climactic years of Weimar Berlin, he hoped to elevate Tel Aviv into a similarly cosmopolitan, open city. By building a collection that represented key avant-garde developments throughout Europe, he sought to initiate dialogues between Tel Aviv and other centers of culture, bringing the world to Israel, and to support the establishment of a thriving cultural scene thoroughly embedded in international networks.

This publication surveys modern art at TAMA today, after nearly a century of collecting. Most of the featured works are paintings, intermixed with sculpture, prints, drawings, and photography—a rare opportunity to consider the Museum's modern holdings across mediums, beyond departmental borders.[3] The works span the years 1880 to 1989 and are made primarily by American and European artists. This stems from the original idea of Dizengoff and Schwarz to focus on modern Jewish art—which meant that from the Museum's founding years, a strong core of works represented late nineteenth- and early twentieth-century developments in France and Germany, countries with significant Jewish populations. As this initial focus gave way to Schwarz's more encompassing vision—which has remained a guidepost for subsequent directors and generous donors, a history of which is outlined in Tania Coen-Uzzielli's Foreword—the collection has preserved its westward orientation. The movements spotlighted in the following pages represent the collection's strengths: Impressionism, Post-Impressionism, the School of Paris, German Expressionism, Surrealism, and European and American postwar art.

The plates proceed loosely by year, with deviations allowing for groupings or sequences to emerge, interweaving chronology with visual delight. When the collection represents an artist in considerable depth, multiple examples of their work are included: in the case of Pablo Picasso, four works made from 1921 to 1953 are shown in adjacent spreads. Artists associated with a particular group often appear together, though when a given work is too far removed stylistically or chronologically, it may be shown among other related works, perhaps giving rise to an unexpected context or correspondence. Some transitions between works stem from purely formal considerations—an Antoine Pevsner Constructivist painting with a spiral form gives way to an Edward Weston photo of a snail shell. Such chance encounters surfaced from ordering and reordering these works over the years in which this book was assembled, inspiring novel perspectives on familiar works.

The nearly sixty catalogue authors are TAMA curators, as well as curators and art historians from Israeli and international museums and universities. Some are intimately familiar with the collection and its changing displays over the years, and in many cases, the works they've written about are "old friends." Other authors had little familiarity with TAMA, applying their fields of expertise to the works, perhaps without having been previously aware of the specific examples or their provenance. Representing a wide variety of specializations and art historical approaches, the authors sought above all to focus on the object at hand. Together, the texts amount to a versatile guide to the Tel Aviv Museum of Art's collection of modern art, offering directions for new research and fresh insights, and renewing our appreciation and wonder.

1 For more about the Museum's early history, see Batsheva Goldman-Ida, "The Child of My Delight: From House to Museum," in *Five Moments: Trajectories in the Architecture of the Tel Aviv Museum* (Tel Aviv: Tel Aviv Museum of Art, 2011), E25–E34.

2 Letter from Chagall to Dizengoff, January 1930, Tel Aviv Museum of Art Archives [Russian; English translation by Benjamin Harshav], *Marc Chagall and His Times: A Documentary Narrative* (Stanford, CA: Stanford University Press, 2004), 369.

3 The Modern Art Department consists mainly of painting and sculpture. Other works in this publication are housed in the Prints and Drawings Department and the Photography Department.

Plates

Pierre-Auguste Renoir
1841, Limoges, France–1919, Cagnes-sur-Mer, France
Nude Seen from the Back, 1880–81
Oil on canvas, 31 ⅞ × 26 in. (81 × 66 cm)

Bequest of Wilhelm Weinberg, Amsterdam-Scarsdale, New York
In memory of his wife and children, 1958

In the 1860s, Pierre-Auguste Renoir, along with a growing number of artists, began painting en plein air, depicting his perception of the effects of light on his surroundings. By the 1870s, he was among the leading figures associated with Impressionism, and he participated in the group's first three exhibitions. He subsequently developed an independent path, and from the 1880s mainly painted young women, mothers, and children—bathing, breastfeeding, or reading. His affinity for depicting women stemmed in part from his regard for the paintings of seventeenth-century artist Peter Paul Rubens and eighteenth-century Rococo artists, which he copied in his youth.

In this painting, a nude woman gazes out at a landscape—or even seems to approach it. Her body fills the entire length of the canvas—from her loosely gathered red hair to her bare buttocks. Fast, free brushstrokes—more typical of Renoir's earlier Impressionist style—describe the green landscape, which appears executed in thinned-out paint, while gentle, caressing, and thicker brushstrokes portray the woman's body, in keeping with Renoir's mature style. His decision to combine purple and green in the skin tones drew mixed responses at the time, including a famous 1876 review in *Le Figaro*, which called on the artist to distinguish between a woman's torso and "a mass of decomposing flesh."[1]

The painting, from the estate of art collector Wilhelm Weinberg, was one of only two paintings not included in the major sale of his art collection at Sotheby's London in 1957. Weinberg, an American banker and philanthropist of Dutch heritage who lost his family in the Holocaust, kept these paintings out of the sale, deciding to donate this Renoir to the Tel Aviv Museum and a painting by Toulouse-Lautrec to the Kröller-Müller Museum in the Netherlands in their memory.

Nathalie Andrijasevic

1 Albert Wolff's review was written after his visit to the second Impressionist exhibition, where he saw Renoir's *Etude. Torse, effet de soleil* (c. 1876).

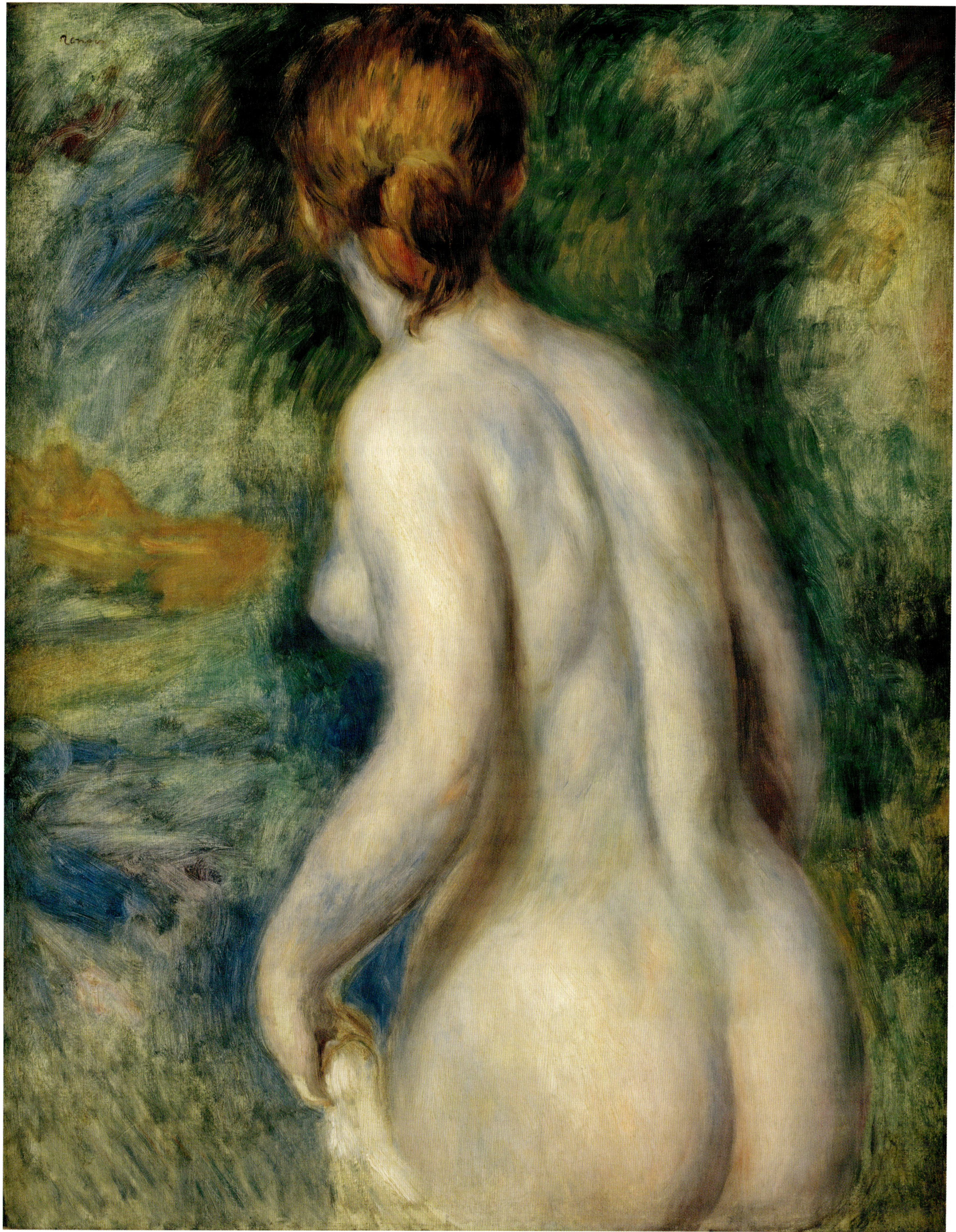

Pierre-Auguste Renoir
1841, Limoges, France–1919, Cagnes-sur-Mer, France
Portrait of Misia Sert, 1904
Oil on canvas, 21 ¾ × 18 ¼ in. (55.5 × 46.5 cm)

Bequest of Dr. Herman Lorber, New York, 1961

Misia Godebska was born in St. Petersburg in 1872 and died in Paris in 1950. In 1893, in Paris, she married Thadée Natanson, the founder and editor of *La Revue Blanche*—an avant-garde periodical devoted to literature and art. Her connection with Natanson, her personal charm, and her musical talent distinguished her as a prominent figure in the Parisian art world. She was admired and celebrated by musicians, poets, and painters who immortalized her in their works. Pierre Bonnard (pp. 56–57), Edouard Vuillard (pp. 58–59), and Henri de Toulouse-Lautrec all painted her; Maurice Ravel and Igor Stravinsky dedicated musical pieces to her; Marcel Proust, Stéphane Mallarmé, and Jean Cocteau mentioned her in their writings. She was a highly influential friend of Sergei Diaghilev and a patron of the Ballets Russes, and also contributed to the success of Coco Chanel. In 1903, she left Natanson and married Alfred Edwards, publisher of the newspaper *Le Matin*, and in 1920 she married her third husband, the Spanish mural painter José Maria Sert.

In her memoir, Misia wrote that Renoir painted six or seven portraits of her, although today only three are known, including this one. Her choice to commission Renoir is an indication of his high status as a portrait painter at that time and attests to the existence of a young generation of collectors who appreciated the artist's late style, characterized by a more fluid and thin paint application than his earlier works more aligned with classic Impressionism. Here, he shows Misia sitting on a sofa, absorbed in her reading. Renoir made this painting when he was confined to a wheelchair due to arthritis. He came to Misia's home three times a week accompanied by his niece Gabrielle—one of his favorite models—who would tie the paintbrush to his hand to allow him to paint with more ease.

Dorit Yifat

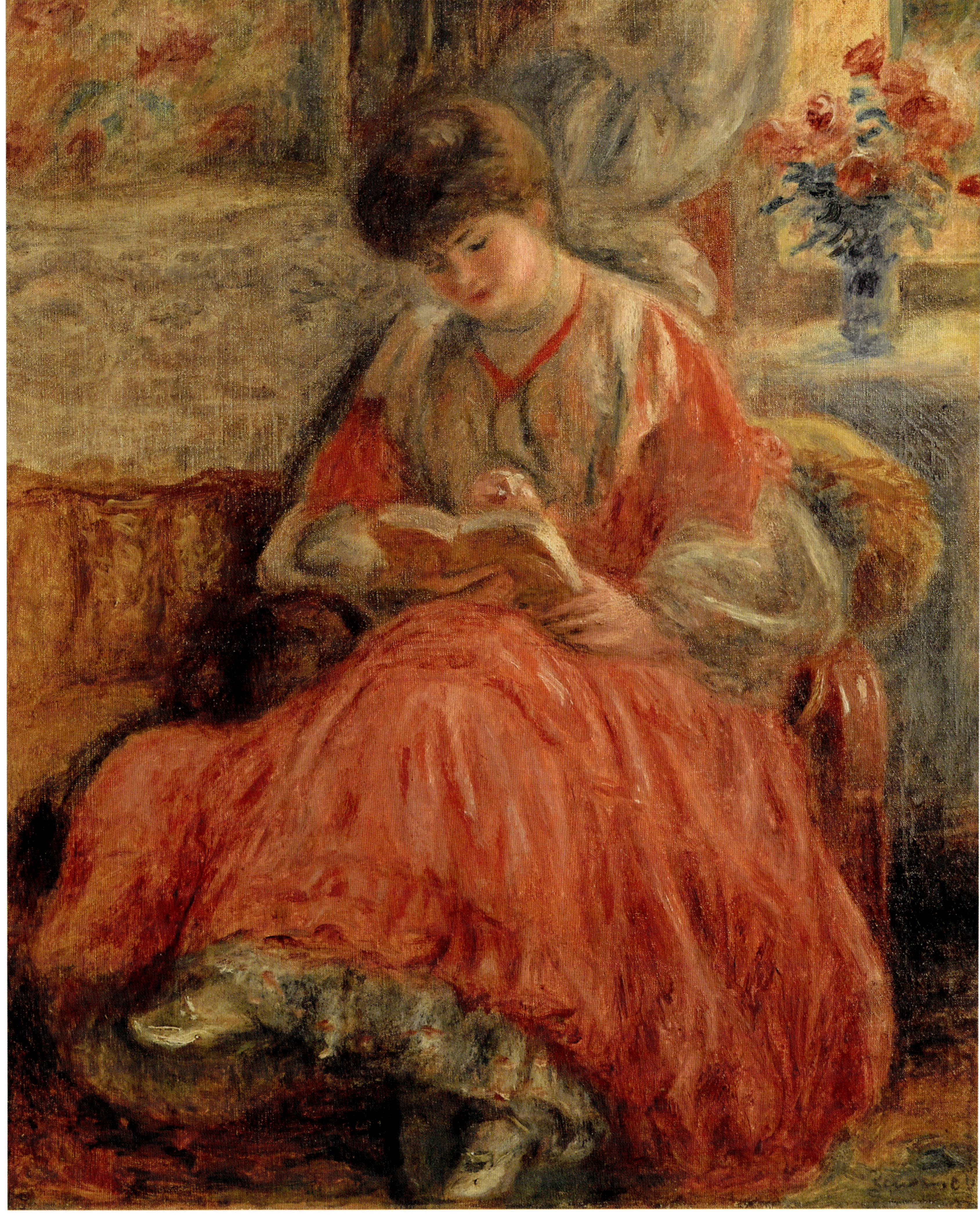

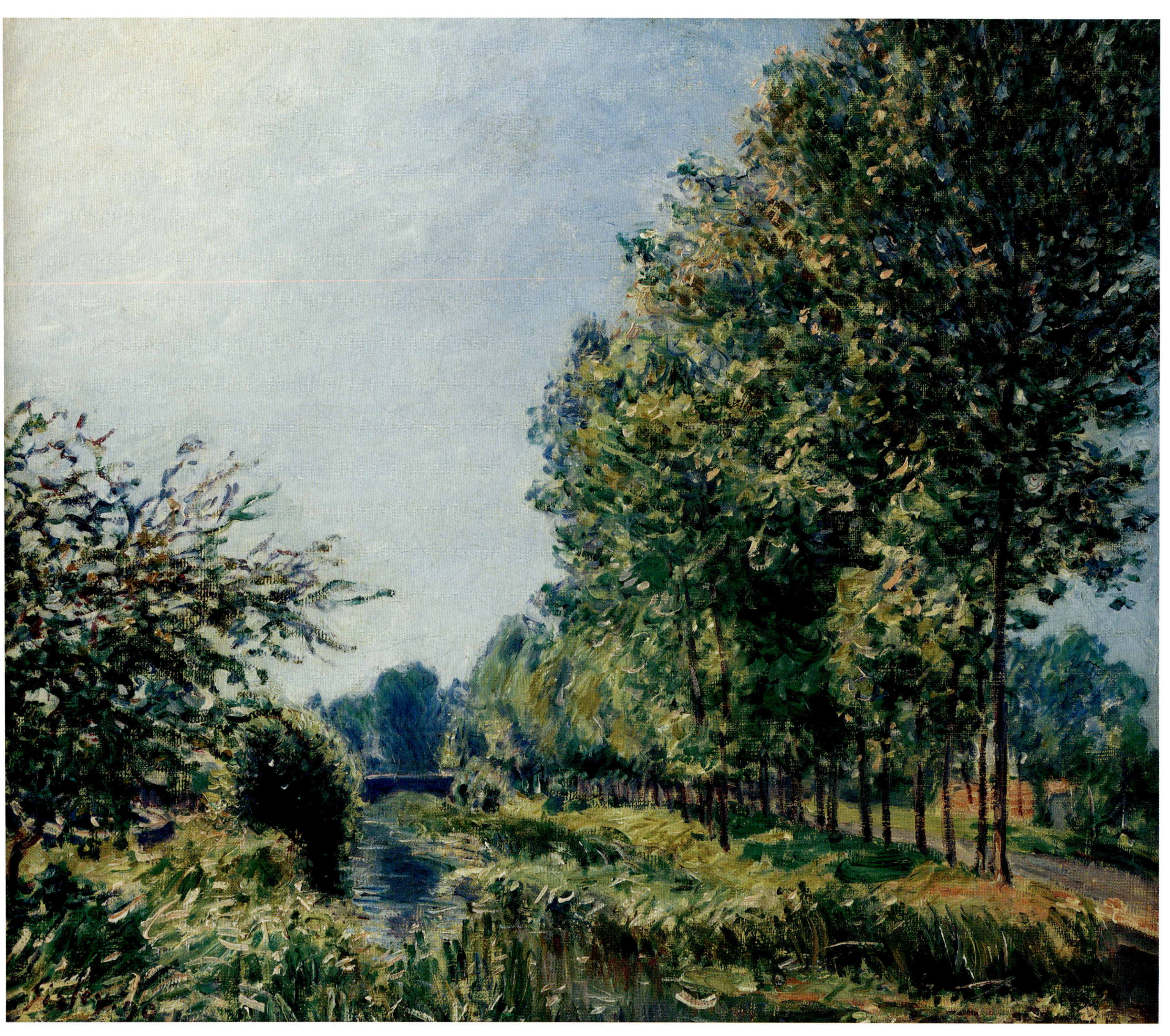

Alfred Sisley
1839, Paris, France–1899, Moret-sur-Loing, France
The Banks of the Orvanne–Morning Effect, 1890
Oil on canvas, 18 ½ × 22 in. (47 × 56 cm)

On long-term loan from the Simon and Marie Jaglom Collection

The Orvanne is a stream feeding into the Loing river near the town of Moret, in the district of Fontainebleau. Alfred Sisley painted the Orvanne twice in the early 1880s and eight more times in the 1890s. The titles of these works often specify the time of day, the month, or the season in which they were painted. In this painting, the composition conveys an illusion of space and distance. Low vegetation bordering the stream fills the foreground, while a row of tall poplars lines the right bank of the river. More vegetation appears beyond the trees, which, painted in an unidentifiable blur, recedes into the background. The composition's dramatic perspective is emphasized by the diagonal lines of the riverbank and of the path running parallel to it along the row of poplars. The sky, which occupies a large portion of the composition, plays a central role. Often a prominent feature of his landscapes, he once wrote "...the sky is never a mere background," as it gives "the picture depth in its successive planes (the sky, just like earth, has planes)..."[1]

Sisley likely painted this scene in the early morning hours, facing eastward, with the sun shining on his left. The strong sunlight is expressed in his choice of tones: the sky is painted in white and pale blue; the leaves of the poplars, facing the river and more exposed to the sun, are rendered in warmer tones of light orange, beige, and wine-red; and the lower vegetation, flooded in sunlight, is partly painted in a rich variety of yellows. The surface of the canvas is composed of areas of thinly applied paint and more thickly painted sections. Discussing the varied texture of his works of the 1890s, Sisley noted that the surface of the painting should reflect the play of light in nature: "I am in favor of a variety of surfaces in the same picture...because when the sun lets certain parts of a landscape seem soft, it brings others into high relief..."[2]

Sisley derived inspiration for *The Banks of the Orvanne–Morning Effect* from seventeenth-century Dutch painter Meindert Hobbema's *Avenue at Middelharnis* (1689), which likewise features a road that passes through field and trees and gradually disappears into the horizon.[3] Sisley saw this painting while living in London, in the years 1858–62, when he frequently visited the National Gallery.

Olga Cohen

1 Iain Gale, *Sisley* (London: Studio Editions, 1992), 37.
2 Gale, *Sisley*, 37.
3 Gale, 25.

Berthe Morisot
1841, Bourges, France–1895, Paris, France
On the Island, 1880
Oil on canvas, 18 ⅛ × 21 ⅝ in. (46 × 55 cm)

On long-term loan from the Moshe and Sara Mayer Collection

On the Island is one of a series of paintings by Berthe Morisot set in the Bois de Boulogne woodland, which bordered Passy, a suburb of Paris where she lived (now in the 16th arrondissement). The depicted female figure is seated and holds an umbrella, while the green background is rendered with quick, loose brushstrokes, creating a sense of swirling motion around her. The dynamic interplay between background and figure is one of Morisot's hallmarks. In her paintings, she reverses the figure-ground hierarchy prevalent in nineteenth-century academic painting: the background is no longer a secondary player but takes on a central role in the composition. Morisot was the sole woman who exhibited with the Impressionists from the movement's emergence in 1874—this painting debuted at the group's sixth exhibition in 1881.[1] Unlike fellow Impressionists, however, she was not concerned with purely external impressions, but also sought to portray the inner world of her primarily female subjects, often expressing stormy emotion and defiant self-possession with erupting lines and color-saturated brushstrokes.

In her groundbreaking 1971 essay "Why Have There Been No Great Women Artists?," American art historian Linda Nochlin argued that nineteenth-century women had no chance of succeeding as artists because they were not allowed to study in art academies, participate in life drawing classes, or sit in cafes and exchange ideas with intellectuals. Morisot succeeded against all odds. Born into a wealthy family, she studied painting privately with Jean-Baptiste Camille Corot, one of the most influential artists of the time. Due to her family lineage, she was also able to spend time with Édouard Manet's family, and thus became acquainted with key figures in Paris's art and literary milieu. Thanks to the financial and emotional support of her parents (and later her husband, Manet's brother, Eugène), Morisot persisted in painting and developed a career as an artist. From the 1870s, a change was evident in her paintings, which resulted from her involvement in the Impressionist movement.

Morisot was one of the few women in the nineteenth century who was able to practice art and gain professional appreciation and financial success without giving up family life. In her paintings, she often portrayed women and girls immersed in their inner worlds. In the painting *On the Island*, the female figure represents the lifestyle of bourgeois women in the Parisian suburbs. The lifeless floral decoration on her hat seems to collide with the erupting inflorescence in full bloom all around.

Shua Ben-Ari

1 When this work was first shown, it was titled *Étude de Plein-Air* (*Study in the Open Air*).

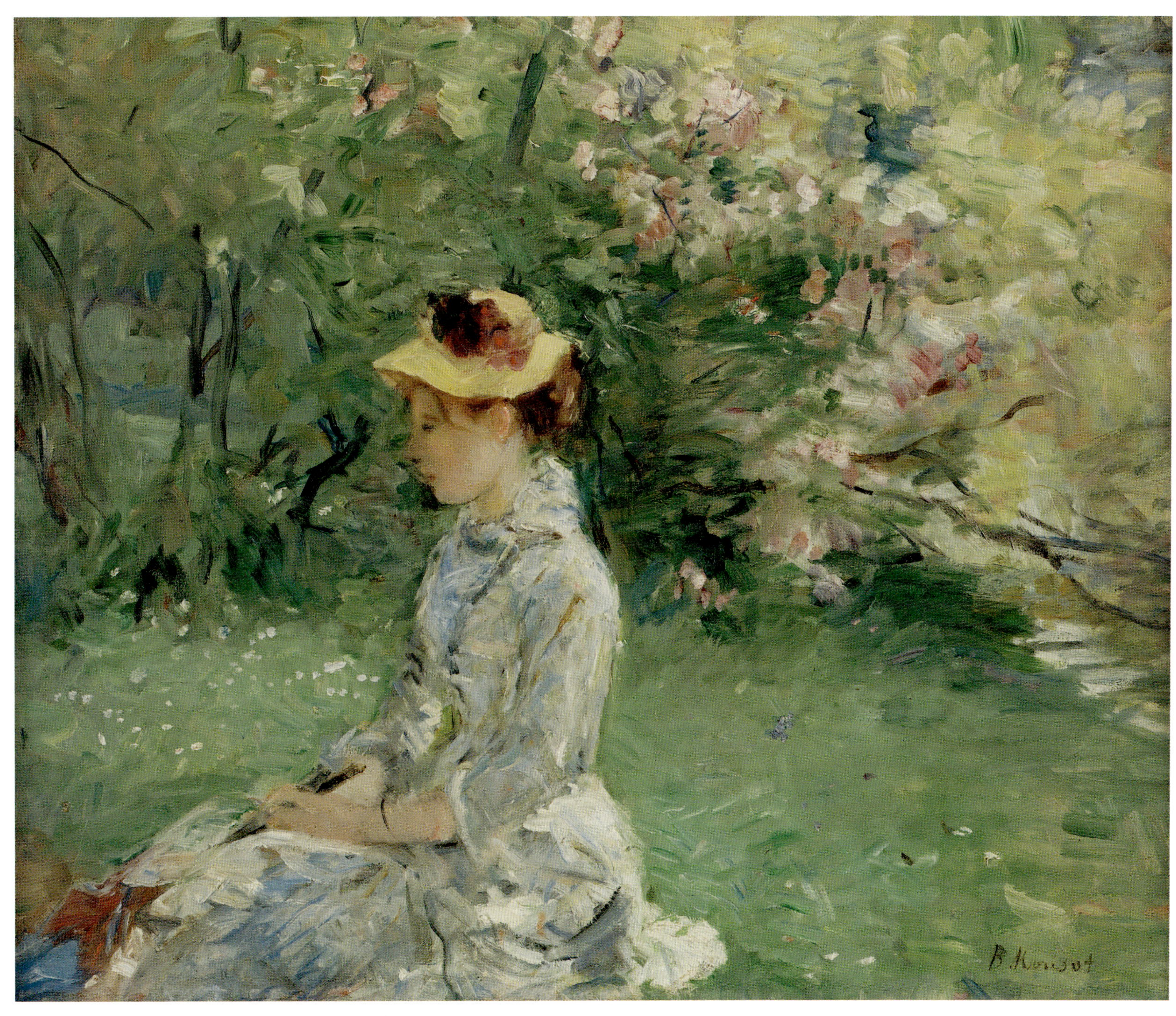
B. Morisot

Claude Monet
1840, Paris, France–1926, Giverny, France
Grainstack at Giverny, 1889
Oil on canvas, 25 9⁄16 × 32 1⁄16 in. (65 × 81.5 cm)

Anonymous gift, 1973

Page 24 *Apple Trees in Bloom*, 1900
Oil on canvas, 35 3⁄16 × 16 1⁄2 in. (89.5 × 92.7 cm)

On long-term loan from the Simon and Marie Jaglom Collection

Page 25 *Water Lily Pond*, 1919
Oil on canvas, 39 3⁄8 × 36 3⁄16 in. (100 × 92 cm)

On long-term loan from the Moshe and Sara Mayer Collection

Claude Monet was both a key figure in the Impressionist movement and arguably its most consistent practitioner. Throughout his long career, he made the constantly changing qualities of natural light and color the defining theme of his art, and strove to capture the very act of perceiving nature on canvas.

Monet's interest in recording perceptual processes reached its height in the series of paintings from the late 1880s and the 1890s—including grainstacks, poplars, and Rouen Cathedral, among others. In each series, Monet painted the same site time and again from slightly different viewpoints, recording how its appearance changed with the time of day and across seasons and weather conditions. In his quest to capture what he called "instantaneous" moments accurately and objectively, Monet worked on several canvases simultaneously, and moved from one to the next as the light changed. Although he painted outdoors, he reworked and completed his canvases in the studio.

Grainstack at Giverny is one of a group of five paintings dating from 1888–89, focusing on stacks of hay-covered grain stalks that Monet spotted in the vicinity of his home. This series precedes a large one on the same theme that the artist would create two years later. The short, distinct, and texturally varied brushstrokes, typical of the Impressionist technique, blur outlines, eliminate details, and dematerialize forms, while the paint acquires an independent presence. This sketchlike style conveys a sense of spontaneity and effortlessness, masking the compositions' careful construction.

Ruth Feldmann

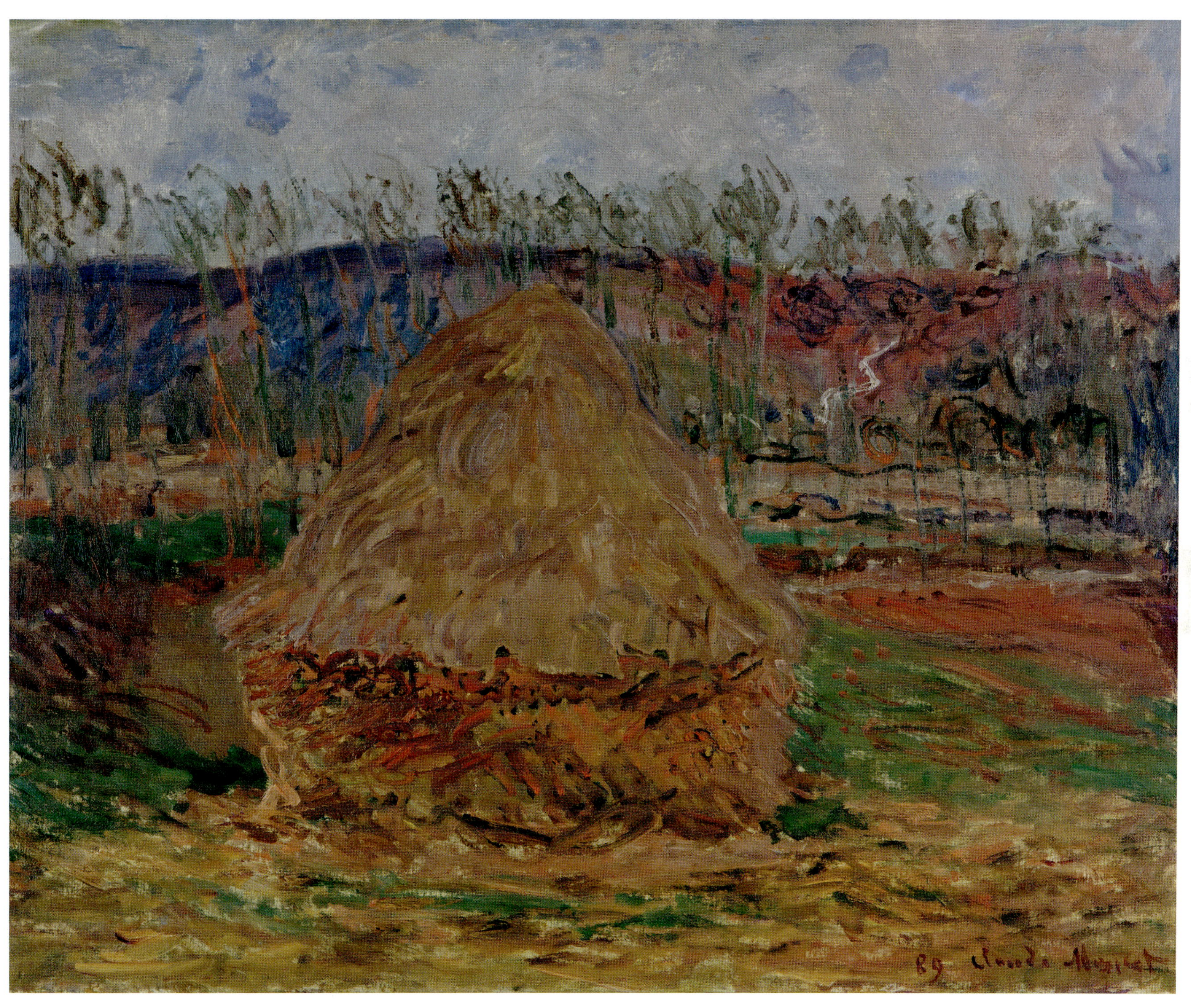
89 Claude Monet

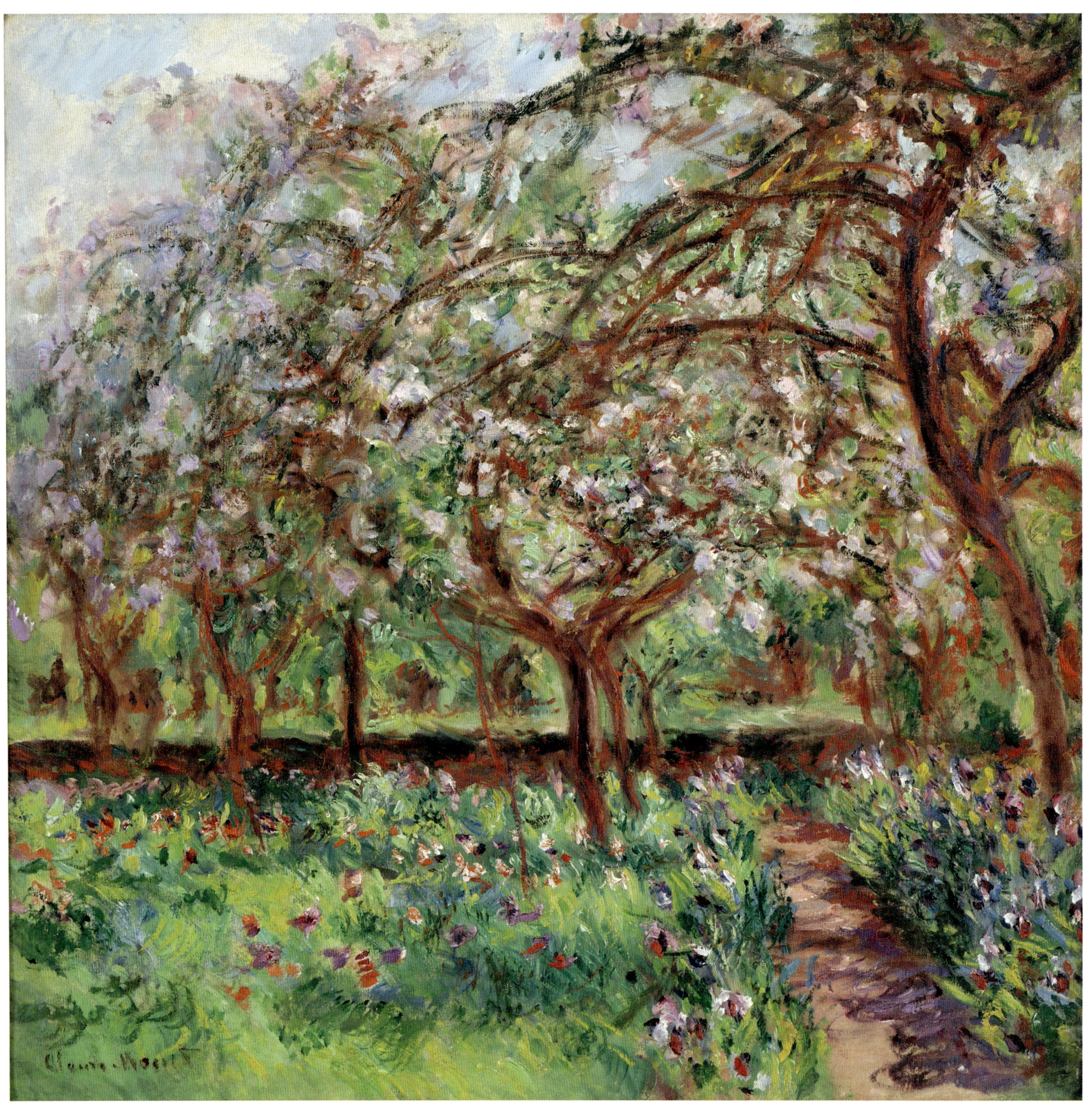

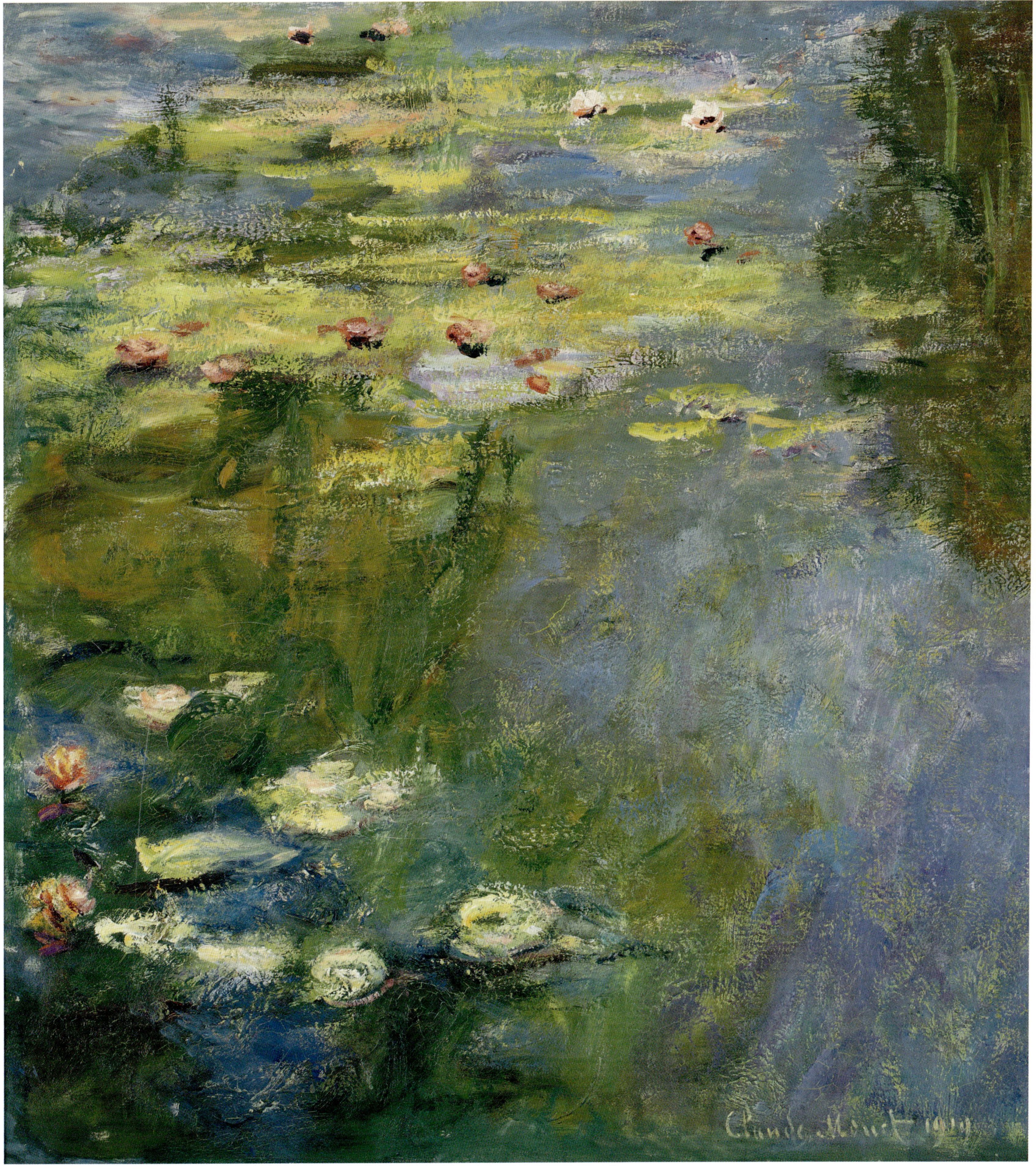
Claude Monet 1919

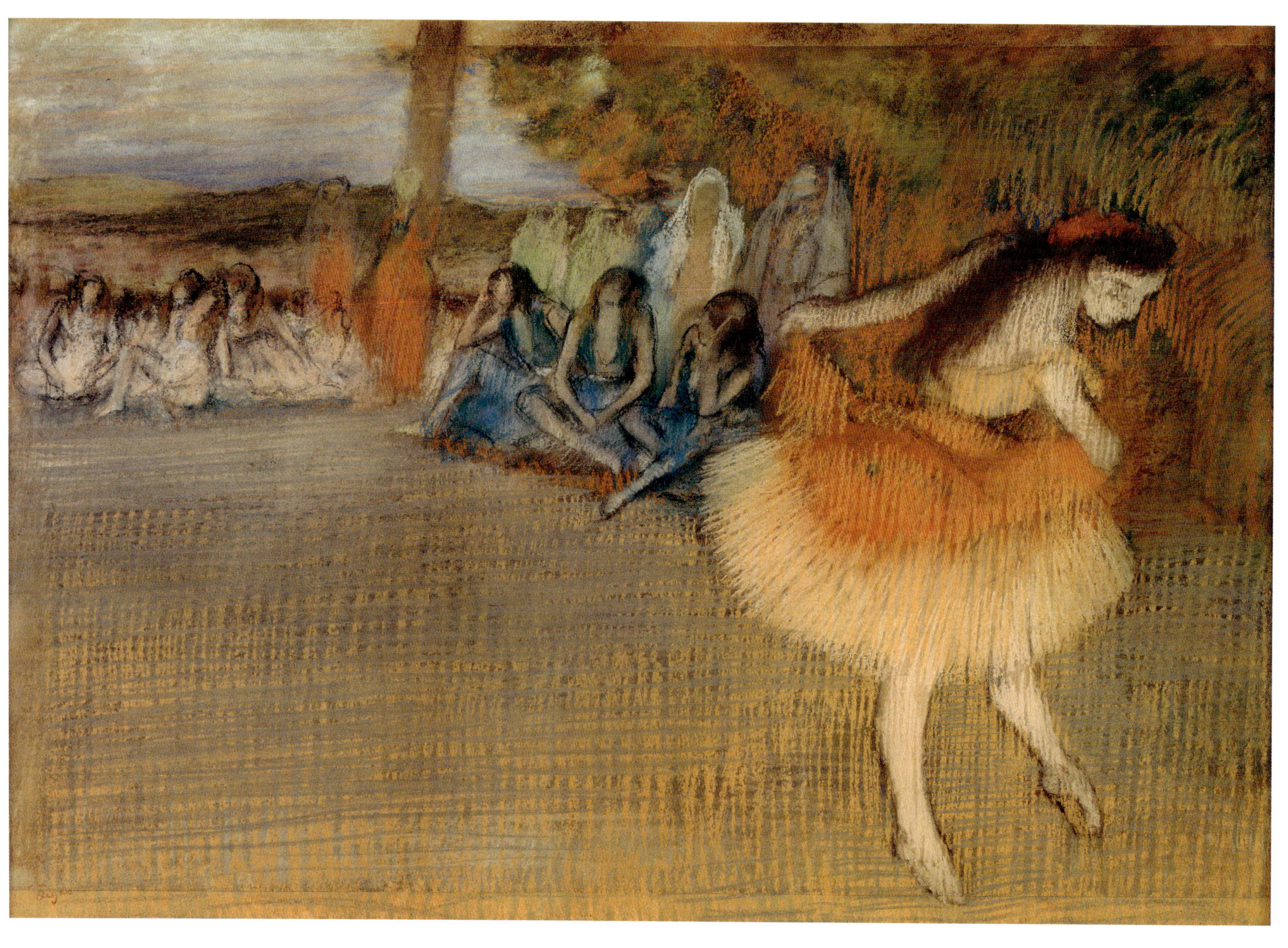

Edgar Degas
1834–1917, Paris, France
Ballet Scene, c. 1887–90
Pastel on paper, 25 9/16 × 37 in. (65 × 94 cm)

On long-term loan from the Moshe and Sara Mayer Collection

Page 28 *Dancer Looking at the Sole of her Right Foot*,
1896–1911 (cast 1919–21)
Bronze, 18 5/16 × 8 1/4 × 8 1/4 in. (46.5 × 21 × 21 cm)

Gift of the Goeritz Family, London, 1956. In memory of Erich Goeritz

Page 29 *Two Dancing Girls*, c. 1880
Charcoal and chalk pastel on paper,
21 5/8 × 26 3/4 in. (55 × 68 cm)

Bequest of Dr. Herman Lorber, New York, 1961

Edgar Degas often attended ballet performances at the Paris Opera, where he made rapid and cursory sketches of the dancers in action. Later in his studio, he executed more exacting and elaborate works based on memory, or from dancers who posed for him. Only rarely—as in *Ballet Scene*—did he record an actual stage performance. This pastel likely depicts a scene from the ballet *Namouna* (music by Édouard Lalo, premiered in Paris in 1882), in which a group of female slaves huddle under a tree on the island of Corfu.[1] This work is outstanding in Degas's production for its detailed representation of the scenery and the individual figures, which, in most of his works, are blurred or played down to the point of abstraction.

Both the asymmetrical composition, with the focus deflected to the side, and the floor, which is allotted a large area, are elements drawn from Japanese art, which exerted a strong influence on Degas, and lend the scene a sense of drama and dynamism. In the late 1880s and early 1890s, the technique of crosshatching of the type seen here in the floor section, and V-shaped strokes, like those delineating the dancer's tutu, became characteristic features of Degas's pastels. During this period, his palette also became more variegated, and he made extensive use of orange and turquoise. In his works on paper, Degas sometimes adapted the format to the demands of the composition by increasing the size of the support as he worked: in this pastel, two strips of paper were tacked on to the upper and lower edges of the sheet.

The ostensibly spontaneous appearance of the composition—which at first glance almost appears as a quick study capturing a moment in a live performance—is in fact the result of meticulous observation, planning, and execution. As Degas himself summarized: "No art is less spontaneous than my own; what I do is the result of reflection and study."[2]

Ruth Feldmann

1 Richard Kendall, in a letter to the author, March 1999, observed the similarity between this work and one of the sets for this production of *Namouna* in an archival photo. See also Jill DeVonyar and Richard Kendall, *Degas and the Dance* (New York: Harry N. Abrams, 2002), 183.

2 Degas, quoted in Theodore Reff, introduction to *Edgar Degas* (New York: Acquavella Galleries, 1978), n.p.

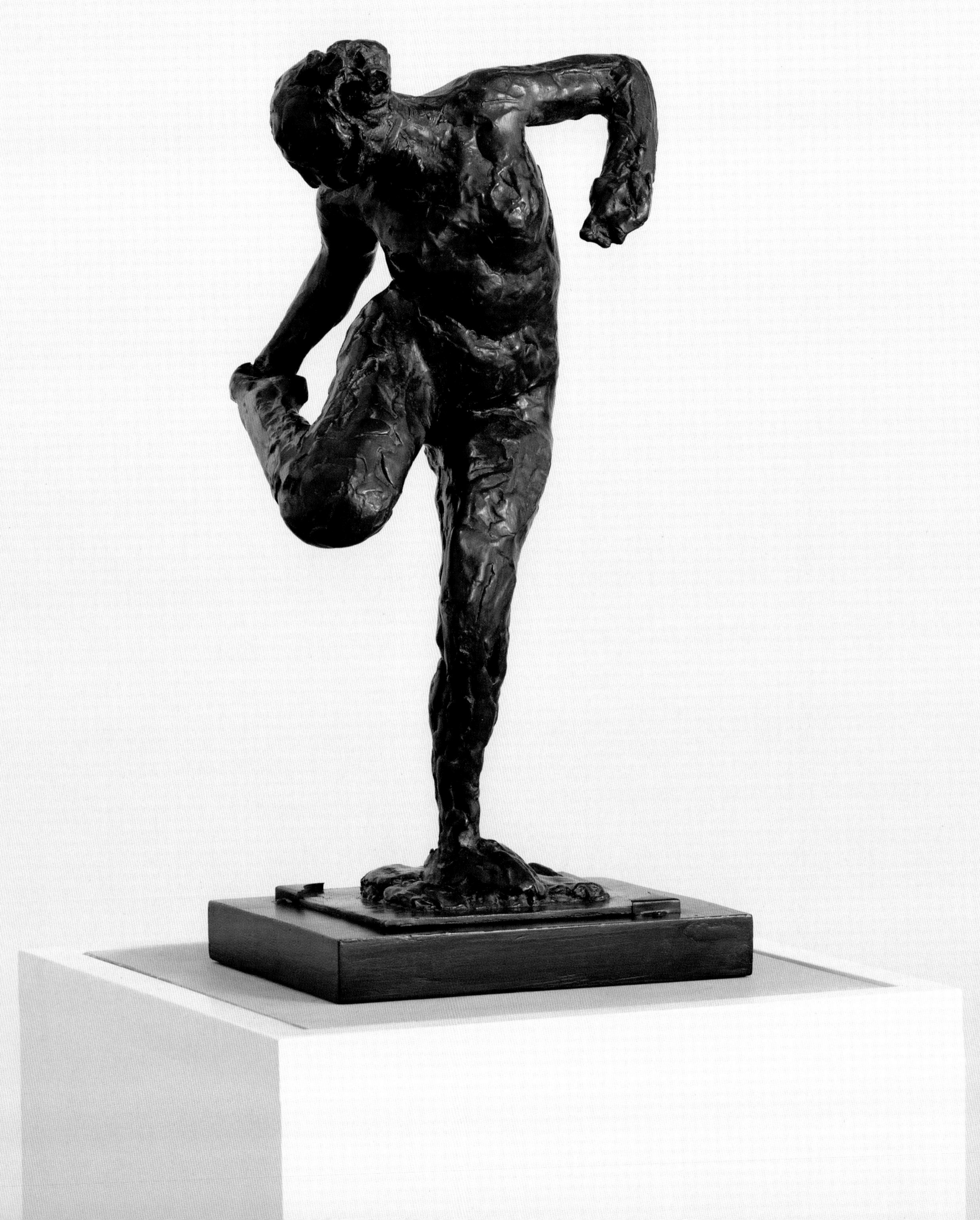

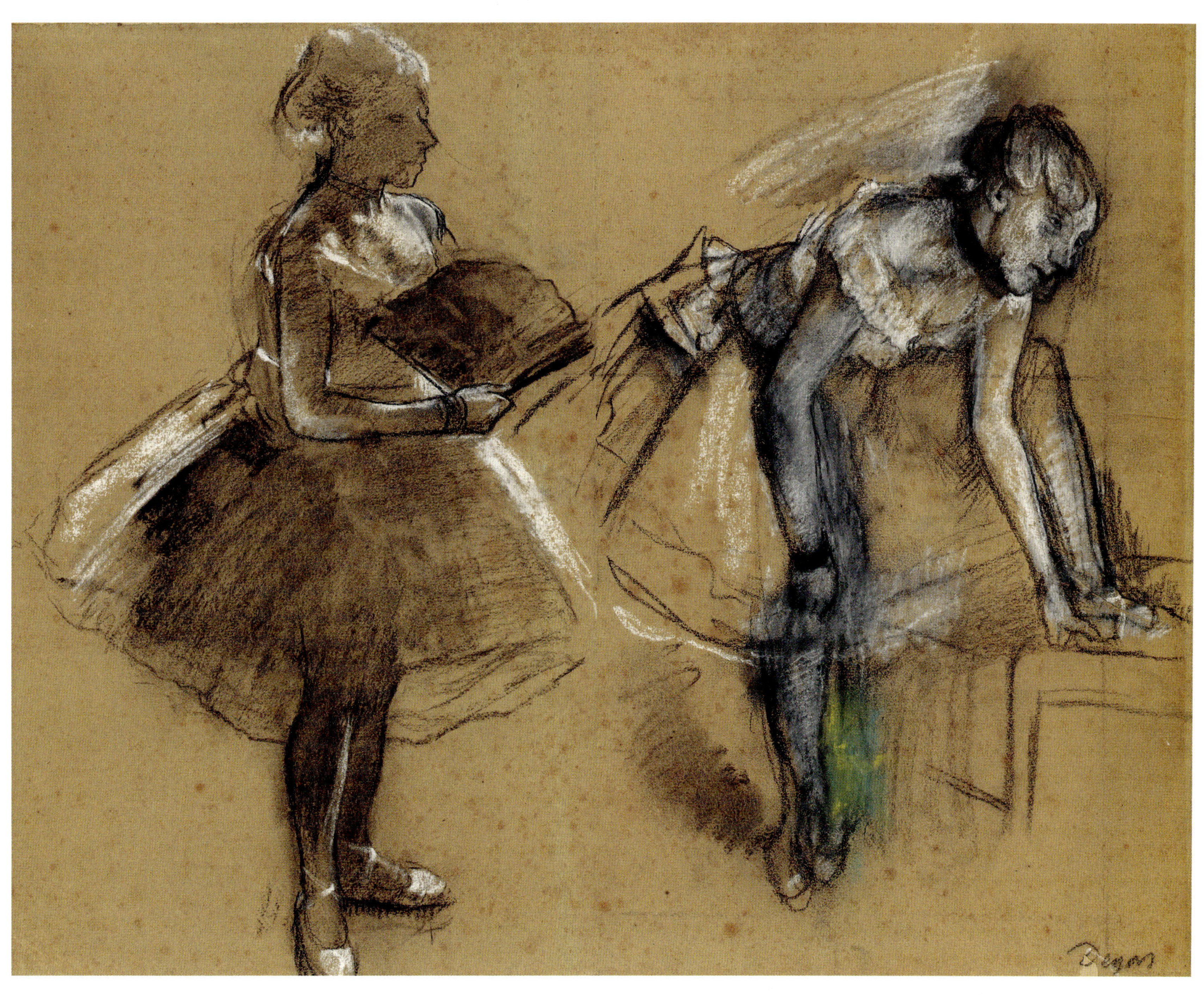
Degas

Paul Cézanne
1839–1903, Aix-en-Provence, France
Houses at the Side of the Road II, c. 1881
Oil on canvas, 21 × 17½ in. (53.3 × 44.5 cm)

On long-term loan from the Moshe and Sara Mayer Collection

Beginning in the early 1870s, Paul Cézanne created a number of oil paintings in which a winding road, or path, recedes from the foreground of the composition, and is abruptly truncated in the middle ground. *Houses at the Side of the Road II* is one of six such paintings that Cézanne created around 1881, and is the only vertical composition among them.

The painting reflects the significance of the decade Cézanne spent working closely with Camille Pissarro (pp. 32–33) in the 1870s, often painting together directly from nature. During that time, Cézanne abandoned the dark colors and impasto that characterized his early works, and adopted a lighter palette. He began applying the paint more smoothly with rounded, patchy brushstrokes, which are visible here in the upper part of the composition. The lower portion of the painting is characterized by a systematic application of paint in dense, parallel brushstrokes that form a topography of sorts. The geometric forms and bold outlines, which endow the clusters of houses and stone walls with a sense of solidity, are common features of Cézanne's work during these years.

Cézanne's goal was to emphasize the two-dimensionality of the painted surface, rather than to create an illusion of perspectival depth. To this end, he used the path strategically to lead the viewer's gaze towards the center of the composition, where it comes up against an impasse—rather than receding in space, the scene appears screenlike. As in the majority of Cézanne's landscape paintings, here too he captures the static and eternal qualities of things, rather than their momentary, ephemeral appearance. The absence of any signs of daily life, such as people or animals in motion, or of details like smoke rising from a chimney or cast shadows, further enhances the scene's sense of calm and immutability.

Ruth Feldmann

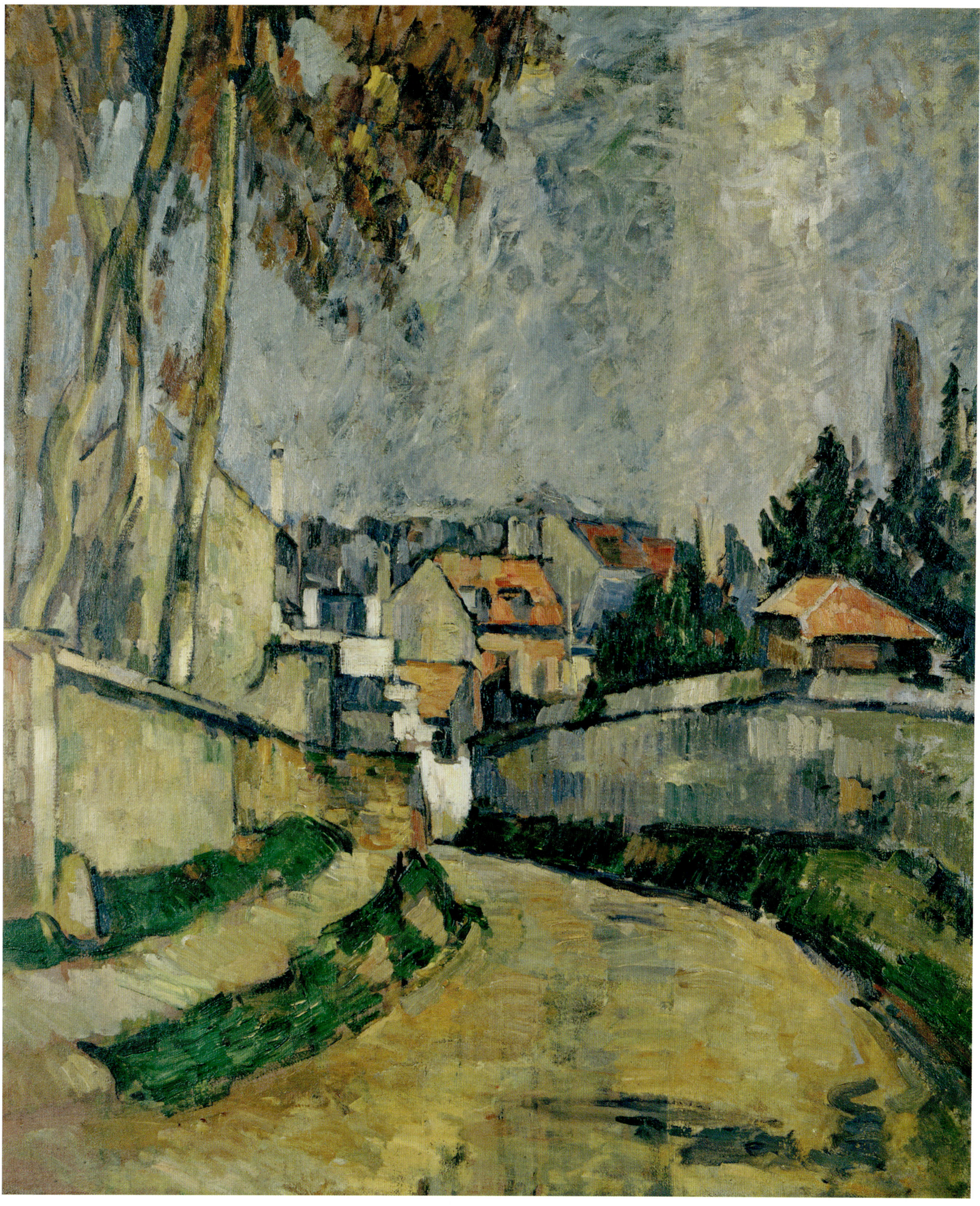

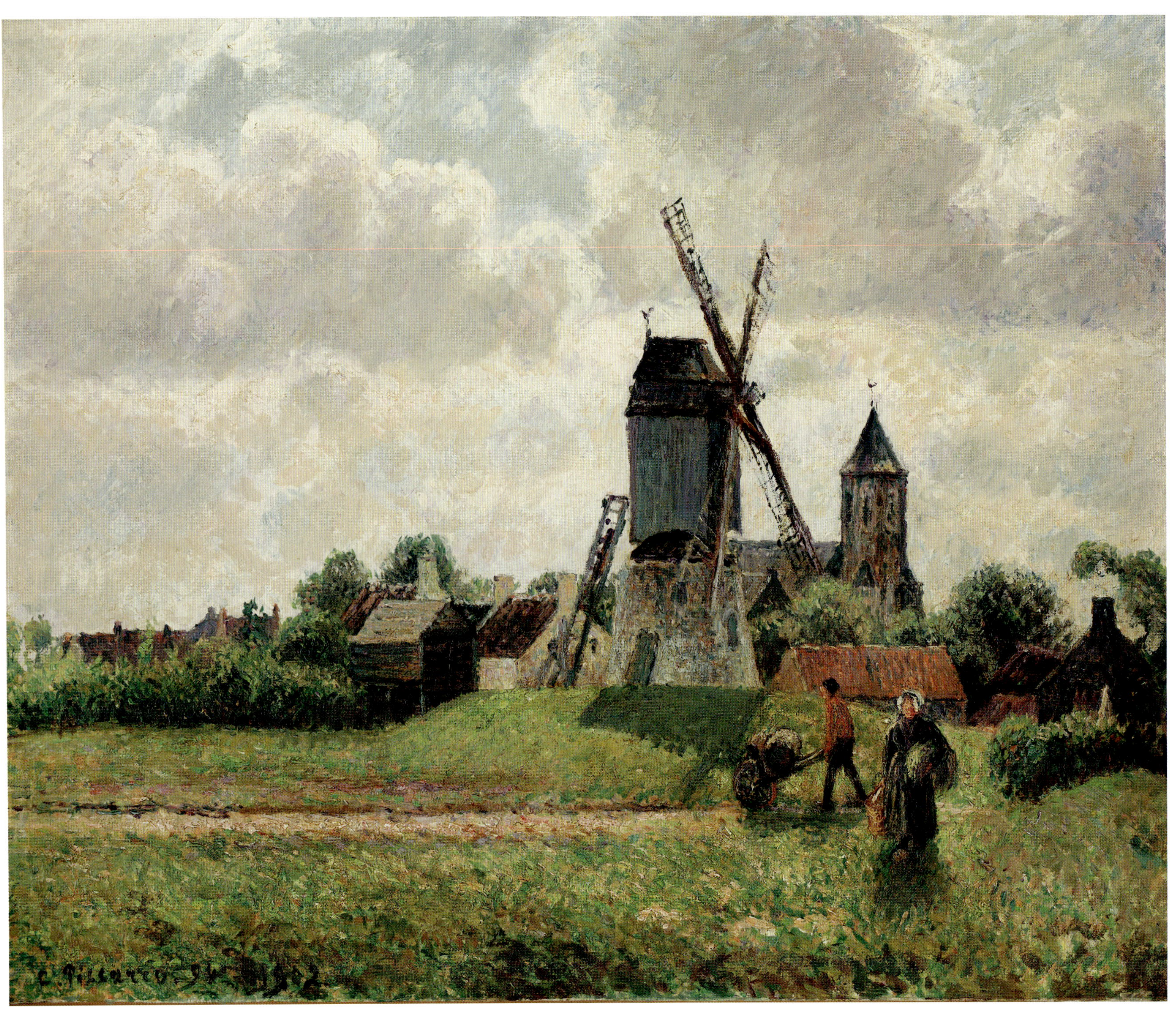

Camille Pissarro
1830, Charlotte Amalie, Saint Thomas, Danish West Indies (now United States Virgin Islands)–1903, Paris, France
The Old Mill in Knokke, 1894/1902
Oil on canvas, 25 ⅞ × 31 ¾ in. (65.8 × 80.7 cm)

On long-term loan from the Simon and Marie Jaglom Collection

Camille Pissarro's painting depicts a quiet moment, with a man pushing a wheelbarrow and a woman holding a basket in front of a large windmill in the Belgian coastal town of Knokke, where the artist spent the summer of 1894.[1] One of thirteen canvases he completed in Knokke, this work features a meadow, a church, and a row of houses peeking through the trees fill the lower part of the painting, while a sky filled with fluffy clouds occupies the upper. Sunlight streaming in from the right extends over the landscape, generating a serene, pastoral atmosphere into which the two figures blend harmoniously.

Born into a well-off Jewish family in Saint Thomas, Pissarro settled in France in 1855 and began painting en plein air, focusing on the countryside and its inhabitants. Over the years he befriended various artists, including Claude Monet (pp. 22–25), and together they developed a new style, soon to be known as Impressionism. The members of the movement translated the effects of sunlight on the ever-changing natural and human-made worlds into loose, interwoven brushstrokes. Between 1874 and 1886, Pissarro exhibited in each of the eight Impressionist exhibitions, a distinction which he alone holds. In the final exhibition in 1886, his paintings were shown alongside the works of Neo-Impressionist artists, including his son Lucien, who advocated the Divisionist, or pointillist, method—placing distinct marks or dots of color adjacent to one another rather than blending them. Pissarro also explored this method briefly, including in *The Old Mill in Knokke*, which is painted with small, stippled brushstrokes. From that time on, his works often contained a synthesis of these styles.

Due to an issue with his eyes that required him to work indoors except in warm weather, in the 1890s, Pissarro painted in a hotel room overlooking Parisian boulevards, or in his home in the suburb of Éragny. For the artist, the summer of 1894 in Knokke was a momentary respite from the pace and stimulation of the city, and a return to the simplicity and beauty of nature, which radiates in this painting.

Nathalie Andrijasevic

1 Pissarro dated the painting twice, in 1894 and 1902, suggesting that he started the work in Knokke, likely painting outdoors, before finishing it at the later date, from memory.

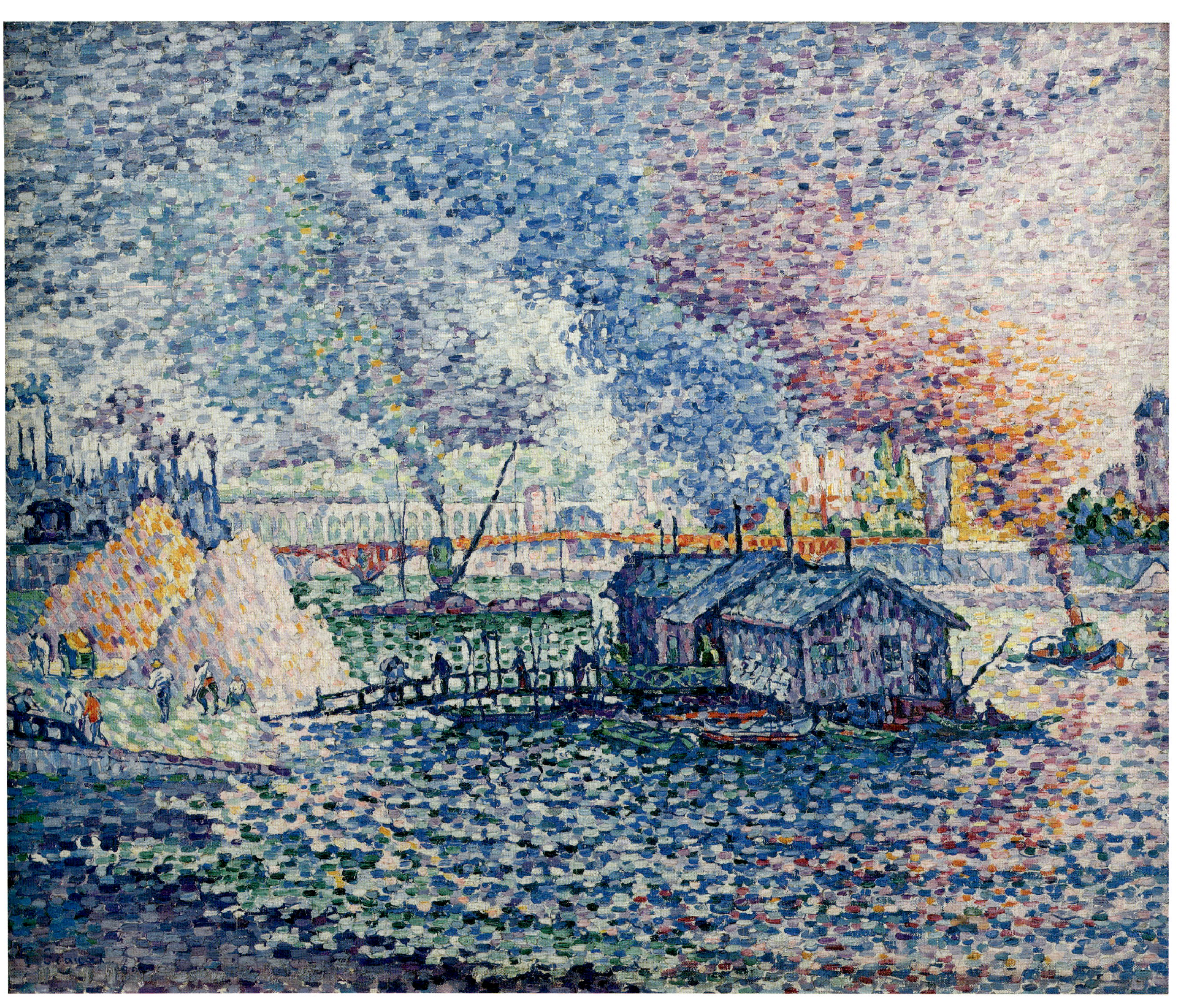

Paul Signac
1863–1935, Paris, France
Pont Mirabeau, 1903
Oil on canvas, 26 × 32 5⁄16 in. (66 × 82 cm)

Bequest of Maurice Lewin, Antwerp, 1934

Early in his career, Paris-born Paul Signac was inspired by the Impressionists, even participating in their eighth and final exhibition in 1886, alongside Georges Seurat, Camille Pissarro (pp. 32–33), and Lucien Pissarro—a group of painters soon to be known as the Neo-Impressionists. Unlike the Impressionists, who relied on their subjective vision to document the effects of light, the Neo-Impressionists sought to develop an objective scientific method to document reality. Their technique was manifested in a meticulous, dense application of tiny dots of pure, unmixed, and contrasting colors to create what they called a "mélange optique," which they believed could faithfully record the brilliance of light. Signac soon became the public representative of the movement, describing its principles in his book *D'Eugène Delacroix au néo-impressionnisme* (1899).

A passionate sailor who owned several sailboats, Signac often depicted views of harbors, seas, bays, and rivers in his work. Towards the end of the nineteenth century, his painting technique changed slightly: the dots transformed into small rectangular brushstrokes, as exemplified by this work, a Parisian landscape. The scene, painted in 1903, represents the river Seine from the banks of the Javel industrial area. The bridge that spans the painting's rear plane—the Pont Mirabeau, completed in 1897—is made up of small orange and red brushstrokes and divides the painting in two like a skyline. Behind it, in light pink coloration, Signac painted the Viaduc d'Auteuil, built in 1865 and replaced in the mid-twentieth century by the Pont du Garigliano. Every element in the painting is treated with the same stippled marks (with the exception of the dark blue contours)—only the direction and color of the brushstrokes generate distinctions between land, water, buildings, and sky. The smoke billowing from several points in the painting creates a visual combination of industry and nature.

Pont Mirabeau[1] was exhibited in 1904 at the Salon des Indépendants, the annual exhibition organized by the Société des Artistes Indépendants, of which Signac was president from 1908 until his death in 1935. Belgian collector Maurice Lewin bought the painting in the early 1930s, and shortly thereafter sent it to the newly inaugurated Tel Aviv Museum. Along with several other paintings bequeathed by Lewin (for example, pp. 48–49), it was one of the first works in the Museum's collection.

Nathalie Andrijasevic

1 Until the 1990s, the work was titled *St. Cloud* in Museum records.

Vincent van Gogh
1853, Zundert, The Netherlands–
1890, Auvers-sur-Oise, France
The Shepherdess (after Millet), 1889
Oil on canvas, 20 7/8 × 16 5/16 in. (53 × 41.5 cm)

On long-term loan from the Moshe and Sara Mayer Collection

Towards the end of September or early October 1889, Vincent van Gogh painted *The Shepherdess*, based on a wood engraving after a painting by Jean-François Millet.[1] "Père Millet," as Van Gogh referred to him, was one of the artist's most important influences throughout his career. A few months earlier, in May, the artist committed himself to a mental health institution in Saint-Rémy-de-Provence, where he painted the lush garden and the landscape beyond the facility's walls. After suffering from a breakdown over the summer, however, he could no longer work outside and instead began to make copies after prints.[2] His brother Theo must have included the print of *The Shepherdess* along with others that he sent to Saint-Rémy after Vincent wrote him, "But how I would like to see more good reproductions of Millet."[3] During the month of September, Van Gogh started copying Millet's *Les Travaux des Champs* (*The Labors of the Field*), a series of ten drawings that focuses on laboring figures, as a way "to console myself, for my own pleasure."[4] *The Shepherdess* likely followed directly afterwards.

This vibrant work exudes a feeling of repose. Van Gogh stayed largely true to the slightly smaller wood engraving, and likely copied the image freehand, choosing his own colors.[5] The solitary shepherdess is resting on a hay bale in the fields, her right hand clasping her staff as her gaze drifts. Van Gogh used different shades of blue for her clothes—round brushstrokes to represent the shape of her body beneath her robes, and firm brushstrokes in deep cobalt for her cape, as well as strong contours to separate the sitter from the background. With a few red brushstrokes, he indicated her features and chose fresh white for the bonnet covering her hair. Due to the poor quality of the print reproduction, her second clog had become invisible, and therefore he depicted just one foot. A flock of sheep is gathered safely behind her to the left, and almost blends into the background because Van Gogh chose similar yellow and beige tones for the fields. He dotted the foreground with grass consisting of contrasting vertical green and red brushstrokes to create a complementary color effect.

Although the figure is still, the skies behind her are full of movement. With white, playful brushstrokes Van Gogh indicated several clouds along the horizon—his own addition, as this area is completely blank on the reproduction that he used—whereas darker blue lines suggest a strong wind. Although he may have been pleased by this endearing work, which he didn't mention specifically in his letters, he informed Theo that "the canvases after Millet … aren't destined for public viewing."[6]

Bregje Gerritse

1 Leo Jansen, Hans Luijten, and Nienke Bakker, eds., *Vincent van Gogh: The Letters. The Complete and Annotated Edition* (Amsterdam/Brussels: Thames and Hudson, 2009), https://vangoghletters.org/vg/. It seems likely that Van Gogh made this work roughly around the same time as his copy after Virginie Demont-Breton (letters 809 and 810), a slightly larger work than *The Shepherdess*, before he started working on a larger, more ambitious series of works after Millet reproductions that Theo sent towards the end of October (letter 815). A slightly broader dating is suggested in Kathrin Pilz et al., "Van Gogh's Copies from Saint-Rémy: Between Reminiscence, Calculation and Improvisation," in *Van Gogh's Studio Practice*, ed. Marije Vellekoop et al. (Amsterdam/Brussels: Van Gogh Museum/Mercatorfonds, 2013), 110 no. 27, 113 no. 43, 130.

2 Letter 793, no. 1, *Vincent van Gogh: The Letters.* There are twenty-two painted copies after Millet known from this period.

3 Letter 789, *Vincent van Gogh: The Letters.*

4 Letter 805, *Vincent van Gogh: The Letters.*

5 See Pilz et al., "Van Gogh's Copies from Saint-Rémy," 112–13.

6 Letter 863, *Vincent van Gogh: The Letters.*

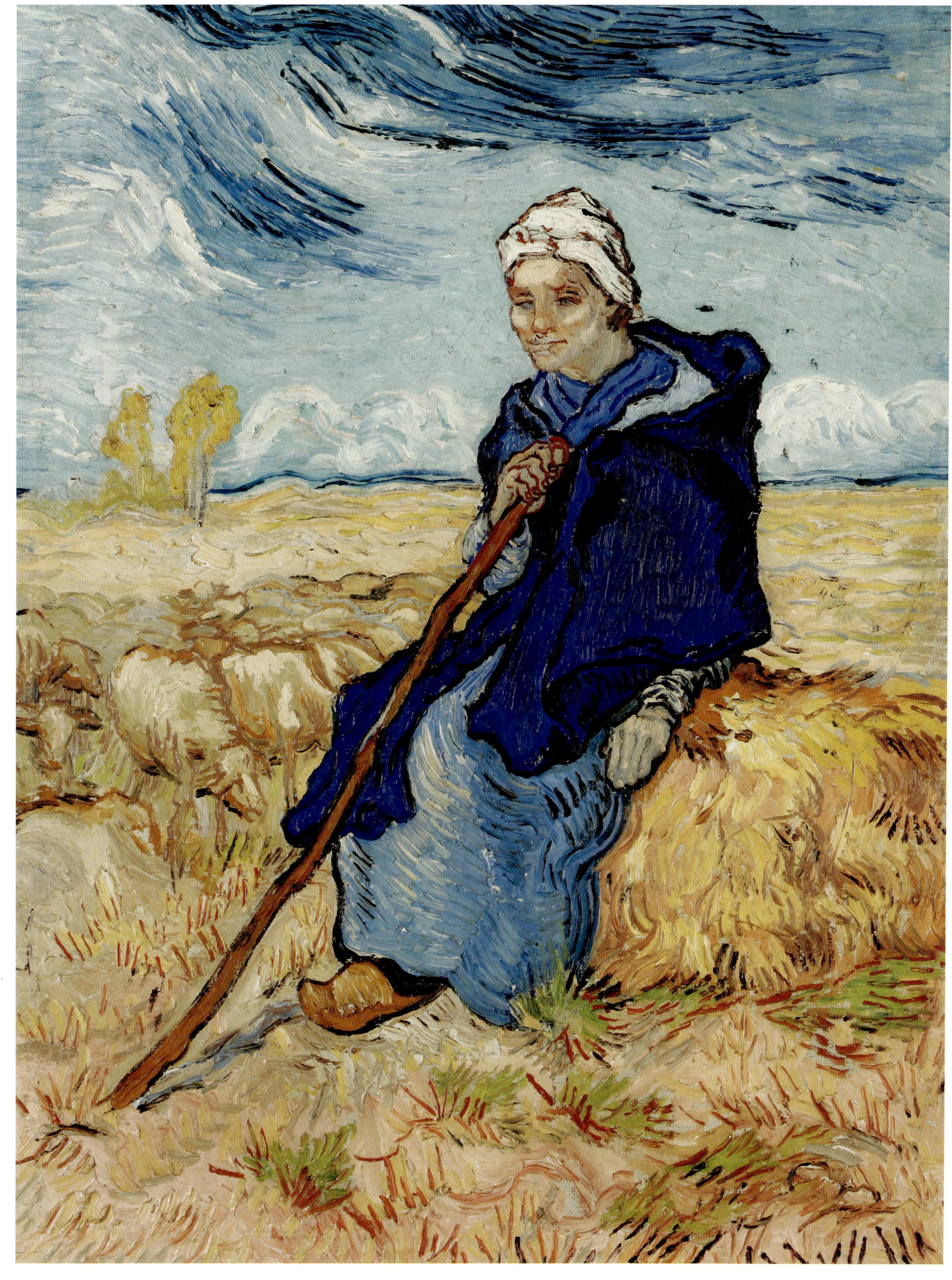

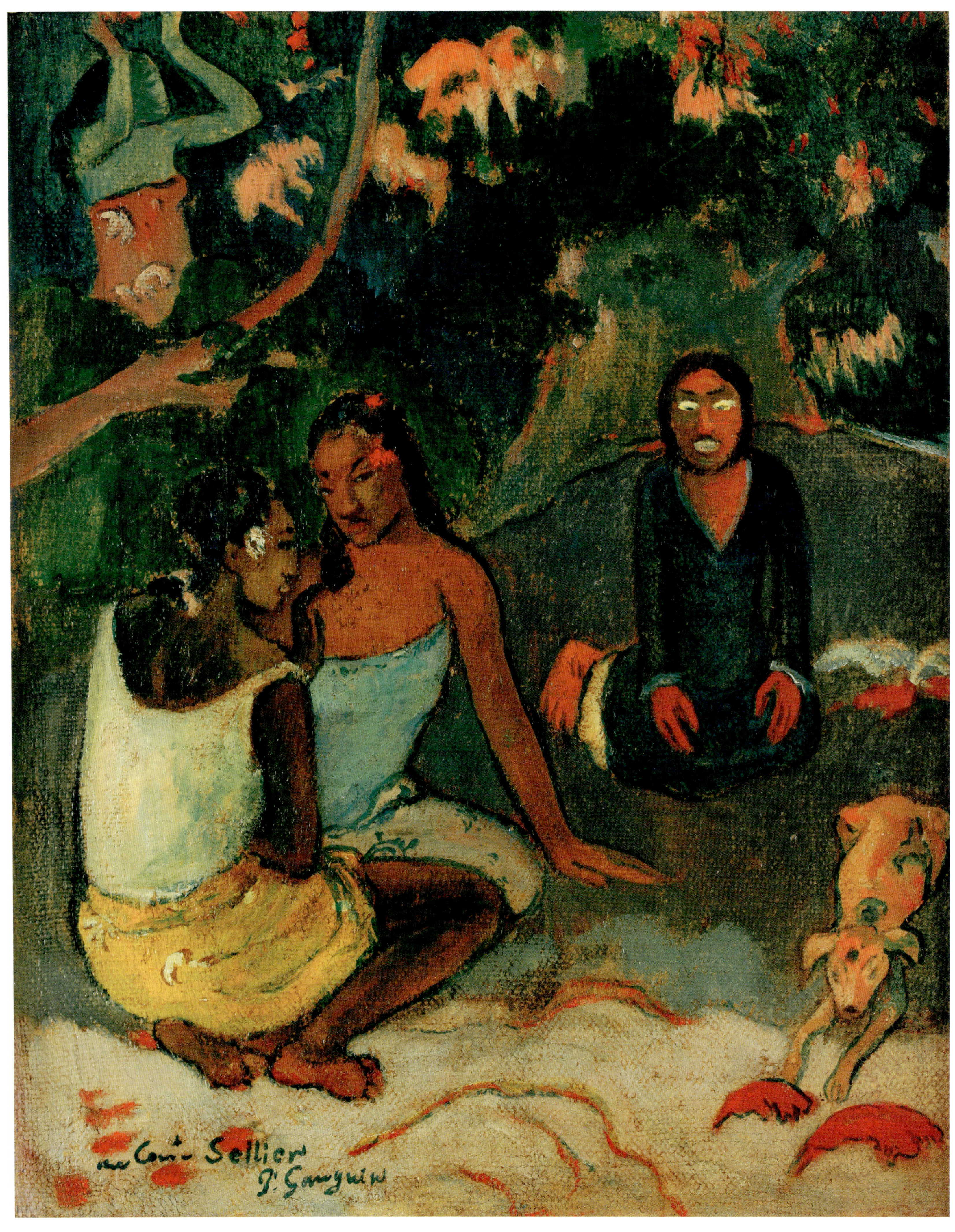
au Comt Sellier
P. Gauguin

Paul Gauguin
1848, Paris, France–1903, Atuona, Hiva Oa, French Polynesia
Barbaric Tales, 1892
Oil on canvas, 15 3/8 × 11 in. (39 × 28 cm)

On long-term loan from the Moshe and Sara Mayer Collection

In an era of high colonialism in Europe in the later nineteenth-century, Polynesia held a popular allure in the French imagination as a region where there allegedly remained abundant belief in supernatural forces.[1] This is one idea that attracted Paul Gauguin to Tahiti, where he spent a two-year sojourn in 1891–93. *Barbaric Tales* (*Contes Barbares*) is one of several paintings from that moment that depict the encounter of the human with the spiritual through exclusively feminine forms.[2] Here, the young, seated women wear clothing typical of Tahiti in the 1890s: wrapped cotton pareu skirts printed with floral motifs, simple blouses, and tropical flowers adorning their hair.

The artist sets these quotidian figures in an encounter with a fantastic and severe female form. Her almond-shaped bright eyes and mouth contrast sharply with her tawny skin, and they resemble the shell inlay features of some of the Pacific masks Gauguin saw in curio shops in Papeete. Her black hood links her to Gauguin's other representations of a Tupapau.[3] The Tupapau were spirits from the realm of the dead that some Tahitians believed to circulate, particularly at dusk and at night, at the edges of the forest, hovering on the fringes of human habitation. In December 1892, Gauguin wrote to his wife Mette about the "phosphorescence of the night that are the spirits of the dead."[4] In the dense green foliage, flashing patches of pink suggest both tropical flowers and the lights at dusk that supposedly announce the presence of these spirits.

In the left background, a woman raises either fruit or flowers, perhaps an offering to the Tupapau. The odd green tint of her skin fuses her with the domain of the forest and with the non-human. Her hieratic profile imitates a style found in the wall paintings of ancient Egypt, an art form that Gauguin knew well from reproductions he kept in his studio. His image thus engages less with the contemporary Tahiti in which he lived and more with a practice of primitivist fantasy, in which he appropriated both ancient and Pacific forms to render a scene of spiritual mystery that he associated with the realm of the feminine.

Elizabeth C. Childs

1 See Elizabeth C. Childs, *Vanishing Paradise: Art and Exoticism in Colonial Tahiti* (Berkeley: University of California Press, 2013), 38–42.

2 Other canvases include *Parau na te varua ino (Paroles du diable)*, 1892 (National Gallery of Art, Washington, DC) and *Parau hanohano (Paroles terrifiantes)*, 1892 (private collection, destroyed in WWII). See the Wildenstein Plattner Institute digital catalogue raisonné, https://digitalprojects.wpi.art/gauguin/artworks, nos. PGQF3L and PG6N5T. The current canvas appears in this database as *La Nuit des contes barbares*, PG5U3P.

3 Such as in his ambitious painting of 1892, *Manao tupapau* (Spirit of the Dead Watching) (Buffalo AKG Art Museum, Buffalo, NY).

4 Letter from Paul Gauguin to Mette Gauguin, December 8, 1892, in *Paul Gauguin: Letters to His Wife and Friends*, ed. Maurice Malingue, trans. Henry J. Stenning (Cleveland: World, 1949), letter 134, 178.

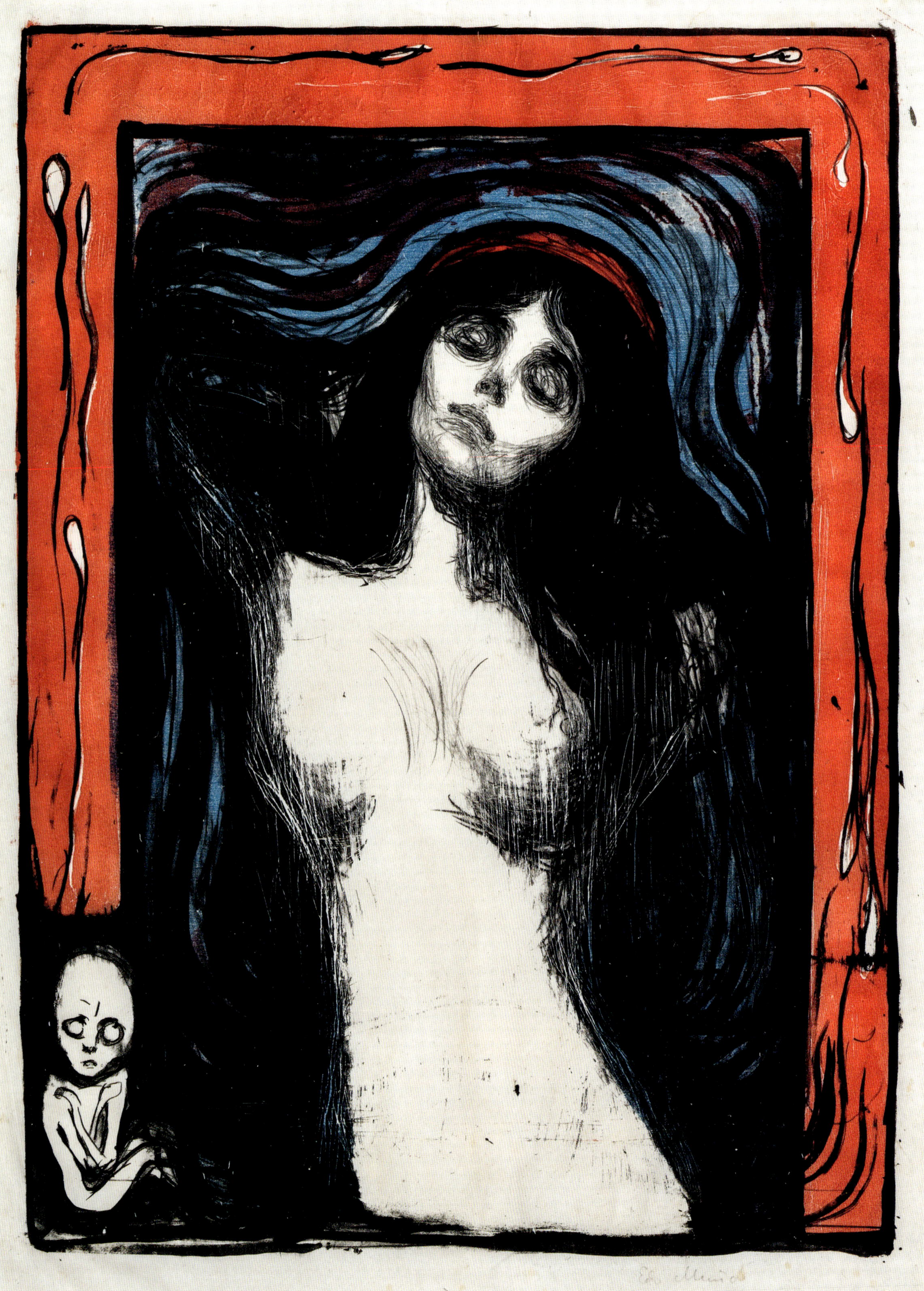

Edvard Munch
1863, Ådalsbruk, Norway–1944, Oslo, Norway
Madonna, 1895–1902
Lithograph, 33 11⁄16 × 23 3⁄8 in. (85.6 × 59.3 cm)
Printed by M. W. Lassally, Berlin, edition of approx. 150

Gift of Charles and Evelyn Kramer, New York, through the American Friends of the Tel Aviv Museum of Art, 1986

Edvard Munch's writings make clear that he intended the swooning, nude woman in *Madonna*, framed by swimming spermatozoa and an embryo, to represent the moment of conception: "The pause when all the world came to a stop—Your face reveals all the beauty of the earthly world—Your lips, crimson as the ripening fruit, part in pain—The smile of a corpse—Now death reaches out a hand to life—The chain is joined that links the thousands of generations that are dead to the thousands that are to come."[1]

The myth of the femme fatale, which polarized women into virtuous Madonnas or dangerous whores, strongly appealed to men threatened by new demands for women's rights and independence. In the circle of writers Munch mixed with in 1890s Berlin, including August Strindberg and Stanislaw Przybyszewski, the theme was rife. Both Przybyszewski and Munch fused alternative clichés concerning women by combining erotic fascination with mystical, spiritual beauty.[2] They were also inspired by current scientific theories about the ongoing, physiological cycle of life and death. Munch's sensual *Madonna* is pictured as both sinner and saint. Closing her eyes in ecstasy, she floats in a fluid, womblike ambience.

Munch created his prints of *Madonna* in parallel with several paintings of the same subject, which he exhibited in his *Love* series and later developed into the visual poem about life, love, and death called "The Frieze of Life."[3] The *Madonna* prints began with a drypoint in 1894, followed a year later by a black-and-white lithograph that restates the painted image in the starkest, most dramatic manner. Almost immediately, Munch began to add hand tints, highlighting, for example, the woman's sensual lips in red. Then, in 1902, he executed his first color prints of *Madonna* using a combination of lithographic and woodcut techniques in a highly experimental way—as in the example shown here.[4] While the red and black areas are printed using two different lithographic stones or plates, the translucent blue is printed from a wooden block, adding texture and creating a watery effect that is visible through the ink.[5] *Madonna* was printed in numerous variant impressions: sometimes an additional stone was used for an olive-green or green-beige skin tone that conveys the impression of gas or candlelight. In other instances, the woman's body emerges like a ghost from thin, white China paper, or thick white card. The vibrant colors and elaborate printing processes result in an overall pictorial richness that reflects the importance Munch attributed to his iconic *Madonna*.

Jill Lloyd

1. Arne Eggum, *Edvard Munch, Livsfrisen fra maleri til grafikk* (Oslo: J.M. Stenersen, 1990), 196, quoted in Ina Johannesen, *Edvard Munch: 50 Graphic Works from the Gundersen Collection* (Bergen Art Museum, 2010), 58.
2. Przybyszewski's novel *The Requiem Mass* (1893) uses religious vocabulary to describe overtly sensual scenes.
3. One of these paintings originally had a frame inscribed with swimming spermatozoa and an embryo. Although this was later discarded, the symbols recur in Munch's lithographic versions of *Madonna*, providing a key to the meaning of the image.
4. According to Gustav Schiefler's early catalogue of Munch's prints, there are only four combination prints of this type.
5. The technique is explained in detail in Gerd Woll, *Edvard Munch: Complete Graphic Works* (Stockholm: Orfeus, 2012), 67.

Edvard Munch
1863, Ådalsbruk, Norway–1944, Oslo, Norway
Vampire II, 1902
Lithograph and woodcut, 22 3/8 × 27 5/8 in. (56.9 × 70.1 cm)
Published by Edvard Munch, Berlin, edition of 150–200

Gift of Charles and Evelyn Kramer, New York, through the American Friends of the Tel Aviv Museum of Art, 1986

The striking motif of a red-haired woman bending over the neck of her lover appears in several of Edvard Munch's paintings dating from 1893–95, the first of which was originally exhibited with the title *Love and Pain*. Under the influence of the Polish writer Stanislaw Przybyszewski, whom Munch met in Berlin at the Black Pig Tavern, its title was changed to *Vampire*, reflecting current literary fascination with the theme of the femme fatale, a malevolent female who deploys her seductive charms to ensnare her lovers.

Both Przybyszewski and the Swedish playwright August Strindberg responded in their writings to Munch's vampire image. Strindberg described the woman's blood-red hair cascading over her shoulders onto the man's back as "showers of golden rain ... golden cords which tie him to earth and to suffering."[1] Later, however, Munch downplayed these literary associations, claiming that this work simply depicts "a woman kissing a man on the back of the neck."[2]

Munch first translated his vampire paintings into a black-and-white lithograph in 1895, adding hand-color to highlight the all-important red hair, while varying its intensity in different impressions. In 1902, when Munch returned to Berlin to exhibit his *Frieze of Life* (see entry on Munch's *Madonna*, p. 41) at the Berlin Secession, which marked his definitive breakthrough in Germany, there was a sudden surge in demand for his work. His prints enabled him to respond to this demand and offered the opportunity to experiment with new techniques.

Vampire II is one of Munch's most innovative prints from this period, combining lithography and woodcut in a groundbreaking synthesis. Munch reused the original black-and-white keystone for the figures, employing a second lithographic stone to delineate the woman's red hair. In addition, he made use of a wooden block cut into four pieces that he inked separately in yellow, blue, and green and then reassembled to create the figure's skin and jacket, as well as the background colors.[3] Munch's transparent printing inks create subtle layering effects and textures, so that the grain of the wooden printing block remains visible in the final image.

Jill Lloyd

1 August Strindberg, 1896, quoted in Ina Johannesen, *Edvard Munch: 50 Graphic Works from the Gundersen Collection* (Bergen Art Museum, 2010), 64. In 1894, Przybyszewski wrote his description of "a broken man with a vampire biting in his neck," in Johannesen, 62.

2 See Ragna Stang, *Edvard Munch. Mennesket og kunstneren* (Oslo: Aschehoug, 1977), 108.

3 "Munch invented the process of sawing his woodblocks into pieces, inking them in different colors, reassembling them, and printing the multihued image all at once." See Elizabeth Prelinger, *Edvard Munch, Master Printmaker* (New York: W.W. Norton & Co., 1983), 149. We are able to reconstruct exactly how Munch made his multicolored *Vampire II* print because the original sawn woodblocks are preserved at the Munchmuseet, Oslo.

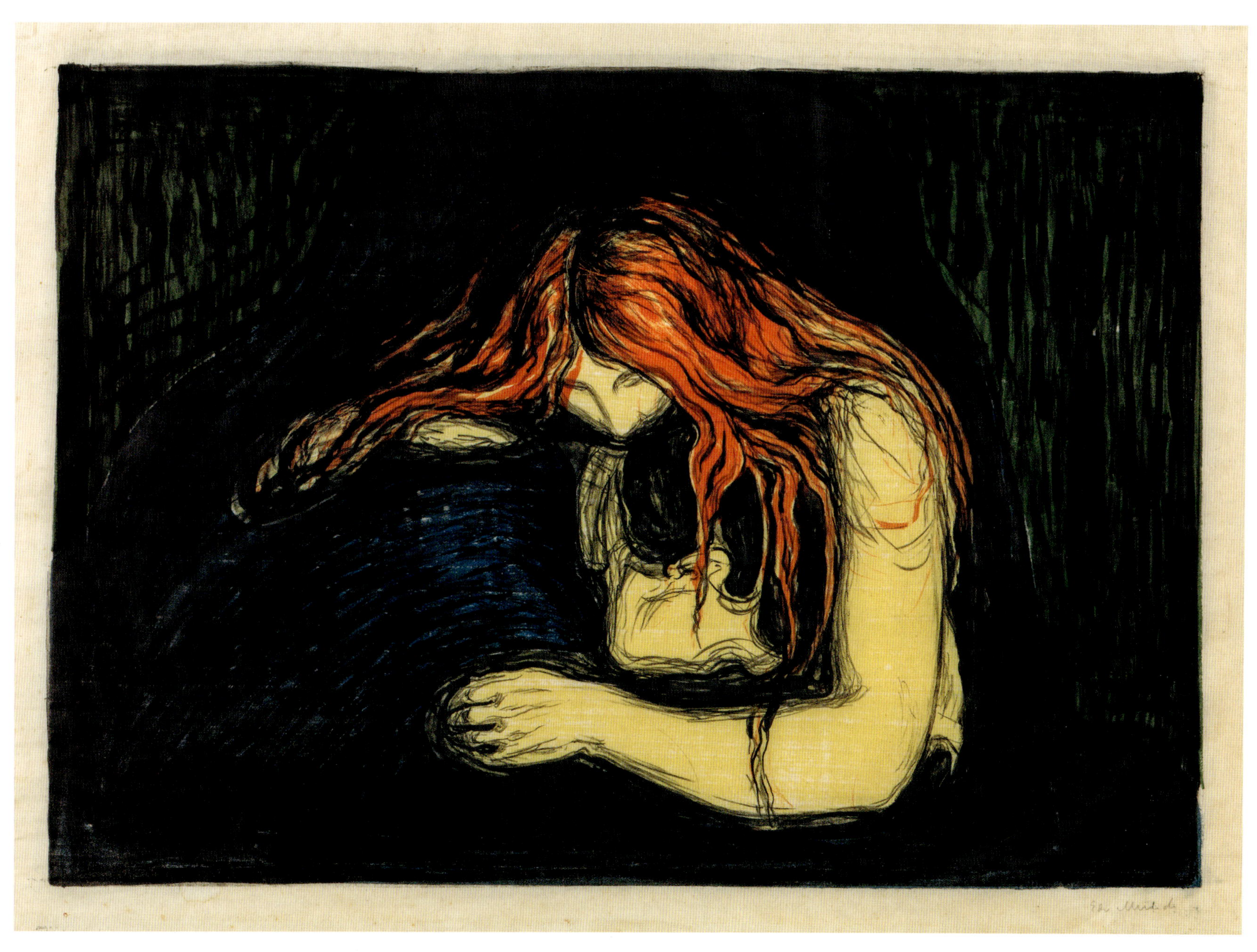

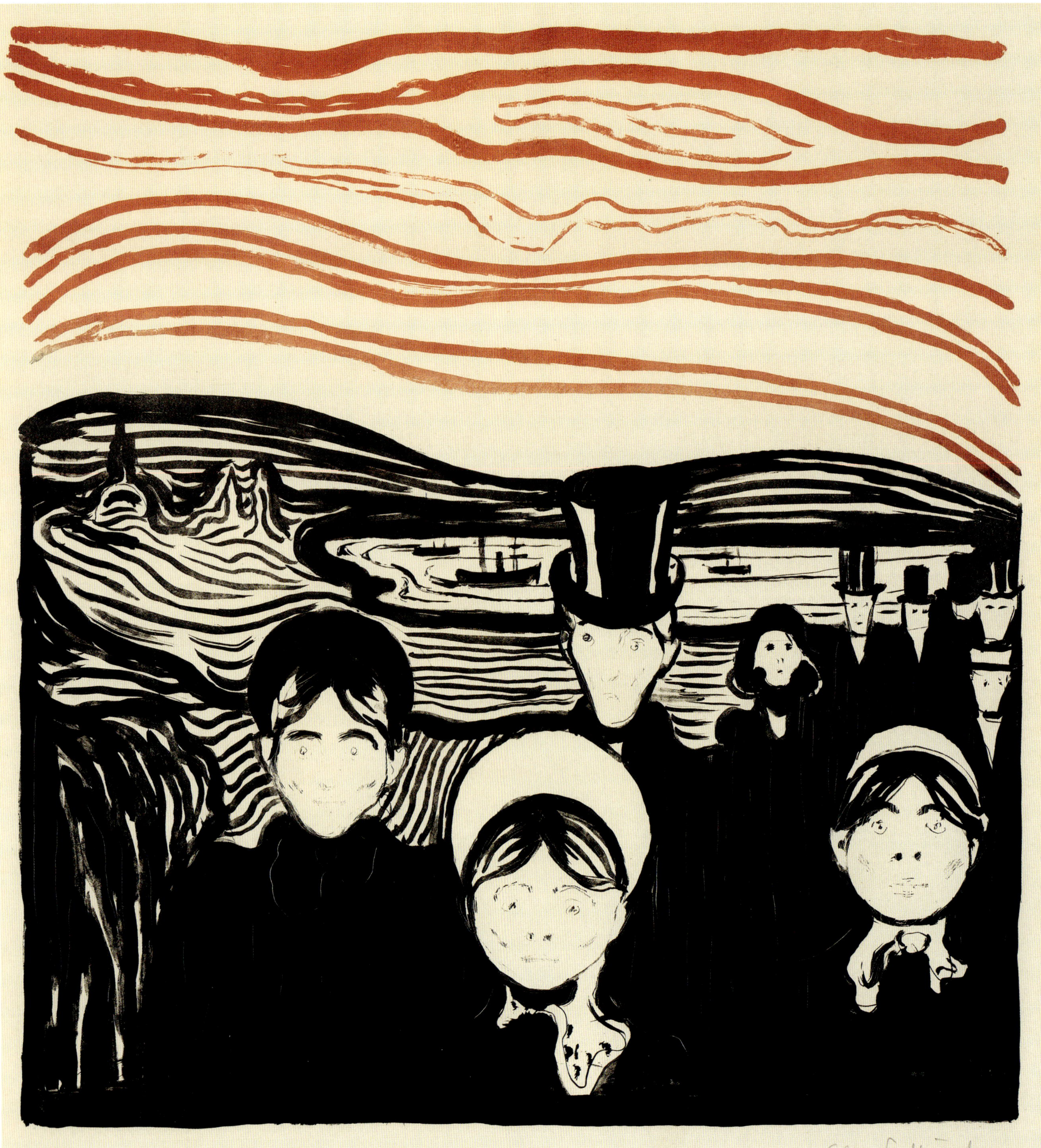
Edvard Munch

Edvard Munch
1863, Ådalsbruk, Norway–1944, Oslo, Norway
Anxiety, 1896
Lithograph, 22 ½ × 16 15⁄16 in. (57.1 × 43.1 cm)
Published by Edvard Munch, Berlin, edition of approx. 150

Gift of Charles and Evelyn Kramer, New York, through the American Friends of the Tel Aviv Museum of Art, 1986

Anxiety (alternatively titled *Angst*) is a print version of Edvard Munch's painting of the same title dating from 1894.[1] The motif of ghostlike figures in city dress pressing forward beneath the vortex of a blood-red sky fuses two of his earlier images, namely the landscape from *The Scream* (1893) and the urban crowd represented in *Evening on Karl Johan Street* (1892). The lone, skull-like creature in *The Scream* has been replaced by a tightly packed crowd advancing along the same elevated roadway with a view over the Oslo Fjord, identified as Ljabruveien on Ekeberg Hill. The faces in the crowd change in different versions of *Anxiety* (which Munch also made as a woodcut), but the skeletal, bonneted woman in center foreground, who has been identified as Munch's ex-lover Milly Thaulow, always appears.

The vertiginous perspective, dramatically contrasting red and black hues, pulsating lines, and masklike facial features communicate a strong sense of urban alienation, which destabilizes both humankind and nature. The image is redolent of Munch's antipathy to the oppressive, hypocritical crowd who disapproved of his art in Norway and of his general sense of existential anxiety. In his literary notes, the artist wrote: "I saw all the people behind their masks—smiling, phlegmatic—subdued faces—I saw through them and there was suffering—in them all—pale corpses—who restlessly nervously—scurried about—along a torturous road whose—end was the grave."[2]

The lithograph was made in Paris, where Munch lived from February 1896 to spring 1897. Inspired by a boom in printmaking in France and by the technical advice of expert printmakers such as Auguste Clot, who printed *Anxiety* in red and black ink for the artist on a single lithographic stone, Munch's printmaking reached new heights.[3] He drew *Anxiety* directly on the stone, using deep, silky areas of brushed black ink or tusche, soft lines in black crayon, and sharp, white, incised lines scraped into the ink. This combination results in the "suppleness and refinement" that characterizes Munch's most powerful prints.[4] Condensed and abstracted, the themes of his *Anxiety* painting reemerged with added conviction and force.

Jill Lloyd

1 Gerd Woll, *Edvard Munch: Complete Graphic Works* (Stockholm: Orfeus, 2012), 91, no. 63.
2 Edvard Munch, literary sketch (undated), Munch museet N625, p. 1.
3 Printing in more than one color on a single stone is rare. The technique is called *à la poupée* and is more commonly used in intaglio printing.
4 Woll, *Edvard Munch*, 14.

James Ensor
1860–1949, Ostend, Belgium
My Favorite Room, 1892
Oil on canvas, 31½ × 39⅜ in. (80 × 100 cm)

Gift of the children of Oscar and Shulamit Fischer, Tel Aviv, 1947. In memory of their parents

For most of his life, until 1917, James Ensor lived in a large corner house on the Vlaanderenstraat in Ostend, with a studio in the attic of his parents' home.[1] In *My Favorite Room*, Ensor probably portrays a dining room he depicted in earlier works, based on the same Neo-Renaissance buffet and the rectangular table, using it as a showcase for his varied interests and valued objects.[2]

A remarkable selection of his own paintings is hung salon-style on the surrounding walls, among them six small satirical and grotesque works that he painted in 1891, as well as three earlier works: *Carnival in Brussels* (1888) and two still lifes featuring fans, vases, and household goods from Japan and China. He also included small and large vases that testify to his love for whimsical and exotic forms. The table itself features drawings, books, and writing utensils that reflect Ensor's literary ambitions, as well as a whistle he always carried. The piano in the back of the room, along with his painting *The Grotesque Musicians* (1888), points to the artist's musical hobby.

Near the scene's center is a portrait of Ensor as a well-dressed dandy, painted by his somewhat older colleague Isidore Verheyden, which was exhibited in 1886 at the avant-garde artist group Les XX, of which Ensor was a founding member.[3] *My Favorite Room* can be considered a kind of allegorical self-portrait, with the room's objects together symbolizing Ensor's various identities and the roles he played, as an artist, musician, writer, and lover of the whimsical.

The representation of the room does not abide by conventions of academic painting. Several parts of the image are shown from different angles: the tabletop seems to have a life of its own, the small paintings are not proportional to their real dimensions, and the fireplace and floor are spatially confusing. Such formal aspects are subordinated to a coloristic design somewhat similar to the intimist Post-Impressionism of Pierre Bonnard (pp. 56–57). In this engrossing composition, colors are variously echoed: the green motifs in the carpet and the green brochure or print on the table; extended—the red carpet ends abruptly on the table's left, but Ensor paints a red surface on the table's right; and transformed—the left wall is light blue, but to the right of the door, the wall color seems to have been adapted to the gilded frames around the paintings.

Herwig Todts

1 On the ground floor, the family ran a large souvenir shop, and they also rented out some of the home's many rooms to summer guests.

2 Earlier works that may feature this dining room include *Le Vieux Meuble* (The Old Furniture; 1885) or *Le Meuble Hanté* (The Haunted Furniture; 1888, destroyed in 1945).

3 It is not known how this portrait came into the artist's possession.

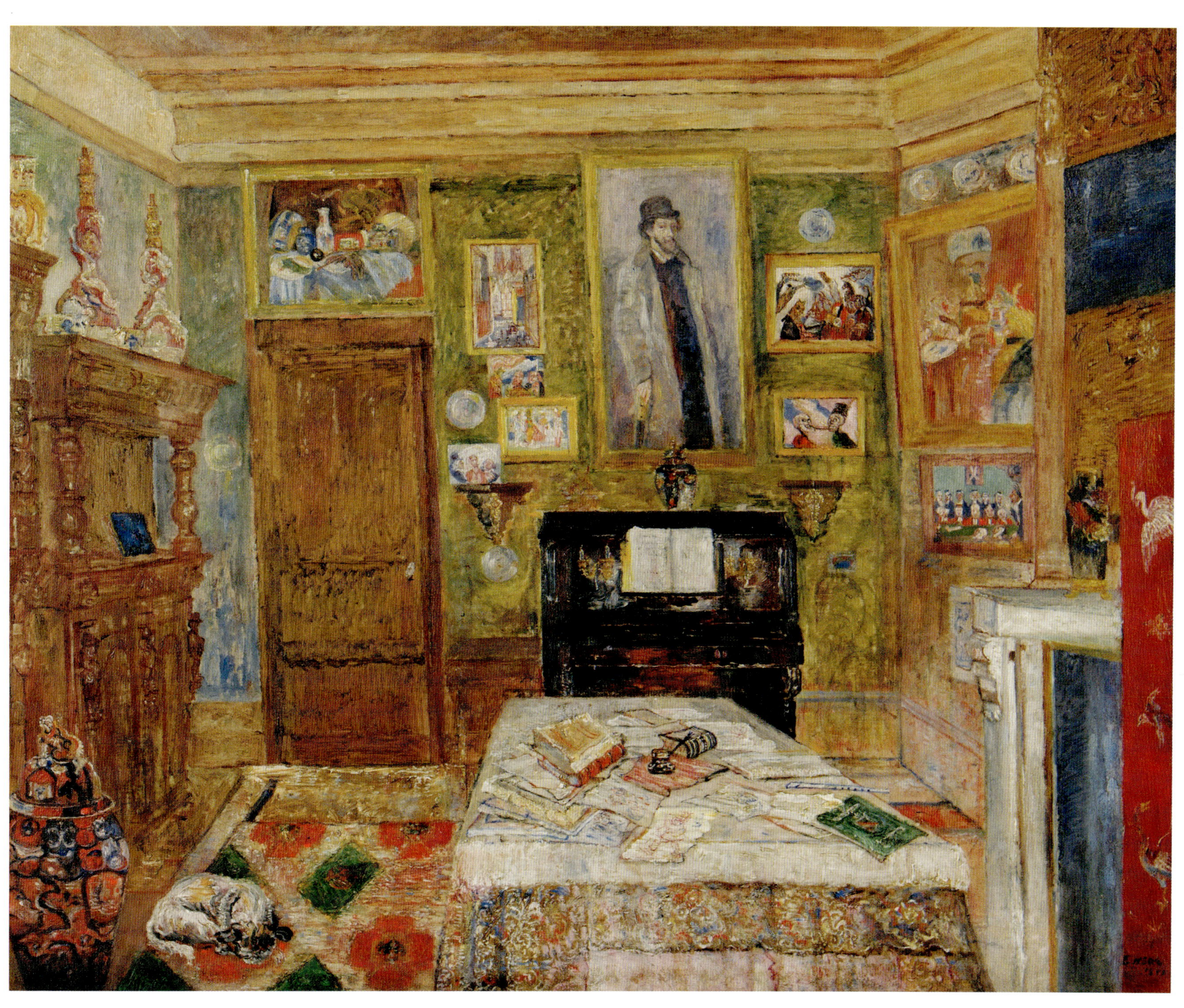

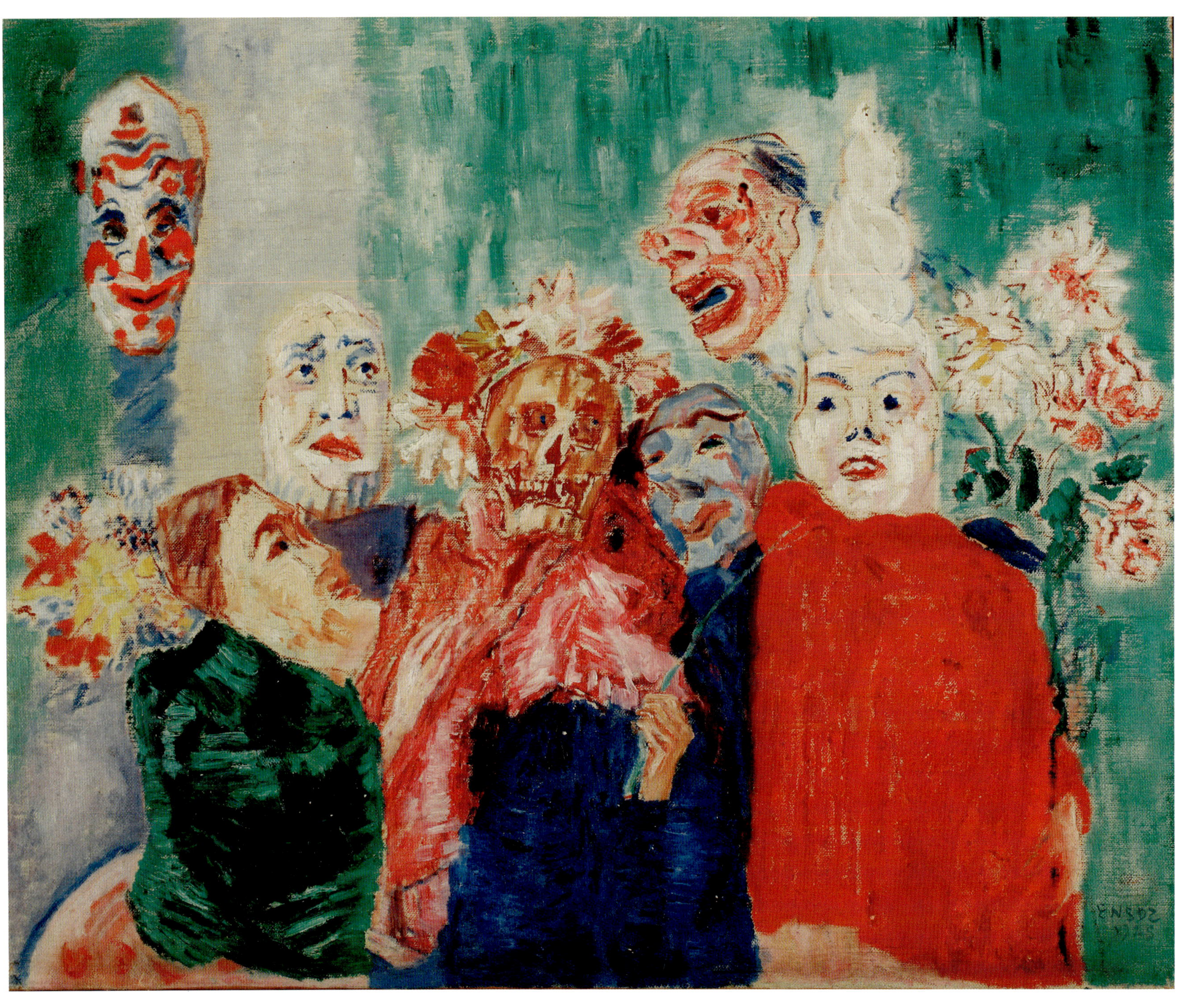

James Ensor
1860–1949, Ostend, Belgium
Masks, 1925
Oil on canvas, 21 7/16 × 26 3/8 in. (54.5 × 67 cm)

Bequest of Maurice Lewin, Antwerp, 1934

James Ensor, dubbed "the painter of masks" by his friend, the Belgian poet Emile Verhaeren, grew up in the resort town of Ostend surrounded by the masks, harlequins, skulls, and animal heads that were available in his family's curiosity shop. The Flemish carnival surely contributed to his fascination with such objects, as did the presence of skulls and bones from the historical religious wars that had taken place in the region. His predilection for masquerade and carnivalesque imagery appeared in his oeuvre as early as 1883. This 1925 painting of masked figures surrounding a grinning skeleton, characteristic of Ensor's late period, reworks earlier symbolic iconography and compositions in a brighter palette and more diluted colors.

The artist confessed that "hounded by hangers-on, [he] was only too happy to shut [himself] away in a solitary environment ruled over by the mask in all its violence, its light and its sharp laughter."[1] He frequently combined play, irony, and ambiguity using these metaphorical and fantastic motifs. In *Masks*, for example, it is unclear whether the figures portrayed are disguised, mask-wearing humans or animated masks and puppets. The three schematic hands are the only tangible signs of human presence. Additionally, the flower-crowned skull in the composition's center serves as a *memento mori*, a reminder of death's certainty, underscoring the hypocritical games of social conventions that Ensor's grotesque figures critique.

By introducing imagination and phantasmagoria to a bourgeois world, and through an unconventionally direct use of paint on the canvas to depict his inner vision, Ensor mediates between symbolism and expressionism while anticipating the concerns of Surrealism. It is no wonder that his work represented a source of inspiration for a range of artists looking for an independent creative path, such as Emil Nolde (pp. 68–69), Felix Nussbaum (pp. 178–79), Paul Delvaux, and Jackson Pollock (pp. 200–203), to name just a few.

Eliad Moreh-Rosenberg

1 James Ensor, "Réflexions sur quelques peintres et lanceurs d'éphémères," *Pourquoi pas?* (Brussels, December 21, 1911), reproduced in *Les Ecrits de James Ensor* (Brussels: Editions Lumière, 1944), 30. English trans. from Danielle Derrey-Capon, "The Masked Soul of James Ensor," in *Ensor*, ed. Gisèle Ollinger-Zinque (Brussels: Musées Royaux des Beaux-Arts de Belgique, 1999), 39.

Kees van Dongen
1877, Rotterdam, The Netherlands–1968, Monte Carlo, Monaco
Active in Paris, France
The Princess of Babylon, 1904
Oil on canvas, 31 7/8 × 25 9/16 in. (81 × 65 cm)

Mizne-Blumental Collection, Bequest of Annette Celine, 2018

Kees van Dongen's portrait, *The Princess of Babylon*, vividly presents fashion's power to establish identity and glamour in a work of art. Van Dongen moved from Rotterdam to Paris at the end of the nineteenth century, and by the 1920s, he had established himself as a prominent artist. In his works, he illuminated those who lived in the shadows and on the fringes of propriety: prostitutes, striptease performers, singers, and dancers, whose occupations were considered dubious at the time. Van Dongen had close relationships in the Parisian couture scene, most notably with the French fashion designer Paul Poiret, who launched an influential orientalist trend in fashion. This trend was characterized by luxurious, boldly colored fabrics, often adorned with intricate embroideries and beading, and exotic prints inspired by Middle Eastern and Asian motifs and costumes. The oriental craze seeped into other cultural realms of the era, such as opera and theater. Most notable were Leon Bakst's designs for the Ballets Russes [see Goncharova's designs, pp. 110–11, for other examples]. Van Dongen became celebrated for his sharp eye for style and his ability to capture the revolutionary cuts and looks of his time.

In *The Princess of Babylon*, van Dongen depicted the soprano Modjesko, the stage persona of African American singer Edward Claude Thompson, who began his career as a performer in minstrel troupes before becoming famous for his drag shows in turn-of-the-century Europe. While orientalist painters of his time gravitated towards passive, nude female figures, such as odalisques in harems, van Dongen placed Modjesko on a princess's throne instead. He treated her body with respect, using the paintbrush as a vehicle of recognition that extolled her beauty, radiance, and couture.

The artist presents Modjesko, in profile, centered in the composition: she wears the most fashionable items of the period—a pearl choker, with a dress that leaves her shoulders bare—subtly signaling a sense of style and elegance. Her head is wrapped in a turban decorated with an aigrette (a headdress adorned with an egret feather). Van Dongen applied paint on the canvas directly from the tube, emphasizing the animalistic quality of the aigrette's feathers. The thick impasto offers a metaphor for "applying" makeup to Modjesko's face, highlighting her red lipstick as well as her blue eyeshadow and eyebrows. Using saturated, anti-realistic Fauvist colors that were groundbreaking for his time, van Dongen wielded them as a tool: as Modjesko's greenish skin merges with her fashionable choker, the fantastical color conjures other realities that make conventional racial paradigms irrelevant.

Ya'ara Keydar

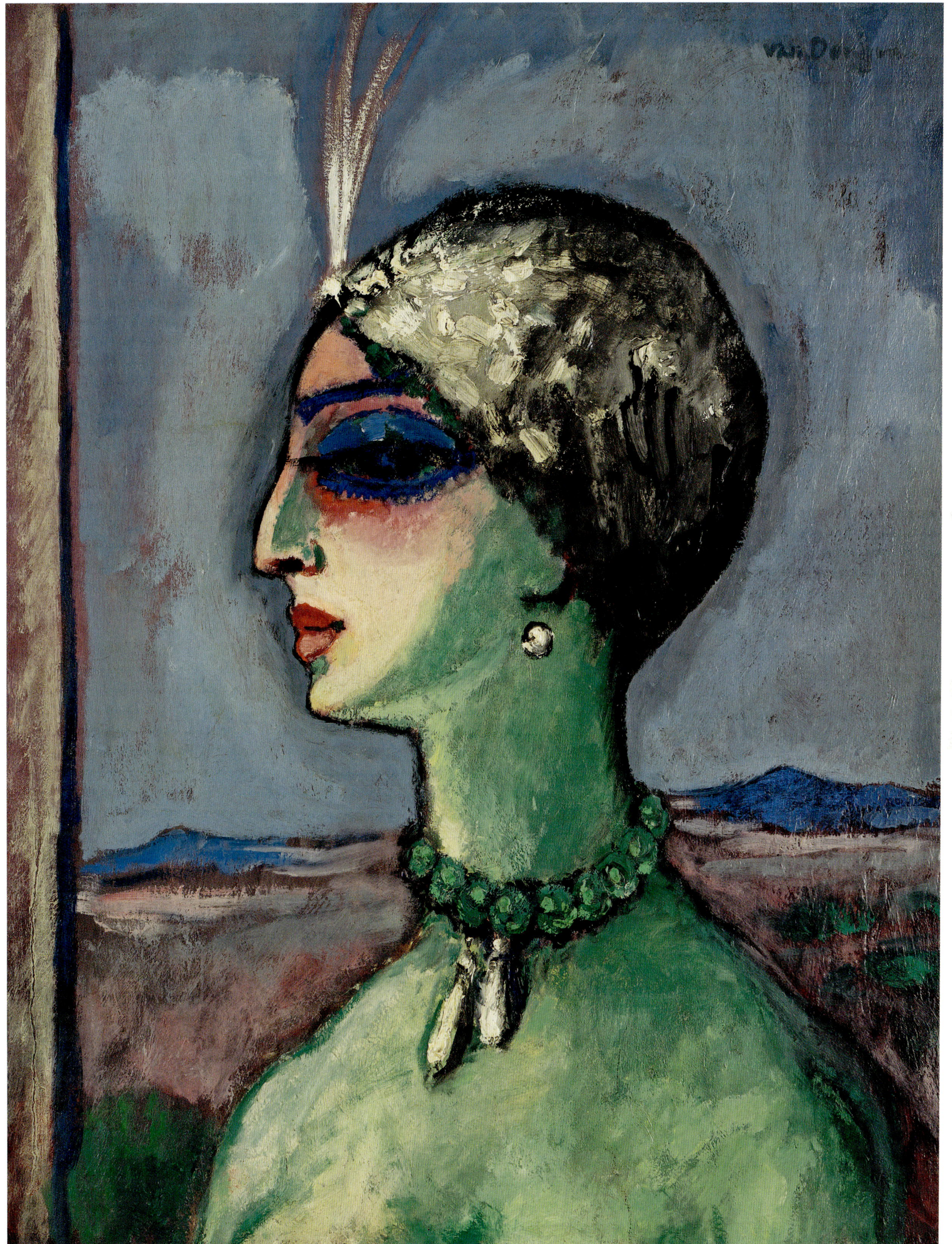

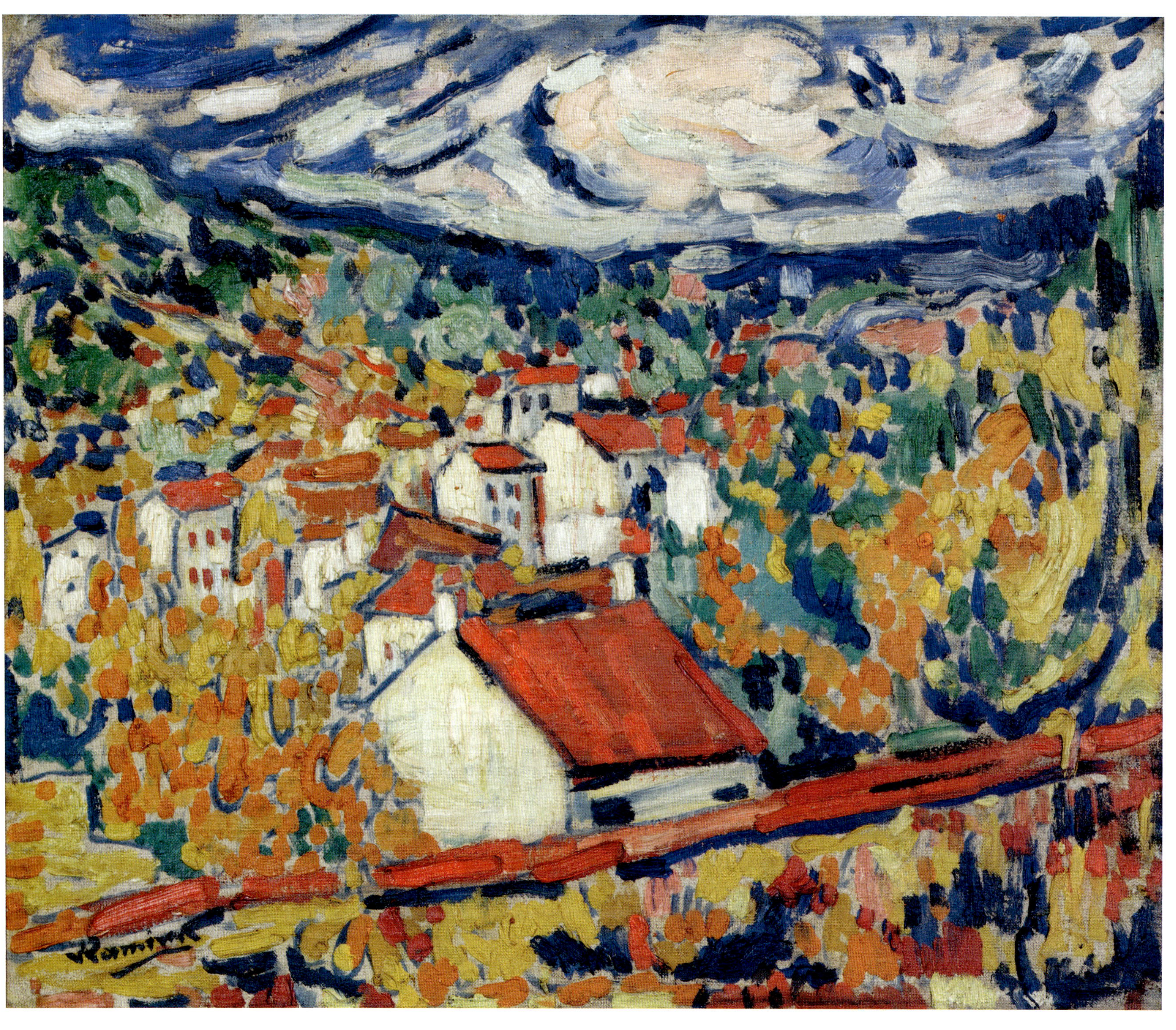

Maurice de Vlaminck
1876, Paris, France–1958, Rueil-la-Gadelière, France
View of Bougival, 1906
Oil on canvas, 18 5/16 × 21 7/8 in. (46.5 × 55.5 cm)

Bequest of Harry and Leah Mecklembourg, New York, 1979

The suburbs of Paris along the banks of the Seine were the primary source of inspiration for Maurice de Vlaminck during his short-lived Fauvist period (1904–07). This scene depicts Bougival, a small town across the river from Chatou, where Vlaminck lived at the time, sharing a studio with friend and fellow artist André Derain. With its radiant, powerful colors and its variegated brushwork, *View of Bougival* exemplifies Fauvism at its peak.

The painting is not stylistically homogenous and features various techniques that Vlaminck employed in these years. The sky is painted mainly in near naturalistic colors, with long, swirling brushstrokes; by contrast, the suburban houses and their surroundings are painted with conspicuously bolder, intense colors and short, oblong, brick-shaped marks. In the period leading up to the summer of 1906, Vlaminck indeed blended these two techniques—the so-called "swirls" and "bricks"—in a number of paintings.

The houses are painted schematically. Their outlines, as well as the more subtle brushstrokes and the large and relatively uniform areas of color, hint at the Gauguin-inspired aspect of Fauvism that Vlaminck began to develop at the time. The combination of different painting techniques in this work demonstrates the synthesis characteristic of Fauvism in general—in which realistic, Impressionist, Post-Impressionist, and abstract elements are interwoven.

Above all, the painting suggests Vlaminck's passion for the local countryside, which he expressed in a letter to Derain around the time he painted this work, explaining his decision to remain at home rather than join him in Paris, where he was renting a studio for the autumn:

> *I had no wish for a change of scene. All these places that I knew so well, the Seine with its strings of barges, the tugs with their plumes of smoke, the taverns in the suburbs, the colours of the atmosphere, the sky with its great clouds and its patches of sun, these were what I wanted to paint.*[1]

Ruth Feldmann

1 Vlaminck, letter to Derain, 1906, quoted in Judi Freeman, *Fauves* (Sydney: Art Gallery of New South Wales, 1995), 220.

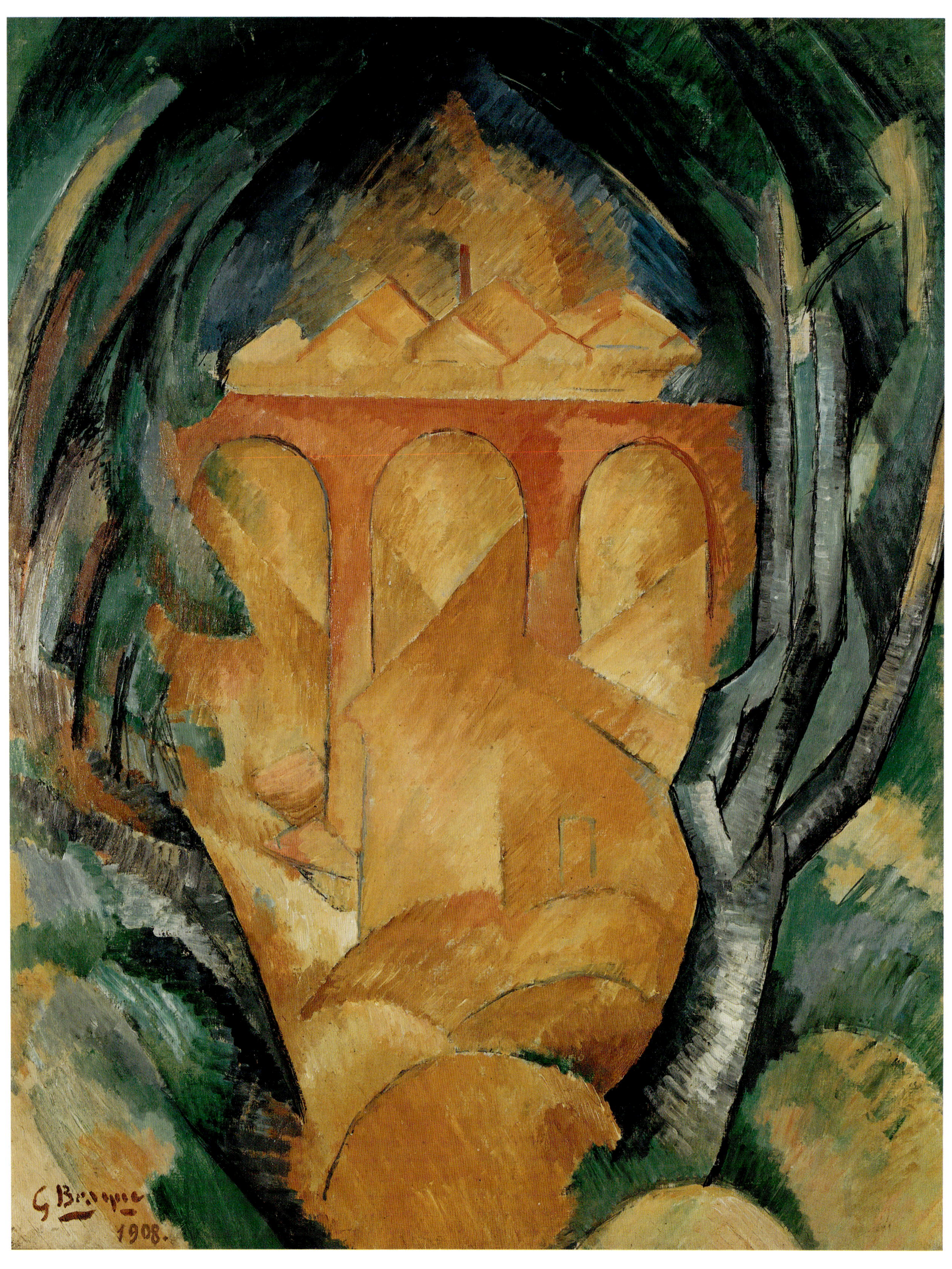
G Braque
1908.

Georges Braque
1882, Argenteuil, France–1963, Paris, France
The Viaduct at L'Estaque, 1908
Oil on canvas, 28 ¾ × 23 ⅝ in. (73 × 60 cm)

Mizne-Blumental Collection, Bequest of Annette Celine, 2018

In 1906, Georges Braque made the first of several visits to L'Estaque, a small port near Marseilles, in search of the bright light that had enamored the recently deceased Paul Cézanne (pp. 30–31), who made over twenty paintings of the fishing village. Braque's fascination with Cézanne's work grew after seeing a posthumous retrospective of his work, and he returned to L'Estaque to further immerse himself in its vistas and atmosphere.

Of the several landscapes Braque made of L'Estaque in 1907, one included a view of the town's rail viaduct—a subject Cézanne also represented, and that Braque would paint twice more.[1] The first view of the viaduct features a Fauvist palette of blues and yellows, while the clarity of the composition and the simplified, geometric forms point to Cézanne's influence. In 1908, in Paris, Braque painted the viaduct again, this time from memory and with a radically reduced palette of greens and ochres. Negating traditional perspective, the viaduct appears to balance precariously on top of a jumble of boxlike houses. Later in 1908, he traveled again to L'Estaque, and made a third painting of the viaduct—the Tel Aviv canvas. Here, the outlines of the houses and the viaduct interpenetrate one another, forming a nearly abstract, flat plane. Dark trees frame the view like stage curtains, reversing conventional pictorial depth by bringing the radiant background forward, generating a screenlike appearance.

When Braque presented his L'Estaque landscapes to the Salon d'Automne in Paris, they were rejected. Art dealer Daniel-Henry Kahnweiler saw the potential in this daring body of work and gave Braque his first solo exhibition, in 1908. The critic Louis Vauxcelles responded unfavorably to the show, writing that Braque "despises form, reduces everything, places and figures and houses to geometrical schemes, to cubes."[2] He had unwittingly announced the emergence of Cubism, and today, Braque's landscapes of L'Estaque are considered the earliest manifestations of the new style. Soon after the debut of these canvases, Pablo Picasso (pp. 124–31) and Braque initiated a storied creative dialogue of six years. Leaving behind the idea that art must imitate nature, they proposed new ways of representing volume in space that emphasized the flatness of the canvas, and the fact of its madeness, permanently upending notions of what a painting can be.

Hillary Reder

1 The first viaduct painting, *The Viaduct at L'Estaque* (1907), is in the collection of the Minneapolis Institute of Art; the second and third, identically titled versions (both from 1908) are in the collections of the Centre Pompidou, Paris, and the Tel Aviv Museum of Art, respectively.

2 Louis Vauxcelles, "Exposition Braques," *Gil Blas*, volume 29, number 10.607.

Pierre Bonnard
1867, Fontenay-aux-Roses, France–
1947, Le Cannet, France
Morning, or The Jams, 1915
Oil on canvas, 49 × 32½ in. (124.5 × 82.5 cm)

On long-term loan from the Moshe and Sara Mayer Collection

Morning, or The Jams depicts a relaxed, seemingly banal moment in the artist's life: his mistress and eventual wife, Marthe, spooning jam into bowls. Working at the turn-of-the-twentieth century, Pierre Bonnard has always defied categorization. He has often been considered as a kind of a Neo-Impressionist trying to capture a glimpse of everyday life. During much of the twentieth century, he was defined as a traditionalist, still working in the manner of Impressionism, and Picasso maintained that he was "not really a modern painter." However, in the 1890s, at the outset of his career, Bonnard was known primarily as a member of Les Nabis, an artist's group that was centered on the symbolic and decorative realms, far removed from a naturalistic portrayal of reality.

Regardless of precisely how Bonnard fit into prevailing narratives of the avant-garde in these years, the unconventional, flattened perspective of *Morning, or The Jams*, dominated by adjacent geometric planes painted in bold colors and patterns, signals that Bonnard was looking beyond the tradition of Western painting. In 1890, a visit to a large-scale exhibition of Japanese prints held at the Parisian École des Beaux-Arts deeply inspired Bonnard, along with other members of Les Nabis. He developed a lifelong appreciation for Japan and its culture, powerfully evident in this painting, created twenty-five years after that exhibition. It possesses several signature principles of Japanese art: eschewing symmetrical or centralized compositions in favor of emphasis on the edges of the canvas, and constructing space through screening techniques and dramatic diagonals.

While Bonnard may have rejected the trends of his era that favored abstraction and a break from tradition—Fauvism and Cubism, for example—his works possess a distinctly modern consciousness. Bonnard's innovation lay in his understanding of art as a reflection of an evolving memory. After a series of quick sketches, intended to capture various poses and situations, he worked with oil paints on canvas to process the initial experience, intermixing the various compositions and visual memories into one image. He depicted Marthe numerous times in their apartment, and the scene here perhaps results not only from modeling sessions but also from an amalgam of countless mornings they shared over their decades together, with Marthe in her signature shade of bright orange-red punctuated with black stockings.

The date of the painting charges the pathos-free domestic moment depicted by Bonnard with a dramatic air: it was made a year after the outbreak of World War I, in which France, like the rest of Europe, suffered heavy losses. Bonnard wanted to enlist along with many of his friends who fought in the trenches but was refused due to his age. It is as though the artist was trying to hold on to the memory of a time of calm and comfort, while the world around him was on fire.

Shua Ben-Ari

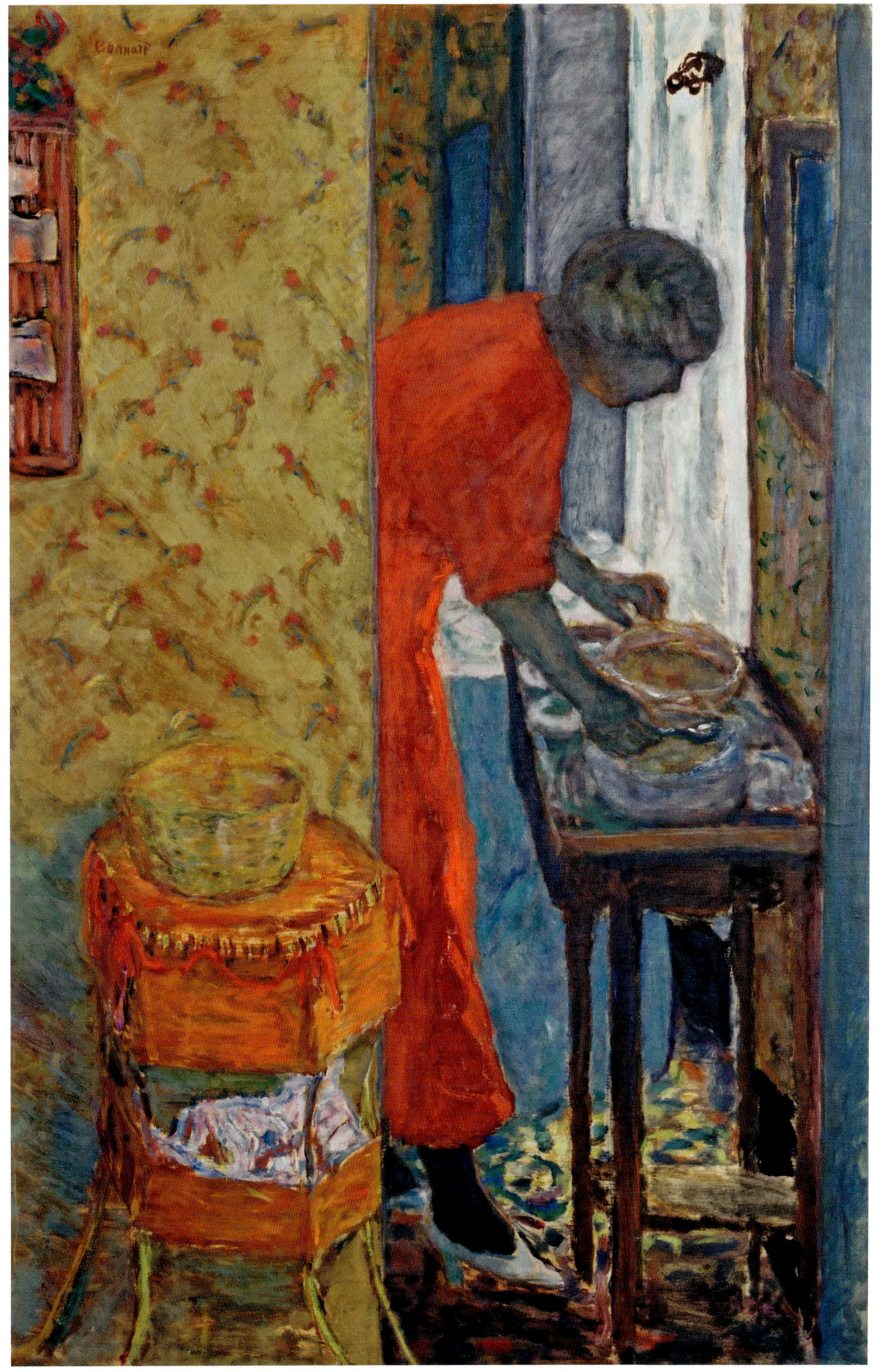

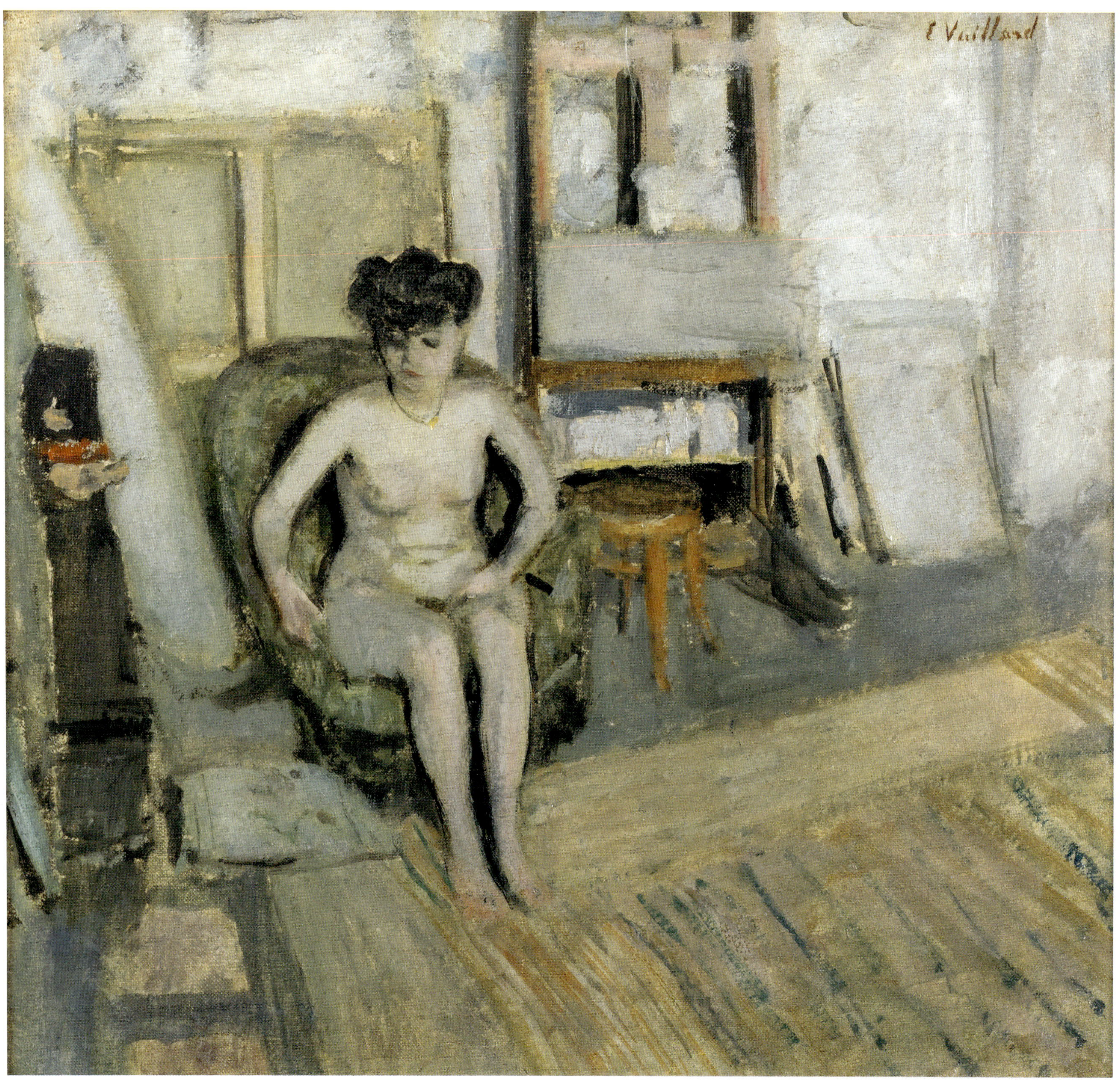
E Vuillard

Édouard Vuillard
1868, Cuiseaux, France–1940, La Baule, France
Small Seated Nude, c. 1903
Oil on canvas, 14 3⁄16 × 14 15⁄16 in. (36 × 38 cm)

Gift of Jacques and Eugenie O'Hana, London, 1972

With its theatrical atmosphere and nearly monochromatic palette, this painting stands out in Édouard Vuillard's oeuvre, which focuses primarily on vibrantly colored and patterned domestic scenes, attesting to a new artistic interest he developed between 1900 and 1907. Vuillard began his career in the late 1880s, when he co-founded the avant-garde group Les Nabis with fellow students from the Académie Julian in Paris. The rebellion against the mainstream art scene was also manifested in his affiliation with the circle of intellectuals behind the influential, eclectic journal *La revue blanche*.

In 1900, Vuillard met Lucie Hessel, a charismatic socialite, who regularly hosted figures from Paris's cultural milieu in her home, and she became his close friend and muse, often appearing in his paintings. In these years, he frequented the Louvre's classical art galleries and expanded his knowledge of Greek and Roman art, which is reflected in more than thirty paintings from this period, depicting countless nudes in various postures. In this painting, the model is seated in an armchair in the studio, wearing only a necklace, flanked by canvases and paintings leaning against the studio wall.

Though the nude was a new subject for Vuillard, this scene shares many of the same characteristics of his earlier interiors. The ostensibly spontaneous composition likely stems from his use of the first Kodak camera, invented in 1888—a portable box camera with which he captured moments in social gatherings. Since the camera did not allow the photographer to preview the frame before it was taken, its lens had to be pointed at a height estimated to yield the desired shot, generating unbalanced, off-center compositions, often containing strong diagonals. Vuillard adopted these transient compositions and translated them into painting. The work thus seems to evoke a fleeting glimpse into an intimate moment, even though it is the result of a lengthy work process between the artist and the model.

Shua Ben-Ari

Eugène Atget
1857, Libourne, France–1927, Paris, France
Viarmes, Château, 1910
Albumen silver print, 8 × 6 11⁄16 in. (20.3 × 17 cm)

Gift of Michael S. Sachs, Westport, Connecticut, through the American Friends of the Tel Aviv Museum of Art, 1992

Eugène Atget documented fin-de-siècle Paris, leaving behind more than 8,000 photographs taken over a period of about thirty years. Atget photographed the city primarily at dusk and dawn, focusing on empty streets shrouded in fog and the city's architecture. His photographs capture a modest Paris, different from its cosmopolitan public image. He used a large-format view camera and glass plates to produce high-definition, detailed images. The lack of human presence in his photographs, along with their soft, diffused light, imbues them with a sense of mystery—a world emptied of its inhabitants. Before World War I, Atget sold his photographs mainly to painters, including Georges Braque (pp. 54–55) and Henri Matisse (pp. 120–23). After the war, his photographs drew the attention of Man Ray and his studio assistant, American photographer Berenice Abbott, who preserved and exhibited his work. Atget received widespread acclaim only after his death.

The Château of Viarmes, documented in this photograph, is located in Île-de-France and was built in 1758 for Jean-Baptiste Élie Camus de Pontcarré, Lord of Viarmes, on the ruins of a medieval fortress. The U-shaped castle was constructed using local stone and that of the fortress's ruins. Heraldic decorations associated with the original owners are visible under the roof. In 1857, the city of Viarmes purchased the château, and today it is used as city hall and a museum dedicated to local history. The park adjacent to the castle in Atget's photograph no longer exists. The photograph shows a view of the back of the castle, with two open windows—in the upper one, bedding is hanging out, being aired. The vegetation in the yard is dry and neglected, with several uprooted shrubs, and the castle appears long past its glory days. The photograph does not seek to aggrandize it, but rather presents it as something of a forgotten monument, emptied of its cultural and historical significance.

Raz Samira

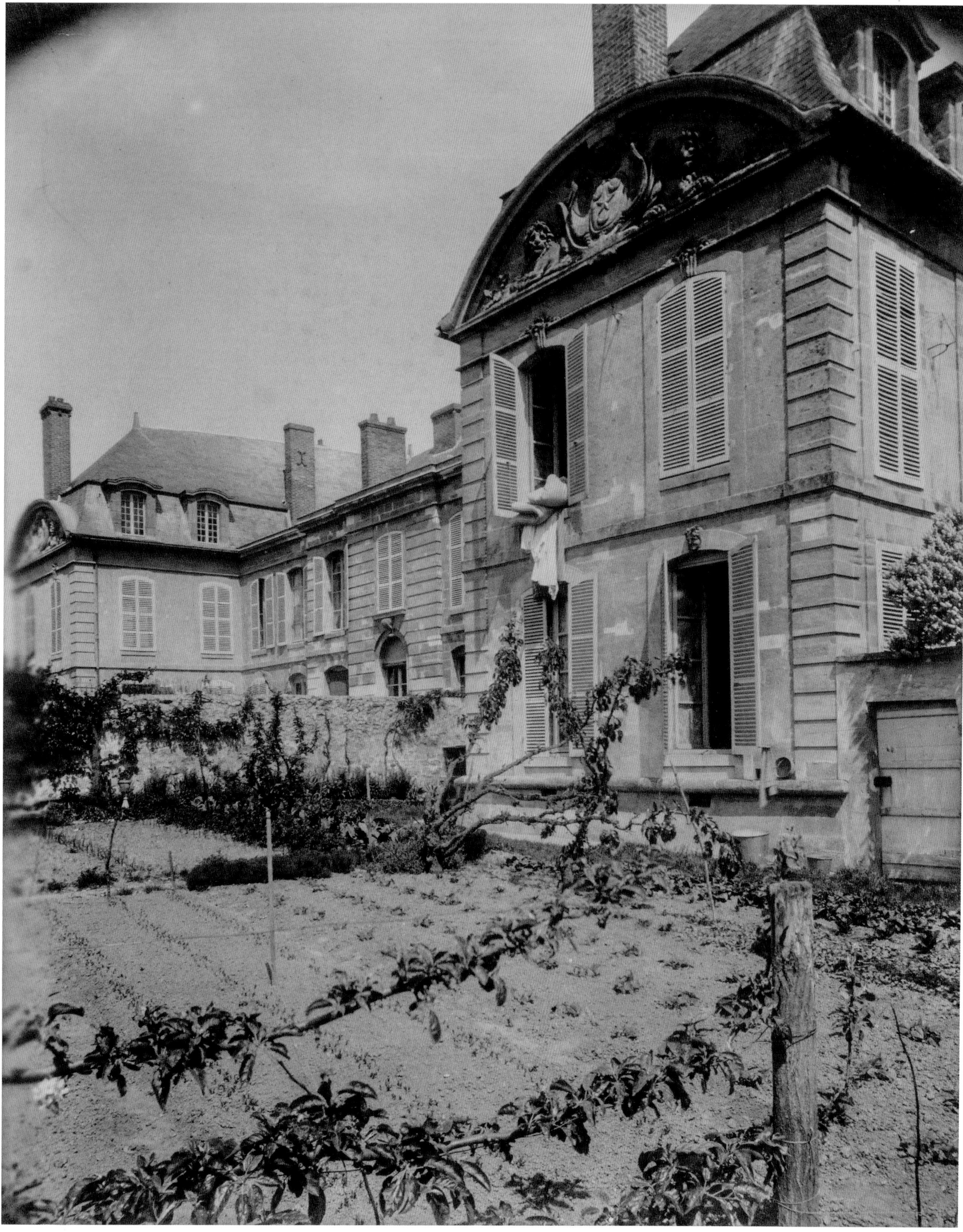

Lesser Ury
1861, Birnbaum, Prussia (now Międzychód, Poland)–
1931, Berlin, Germany
Holstein Switzerland, 1908
Oil on canvas, 39 3/8 × 27 9/16 in. (100 × 70 cm)

Purchased through a contribution from Arieh Shenkar, 1944

This work portrays a resort area in the north of Germany known as Holstein Switzerland for its resemblance to picturesque Swiss landscapes. Lesser Ury occasionally vacationed there.

In this painting, absolute stillness reigns. No living creature disrupts the tranquility, which is at once pastoral and slightly menacing. In the foreground, dark trees with greenish-brown foliage are bathed in dazzling light; they form a frame for the expanse of the sky and the lake, which are painted an identical yellowish-white, and are separated by a narrow strip of earth. Although this is an oil painting, the paint is thinly applied and the surface is unsaturated and finely textured, as if it had been smoothed with the palm of a hand. These qualities lend it the appearance of a pastel—a medium closely associated with Ury. Indeed, a pastel study with an identical composition is in a private collection in New York.

Along with Max Liebermann (pp. 64–65), Lovis Corinth, and Max Slevogt, Ury was a prominent German Impressionist painter—together, these artists played a key role in establishing modern art in Germany. Ury was deeply influenced by French Impressionism, and by Edgar Degas in particular, which is apparent in the uncanny nature and somber palette of this work.

In addition to painting landscapes and Jewish subjects, Ury is celebrated for his images capturing the bustle of Berlin, his home from 1887 until his death in 1931. Even though he was considered something of an introvert, many of his works feature cafe scenes and city streets, making him an important forerunner of the German Expressionists, who enshrined the modern metropolis in their works. This landscape painting, with its static character, stands in sharp contrast to the dynamism of early twentieth-century Berlin.

Alisa Padovano-Friedman

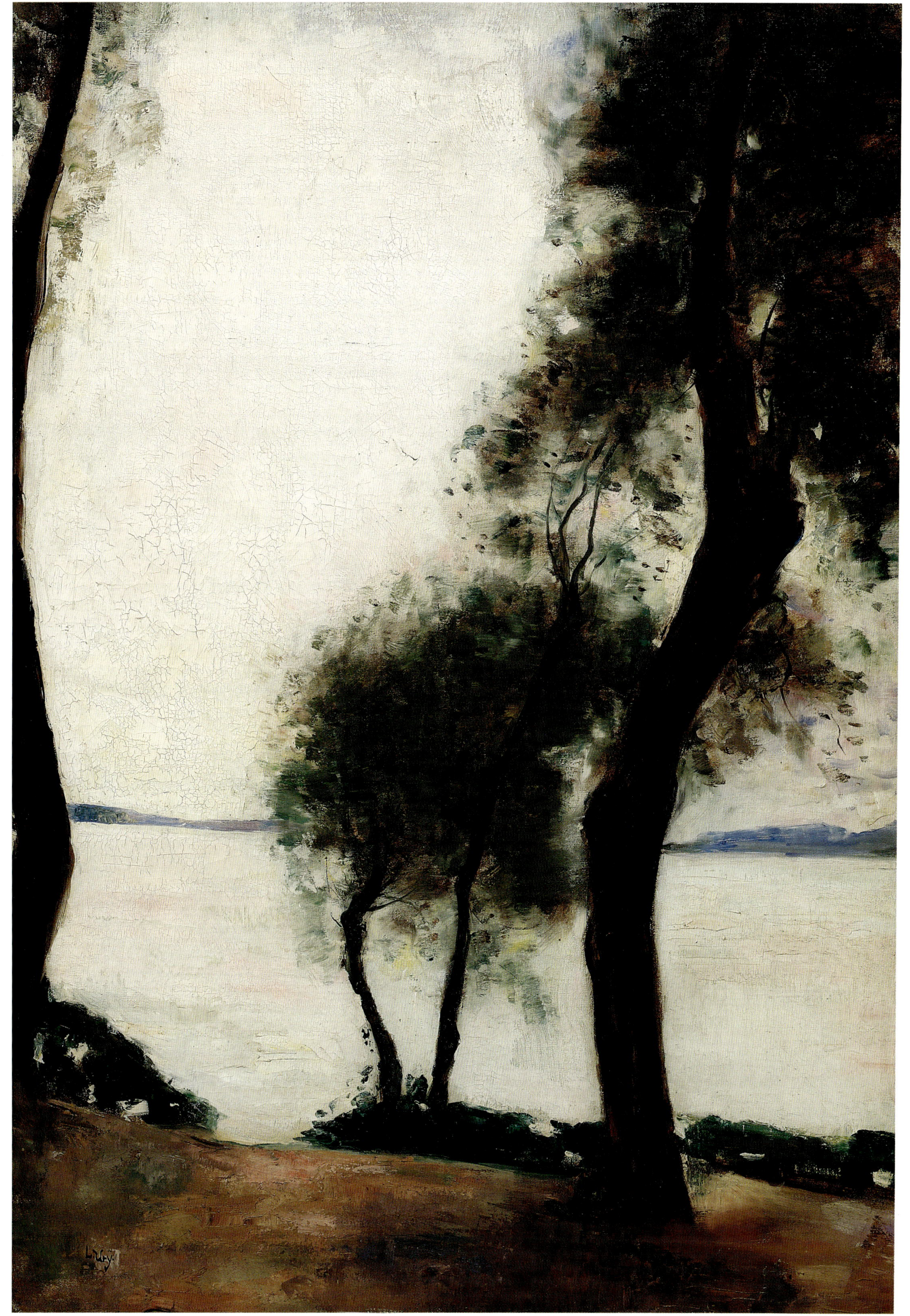

Max Liebermann
1847–1935, Berlin, Germany
Self-Portrait, 1911
Oil on canvas, 21 5⁄8 × 18 1⁄8 in. (55 × 46 cm)

Gift of Dr. Walter Feilchenfeldt, Amsterdam, 1938

This self-portrait by the German painter Max Liebermann arrived at the Tel Aviv Museum in the spring of 1940. It was a gift from Dr. Walter Feilchenfeldt, owner of the Paul Cassirer gallery in Amsterdam, and was received by the Museum's director, Dr. Karl Schwarz, who visited Amsterdam in November 1938 on his last trip to Europe before the outbreak of World War II. The sixty-four-year-old artist portrays himself frontally against a neutral background. Vivid, impressionistic brushstrokes articulate the modeling of his head as a subtle light from the left intensifies his physical presence. His eyes are fixed upon the viewer, in this case the actual recipient of the painting, whom he addresses with his brush in the upper right-hand corner: *to Paul Cassirer / M Liebermann.*

Paul Cassirer was one of the most influential and innovative promoters of modernism in Germany. Founded in 1898, his gallery, the Kunstsalon Cassirer, presented French and German Impressionist paintings to Berlin's emerging art scene. Both the painter and the dealer were mediators between French and German art and ardent supporters of the Berlin Secession. A revolt against the dominant yet stagnant artistic establishment, the Berlin Secession was an independent artists' association—founded in 1898 with Max Liebermann as its president—which championed individual artistic freedom and international collaboration. Liebermann stepped down from his leadership role in 1911, the year of this self-portrait, following fierce battles between adherents of Impressionism and Expressionism, exacerbated by virulent anti-Semitic attacks against Cassirer and Liebermann in the German nationalist press.

Paul Cassirer died in 1926 and his daughter, Suzanne Bernfeld-Cassirer, inherited his collection. After the National Socialists seized power in January 1933, she was desperate to raise funds in order to immigrate with her family to the United States. To support her, Walter Feilchenfeldt, who ran the gallery with Grete Ring after Cassirer's death, bought every picture, piece of furniture, and book from her holdings. As his widow, Marianne Feilchenfeldt, wrote to Dorit Yifat, a former curator at the Tel Aviv Museum of Art: "You may realize that paintings by Liebermann were more or less impossible to sell and [Feilchenfeldt] would not have sold it being a gift to his former 'chef' Paul Cassirer."[1]

When, in 1937, Walter Feilchenfeldt was forced to liquidate the Kunstsalon Cassirer in Berlin, he transferred the remaining artworks, including Liebermann's self-portrait, to the Amsterdam branch. Before the German invasion of Holland in May 1940, the Feilchenfeldts moved to Switzerland and donated the painting to Tel Aviv along with other important graphic works by Ernst Barlach, Max Slevogt, and Käthe Kollwitz (pp. 176–77).

Chana Schütz

1 Letter from Marianne Feilchenfeldt, Zurich, to Dorit Yifat, December 3, 1980, Tel Aviv Museum of Art object file.

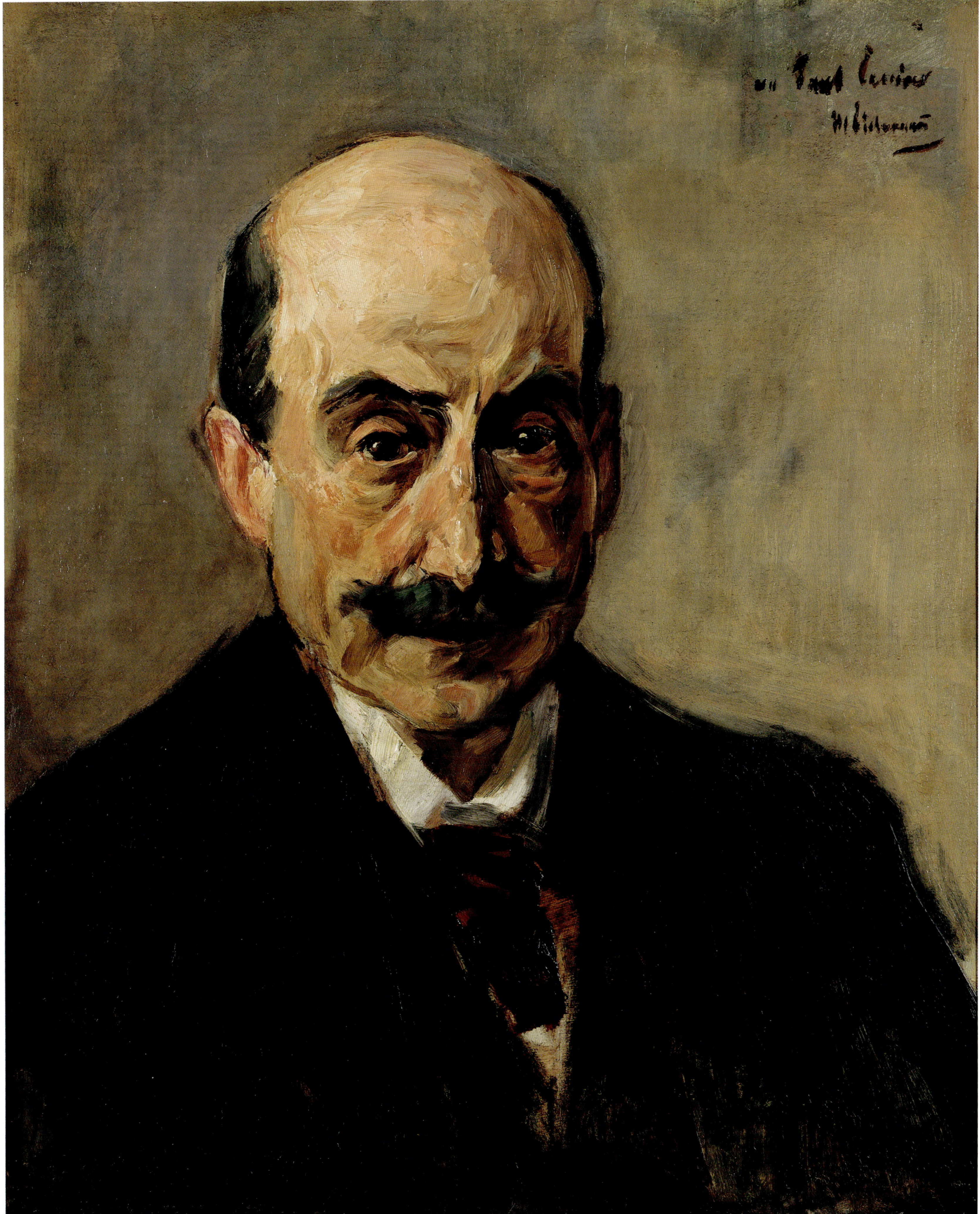

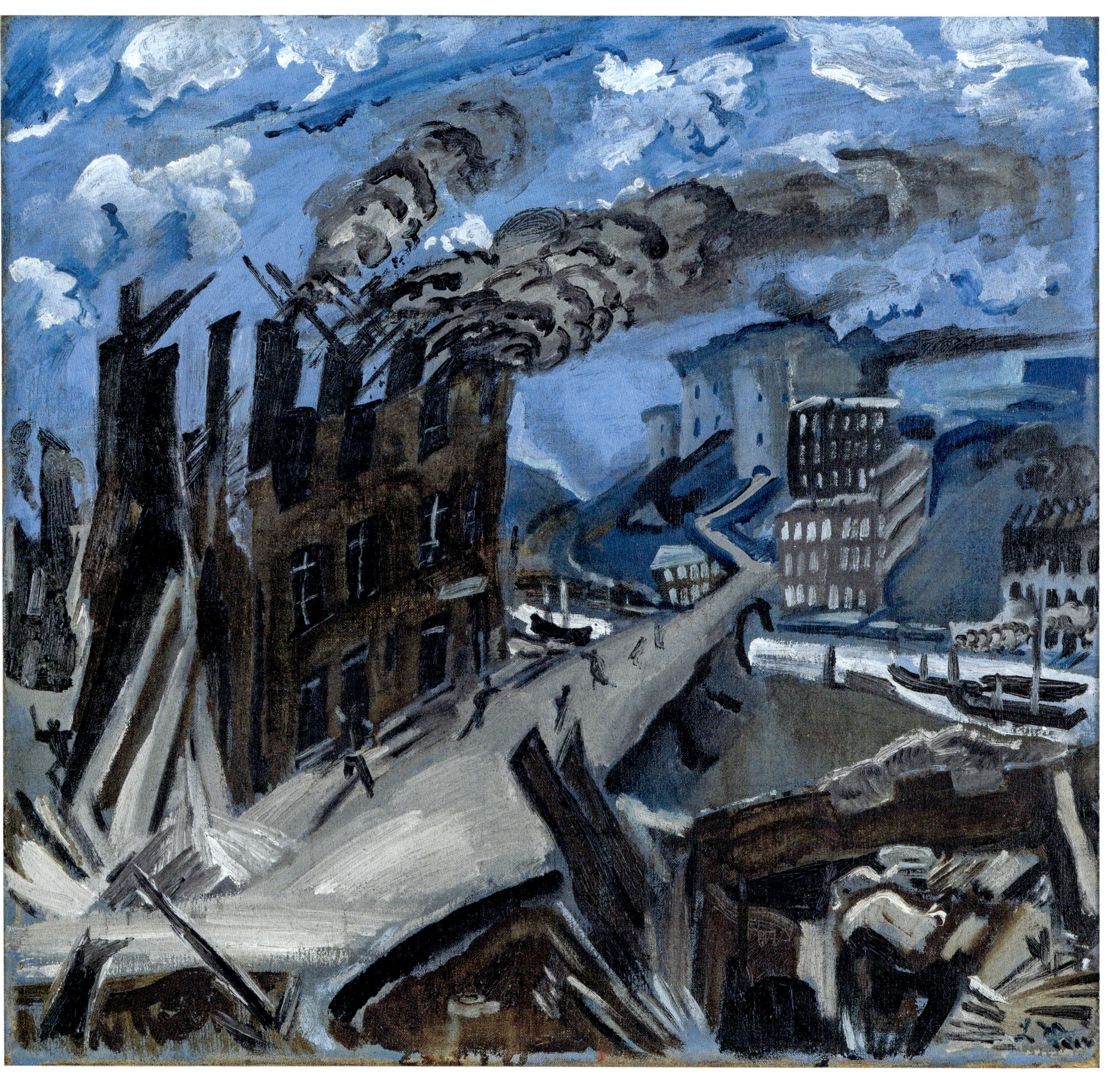

Ludwig Meidner
1884, Bernstadt, German Empire (now Bierutów, Poland)–1966, Darmstadt, Germany
Burning Factory Building, 1912
Oil on canvas, 18 ⅛ × 19 11⁄16 in. (46 × 50 cm)

Acquisition, 1942

Burning Factory Building is among the first of approximately fifteen works in the *Apocalyptic Landscapes* series that Ludwig Meidner painted between 1912 and 1916 on the theme of a burning and collapsing city. Like many paintings by Meidner, a prominent representative of the Expressionist avant-garde in Germany, this work is characterized by loose, vigorous brushstrokes and a distortion of form and perspective. In contrast to most of his paintings, however, here the artist limited himself to a restrained, minimalist color scheme of black, gray, and blue. This painting also reflects a stylistic turning point for Meidner, who for several years had painted tranquil suburbs in light colors.

The dark, devastated streets in *Apocalyptic Landscapes* are not based on real scenes, but rather express the artist's personal mindset and the spirit of the time. Meidner represented the industrialized metropolis in general, and Berlin in particular, as a menacing, alienating site of inevitable catastrophe. Writing of the period when he painted this work, Meidner recalled, "I trembled in front of steaming canvases, whose every part, every tattered cloud, and every torrential stream foreshadowed the misery of the earth. I shattered countless tubes of indigo and ochre paint and had a painful urge to break apart everything linear and vertical, to scatter debris, scraps, and ashes across all of the landscapes."[1]

One cannot dissociate the iconography of the *Apocalyptic Landscapes* from the writings of Nietzsche, and especially from *Thus Spoke Zarathustra* (1883), where the collapsing city is an analogy for the end of the world. Meidner, who wrote poems himself, was influenced by the German apocalyptic poetry of his time—especially by that of his friend Jakob van Hoddis, whose well-known *Weltende* (*End of the World*, 1910) is considered the first Expressionist poem.

Ruth Feldmann

1 Ludwig Meidner, "Vision des apokalyptischen Sommers," in *Septemberschrei* (Berlin: Kunstsalon Cassirer, 1920), 8, quoted in Erik Riedel, *Ludwig Meidner: Catalog Raisonné of the Paintings Until 1927* (Berlin: Gebr. Mann Verlag, 2023), 29.

Emil Nolde
1867, Nolde, Prussia (now Denmark)–1956, Seebüll, Germany
Prophet, 1912
Woodcut, 12 5⁄8 × 8 7⁄8 in. (32 × 22.5 cm)
Unpublished, unknown edition (approx. 20–30)

Gift of Dr. Pulvermacher, 1952

Emil Nolde's woodcut *Prophet* is characterized by its bold and simplified forms. It portrays a male figure with a long, flowing beard and a gaze that emanates intensity. His face exhibits striking features, with deeply shaded, sunken eyes, furrowed brows, and hollowed cheeks. Although the figure is posed frontally, directly facing the viewer, the work nonetheless conveys a sense of contemplation and introspection.

The artist's use of woodcut as a medium—with its rough contours, frayed and jagged lines, and richly textured wood grain—adds a raw and tactile quality to the image. Nolde enhanced the expressive tension of the work by using stark contrasts between light and dark areas, dramatically accentuating the force and seriousness of the prophet's expression.

Nolde joined the artist group Brücke in 1906, a year after its formation. Together, these artists aimed to break away from academic traditions and create art that was unrestrained by convention and could authentically reflect inner experiences. Although Nolde was an active member of Brücke only until November 1907, the group played a crucial role in his artistic development and provided a platform for his creative expression. He contributed significantly to its innovations in graphic art, introducing his colleagues to etching while learning the art of woodcut from them. However, he maintained his individuality within the group, and his work from this period does not resemble the other members' work in terms of style and motif.

Nolde is a controversial figure within the Expressionist movement. The artist himself held a favorable view of the nationalist ideology, and his anti-Semitic views are clearly stated in his private writings.[1] Initially his style was highly popular among officials; however, it was later prominently condemned by the Nazi regime. As a result, many of his works were confiscated from public collections and displayed in the propaganda exhibition *Entartete Kunst* (Degenerate Art), organized by the regime in 1937.

Elena Schroll

1 For further reading, see Bernhard Fulda, Christian Ring, and Aya Soika, eds., *Emil Nolde. The Artist during the Third Reich* (Munich: Prestel, 2019).

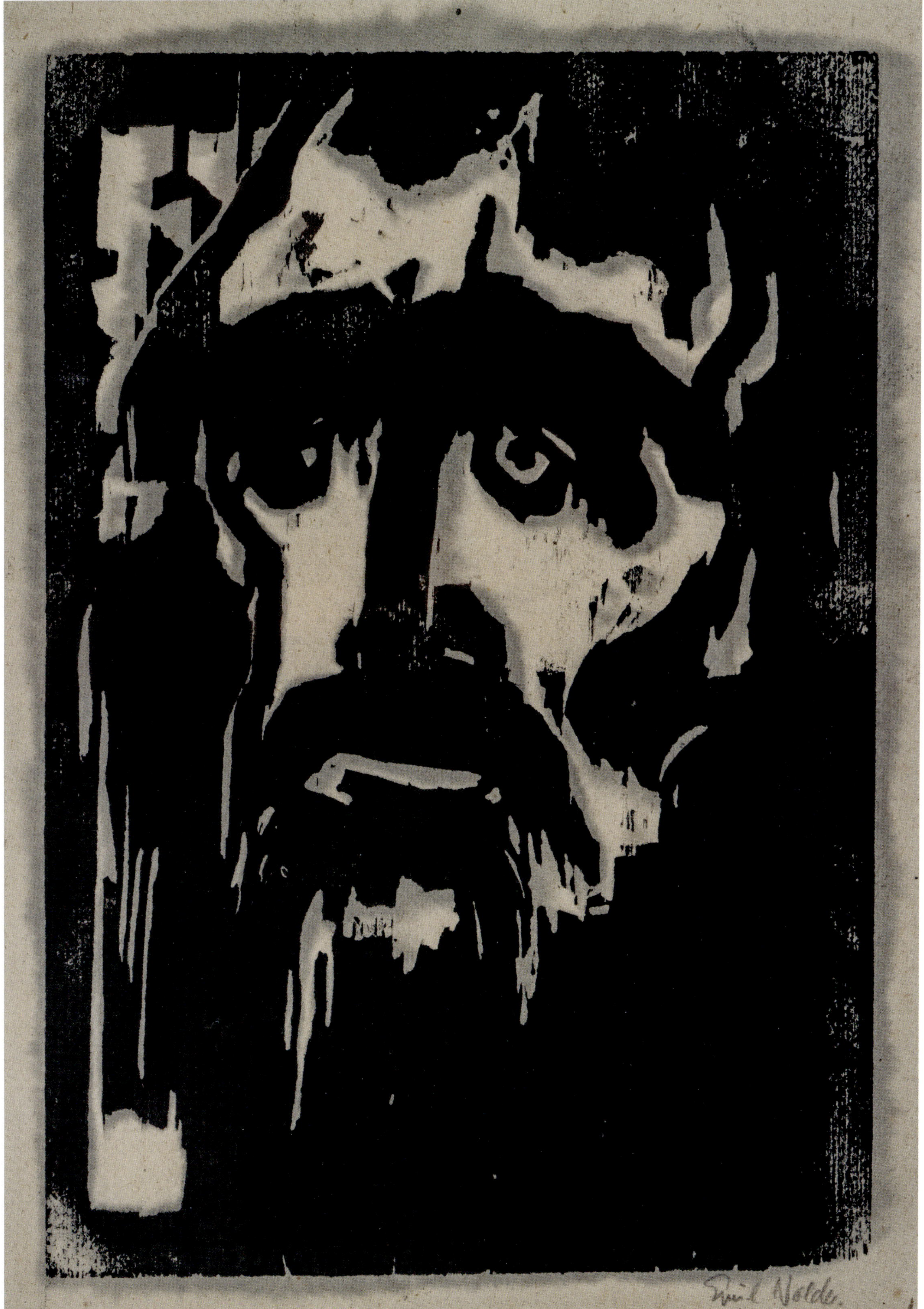
Emil Nolde.

Alexej von Jawlensky
1864, Kuzlovo, Tver Governorate, Russia–
1941, Wiesbaden, Germany
White Turban, 1912
Oil on cardboard mounted on Masonite,
21 ¼ × 19 ½ in. (54 × 49.5 cm)

Mizne-Blumental Collection, Bequest of Annette Celine, 2018

In 1910, Alexej von Jawlensky began painting his series *Heads*, characterized by clashing colors, dark, thick outlines, and unrestrained brushwork. Most of these portraits depict women the artist knew, usually wearing hats or headdresses. In *White Turban*, Jawlensky used both warm and cool colors against a dark ground, creating jarring contrasts, while the woman's features are dominated by reds and turquoises. The "white" of the turban is made up of a prismatic array of squiggly lines. The woman's head is in three-quarter profile, and the neck and shoulders fill the lower half of the painting. Despite the tilt of her head, both of her long, narrow eyes are entirely visible, wide open and staring out with an otherworldly gaze. While Jawlensky avoided identifying details in these works, many of his heads from those years are recognizable as his wife's maid, Helene Nesnakomoff—who was likely the model for this painting. He eventually left his wife, the artist Marianne von Werefekin, and married Nesnakomoff, with whom he already had a child, in 1922.

The rapid, direct brushstrokes and vibrant colors are characteristic of Jawlensky's paintings in this period. They suggest the influence of Vincent van Gogh (pp. 36–37) and the Fauves, and reflect his association with the Blue Rider, the German Expressionist artists' group he co-founded. Using dynamic color combinations and symbolic forms, these artists sought to manifest spiritual expression in their work. Jawlensky turned in particular to Russian icon paintings, familiar to him since his childhood, growing up in a pious Russian Orthodox family. This work references the intense red, blue, and green palette typical of icons. The figure's oversized, slanted eyes and the halo-like turban reinforce this link. Profoundly connected to his heritage, he also drew inspiration from other ancient forms of sacred art as a model for his own, as he attested: "My Russian soul has always been close to the art of old Russia, the Russian icons, Byzantine art, the mosaics in Ravenna, Venice, Rome, and to Romanesque art. All these artworks produced a religious vibration in my soul, as I sensed in them a deep spiritual language. This art was my tradition."[1] Heads would remain central to Jawlensky's art for the remainder of his career—he endowed them with a mystical, saint-like status.

Sophia Berry-Lifschitz

1 Jawlensky, quoted in Volker Rattemeyer, "From the Large Figural Representations to the 'Meditations': Jawlensky's Series," in *Alexej von Jawlensky* (Rotterdam: Museum Boijmans Van Beuningen, 1994), 24.

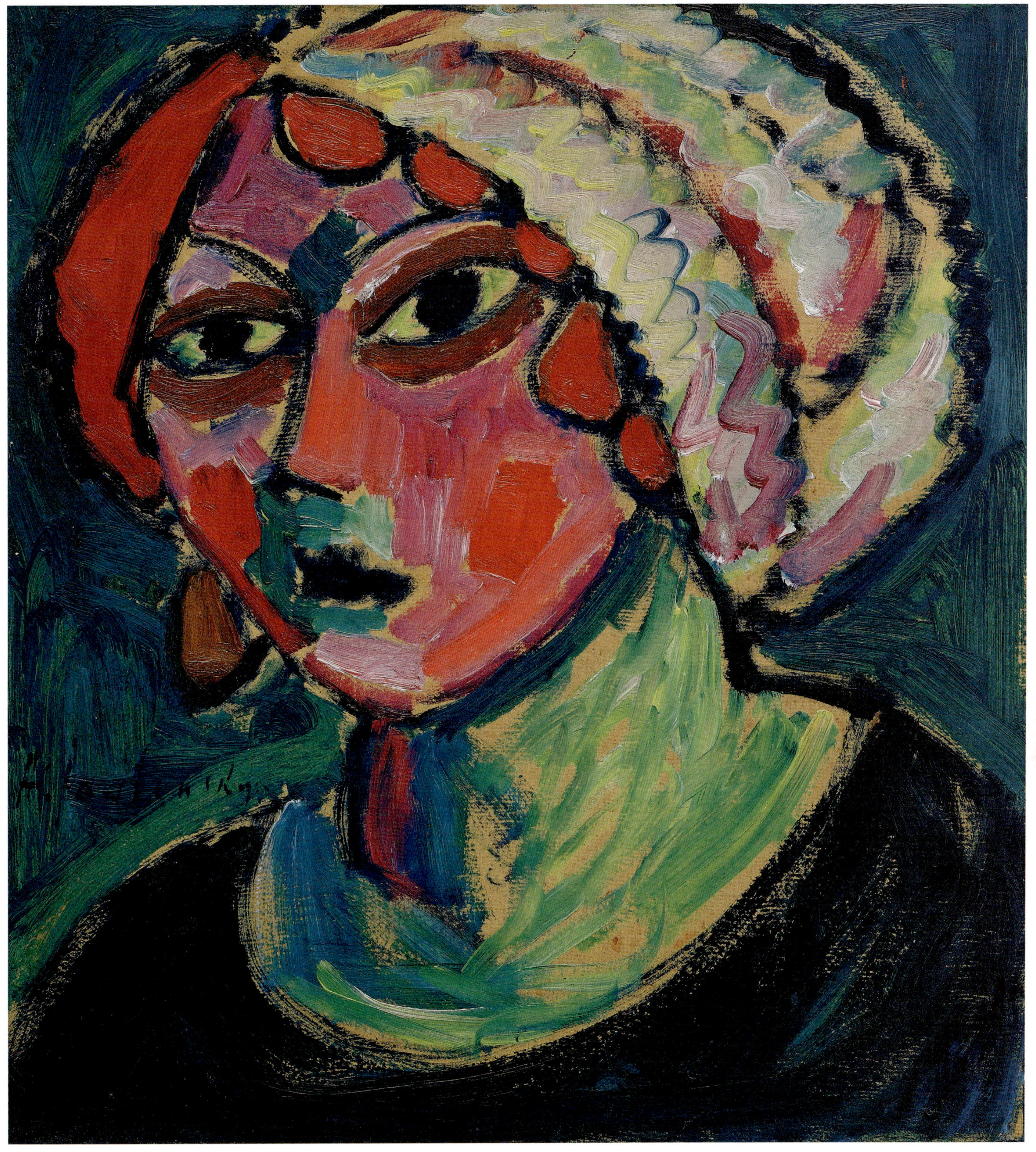

Alexej von Jawlensky
1864, Kuzlovo, Tver Governorate, Russia–
1941, Wiesbaden, Germany
Savior's Face: Dolorosa, 1920
Oil and graphite on paper, mounted on cardboard,
14 9⁄16 × 10 11⁄16 in. (37 × 27.2 cm)

Bequest of Lilly Schwabacher, Ascona, Switzerland, 1989

At the outbreak of World War I, Alexej von Jawlensky, already an established artist in Munich, was forced to flee to Switzerland. During his stay in the town of Saint-Prex, he began to develop a new body of work later to be known as *Variations*. Jawlensky abandoned the crude brushstrokes and vibrant colors that characterized his series *Heads* (p. 71), and shifted to lighter, pastel tones, applied in a thin, uniform layer. Depicting views from the window of his bedroom overlooking the shores of Lake Geneva, the landscapes became increasingly abstract as the series progressed.

In 1917, still in Switzerland, Jawlensky began to paint the series *Mystical Heads* (later titled *Abstract Heads*), to which this painting belongs. He worked on the series with greater devotion upon his return to Munich in 1920, and continued until 1933. Initially based on the likeness of artist and dealer Galka Scheyer, a close friend of the artist who played a major role in promoting his works, the schematic face soon transformed into an independent entity. All the paintings in the series are constructed in a similar way: two horizontal or rounded lines to indicate the eyes, a long vertical line for the nose, a horizontal line, a curved line, or both, for the mouth, and an oval for the chin. Only chromatic nuances and minor compositional changes distinguish the various works from each other.

Jawlensky's adherence to one subject represented in nearly the same composition over many years attests to his desire to explore the expressive qualities of color application, alongside a deep religious sentiment spurring from his Russian Orthodox upbringing. Jawlensky believed that "the work of art is a visible god, and art is 'desire for god.'"[1] The paintings in the series, with their recurring features and meticulous formal reduction, are a kind of modern-day icon. They evoke a deep meditative quality, manifesting Jawlensky's attempt to access the divine through seemingly simple and mundane repetition.

Sophia Berry-Lifschitz

1 Jawlensky, quoted in Silke Thomas, *Alexej von Jawlensky* (Munich: Galerie Thomas, 2015), 50.

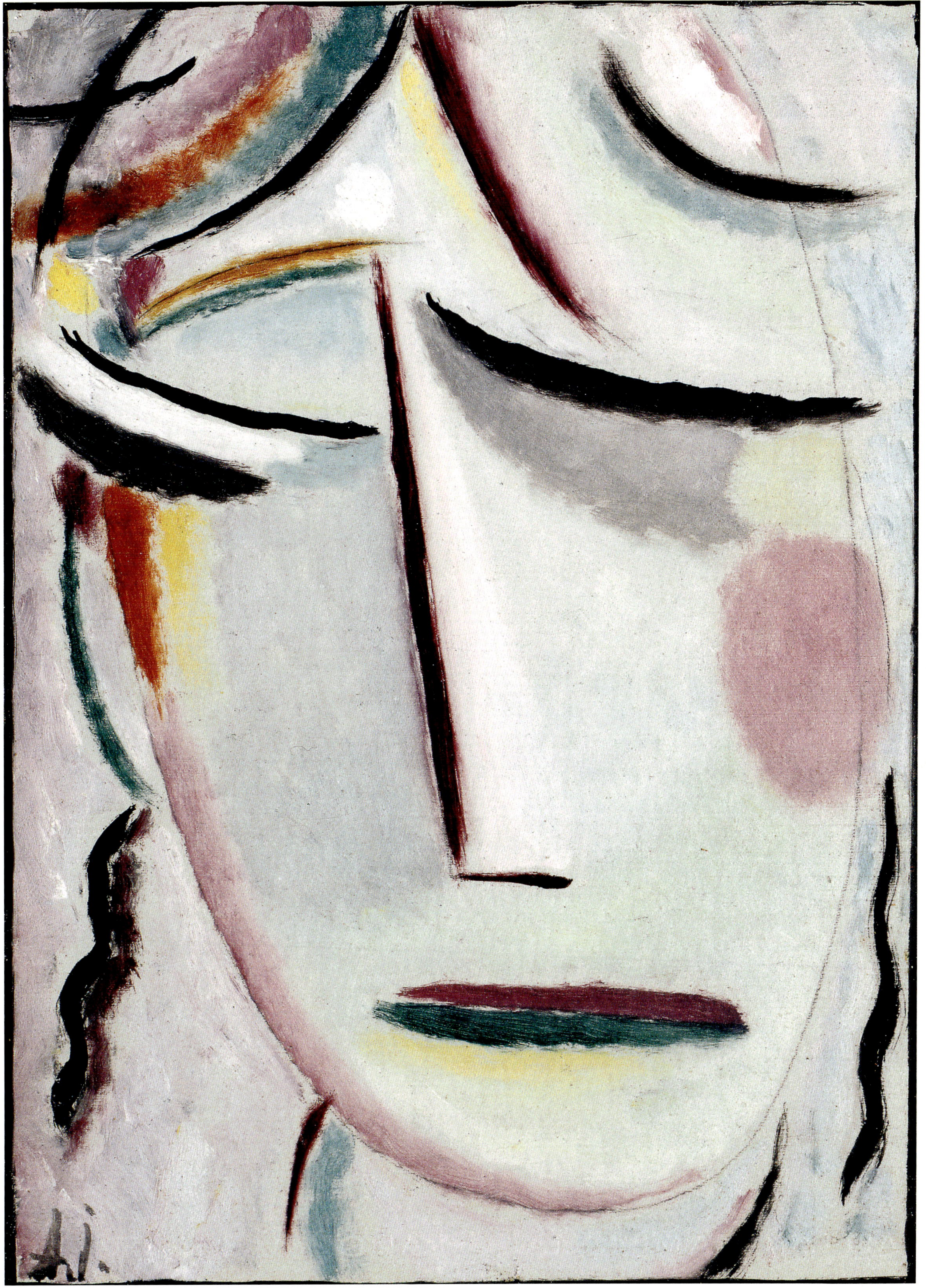

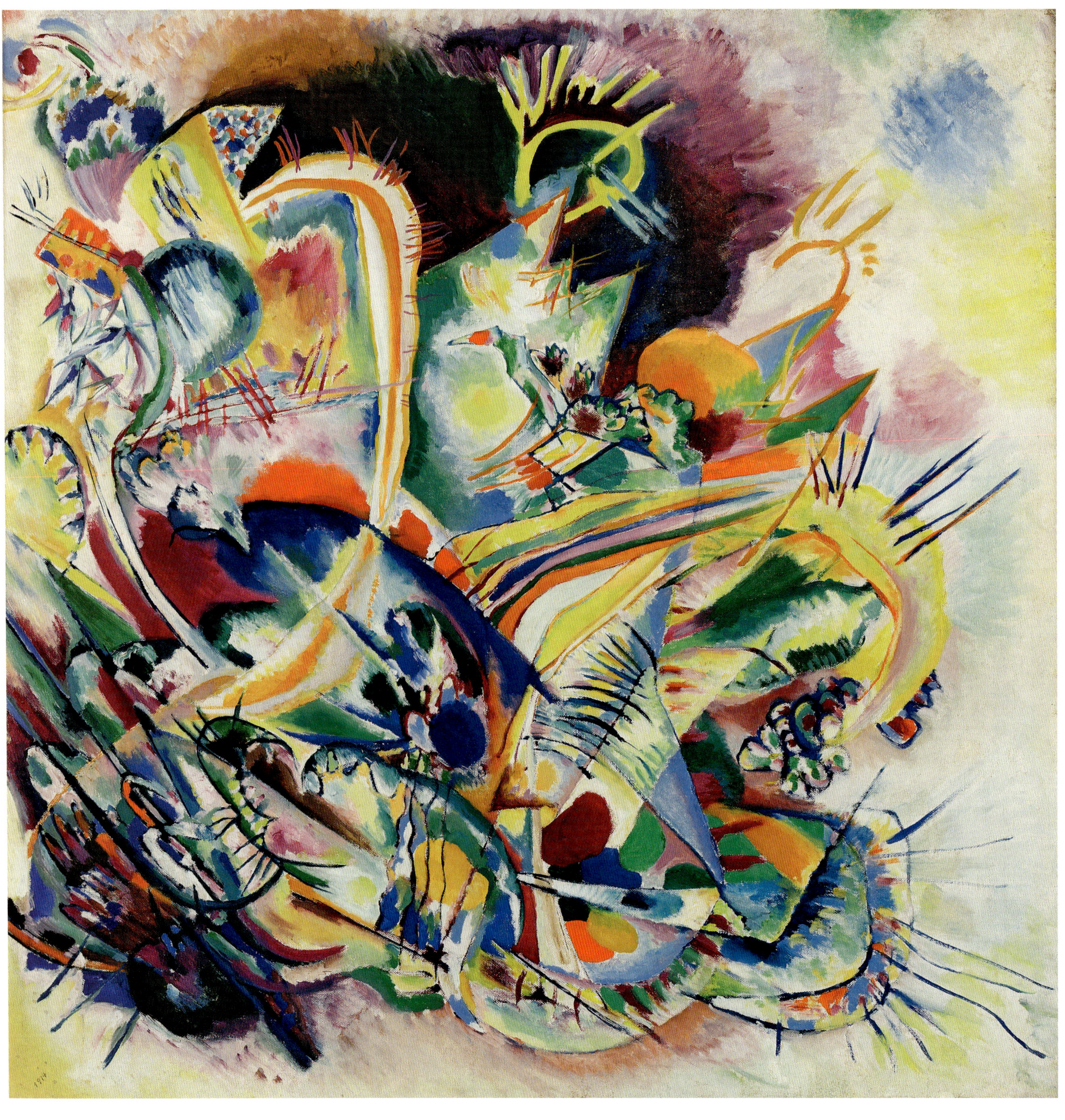

Wassily Kandinsky
1866, Moscow, Russia–1944, Neuilly-sur-Seine, France
Untitled (Improvisation V), 1914
Oil on canvas, 43 11⁄16 × 43 11⁄16 in. (111 × 111 cm)

Mizne-Blumental Collection, Bequest of Annette Celine, 2018

Wassily Kandinsky is recognized as a leading painting theorist and innovator whose experiments with abstraction proved consequential in the broader shift towards nonrepresentational art in the early twentieth century. The Russian-born artist began his career while living in Munich and its environs from 1896 until the outbreak of World War I in 1914. Kandinsky promoted art's ability to transform self and society; pastoral landscapes and apocalyptic imagery emerged in the late 1900s from his dissatisfaction with urban industrialization and materialism. Notably, in 1911, the same year in which he published his groundbreaking treatise *Über das Geistige in der Kunst* (*On the Spiritual in Art*), Kandinsky and the German artist Franz Marc formed Der Blaue Reiter (The Blue Rider). Shared interest in the expressive potential of color and the symbolic resonance of forms united this loose, transnational confederation of artists, writers, and musicians. What Kandinsky called the artist's "inner necessity," or the impulse for spiritual expression, remained his guiding principle.[1]

Later assigned the Roman numeral "V," this painting is associated with Kandinsky's *Improvisations* (1909–14), a group of works that uses musical terminology and seeks to convey internal forces.[2] Kandinsky was interested in synesthesia, a phenomenon in which the senses are commingled and felt simultaneously, such as experiencing color as a tone. Here, sweeping arcs and explosive rays animate the centralized composition. The confluence of overlapping planes and riotous colors suggests a spontaneity of execution that belies the existence of at least one related drawing.[3] While a dark passage looms in the top background, patches of pastel colors create soft atmospheric effects at the right and bottom of the canvas.

As Kandinsky's practice evolved, the representational origins of his rhythmic forms became secondary to line and color. Yet one may still discern in *Untitled (Improvisation V)* evocations of rolling hills, stalwart mountain peaks, and clustered trees. Some art historians have additionally suggested the presence of a horse, a recurrent motif for Kandinsky and a vehicle for spiritual revolution or upheaval. The artist would not abandon the precedents of representation or of his own early work altogether, even as he explored the transcendent possibilities of abstract forms.

Megan Fontanella

1 Wassily Kandinsky, "On the Spiritual in Art," in Wassily Kandinsky, *Kandinsky: Complete Writings on Art*, eds. Kenneth C. Lindsay and Peter Vergo (1982; repr., New York: Da Capo Press, 1994), esp. 127–30, 165. Originally published as *Über das Geistige in der Kunst. Insbesondere in der Malerei* (Munich: R. Piper & Co., 1912).

2 This painting is not recorded in Kandinsky's *Hauskatalog* (Handlist), his system for documenting the production and transfer of his artwork. It was later exhibited as *Improvisation*. Hans K. Roethel advanced the title "Improvisation V"; see Roethel and Jean K. Benjamin, *Kandinsky: catalogue raisonné of the oil-paintings* (Ithaca: Cornell University Press: 1982): no. 505, 510.

3 See Vivian Endicott Barnett, *Kandinsky Drawings: catalogue raisonné*, vol. 1 (London: Philip Wilson, 2006), no. 347, 180.

Gustav Klimt
1862–1918, Vienna, Austria
Friederike Maria Beer, 1916
Oil on canvas, 66 1/8 × 51 3/16 in. (168 × 130 cm)

Mizne-Blumental Collection, Bequest of Annette Celine, 2018

Gustav Klimt's life-size portrayal of socialite Friederike Maria Beer (1891–1980) is an evocative depiction, brilliantly conveyed through her face and hands. Dozens of preparatory drawings affirm Klimt's devotion to capturing these features. Beer recalled that Klimt would "take my hand and just stand there, holding it, studying it, turning it over without speaking—so long that it made me feel eerie."[1]

Photographs were another aspect of Klimt's process. His sister Hermine recounted that he made "countless enlarged drawings from photographs."[2] A 1916 photograph, which he may have used when she was unavailable, shows Beer in a similar pose.

A visitor to the first Klimt exhibition held in the United States was awestruck upon encountering Beer's portrait. He dashed off a letter to her: "And, there was your portrait! Very beautiful. I didn't know he ever painted you—or knew you. I recognized you immediately. He captured so much of your charm!"[3]

Beer is transfigured against a lushly ornamented scene, awash in decorative effusion, and accompanied by figures derived from a Chinese vase.[4] Beer's boast that she was a "walking advertisement for the Wiener Werkstätte,"[5] a modernist Viennese workshop of artists and designers, is confirmed by her fashionable dress made with Dagobert Peche's *Marina* pattern and a fur coat worn inside out to highlight the silk lining made with Leo Blonder's *Flora* textile design.[6] According to Beer, portraying her in a long and narrow so-called "hobble skirt" was artistic license on Klimt's part.

Typically, Klimt's sitters were the wives or daughters of wealthy industrialists. For this work, Beer's romantic partner, artist Hans Böhler, paid Klimt's fee. While walking along Vienna's Neuer Markt, Böhler offered Fritzi, as Beer was known, a lavish gift. She demurred, preferring to have her portrait painted by Klimt. Surprised, Böhler wept in joy and kissed her in delight, thrilled that Fritzi "chose art over jewels."[7]

Klimt's decision to situate Beer in a fantastical and exotic landscape was an acknowledgment of the cosmopolitan lifestyle of his sophisticated patrons and his own fascination with non-European art. When the commission was completed, Klimt exclaimed, "Now people can no longer say that I paint only hysterical women!"[8]

Photographs from the summer of 1916 show a camaraderie between artist and sitter, perhaps contributing to Beer's willingness to lend her portrait to a 1917 Stockholm exhibition. By the time the painting was unveiled in Vienna at the *Kunstschau 1920*, Klimt had died, Beer and Böhler were no longer a couple, and Vienna was reborn as a republic in War World I's aftermath, thus marking the end of an era.

Janis Staggs

1 Alessandra Comini, *Egon Schiele's Portraits* (Berkeley: University of California Press, 1974), 127–32, esp. 130 for the anecdote about Beer's hand.
2 Franz Eder, "Gustav Klimt and Photography," in Tobias G. Natter and Gerbert Frodl, eds. *Klimt's Women*, exh. cat., trans. Nikolas Bertheau et al. (New Haven, CT: Yale University Press; Cologne: DuMont, 2000), 50.
3 Norman Carton in a letter to Beer dated May 8, 1959, held in the Artists' Gallery Records, 1929–67, Archives of American Art, Smithsonian Institution. Beer was able to bring the Klimt portrait and two other pictures to the United States with the help of Hugh Stix, founder of the Artists' Gallery in New York City.
4 In an interview with Butler Coleman, Beer said that the background motifs came from a Chinese vase. Oral history interview with Federica Beer-Monti, November 1, 1967. Archives of American Art, Smithsonian Institution.
5 Comini, *Egon Schiele's Portraits*, 127.
6 Beer donated the hand-blocked silk dress that she wore for the Klimt portrait to the Costume Institute at the Metropolitan Museum of Art in 1964.
7 Beer related that Böhler offered her a choice between a pearl necklace or having her portrait painted by Klimt, and confided the anecdote about "choosing art over jewels" to Andy Satter in October 1976, as related to the author by Satter, April 22, 2023, and based upon a transcription from 1976.
8 According to Beer, Klimt included her name to immortalize her as related in a 1967 oral history interview (see note 4).

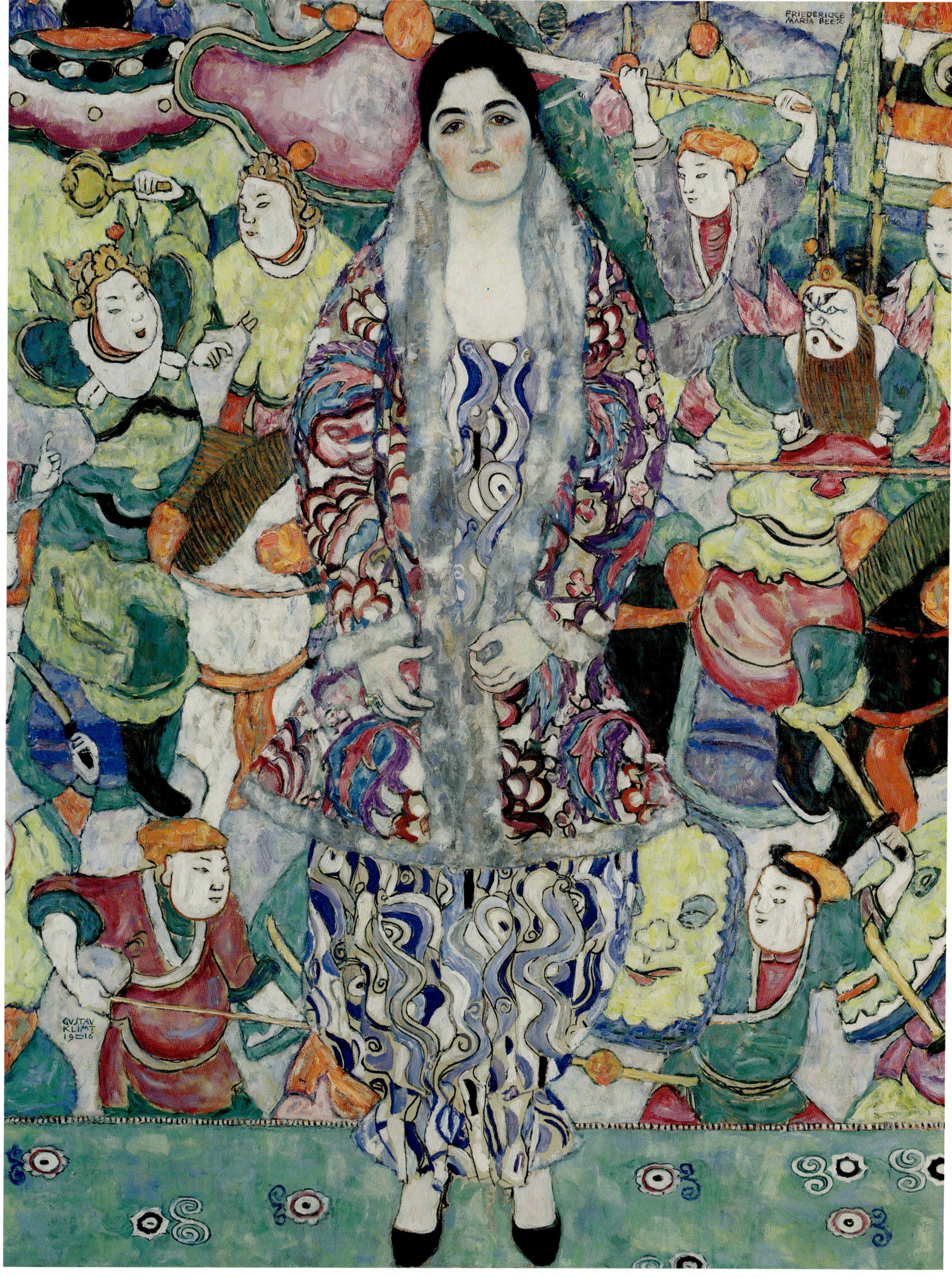
FRIEDERICKE
MARIA BEER
GUSTAV
KLIMT
1916

Egon Schiele
1890, Tulln, Austria–1918, Vienna, Austria

Left *Woman with Mirror*, 1915
Pencil and gouache on paper, 19 ½ × 12 ¾ in. (49.6 × 32.6 cm)

Right *The Prostitute*, 1913
Pencil and gouache on paper, 18 ⅞ × 12 ⅜ in. (48 × 31.5 cm)

Acquisition, c. 1953

From the outset of his artistic career in the opening years of the twentieth century until his death of Spanish flu in 1918, at the age of twenty-eight, portraiture was a central theme in Egon Schiele's work. The Austrian artist frequently made self-portraits as well as portraits of women and girls, relatives, lovers, and models, in different variations, which reflected an ongoing attempt to capture the essence of the human experience and fragile existence in the turbulent modern world. Schiele depicted the body in a sensual and often grotesque manner—fluid bodies with limbs twisted, stretched, or contorted, extending across the entire painterly surface. The background is often left bare and empty, enhancing the sense of alienation and detachment of the vulnerable body.

The 1913 drawing *The Prostitute* attests to Schiele's extensive engagement with figures from the margins of society, such as beggars, or those in throes of nonconforming psychological states—a fascination that was prevalent among modern painters at the turn of the century, who attempted to create a new, frenzied, and deconstructed representation of reality, undermining the old, conservative world of values. Unlike Edgar Degas (pp. 26–29) or Toulouse-Lautrec, who depicted figures embedded within their environments, Schiele extracted his figures from a specific time and place, and left them hanging, exposed and bereft, without context. The portrayal of the prostitute here also resembles a marionette, referencing the artist's fondness for the world of children and for theater puppets, and hinting at a lack of control. The figure embodies a tension between life and death, Eros and Thanatos, or the death drive: on the one hand—the frozen gaze, the limpness of the body threatening to collapse, and the mechanical gesture of the arms from which torn threads hang; on the other hand—the "flesh," which is rendered with watery red dabs, also discernible in the figure's hands and face and in the lining of the dress that accentuates the loins.

Anat Danon-Sivan

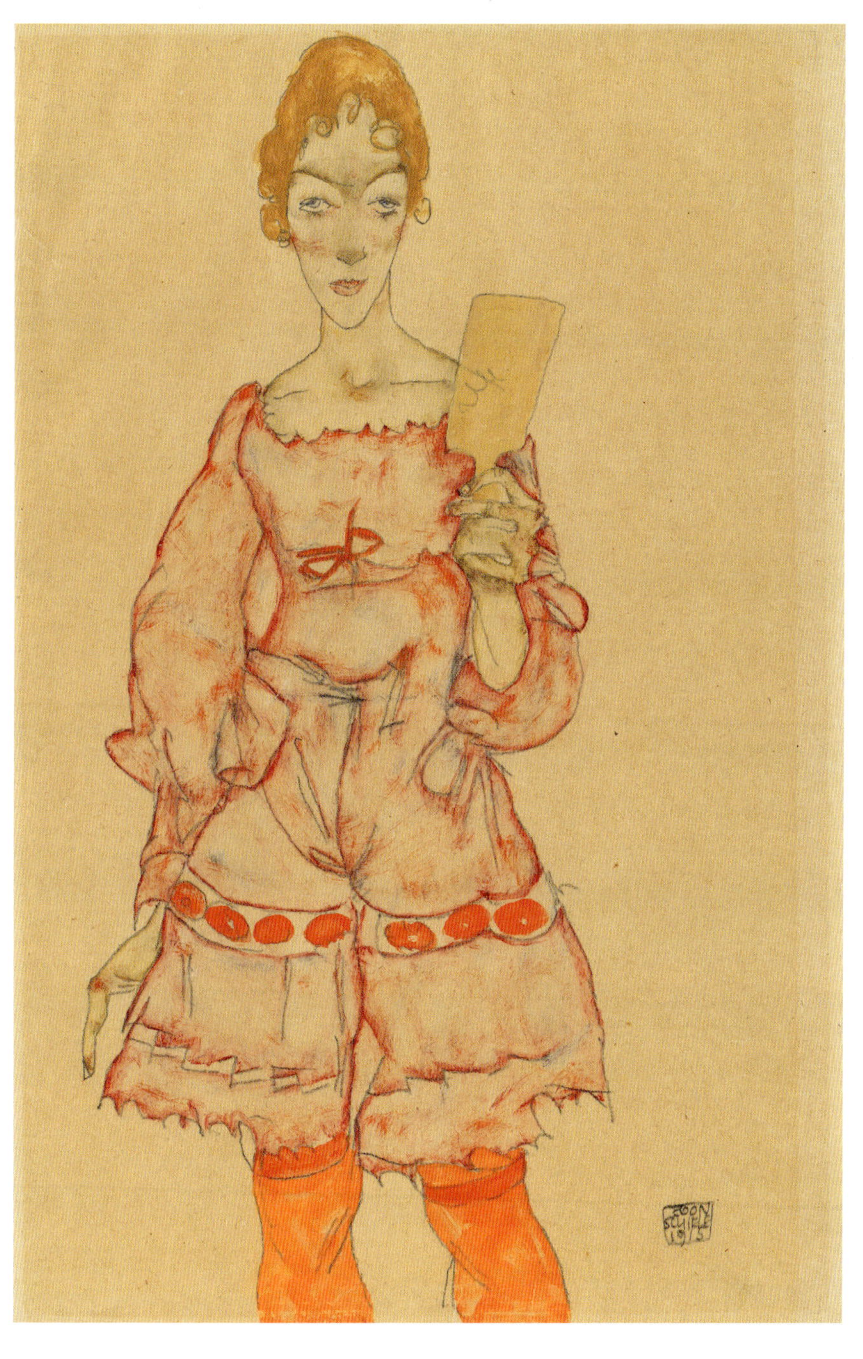

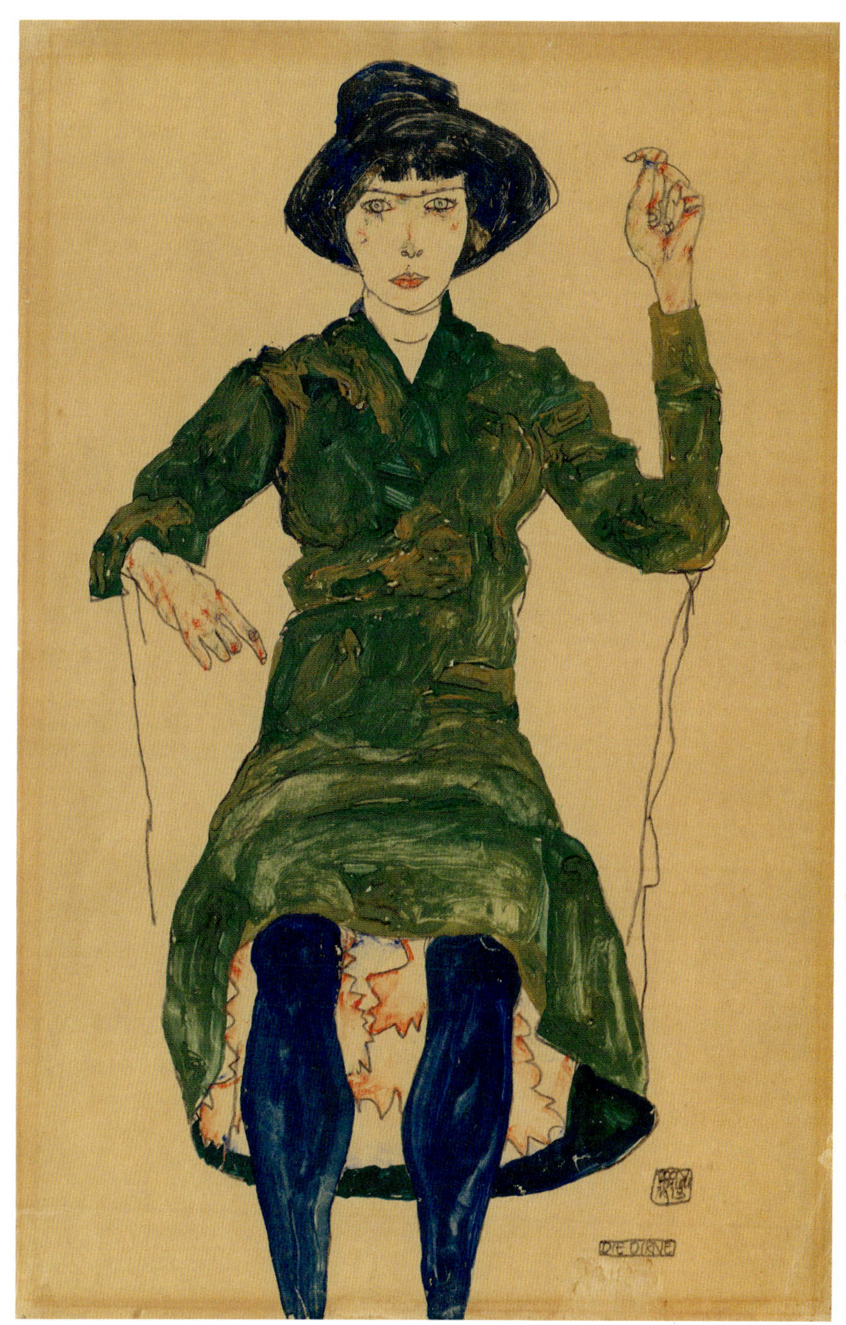

DIE DIRNE

Wilhelm Lehmbruck
1881, Duisburg, Germany–1919, Berlin, Germany
Bust of the Rising Youth, c. 1914
Cast stone, 21¼ × 20 1⁄16 × 7½ in. (54 × 51 × 19 cm)

Gift of the Goeritz Family, London, 1956, in memory of Erich Goeritz

Wilhelm Lehmbruck conceived *Bust of the Rising Youth* as part of his monumental sculpture *The Rising Youth* (*Der Emporsteigende Jüngling*), 1913–14. To make this work, the artist cut back the larger-than-life figure to focus only on the bust. It features the head of a pensive young man, leaning forward slightly, who appears to be hesitantly waiting. The viewer is confronted with multiple layers of tension. The whole situation is rather ambiguous, a possible reflection of the existential anxieties felt by many, particularly by German artists, around the outbreak of the First World War.

Lehmbruck's earlier work was strongly influenced by Auguste Rodin. Following his studies at the Kunstakademie Düsseldorf, he moved to Paris in 1910, where he became familiar with the medieval technique of cast stone. He also made use of recently invented cement mixtures, which allowed greater possibilities in creating freestanding figures. Deeply influenced by Gothic art, Lehmbruck experimented with a notably long neck in his *Bust of the Rising Youth*. Several contemporary versions of the bust are known, mainly in terracotta and tinted cement casts, such as this version.[1]

In Paris, Lehmbruck became part of a cosmopolitan art scene that opposed nationalist and xenophobic trends. In association with the sculptors Constantin Brancusi and Alexander Archipenko (pp. 82–89), he searched for new ways to create three-dimensional representations of the human figure. In 1913, two of his monumental sculptures were exhibited in the Armory Show in New York City, and his international reputation grew considerably. But in the face of the devastation of the First World War, the artist sank into a deep depression and committed suicide in Berlin in 1919.

Lehmbruck's monumental sculptures, including *The Rising Youth*, are considered pioneering works of German Expressionist sculpture, and were targeted by Nazis as "degenerate." As early as 1930, three years before the Nazis seized power, the Weimar Schlossmuseum purged its collection of Lehmbruck's works.

In 1933, Lehmbruck's *Bust of the Rising Youth* and three other works by the artist arrived at the Tel Aviv Museum from Berlin together with hundreds of other artworks. They belonged to Senta and Erich Goeritz, prominent collectors and patrons of art in 1920s Berlin. Due to the increasingly unstable atmosphere, they sent much of their collection to the Museum for safeguarding. Many of their works later joined the permanent collection, including their holdings of Archipenko, selections of French and German Impressionism, and examples from the Berlin Secession and Brücke artists, playing a vital role in shaping the Museum's representation of modern art.

Chana Schütz

1 Dietrich Schubert, "Wilhelm Lehmbruck: Büste des emporsteigenden Jünglings," in *Lehmbruck, Brancusi, Léger, Bonnard, Klee, Fontana, Morandi. Texte zu Werken im Kunstmuseum Winterthur*, ed. Dieter Schwarz (Düsseldorf: Richter, 1997), 11–33.

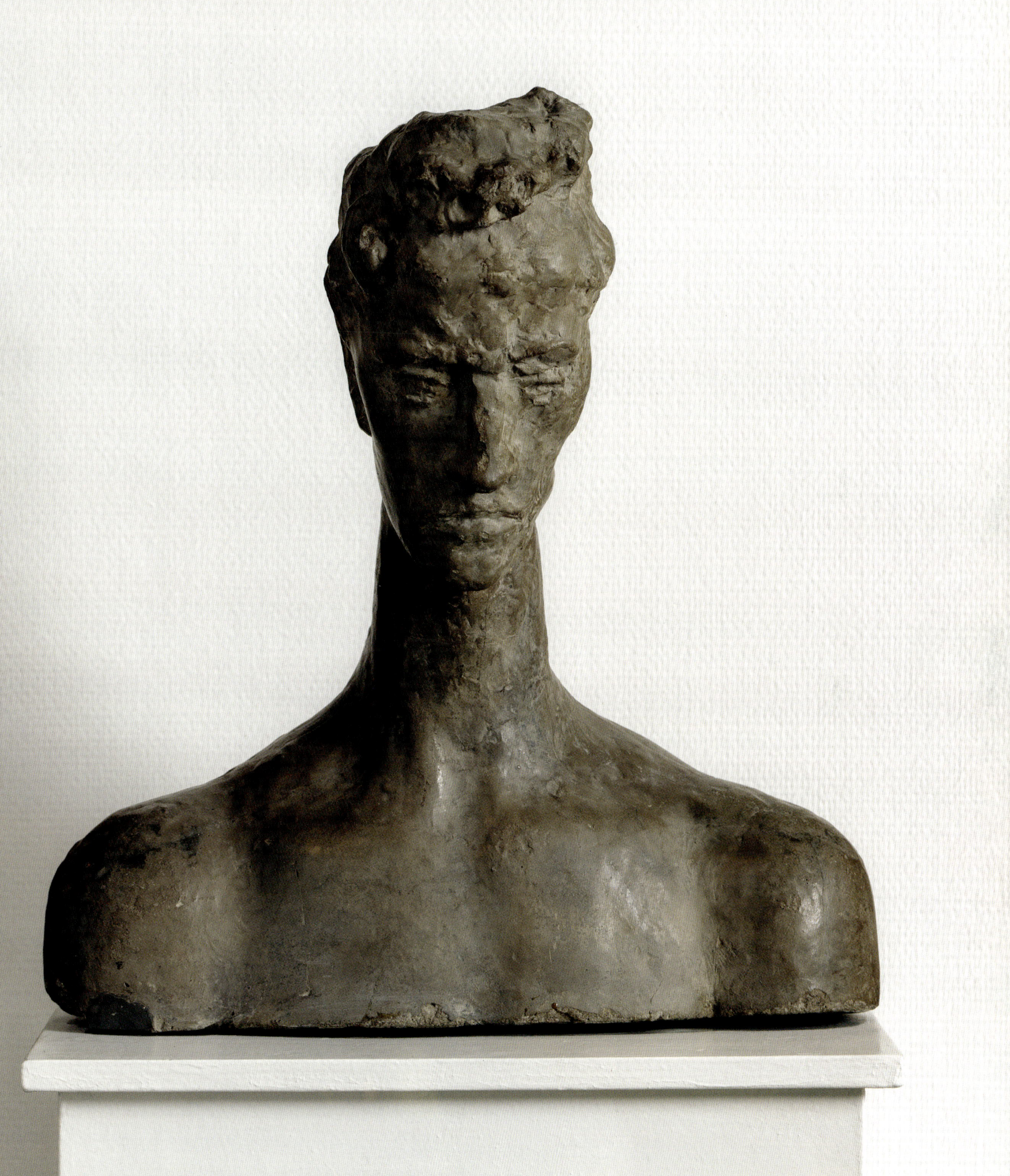

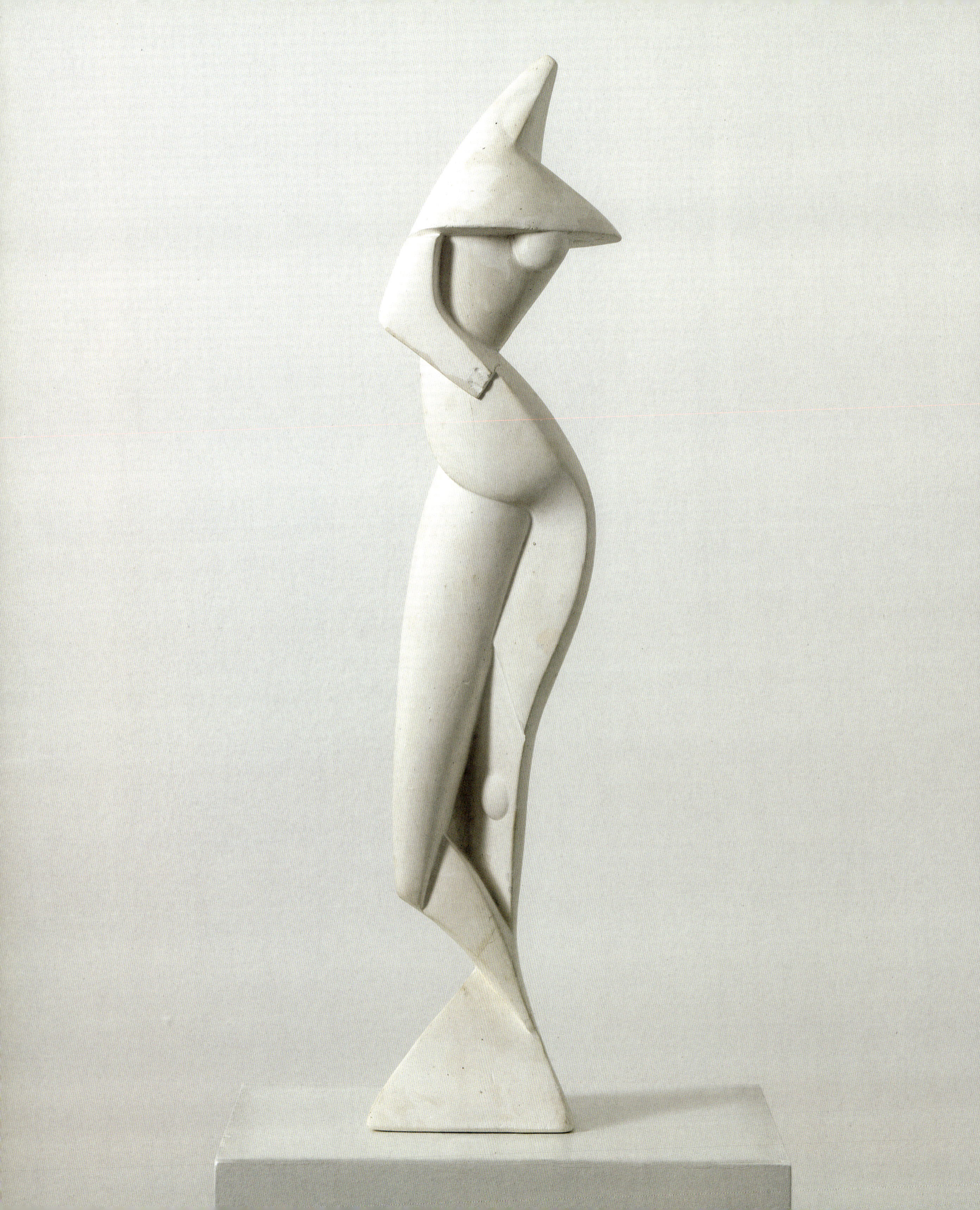

Alexander Archipenko
1887, Kyiv, Russian Empire (now Ukraine)–
1964, New York, NY, United States
Statue on a Triangular Base, 1914
Plaster, 31 ⅛ × 7 ⅞ × 7 ⅞ in. (79 × 20 × 20 cm)

Page 85 *Leaning Woman*, 1913–14
Polished bronze, 16 9⁄16 × 9 13⁄16 × 2 ¾ in. (42 × 25 × 7 cm)

Page 86(l) *Seated Woman*, 1920
Gouache on paper, 12 7⁄16 × 9 7⁄16 in. (31.6 × 24 cm)

Page 86(r) *The Kiss (Composition: Dancers I)*, 1914
Pastel and pencil on cardboard, 19 5⁄16 × 12 ⅝ in. (49.1 × 32 cm)

Page 87 *Seated Woman*, 1920
Painted plaster, 22 7⁄16 × 7 ⅞ × 5 ⅛ in. (57 × 20 × 13 cm)

Page 88 *Woman in Armchair*, 1918
Painted wood, painted sheet metal, and found objects on oil on panel, 22 13⁄16 × 15 15⁄16 × 1 7⁄16 in. (58 × 40.5 × 3.7 cm)

Page 89 *Woman*, 1920
Construction, painted and unpainted sheet metal, on oil on burlap, 73 ⅝ × 32 5⁄16 × 5 ⅛ in. (187 × 82 × 13 cm)

Gift of the Goeritz Family, London, 1956. In memory of Erich Goeritz

The Tel Aviv Museum of Art holds the largest public collection of Alexander Archipenko's early works. Twenty-four of its thirty-two sculptures, "sculpto-paintings," and works on paper—spanning the years 1908 to 1920—were gifts of the Erich Goeritz Collection.[1] In the late 1920s, Goeritz, a German-Jewish collector, bought a group of Archipenko's works first assembled by a major early supporter, Sally Falk.[2] Following the Nazi ascent to power, Goeritz had the foresight to send his collection for safeguarding to the newly established Tel Aviv Museum in 1933. Upon his death in 1955, his family donated most of the collection to the Museum in his memory.[3] Archipenko learned that these works survived only in 1947—an important discovery given that much of his early output was lost or destroyed during the two World Wars.

1 Their secure dating to pre-1921 is particularly significant since Archipenko recreated many of his early works after moving to the United States in 1923 and always backdated them to their original creation date.

2 Sally Falk, a Mannheim-based textile heir, organized Archipenko's traveling exhibition in 1919 and acquired the bulk of these works in 1919–21. For more on Falk's support, see Vita Susak, "The Swiss Secrets of Alexander Archipenko," *Harvard Ukrainian Studies* 36, nos. 3–4 (2019): 415–46.

3 The first comprehensive publication on this collection is Donald Karshan, *Archipenko: The Early Works, 1910–1921. The Erich Goeritz Collection at the Tel Aviv Museum* (Tel Aviv: Tel Aviv Museum, 1981).

The powerful diagonal composition and sensuous surface of *Leaning Woman* exemplify poet and critic Guillaume Apollinaire's assertion that Archipenko's sculpture "unites internal plastic structure with the supreme charm of a sensuously beautiful surface."[4] It builds on the artist's earlier carved sculptures of dancers, further abstracting and streamlining their form.[5] A similar composition defines the pastel drawing *The Kiss (Composition: Dancers I)* (1914), with the strong contrast between its curving lines and round forms and the tense, stretched diagonal tilt of the body. The subtle shading of the creamy pastel colors set against the brownish ground of the cardboard support creates an effect of a lush surface.

In Paris, where Archipenko moved in 1908 from his native Kyiv, he joined the international community of artists at La Ruche in Montparnasse. He attended weekly gatherings of the Cubist Puteaux group formed around the Duchamp brothers but claimed that his real school was the Louvre. Apollinaire was instrumental in bringing early recognition to Archipenko's work, writing that he "constructs reality, and his art is drawing closer and closer to pure sculpture."[6] Apollinaire introduced Archipenko to the Berlin art dealer Herwarth Walden, who launched the artist's reputation in Germany with a solo show in 1914, followed by exhibitions in Geneva, Zurich, Venice, and New York in 1919–21.

Archipenko developed a geometricizing formal language inspired by the Cubists, and found inspiration in the dynamism of the Italian Futurists. The visual power of the female figure in *Statue on a Triangular Base* (1914) derives from the contrast of its curving silhouette with the strongly geometric lines of the abstracted torso and head, echoed by the integrated triangular base. The pristine white of the original plaster—a rare extant original—further underscores the figure's sinuous elegance.

A work in painted plaster, *Seated Woman* (1920), comprises ribbonlike shapes that appear to flow down over the empty space. Its composition is likely related to the gouache of the same title and year, suggesting that Archipenko conceived his three-dimensional forms on paper. Its multiplanarity is underscored by a striking polychromatism and multitextural composition, characteristic of the artist's works in these years.

Archipenko's experiments with faceted geometries, distinct textures, and colors came together powerfully in the pioneering works he called sculpto-paintings, which incorporated various materials, including glass, metal, wood, and papier-mâché. A prominent example, *Woman in Armchair* (1918), integrates curved sculptural elements with painted sections that appear modeled, mounted on a wooden support—it hangs on the wall like a traditional painting, yet protrudes from its frame.

Archipenko's sculpto-paintings reached their pinnacle with the monumental *Woman* (1920), nearly two meters tall, made of unpainted, shiny sheet metal placed on top of oil-covered burlap. An amalgamation of human and machine forms, the work parallels the mechanized style of his friend Fernand Léger (pp. 92–93). Radical in its geometry and scale, and defying materiality by reflecting its surroundings in its polished surface, *Woman* made a deep impression on the critic Ivan Goll, who described it as "a window open to all the world's horizons, like a diamond that absorbs all the multicolored flames, a recipient of external movements."[7]

Masha Chlenova

4 Guillaume Apollinaire, "Alexander Archipenko," review of *Siebzehnte Ausstellung: Alexander Archipenko*, Galerie Der Sturm, 1913, reproduced in *Apollinaire on Art: Essays and Reviews 1902–1918*, ed. LeRoy C. Breunig, trans. Susan Suleiman (Boston: MFA Publications, 2001), 364.

5 *Leaning Woman* is related to the now lost *Salome* (1910), reproduced in *Archipenko* (Paris: Galerie Maeght, 1997), 30. For other early sculptures with diagonally tilted dancers' bodies, see Herwarth Walden, ed. *Siebzehnte Ausstellung: Alexander Archipenko* (Berlin: Der Sturm, 1913).

6 Guillaume Apollinaire, preface to *Siebzehnte Ausstellung: Alexander Archipenko* in Ibid., 363.

7 Ivan Goll, "Une Sténographie Artistique," *Die Action* 5 (Oct. 1925), reproduced in *Archipenko* (Paris: Galerie Maeght, 1997), 33 [author's translation].

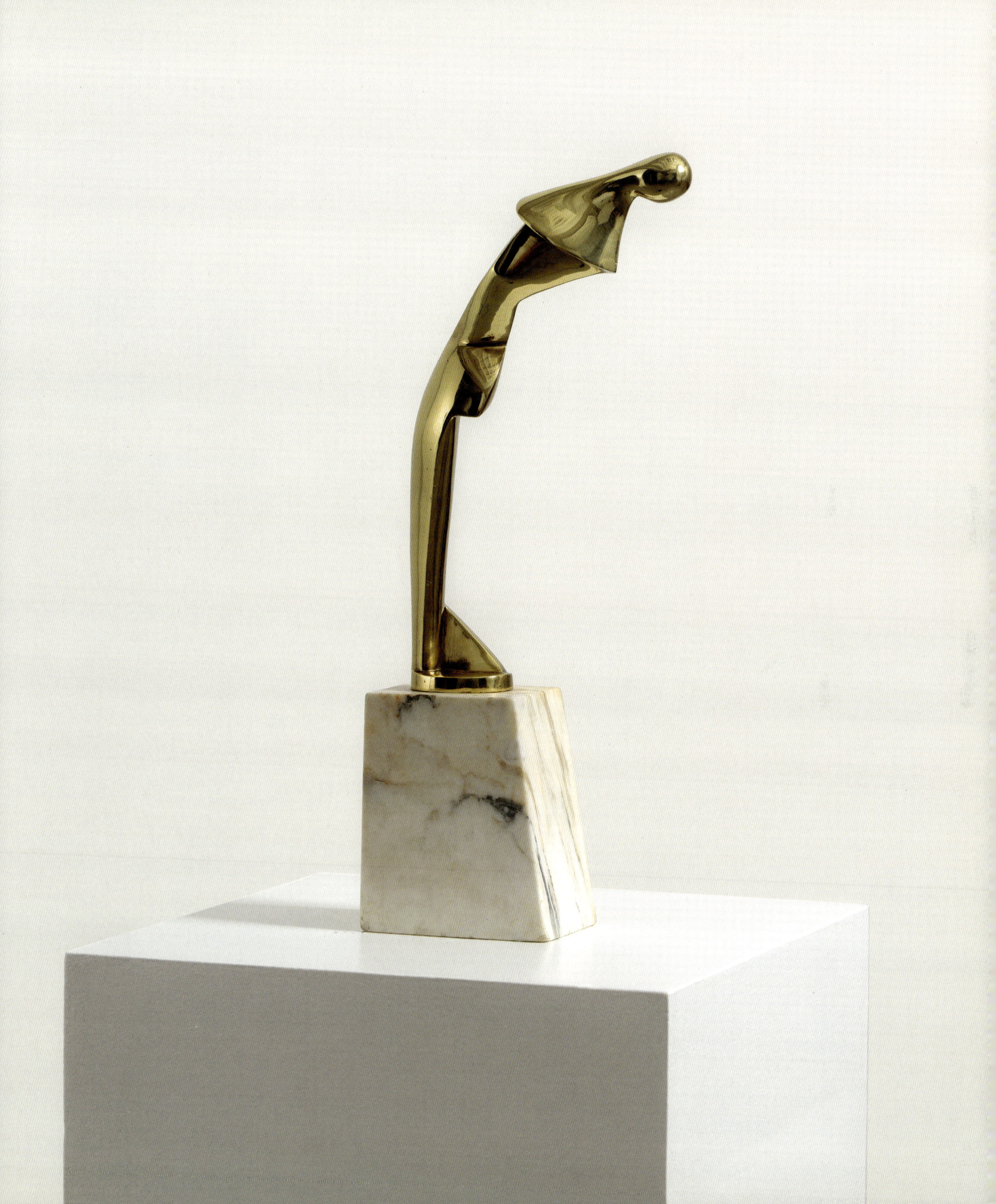

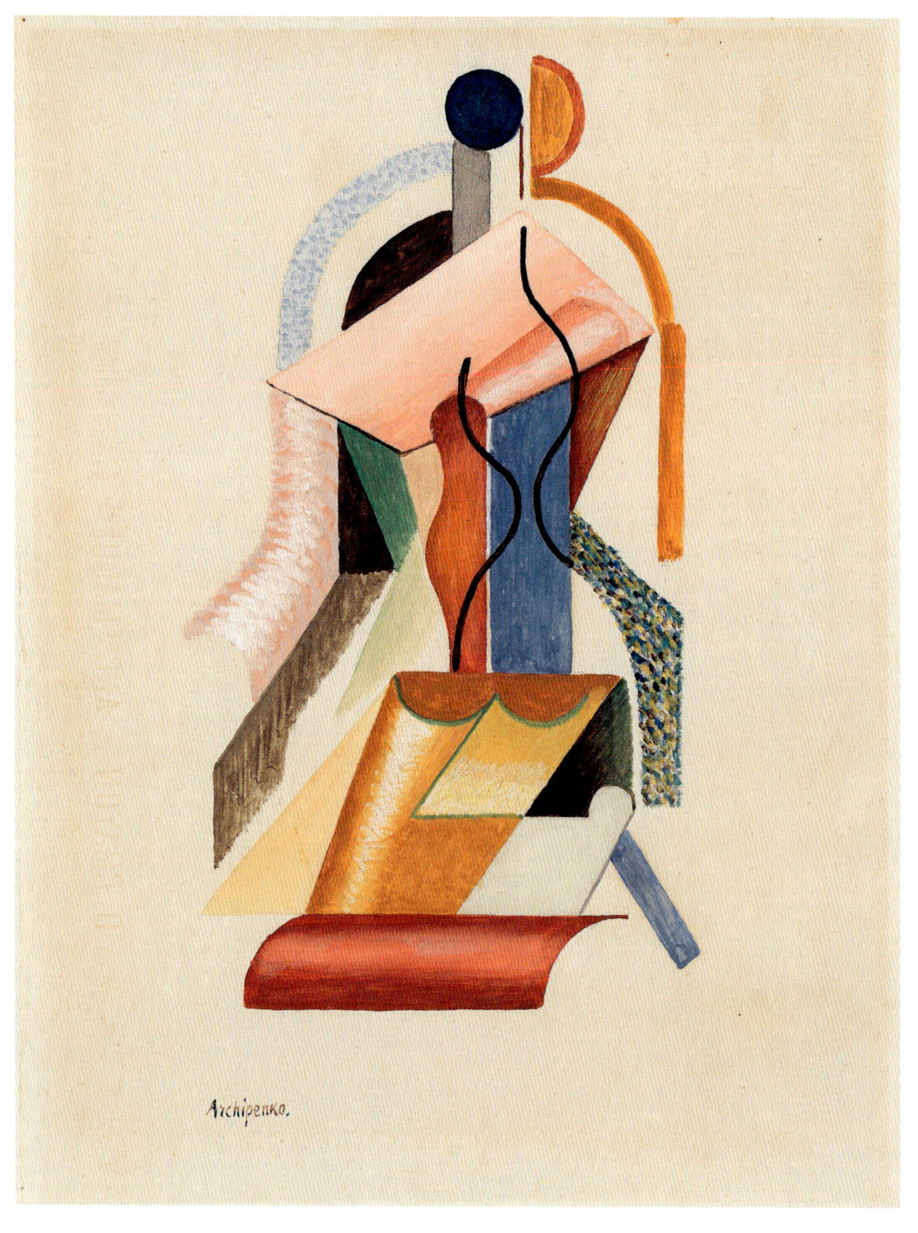
Archipenko.

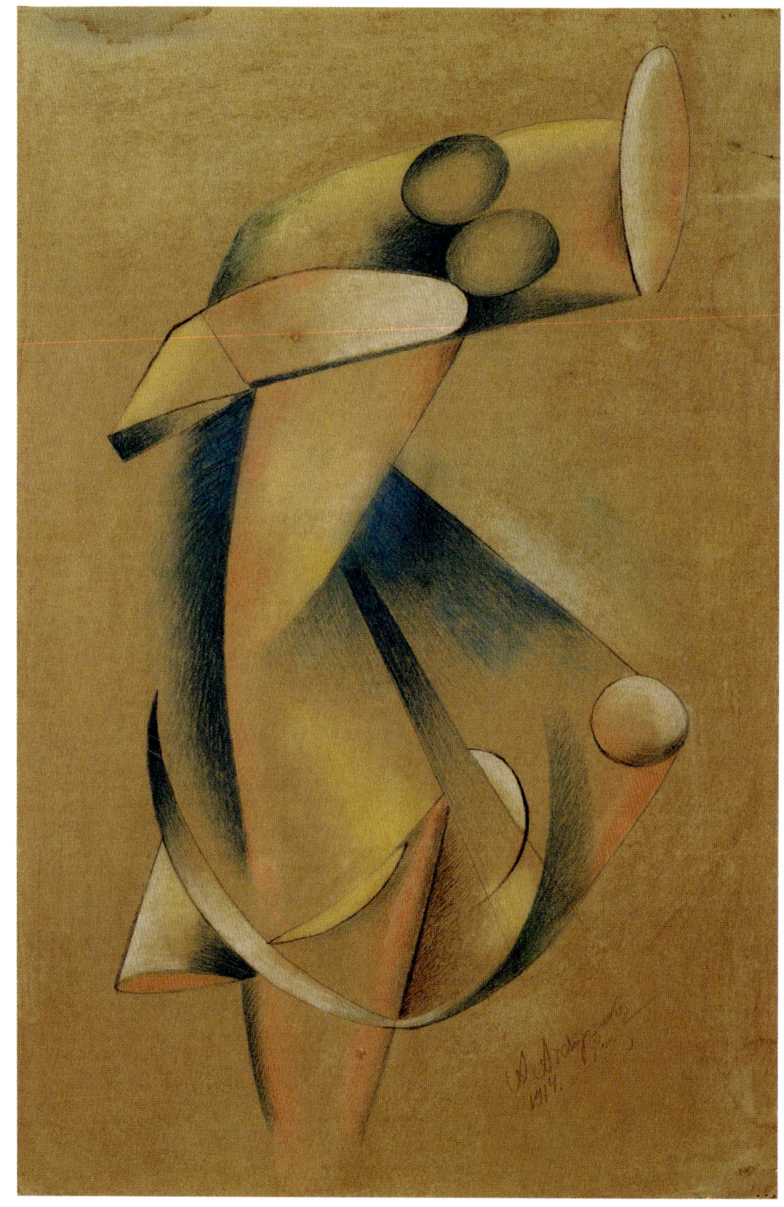

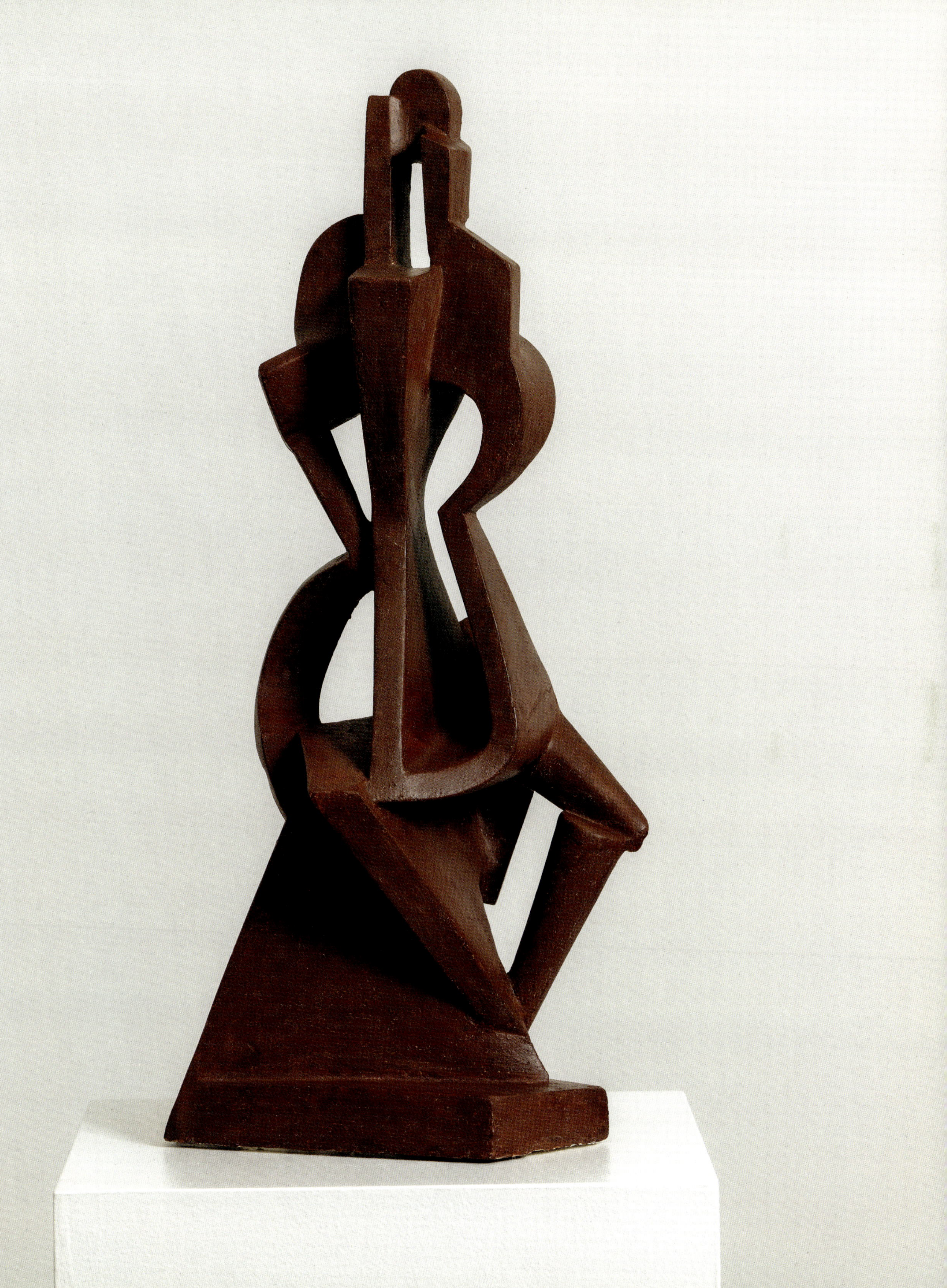

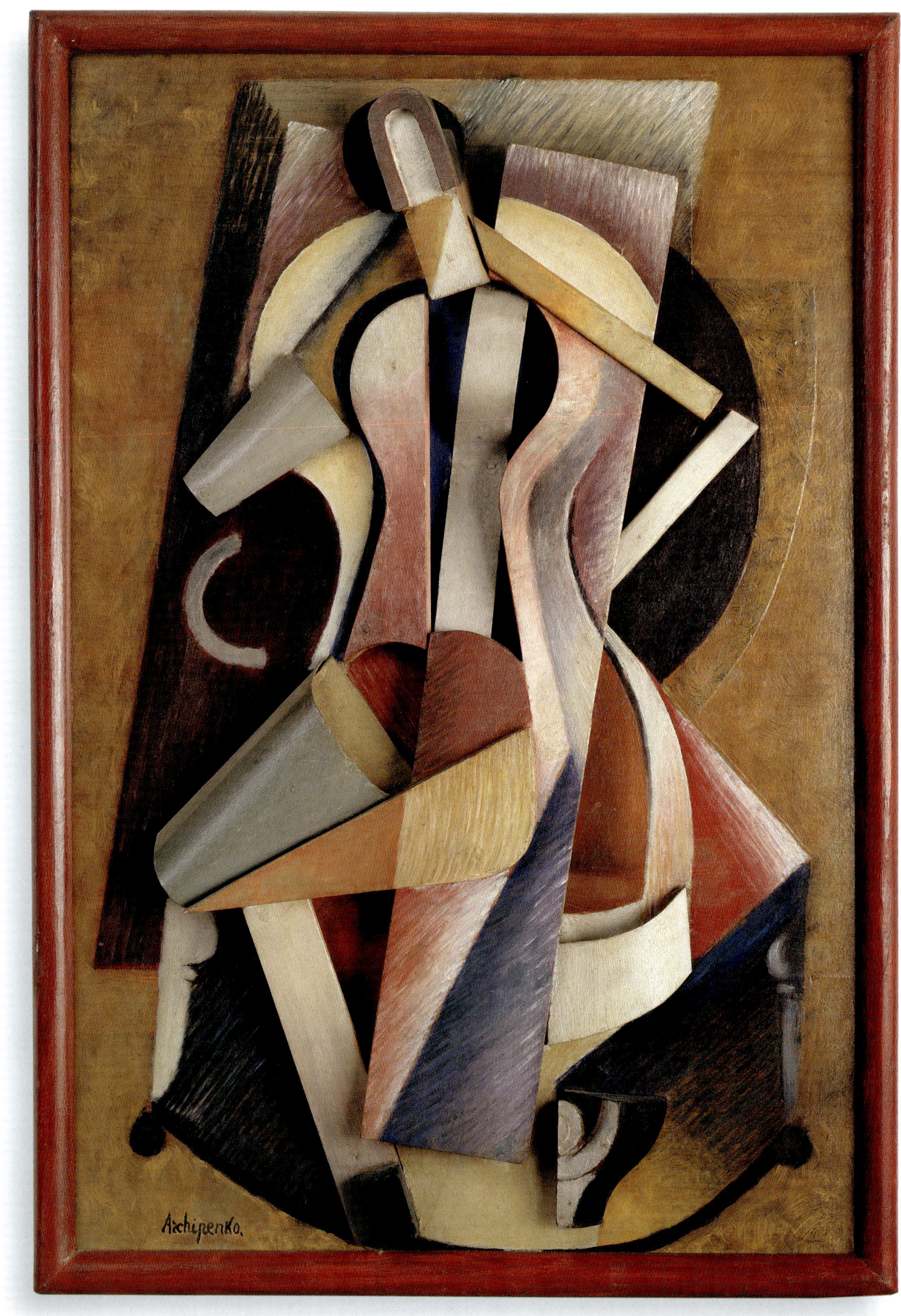
Archipenko.

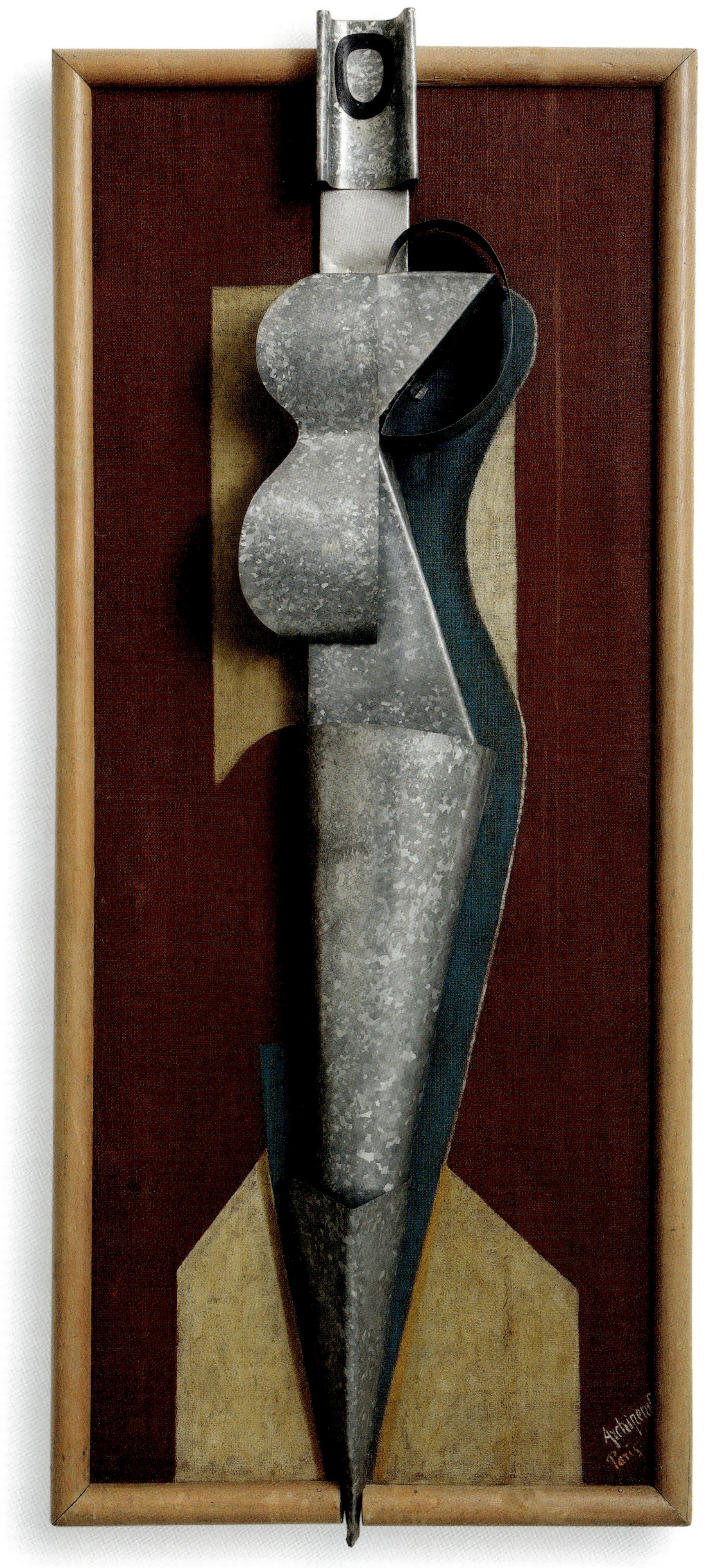
Archipenko
Paris

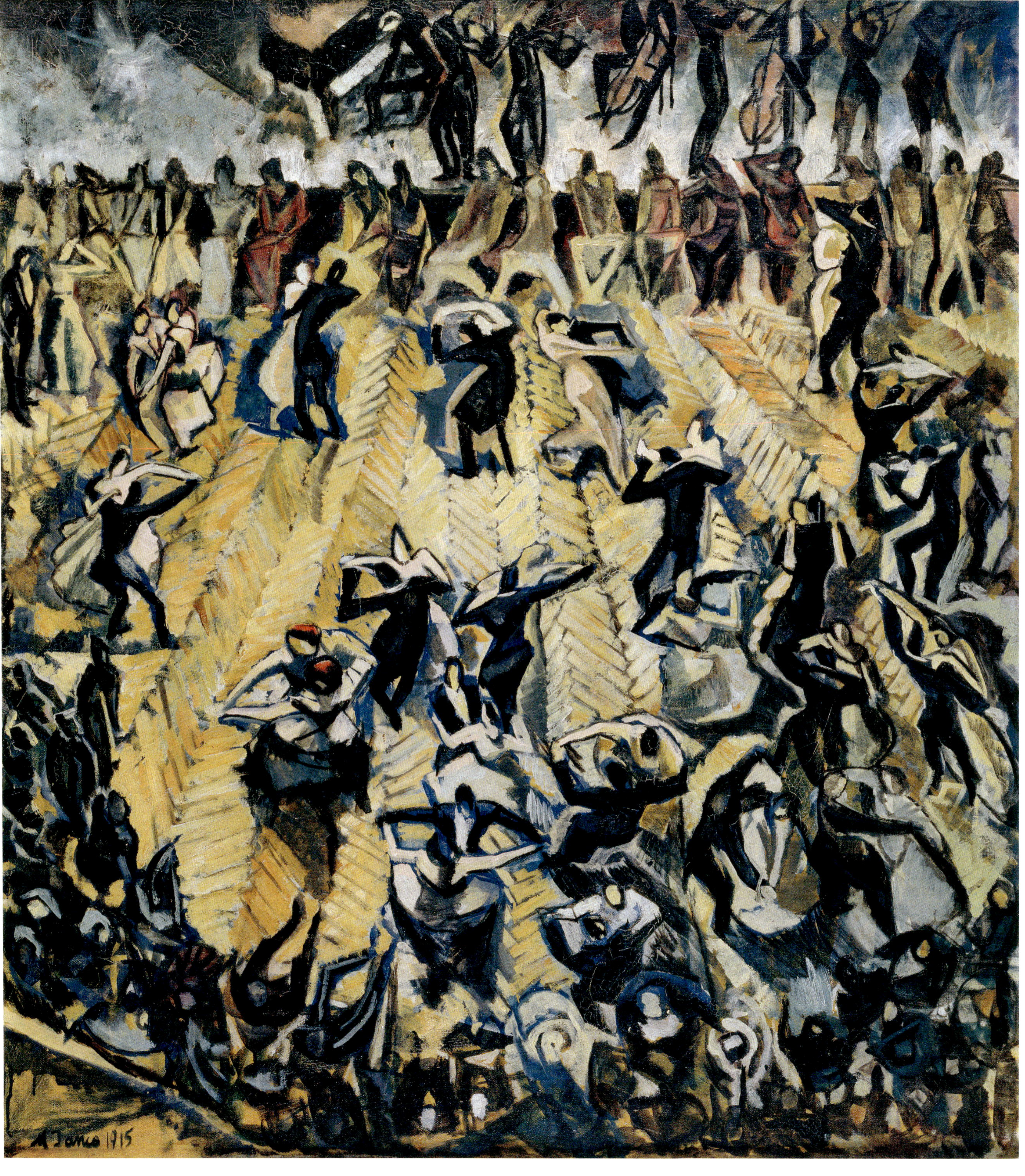

Marcel Janco
1895, Bucharest, Romania–1984, Ein Hod, Israel
Ball in Zurich, 1915
Oil on canvas, 39 3/8 × 35 7/16 in. (100 × 90 cm)

Gift of S. Wyler, through the Tel Aviv Foundation for Development, 1986

Ball in Zurich, one of a series of works on the same theme that Marcel Janco painted between 1915 and 1917, is a motion-filled painting with a dizzying rhythm. The composition's perspective blends a bird's-eye view with a frontal view. An orchestra on a narrow stage appears to hover in midair at the painting's top edge. The couples dancing in the center of the ballroom are rendered as sharp and angular. The zigzag pattern of the parquet floor and the alternating blue and light yellow hues accentuate the sense of rhythmic movement and overall agitation.

During World War I, Zurich was a center of vibrant social and cultural activity, and intellectuals from all over Europe found refuge there from the horrors of the war. Its cosmopolitan atmosphere and cultural interchanges led to the development of innovative ideas, which cut across the boundaries of national traditions. Janco arrived in Zurich in 1915 to study architecture, accompanied by his brother Julius. To earn their living, they sang and played piano in cafes. In *Ball in Zurich*, as in other paintings of dances from this period, Janco succeeded in creating a visual analogy to the animated musical rhythms that were being played across the city.

While performing in cafes, Janco met Hugo Ball, the manager of a cabaret in the old part of the city, and together, along with a group of artists, founded the famous Cabaret Voltaire.[1] They held a series of experimental artistic and political events over the course of 1916 that led to the emergence of Dada. Railing against the stupidity of the war, Dada artists sought to destroy the foundations of bourgeois society and undermine its artistic conventions, fostering one of the early twentieth-century's most provocative art movements.

Alisa Padovano-Friedman

1 In addition to Janco, the group of artists who founded Cabaret Voltaire includes Richard Huelsenbeck, Tristan Tzara, and Sophie Taeuber-Arp and Jean Arp.

Fernand Léger
1881, Argentan, France–1955, Gif-sur-Yvette, France
Contrast of Forms, 1913
Oil on canvas, 39 ⅜ × 31 ⅞ in. (100 × 81 cm)

Mizne-Blumental Collection, Bequest of Annette Celine, 2018

After working in an idiom close to the Analytic Cubism pioneered by his peers Georges Braque (pp. 54–55) and Pablo Picasso (pp. 124–31), Fernand Léger began his series *Contrasts of Forms* in 1912. In these works, Léger adhered to certain Cubist fundamentals, such as reducing formal elements and using fragmentation to create a flattened perspective. However, he rejected the dark, monochromatic palette that typified Cubist works, favoring pure, bold colors instead. The works that make up *Contrasts of Forms* also hold the distinction of being among the most baldly abstract of the early twentieth-century French avant-garde.

From 1912 to 1914, Léger created more than fifty canvases that constitute the series, along with dozens of works on paper. This body of work developed from Léger's law of contrasts, a theory that advocated for the creation of compositions based on simultaneous oppositions between the three compositional elements: line, form, and color. Léger implemented the same elements in different variations throughout the series: all the paintings include geometric forms (combinations of cubes, cylinders, and cones), and a palette limited to the primary colors, supplemented with white and black contours. Each work in the series stands on its own, unnumbered—there is no progression that dictates a specific viewing order. While the compositions seem to reference elements drawn from reality, whether a landscape or still life, ultimately, they eschew visual representation, remaining in the realm of abstraction.

This painting features a central vertical axis composed of squares piled diagonally—like a precarious house of cards on the verge of collapse—flanked on either side by rounded shapes divided into planes by means of light color stripes. The azure stripes lining the edges of the composition seem to recede in space, yet their bright tone creates an optical effect of bringing them forward, enhancing the work's overall quality of flatness. The speed of the artist's hand is apparent in the way the pigment is applied freely on the coarse burlap, enhanced by the occasional layer of paint added to adjust the black contours. The geometric shapes generate a rhythm and movement that recall the world of machines and technology—a theme that would emerge more forcefully in the artist's work a few years later, after returning from his service in World War I in 1917.

Sophia Berry-Lifschitz

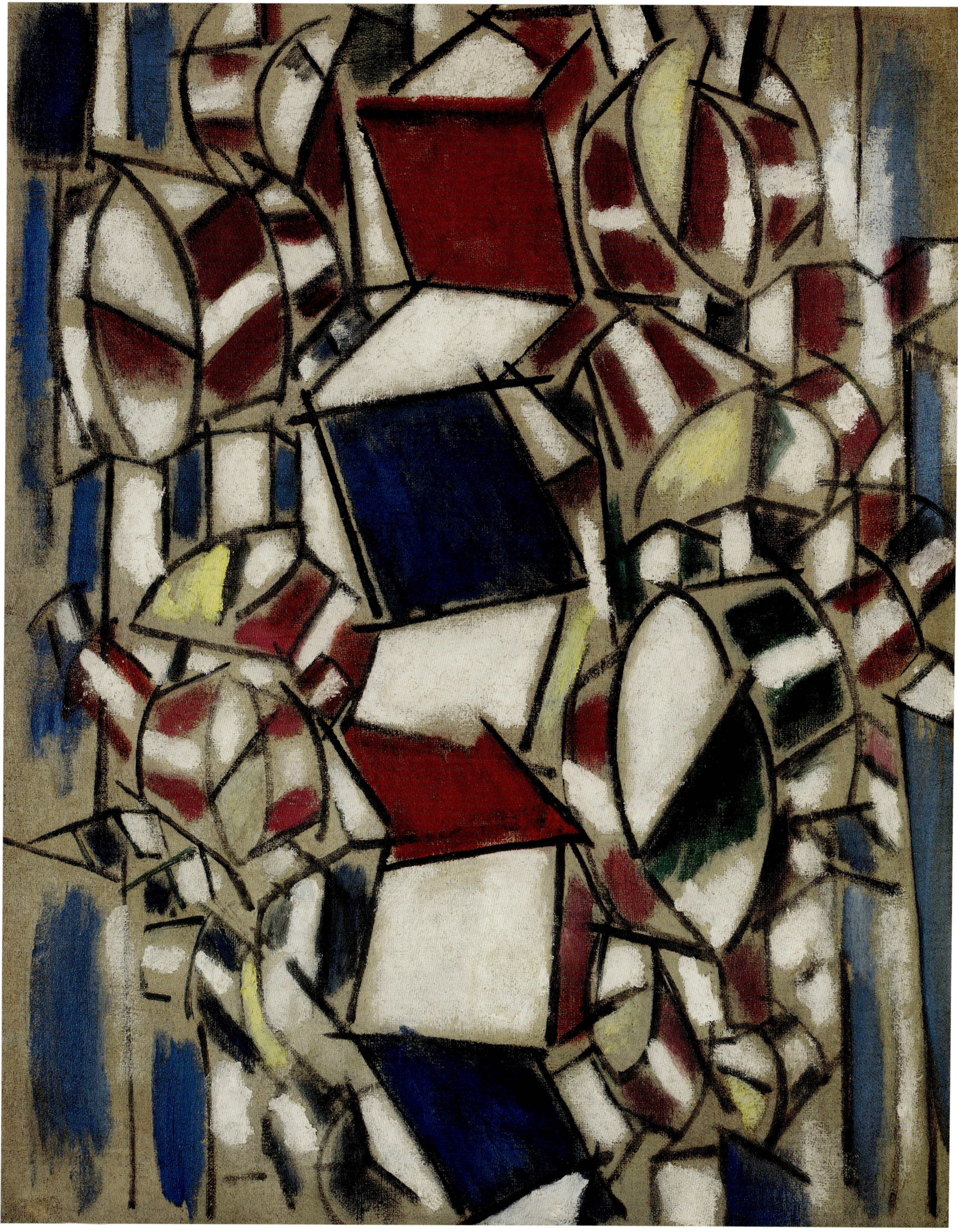

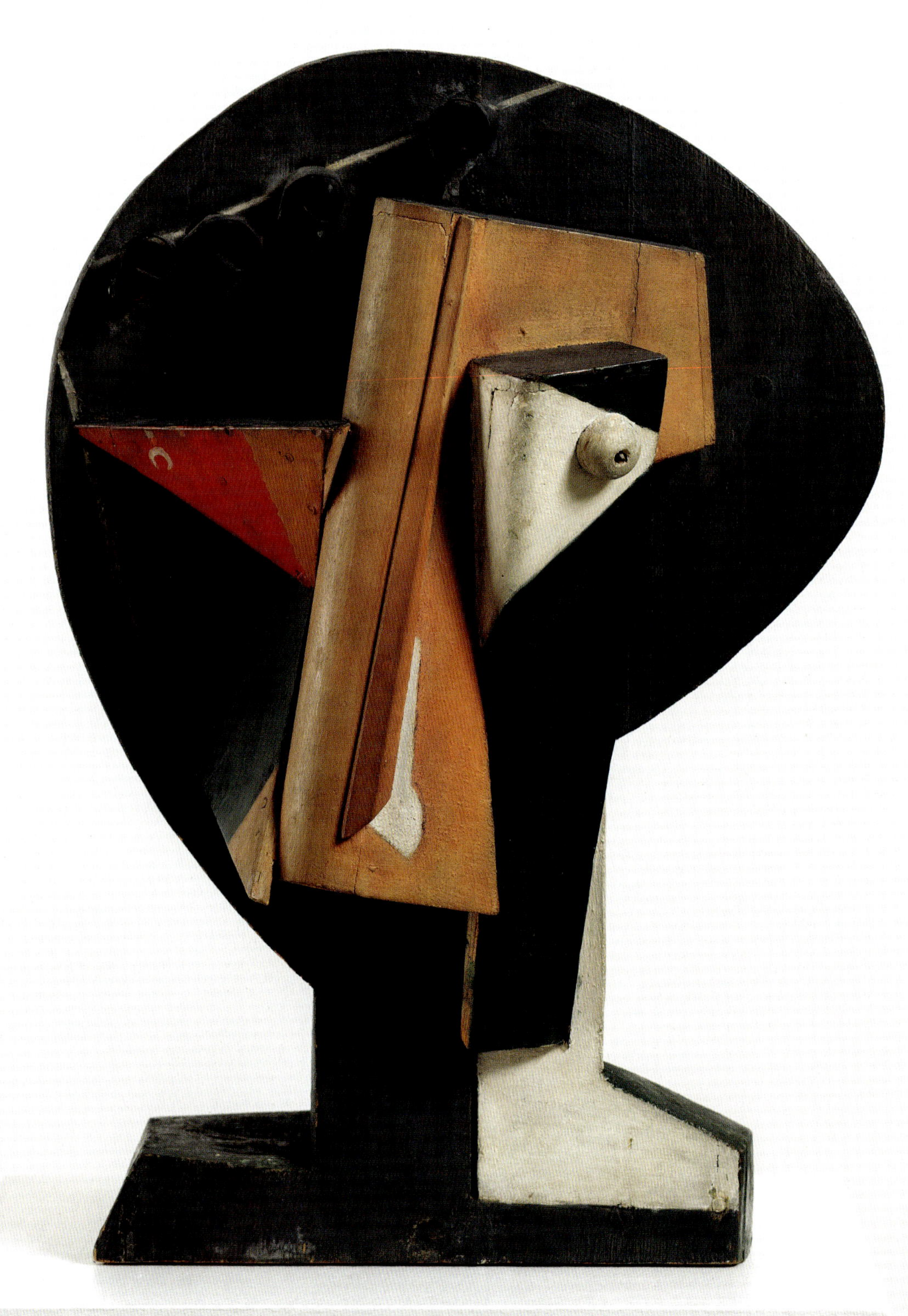

Henri Laurens
1885–1954, Paris, France
Head of a Woman, 1916–17
Painted wood and sheet metal, 17 11/16 × 13 × 14 9/16 in.
(45 × 33 × 37 cm)

Gift of the Goeritz Family, London, 1956. In memory of Erich Goeritz

Head of a Woman by French Cubist sculptor Henri Laurens combines aspects of sculpture and painting: it is freestanding and constructed from geometric pieces of wood and sheet metal, and yet, each element is painted, and the sculpture includes decorative details, such as an engraved zigzag pattern and metal curlicues that represent locks of hair. At the time he created this sculpture, Laurens had befriended Pablo Picasso and Georges Braque, and he began to apply their Cubist innovations to his sculptural work. While their two-dimensional Cubist works disrupted single-point perspective by fragmenting the composition's elements and tilting the picture plane to introduce multiple perspectives, Laurens likewise "constructed" rather than sculpted or carved his forms, eschewing traditional illusionistic representation. His sculptural heads are planar and fragmented and possess no ideal vantage point. For example, when viewing this sculpture frontally, it appears nearly flat—from other angles, it is surprising to see how far back the mass of her hair, gathered into a coiffure, extends.

When the sculpture arrived at the Tel Aviv Museum in November 1933 as part of a group of 500 works on long-term loan from the Erich Goeritz Collection, there were no supporting documents, and the work was unsigned and undated. Stylistically similar to a group of thirty Archipenko sculptures that were also included in the loan (pp. 82–89)—particularly the Cubist-inflected sculpto-paintings, which similarly balance elements of both painting and sculpture—the work was misattributed to Archipenko. In 1986, dissatisfied with this attribution after noting too many discrepancies between this work and Archipenko sculptures from the same period, Nehama Guralnik, who headed the Museum's Modern Art Department at the time, undertook a major research project. She compared the sculpture to Laurens's collages and to a similar 1915 sculpture by the artist in the collection of the Museum of Modern Art, New York, and identified elements common to both. After sharing the data with the artist's foundation and acquiring its confirmation, the sculpture was reattributed to Henri Laurens.

Sophia Berry-Lifschitz

Juan Gris
1887, Madrid, Spain–1927, Boulogne-Billancourt, France
Ace of Spades, 1916
Collage and colored pencil on paper, 11 7/16 × 8 11/16 in. (29 × 22 cm)

Bequest of Alma Morgenthau, New York, through the America-Israel Cultural Foundation, 1955

Ace of Spades is typical of the restraint practiced by Juan Gris, and by Cubist artists in general, at the height of and immediately after World War I. Nevertheless, it contains an interesting complexity, since this piece of glued reality, which is supposed to demonstrate certainty—like the trompe l'oeil nail in Georges Braque's (pp. 54–55) renowned painting *Violin and Palette* (1909)—emerges in Gris's collage as a printed cutout of a Cubist poem, whose words and form are as follows:

> Ace of spades
> This glass
> The ash of the pipe
> Extinguished candle set over my loves
> Rainy morning
> And this boredom which weighs upon
> The game of cards, in which the future dreams[1]

Unsigned, the poem was written by Belgian poet Paul Dermée (the pen name of Camille Jansen), an acquaintance of Gris's and others associated with literary Cubism. The cutout is glued to the center of an illustration from which everyday objects flicker. The Cubist deconstruction-construction arranges them randomly during or after use, in a space whose reality is credible despite being obviously imagined. Indeed, the illustrated and the written echo and enhance each other with the utmost harmony. Together, they deliberately and thoughtfully constitute unraveled sequences, seeking to present a new, distinct, and associative mood whose codes are concealed within the tears and cracks. Both express a measure of melancholy in which reference to the banality of mundane objects inundates the surface with an awareness of the margins of elusive passing life.

Irith Hadar

1 Paul Dermée, "Poème," originally published in *Nord Sud*, no. 11 (January 1918): 5, English translation in *The Cubist Poets in Paris: An Anthology*, ed. LeRoy C. Breunig (Lincoln, NE: University of Nebraska Press, 1995), 149.

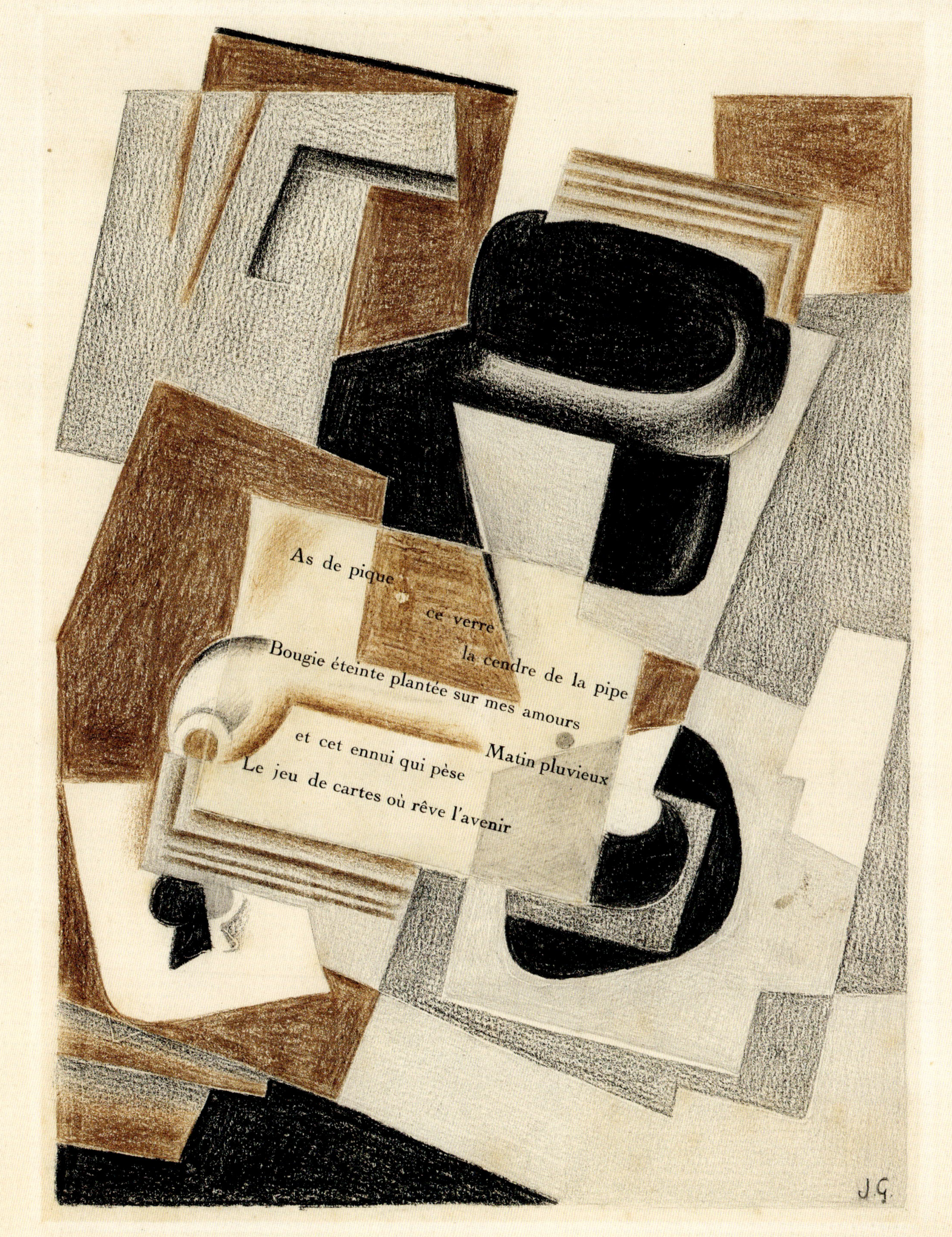
As de pique
ce verre
la cendre de la pipe
Bougie éteinte plantée sur mes amours
Matin pluvieux
et cet ennui qui pèse
Le jeu de cartes où rêve l'avenir
J.G.

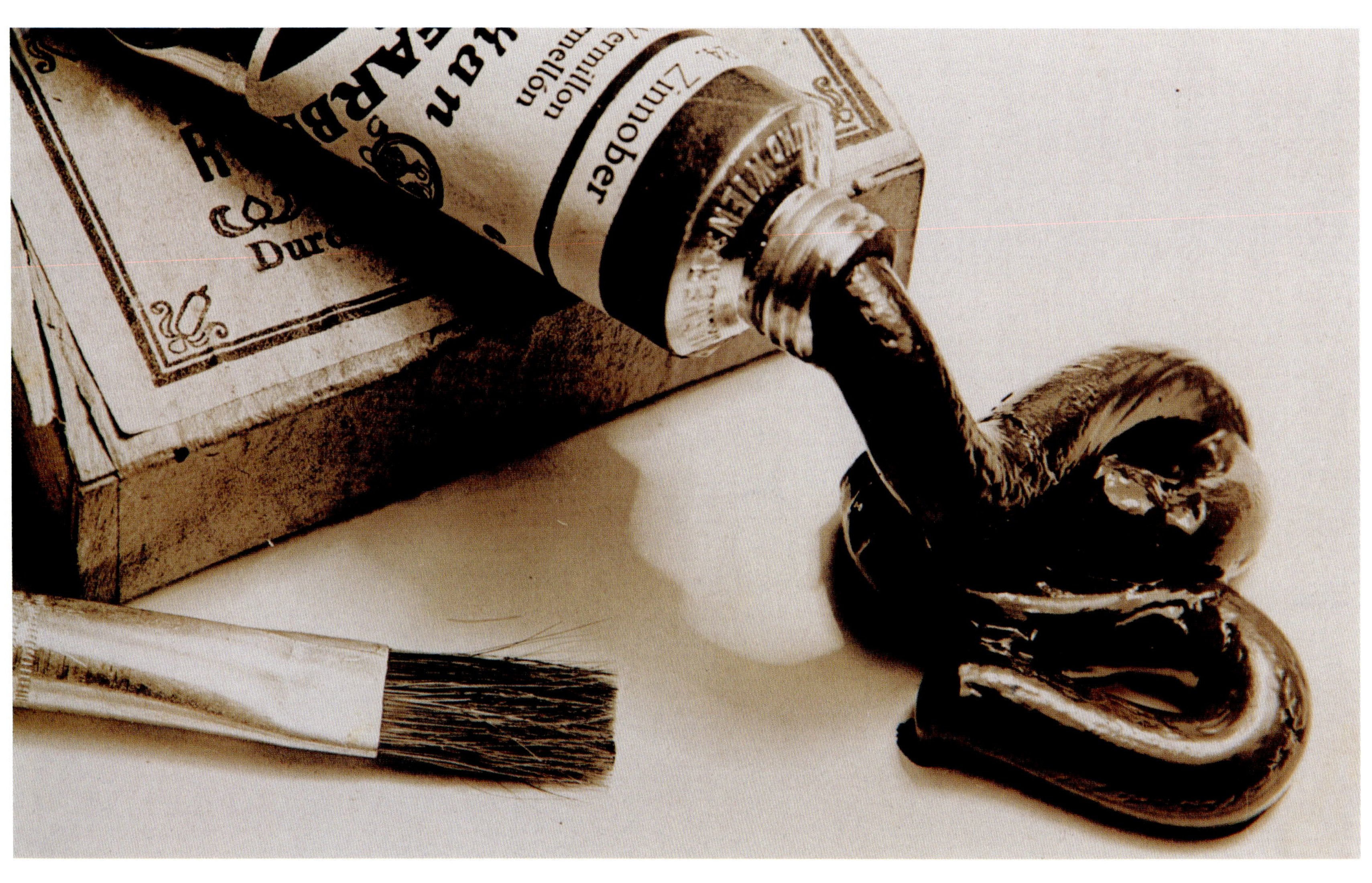

Lucia Moholy
1894, Prague, Austria-Hungary (now Czech Republic)–
1989, Zurich, Switzerland
Color Tube, c. 1920s
Gelatin silver print, 3 9⁄16 × 5 7⁄8 in. (9 × 15 cm)

Gift of Michael S. Sachs, Westport, Connecticut, through the American Friends of the Tel Aviv Museum of Art, 2008

How does one photograph color, capturing the vividness of color as a material—especially a color as bright as vermilion—in a black-and-white photograph? This is the task photographer Lucia Moholy set for herself in this work. Moholy depicts the pigment itself as it oozes out of the tube. From the upper left to the bottom right, the paint pours onto the white ground in an amorphous, snakelike form. She depicts the color in a dynamic stage—in motion—and one cannot tell if it is already solidifying or if someone outside the frame is pressing the tube further to squeeze out more paint. The impression of active flow is reinforced by the material's prominent shadow.

Although quite a lot of packaging material is visible—the paint tube lies on a box with a label—the photograph is clearly not meant for advertising purposes. It is not about the manufacturer, or the company's logo, but about the photographic depiction of color. Apart from the word "Zinnober"—the German name of the color—at the end of the label, accompanied by the French ("Vermillon") and Spanish ("Bermellón") terms, as well as the slightly cropped word "Farbe" ("color" in German) a bit further down on the tube, one cannot decipher other words from the additional visible letters. As if to avoid misunderstandings even among those who did not comprehend her subtle game of naming the photograph's topic through the packaging text, Moholy also foregrounds a paintbrush in the lower left corner of the picture.

Moholy came to the Bauhaus in Weimar in 1923, as the spouse of Bauhaus master László Moholy-Nagy. She already worked as a writer, editor, and photographer before arriving at the Bauhaus, where she continued to develop her technique, embracing an increasingly experimental approach. While she was neither employed by Walter Gropius, the school's founder, nor enrolled as a student, she provided the crucial visual material that made the Bauhaus visible and, above all, kept it visible after its closure in 1933. Today, she is considered the most important chronicler of the Bauhaus, a role that was not recognized for several decades. With her special perspective, one that experiments with art's raw materials and with the fundamental qualities of photography, she literally shaped the image of the Bauhaus.

Tobias Hoffmann

Amédée Ozenfant
1886, Saint-Quentin, France–1966, Cannes, France
Sisteron, 1918–20
Oil on canvas, 27 3⁄16 × 23 7⁄16 in. (69 × 59.5 cm)

Mizne-Blumental Collection, Bequest of Annette Celine, 2018

In an architectural context, the term "vernacular" typically designates the constructed works of those who exercise their design skills as builders, carpenters, or masons rather than academically trained architects. The houses of Sisteron, a village in the Southern French region of Provence, result from the labor of these vernacular figures.[1] In his 1918–20 painting titled *Sisteron*, Amédée Ozenfant depicts interlocking hillside houses and the Porte du Dauphiné, one of the gates of the village's citadel.[2]

Aside from these recognizable motifs, the painting is more informative of Ozenfant's creative agenda than of the architectural actuality of Sisteron at the time of his visit. The artist visibly departs from naturalism by rendering Sisteron's beige facades in shades of burnt orange and deep crimson. Most importantly, Ozenfant does not represent doors, windows, or shutters that punctuate these facades, thus depicting these vernacular buildings as abstract geometrical volumes more akin to Platonic solids than lived-in dwellings. When represented in this abstracted manner, the architecture of the village is hardly distinguishable from the rocky hill on which it stands. While pyramidal volumes may be interpreted as slanted roofs, the cubic masses at the center of the composition cannot be strictly identified as either natural or architectural.

In his autobiography, Ozenfant recalls appreciating Sisteron for its geometry: "I saw Provence for the first time in Sisteron, where I stopped for two days [in 1914] to draw because I was in awe of the admirable alliance between the strongly calculated architecture of the star-shaped citadel *à la* Vauban and the natural architecture of the rock, which appealed to my spirit's geometrical taste."[3] In his painting, Ozenfant emphasized the features of Sisteron that he appreciated the most, geometry in nature and architecture, thus proposing an idealized and fundamentally subjective depiction of the Provençal village. Like Ozenfant, several other key figures of the European avant-garde—including Raoul Hausmann, Georges Braque (pp. 54–55), and Le Corbusier—expressed their deep interest in Mediterranean vernacular architecture and its geometrical predisposition.[4] *Sisteron* is an essential instance within this extended history of creative interaction between modern art and Mediterranean vernacular architecture.

Jacobé Huet

1 Christian Bromberger, Jacques Lacroix, and Henri Raulin, *L'Architecture rurale française: Provence* (Paris: Berger-Levrault, 1980), 17, 62–63.

2 The arch on the lower left of the painting is identified as the Porte du Dauphiné in Raz Samira, ed., *The Mizne-Blumental Collection* (Tel Aviv: Tel Aviv Museum of Art, 2017), 119.

3 Amédée Ozenfant, *Mémoires 1886–1962* (Paris: Seghers, 1968), 78 [French, author's translation].

4 On the broader modernist attraction for Mediterranean architecture, see Jean-François Lejeune and Michelangelo Sabatino, eds., *Modern Architecture and the Mediterranean: Vernacular Dialogues and Contested Identities* (London: Routledge, 2010).

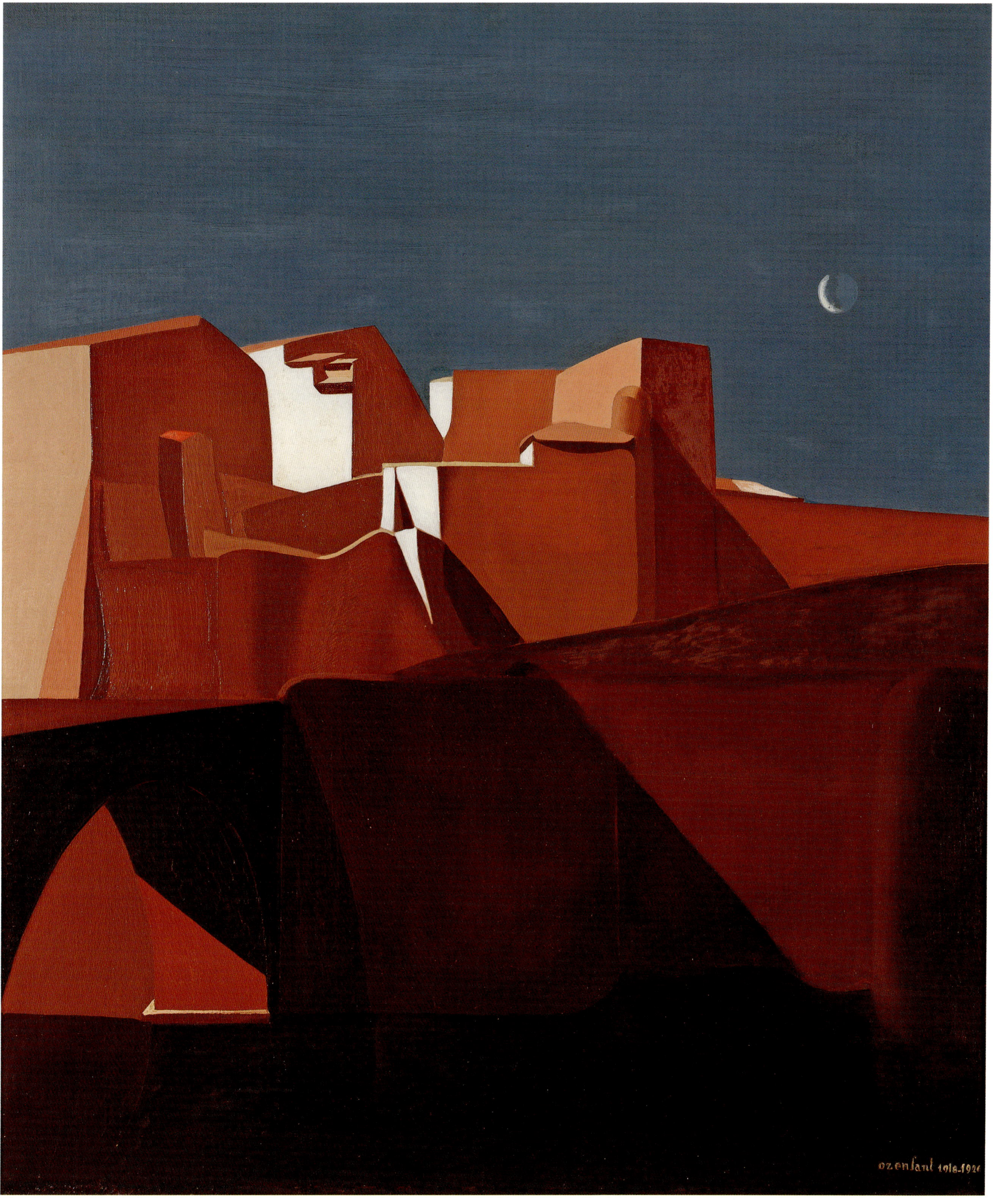
ozenfant

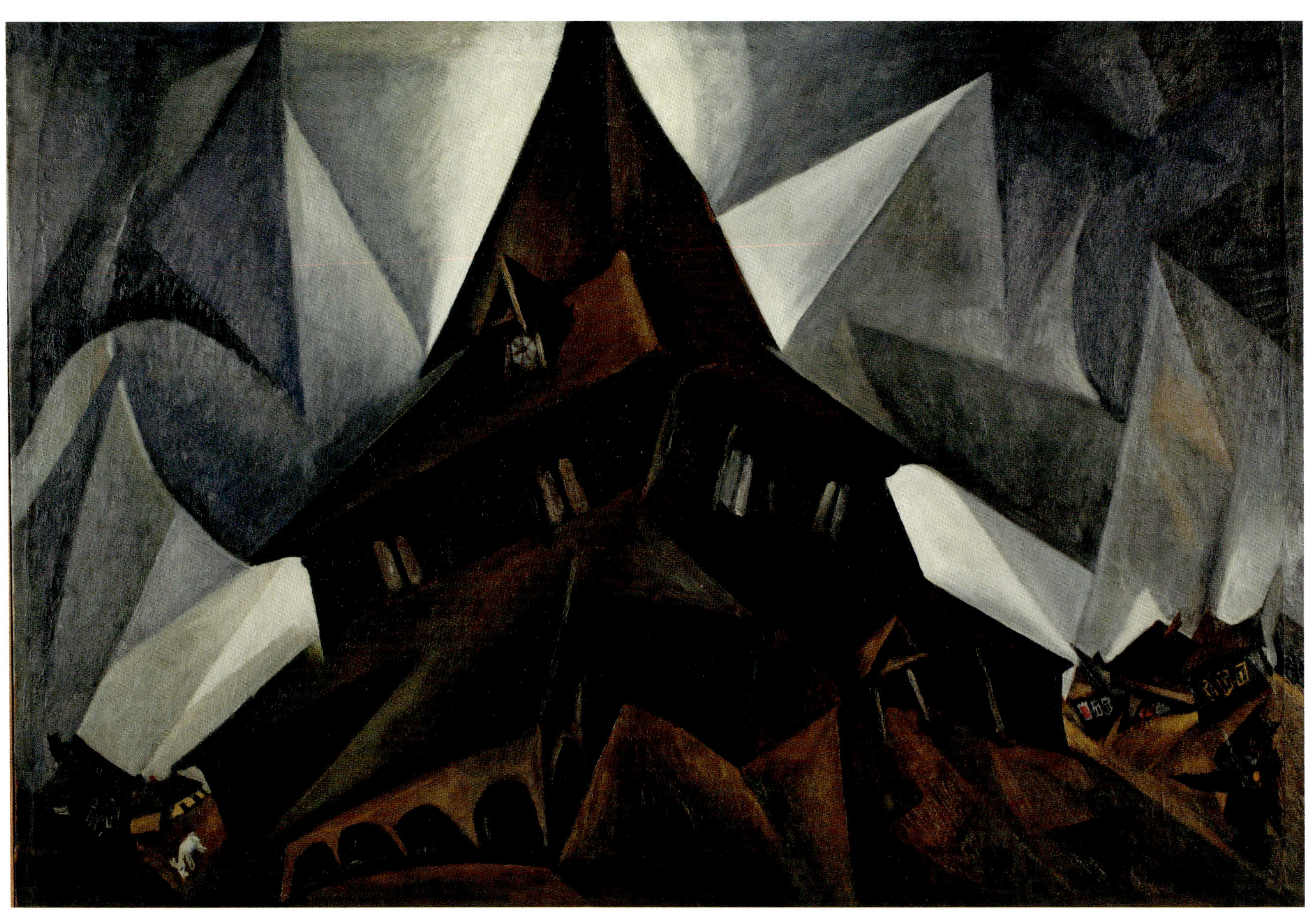

Issachar Ber Ryback
1897, Yelisavetgrad, Russian Empire (now Kropyvnytskyi, Ukraine)–1935, Paris, France
The Old Synagogue, 1917
Oil on canvas, 38 3⁄16 × 57 ½ in. (97 × 146 cm)

Acquisition, 1951

The Old Synagogue is one of a series of oil paintings created by Issachar Ber Ryback in 1917–18 depicting daily life in Jewish shtetls in current-day Belarus and Ukraine, a region undergoing a tumultuous period due to the Russian Revolution, which was unfolding the year this work was made. The painting's somber subject erupts from broken, collapsing forms, a cross between Cubism and Expressionism. Instead of a single pure style, Ryback, a member of the avant-garde Yidishe Kultur-Lige (Yiddish Culture League), harnessed various modernist styles to represent the violence and horror of the pogroms and persecution experienced by the Jewish community in these cataclysmic years when anti-Semitism was on the rise throughout Europe. The painting portrays a synagogue in the town of Dubrouna in Belarus. The monumental, tapering building dominates the town, with small, simple houses jutting out from the undulating land surrounding it. To its left is a wandering goat, and to its right, a mysterious figure, perhaps an old merchant or vagabond. The town appears nearly deserted. Flame-like reddish-yellow lights burning in the windows are the only hint of habitation.

Ryback grew up in a Hasidic family in the town of Yelisavetgrad. Early in life he learned to paint, and as a youth he was exposed to Russian folk art while performing restoration work in monasteries. During his studies in Kyiv, he joined several expeditions to study Jewish folk art and regional synagogues. In 1916, Ryback and El Lissitzky (pp. 104–105) encountered a synagogue in the town of Mogilev on the banks of the Dnieper River, which profoundly impacted both artists. A wooden building with a peaked roof, its interior was bedecked with countless paintings and decorations, which provided an inexhaustible source of inspiration for Ryback. In some respects, it seems Ryback never returned from the shtetls that so totally occupied his artistic imagination. The sense of dread that characterizes many of his works suggests he may have foreseen their impending destruction. Ryback never ceased depicting the landscapes, the dilapidated buildings, and the life of the Jews in these rural areas—his works are a dark monument to their existence.

In 1950, Sonia Ryback, the artist's widow, came to Israel for the first time to visit a retrospective held in his memory at the Tel Aviv Museum. Several years later, the first mayor of Bat Yam, David Ben Ari, invited her to live in the coastal town south of Tel Aviv, where the Ryback House would be designed for her as a residence and a museum for the estate of her husband. Upon her passing, the works were donated to the city and are currently in the collection of the Museums of Bat Yam (MoBY), the most important center dedicated to Ryback's work and legacy.

Hila Cohen-Schneiderman

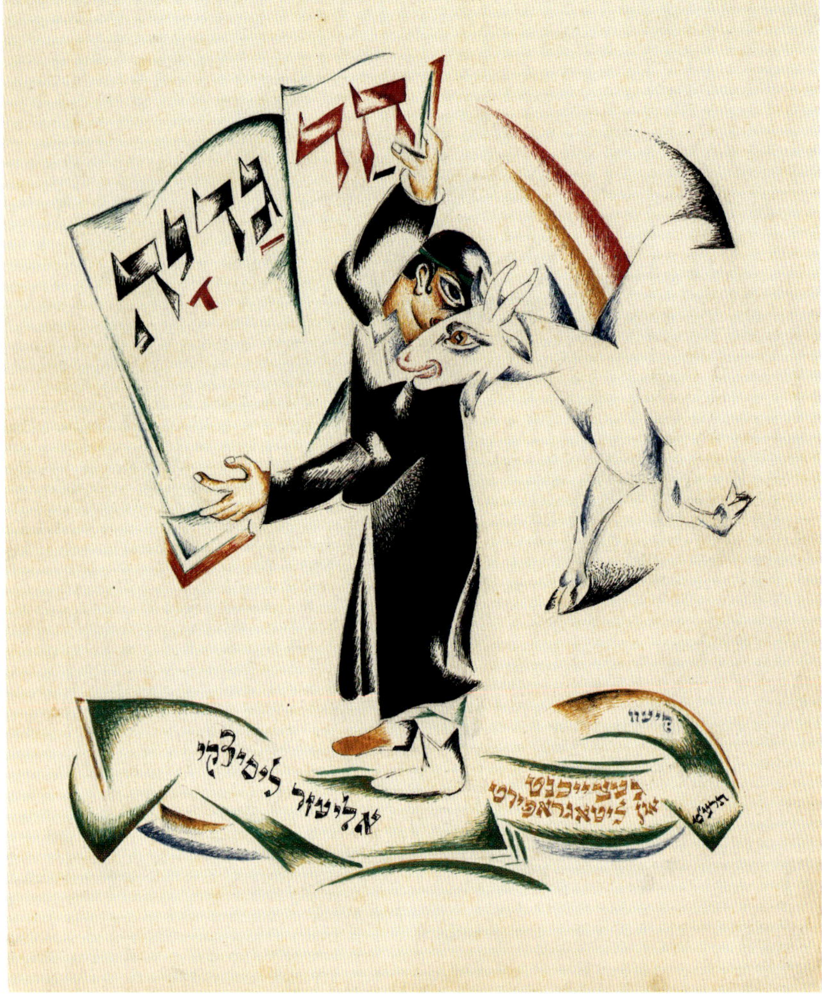

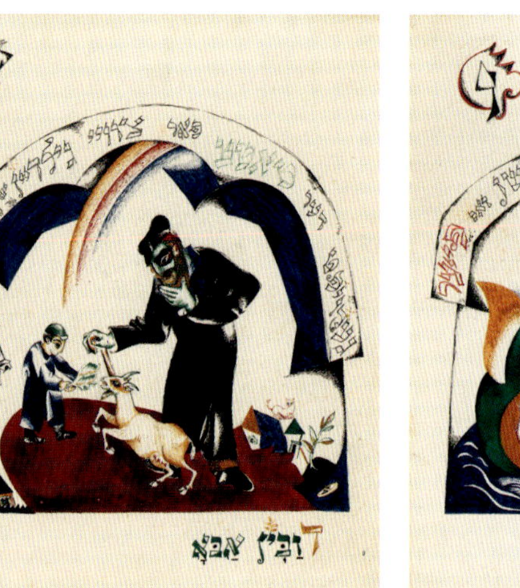

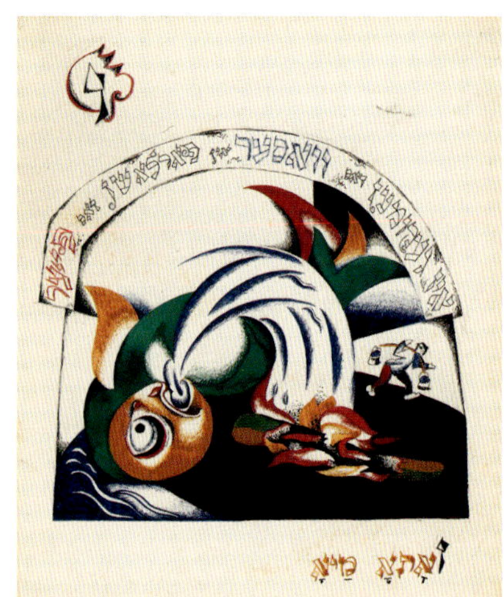

ואתא שונרא

ואתא כלבא

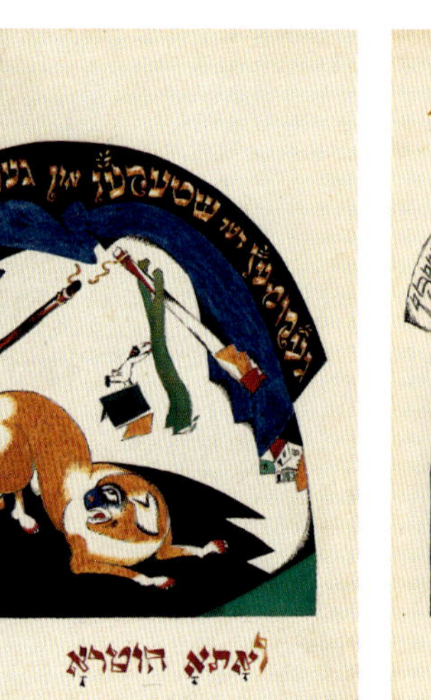

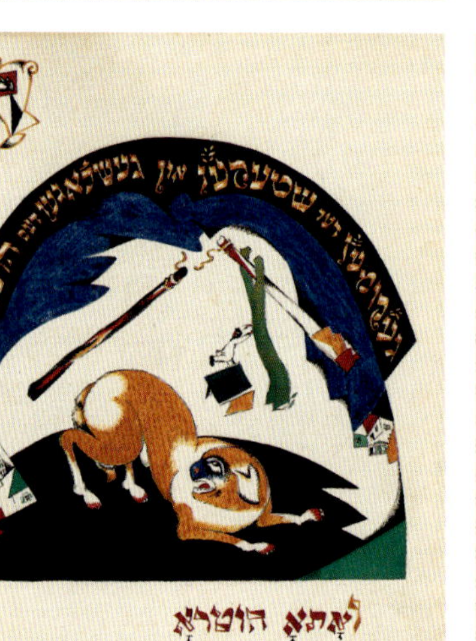

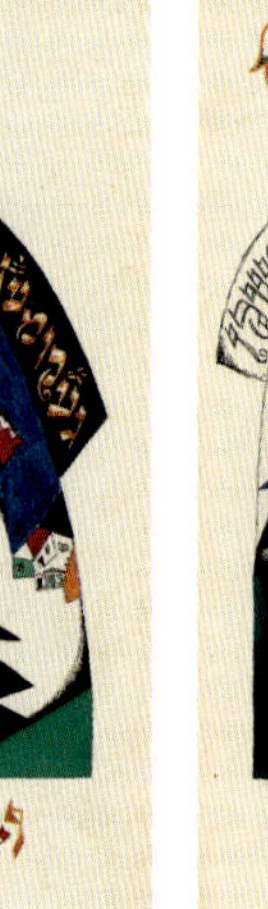

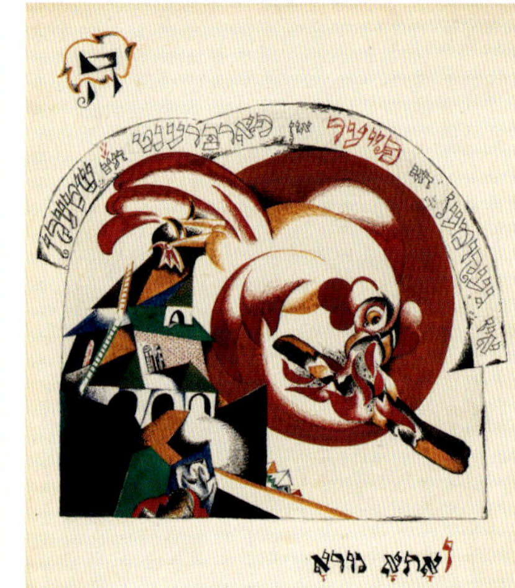

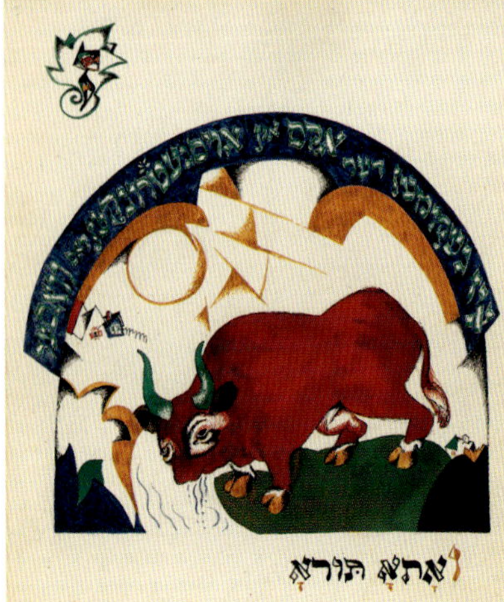

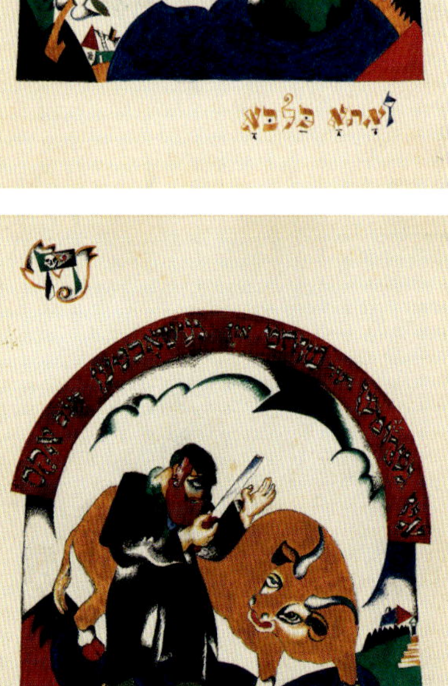

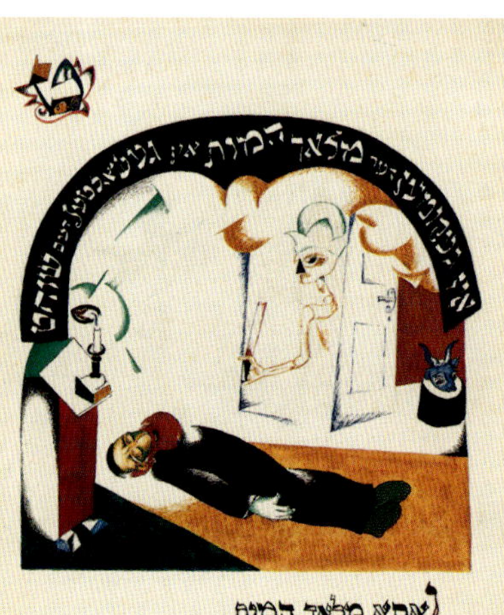

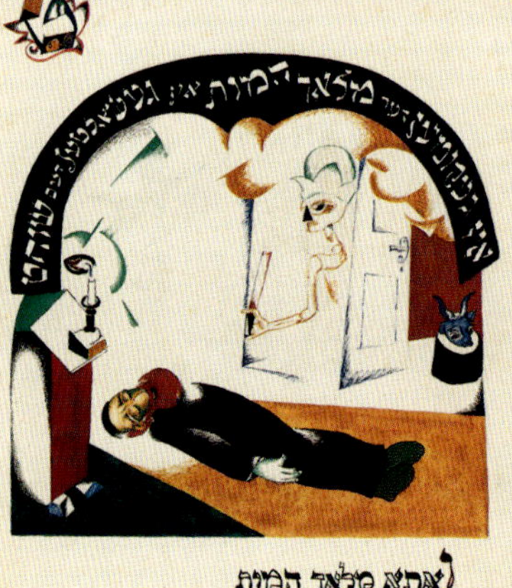

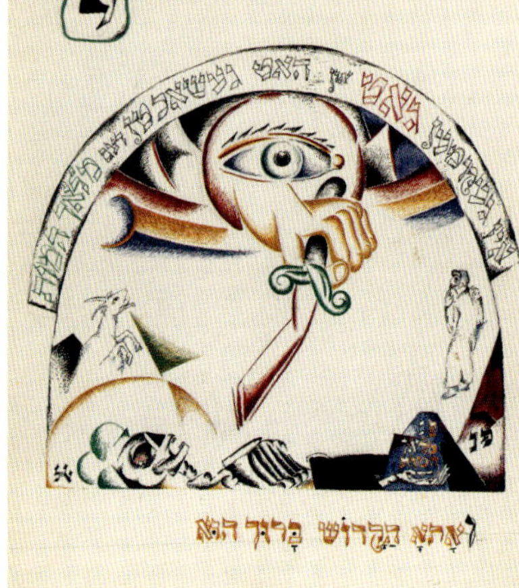

El Lissitzky
1890, Pochinok, Smolensk Governorate, Russia–1941 Moscow, Russia
Had Gadya, 1918–19
Gouache on paper, 11 sheets, each 11 × 9 1/16 in. (28 × 23 cm)

Donated by Israel Pollak, Tel Aviv, with assistance from the British Friends of the Art Museums in Israel, London, 1979

While El Lissitzky made great contributions to the Russian avant-garde as a painter, architect, and advertisement designer, he is equally remembered for rethinking the concept of the printed book.[1] Like many other Jewish artists of the period, he considered book design a primary creative sphere.

Lissitzky was immersed in a Jewish cultural renaissance that flourished from about 1912 to the early 1920s. In 1911, he sketched various Jewish monuments in Germany. In the summer of 1916, together with Issachar Ber Ryback (pp. 102–103), Lissitzky explored some two hundred synagogues in towns and shtetls along the Dnieper River, carefully studying and copying their decorations. From 1916 to 1919, the artist created approximately thirty works on paper, exploring the possibilities of avant-garde syntax within Jewish cultural traditions.

Between 1917 and 1923, Lissitzky illustrated Yiddish and Hebrew books for various publishing houses in Kyiv and Petrograd (today's Saint Petersburg). When he made *Had Gadya* (*The Only Kid*), an illustrated version of the Aramaic song that closes the Passover Haggadah, Lissitzky was a member of the Art Section of the Kultur-Lige in Kyiv, which promoted the development of Jewish secular culture. In each verse, the song introduces a new character who destroys the previous verse's character, beginning with a young goat—until, at song's end, God slays the Angel of Death to end this cycle of violence. An allegory for the hardships of the Jewish people in their exiles in Babylon and Egypt, Lissitzky's *Had Gadya* exemplifies his search for a modern Jewish national style. While creating his illustrations for *Had Gadya*, the artist was inspired by medieval Jewish illuminated manuscripts as well as by the imagery in old painted wooden synagogues. Lissitzky's illustrations include arcs of ribbons crowning the images, suggesting synagogue arches inscribed with sacred texts. The artist chose Yiddish for the song's verses, but introduced each verse with an Aramaic phrase, written using the Hebrew alphabet.

The artist's earliest watercolors for *Had Gadya* were created in 1917. This version, completed in gouache in early 1919, served as the basis for a lithographic portfolio, printed later in 1919 in an edition of seventy-five. Unlike his earlier sketches for *Had Gadya*, which are narrative and figurative, in the 1919 version geometric shapes dominate the imagery, attesting to Lissitzky's interest in Cubist and abstract forms.

Alla Rosenfeld

1 See Arnold J. Band, ed. *Had Gadya (The Only Kid): Facsimile of El Lissitzky's Edition of 1919* (Los Angeles: Getty Research Institute, 2004); Alexander Kantsedikas, *El Lissitzky: The Jewish Period* (London: Unicorn, 2017); Hillel Kazovsky, *Knyzhkova hrafika myttsiv Kultur-Ligy* (*The Book Design of Kultur-Lige Artists*) (Kyiv: Dukh i litera, 2011); and Nancy Perloff and Brian Reed, eds., *Situating El Lissitzky: Vitebsk, Berlin, Moscow* (Los Angeles: Getty Research Institute, 2003).

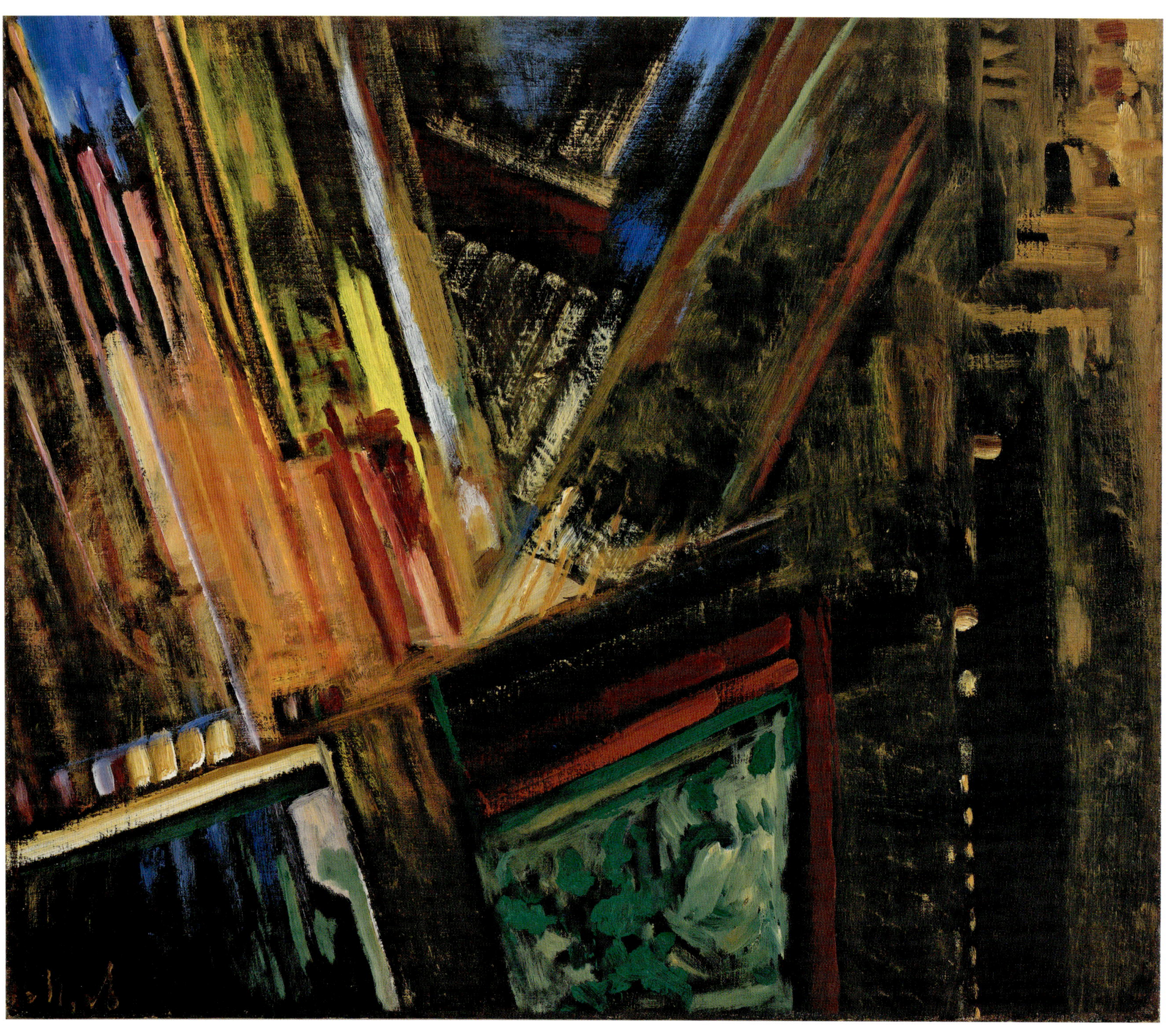

Mikhail Larionov
1881, Tiraspol, Russian Empire (now Moldova)–
1964, Fontenay-aux-Roses, France
A Street in Moscow, 1914–15
Oil on canvas, 22 1/16 × 26 in. (56 × 66 cm)

Mizne-Blumental Collection, Bequest of Annette Celine, 2018

In the years leading up to the execution of this painting, Mikhail Larionov created a series dedicated to Venus (1909–12), in which he initiated a dialogue with classical art—from Titian's *Venus* to the most scandalous painting of the nineteenth century, Édouard Manet's *Olympia* (1863)—to explore national-cultural identity and new approaches to image-making. According to Larionov, an artist must be able to work simultaneously in completely different styles. He went through Impressionist and Pointillist periods, and subsequently made powerful contributions to Russian Neo-Primitivism before his work changed decisively in 1913 with the development of Rayonism—a non-objective style of painting that depicts dynamic rays of light imagined to be emanating from unseen objects.

This painting displays clear characteristics of Larionov's Rayonism. Recognizable objects (houses, landscapes, soldiers, or flowers) have disappeared. Instead, the space of the picture is filled with intersecting, brightly hued diagonal lines, and the artist leaves it to the viewer whether to "create" some semblance of an object or allegory within. The written word, which coexisted so comfortably with the image in his Neo-Primitivist paintings, is resolutely forced out of this painting, with only the artist's initials "*МЛ*" remaining. The image and its title—the two fundamental aspects of European easel painting—maintain a relationship of maximum independence typical of such avant-garde work: if not for the title, we would never know the work's subject.

The painting is inscribed with the date 1909 on the verso, reflecting a common practice among Russian avant-garde artists, who manipulated signatures and dates to dictate the desired trajectory of their artistic development.[1] Here, Larionov not only backdated the work but also signed his name in Cyrillic, falsely indicating that the picture was painted before he left Russia for Paris in 1915. However, the general opinion of specialists today is that Larionov deliberately dated some of his Rayonist paintings to an earlier time in an effort to prove that he "invented" non-objective art as part of an ongoing dispute with Wassily Kandinsky and his supporters.

Kira Dolinina, Roman Grigoryev

1 Kazimir Malevich and Vladimir Tatlin, for example, often put earlier dates on their paintings.

Natalia Goncharova
1881, Nagayevo, Tula Governorate, Russia–1962, Paris, France
Magnolias in a Vase, early 1920s
Oil on canvas, 13 × 9 7⁄16 in. (33 × 24 cm)

Page 110 *Sadko*, costume design for the ballet *Sadko*, 1916
Watercolor, gouache, graphite, and silver leaf on brown paper mounted on white paper, 14 7⁄8 × 10 7⁄16 in. (37.8 × 26.5 cm)

Page 111 *Seraph*, costume design for the ballet *Liturgy*, 1915–27
Stencil with gouache on paper, 23 1⁄16 × 13 9⁄16 in. (58.5 × 34.4 cm)

Bequest of Boris and Alexandra Pregel, 1986

These three works by Natalia Goncharova showcase the breadth of her work across painting, print, and design. The costume sketch for the ballet *Sadko* (premiered Paris, 1916) reflects Sergei Diaghilev's typical productions: famous Russian music accompanied by innovative choreography and costumes. The protagonist wears a pseudo-Russian costume, representing a fantasy that only remotely resembles elements of antique Russian dress. The character's identifying harp on his left shoulder is his source of strength, marking him as the epic hero. The gouache and watercolor drawing is complemented by glued pieces of silver foil—a tribute to the fashionable papier collé technique widely used at the time by modernists. *Seraph* was created for the ballet *Liturgie*, which sought to combine sacred music and rich imagery inspired by the Florentine painter Cimabue, part of the repertory *Russian Seasons* by Diaghilev. Although the ballet was never performed, Goncharova's sketches were published as an album that became famous in 1927. Goncharova often referred to Christian images in these works, and the pose of a seraphim (the highest angelic rank in the Jewish and Christian traditions) was invented by the choreographer and ballet dancer Leonid Myasin himself, who wrote: "For the scene 'Ascension,' I built many groups of angels whose arms were turned up and crossed, which created the illusion of wings raising to heaven."[1] The stencil (*pochoir*) technique of the entire album, and of *Seraph* in particular, carries a message associated with the archaic, aligning it with traditional lithography and Russian popular prints (*lubok*), which actively circulated across Russia and were an important source for Goncharova's imagery. *Magnolias in a Vase* stylistically refers to Goncharova's early 1920s work. The motif of flowers occupies an important place in the artist's oeuvre, helping trace her aesthetic evolution, from her fascination with Paul Gauguin (pp. 38–39) in the 1900s and Paul Cézanne (pp. 30–31) in the 1910s to her Rayonist *Flowers* (1912) and the development of Cubist techniques and decorative qualities in her works of the 1920s. Her combination of different viewpoints simultaneously (from the front and from above), the deliberate decorativeness and use of pure, unmixed colors, and an eschewing of perspective underscore Goncharova's focus on building a composition balanced in a two-dimensional space.

Kira Dolinina, Roman Grigoryev

1 Leonid Myasin, *My Life in Ballet* (Moscow: Artist, Rezhisser, Teatr, 1997), 63.

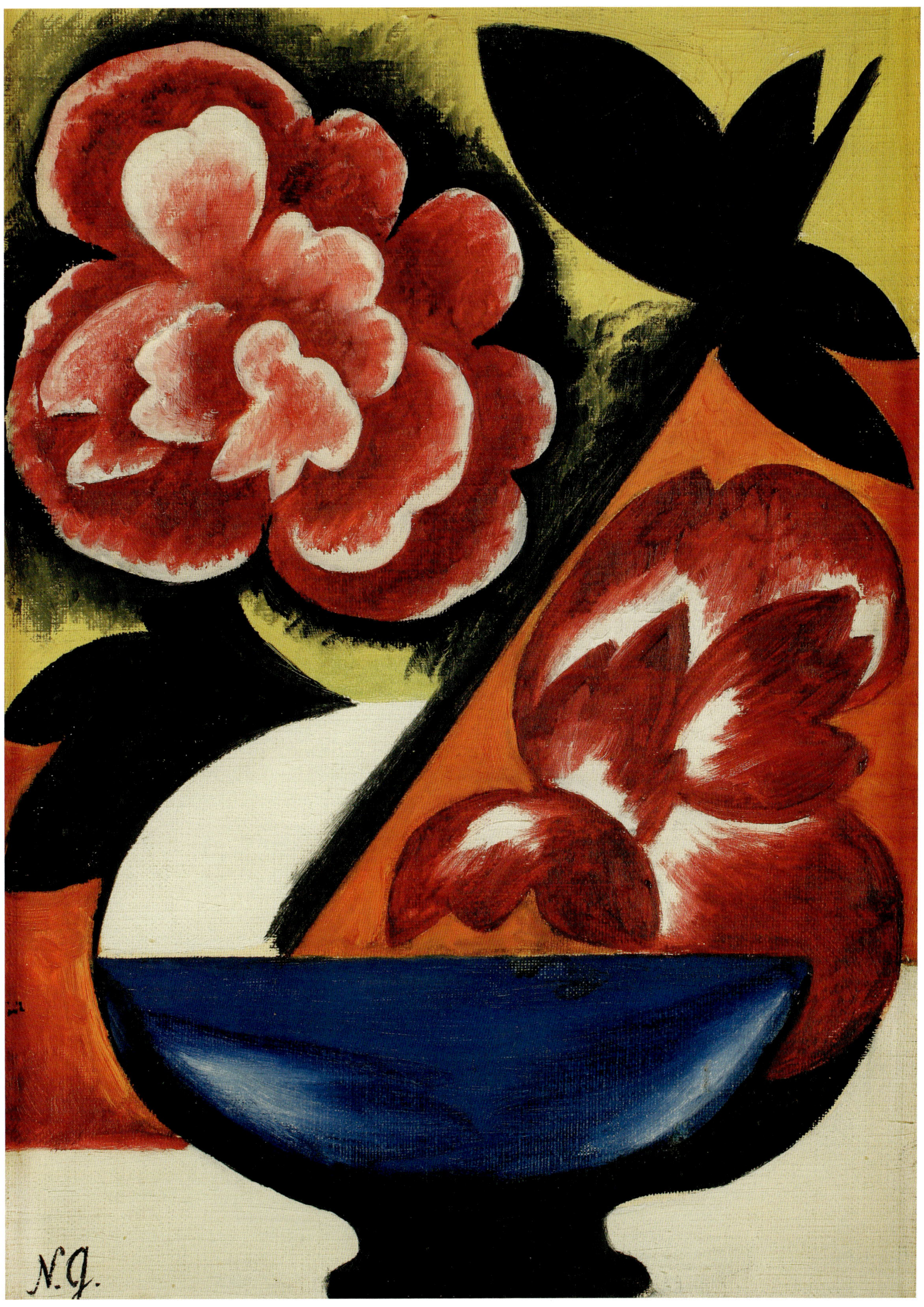

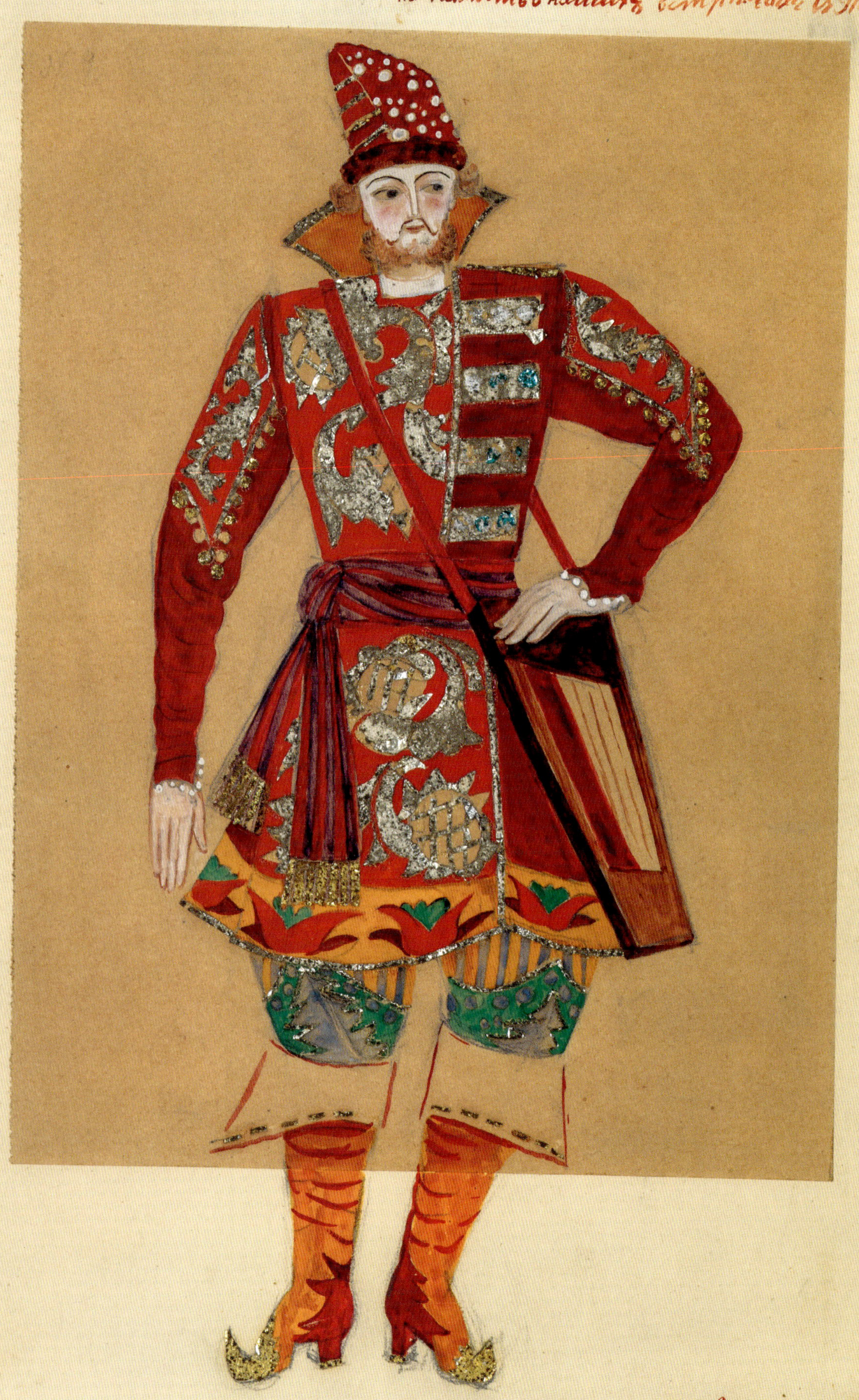
Самому милому доктору философiи
Марiи Самойловнѣ Цетлинъ
на память о нашихъ встрѣчахъ въ Парижѣ.
N. Gontcharowa.

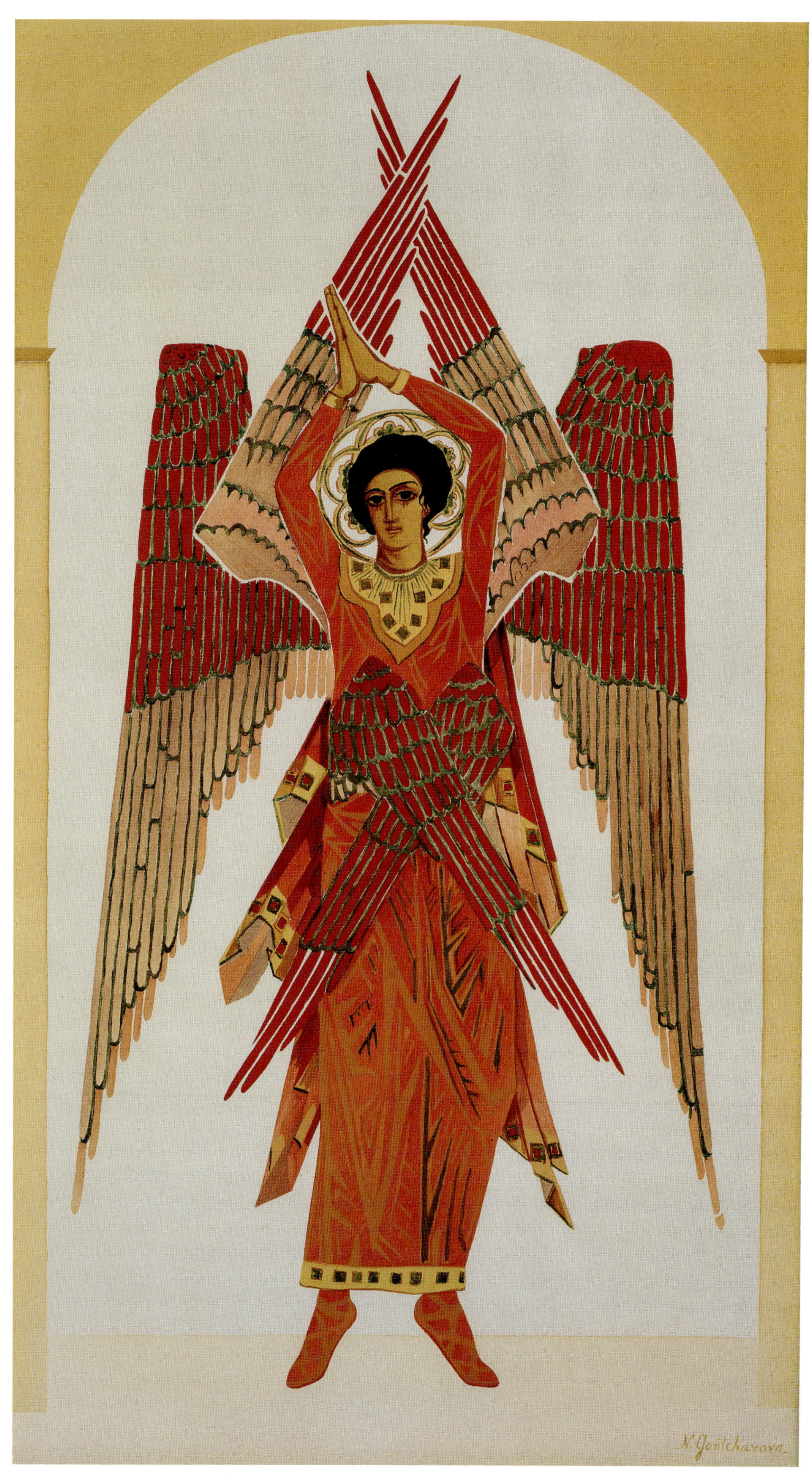
N. Gontcharova

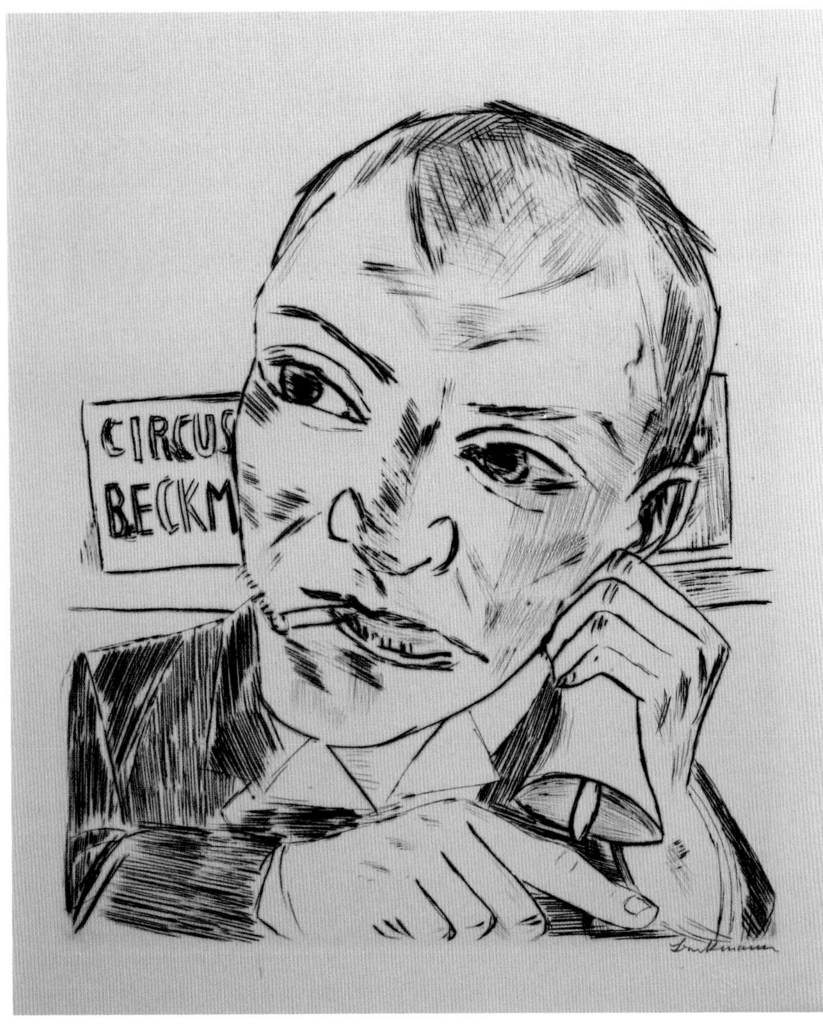
CIRCUS
BECKM

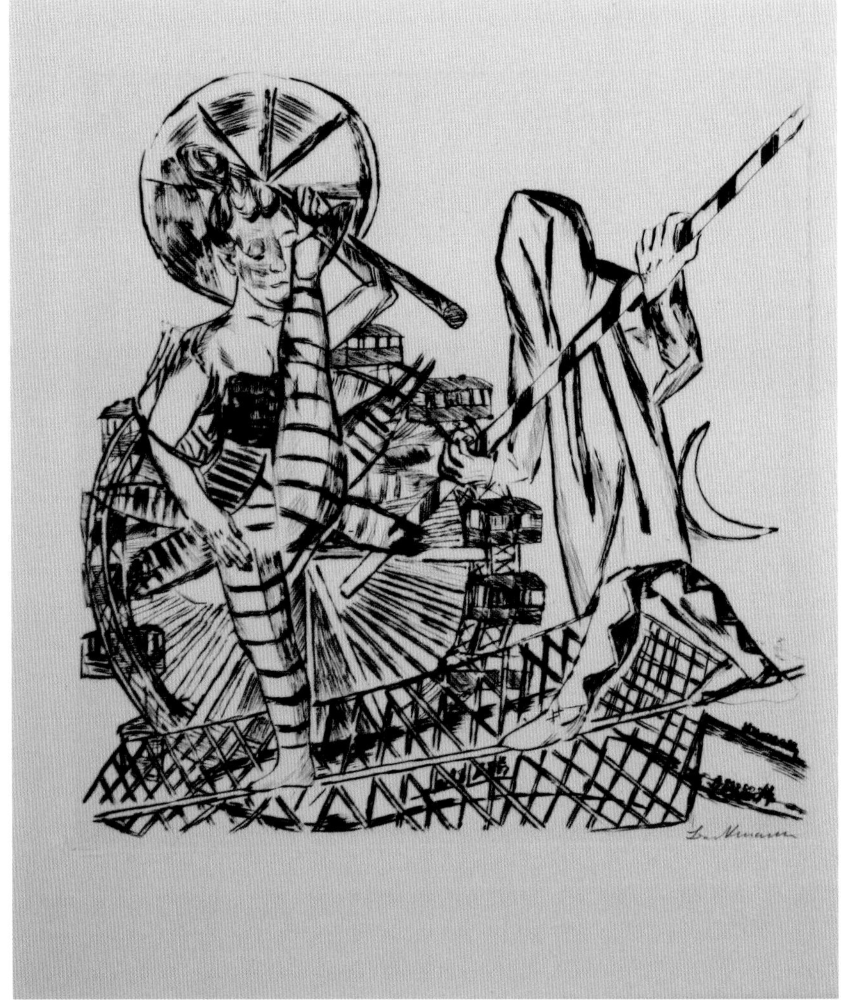

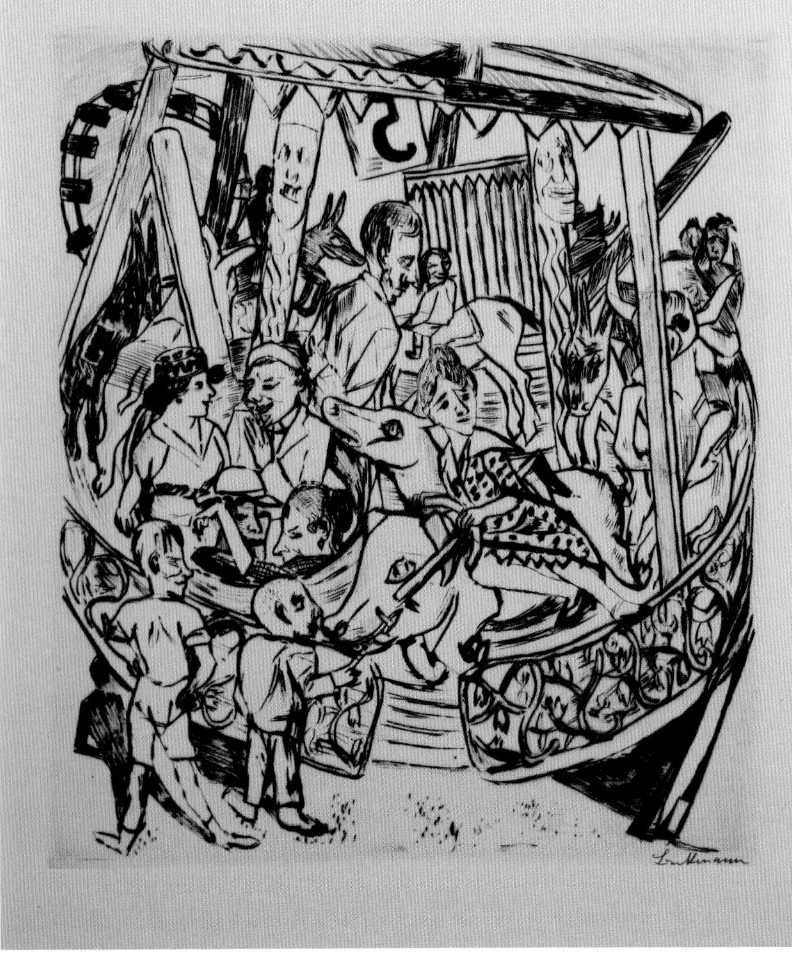

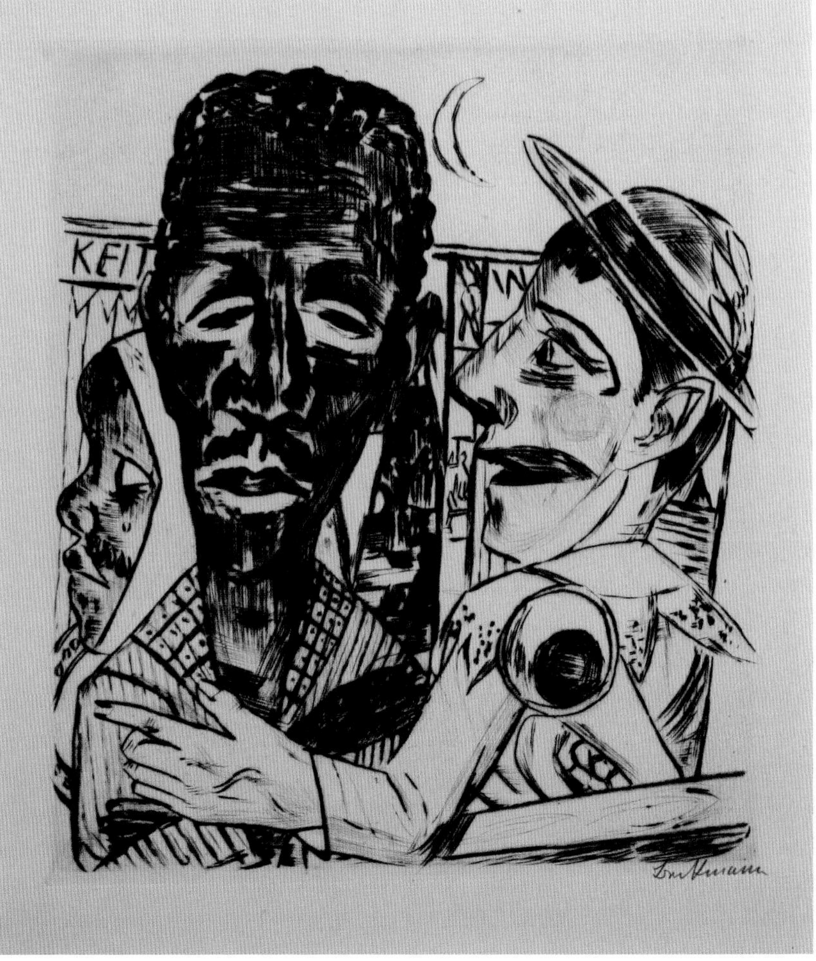
KEIT

Max Beckmann
1884, Leipzig, Germany–1950, New York, NY, United States
Annual Fair, 1921 (published 1922)
Four from a portfolio of ten drypoints, published by Marées-Gesellschaft, R. Piper & Co., Munich, edition of 200

Left to right by row:

The Barker (Self-Portrait)
13 1/4 × 10 3/16 in. (33.6 × 25.6 cm)

The Tightrope Walkers
10 3/16 × 10 in. (26 × 25.3 cm)

Merry-Go-Round
11 7/16 × 10 1/8 in. (29.1 × 25.5 cm)

The Negro
11 7/16 × 10 1/4 in. (29 × 25.4 cm)

Gift of Dr. Abraham Horodisch, Amsterdam, 1986

Max Beckmann—a painter, printmaker, teacher, and thinker—volunteered for the German medical corps in 1914, during World War I. A year later he was discharged due to ill health and settled in Frankfurt. The difficult experiences he endured during the war changed his worldview and led to a dramatic change in his artistic style. Beckmann, like other artists who returned from the war, including Otto Dix and George Grosz, rejected the conventional depiction of space in their works in favor of compressed compositions marked by distortion, which sought to present the sense of instability and anxiety that flooded interwar Germany. While Beckmann did not belong to a defined artistic movement, he was associated with German Expressionism and Neue Sachlichkeit (New Objectivity). In his works, he often combined motifs from the worlds of theater, circus, mythology, and religion as allegories for the human tragedy.

In 1921, Beckmann started working on *Annual Fair* (*Jahrmarkt*), in which the circus is a metaphor for the world. The print portfolio opens with a self-portrait, in which Beckmann presents himself as the ringmaster, pointing to the edge of the title page, inviting the viewers to witness the carnivalesque reality unfolding within. Some of the compositions focus on individuals—a woman with a snake wrapped around her neck, two tightrope walkers, a performer getting ready backstage—while others feature a crush of people, such as a merry-go-round nearly overflowing with passengers. Two prints, *The Negro* and *Negro Dance*, depict people of African descent, displayed as an attraction—a widespread practice in fairs and circuses in the nineteenth and early twentieth centuries, implying the superiority of white people over "primitive" natives. In *The Negro*, Beckmann portrays a red-cheeked clown next to a pair of African figures presented as a popular and commercial attraction. *Negro Dance* features a group of African dancers and musicians on a stage. One dancer stands out with her lighter skin, covered by a transparent veil that signals mystery and exoticism.

The ten drypoints in the portfolio lay out the circus of life from Beckmann's perspective, and may be seen as a poignant personal document, and at the same time, as a broad examination of role-playing, artificiality, and identity in Weimar Germany. With the Nazi rise to power in 1933, Beckmann's art was declared "degenerate," and in late 1937 he permanently left Germany.

Naama Bar-Or

Erich Heckel
1883, Döbeln, Germany–1970, Radolfzell, Germany
Self-Portrait, 1919
Woodcut, 18 1/8 × 12 13/16 in. (46 × 32.5 cm)
Printed by J. B. Neumann, Berlin, edition unknown (approx. 60)

Gift of Dr. Karl Schwarz, 1936

In this self-portrait, Erich Heckel depicts himself in a pose of contemplation with folded hands brought to his chin, recalling traditional representations of prayer. His solemn gaze is turned inward; he seems to be completely absorbed in himself. His features are exaggerated with a high forehead, narrow cheeks, and a downward tapering face. Marked by dark, rough lines, his face appears sunken and wrinkled, underscoring the portrait's melancholic and tense mood. This effect is heightened by the print's dark and earthy tones, as the black areas of the upper body and hair contrast with the blue and red fields of color in the background. Particularly striking is the olive-gray skin, which gives Heckel a sickly appearance.

This work was presumably created during a stay in Osterholz on the Flensburg Fjord. The artist and his partner Siddi spent many summer and autumn months in the small fishing village, where he returned in 1919 after his service in World War I. Heckel volunteered for the army in 1914 but was deemed unfit for combat and subsequently stationed as a medical orderly in Flanders, Belgium. His artistic production during that time depicts people marked by war and suffering, although it does not explicitly show the horrors of battle. In a letter to his artist friend Lyonel Feininger dated May 1919, Heckel wrote that the tranquility of Osterholz revived his memories of the war. *Self-Portrait* might be a testament to this.

Like his colleagues from the artist group Brücke, Heckel was heavily engaged with graphic techniques and, in particular, explored the possibilities of woodcut, which had a centuries-old tradition in Germany. Brücke artists considered woodcut as an independent artistic medium, detached from purely reproductive uses or as a preparatory function in relation to oil painting. Unlike their contemporaries, they did not polish the surfaces of their printing blocks. Instead, they emphasized a rough, angular visual language with flat areas of color that incorporated the unevenness of the material, as well as the wood's natural grain and cracks. *Self-Portrait* still exhibits stylistic elements characteristic of Brücke, although it was created six years after the group's dissolution.[1]

Elena Schroll

1 For further reading, see *Geheimnis der Materie. Kirchner, Heckel, Schmidt-Rottluff*, ed. Regina Freyberger (Frankfurt: Städel Museum, 2019).

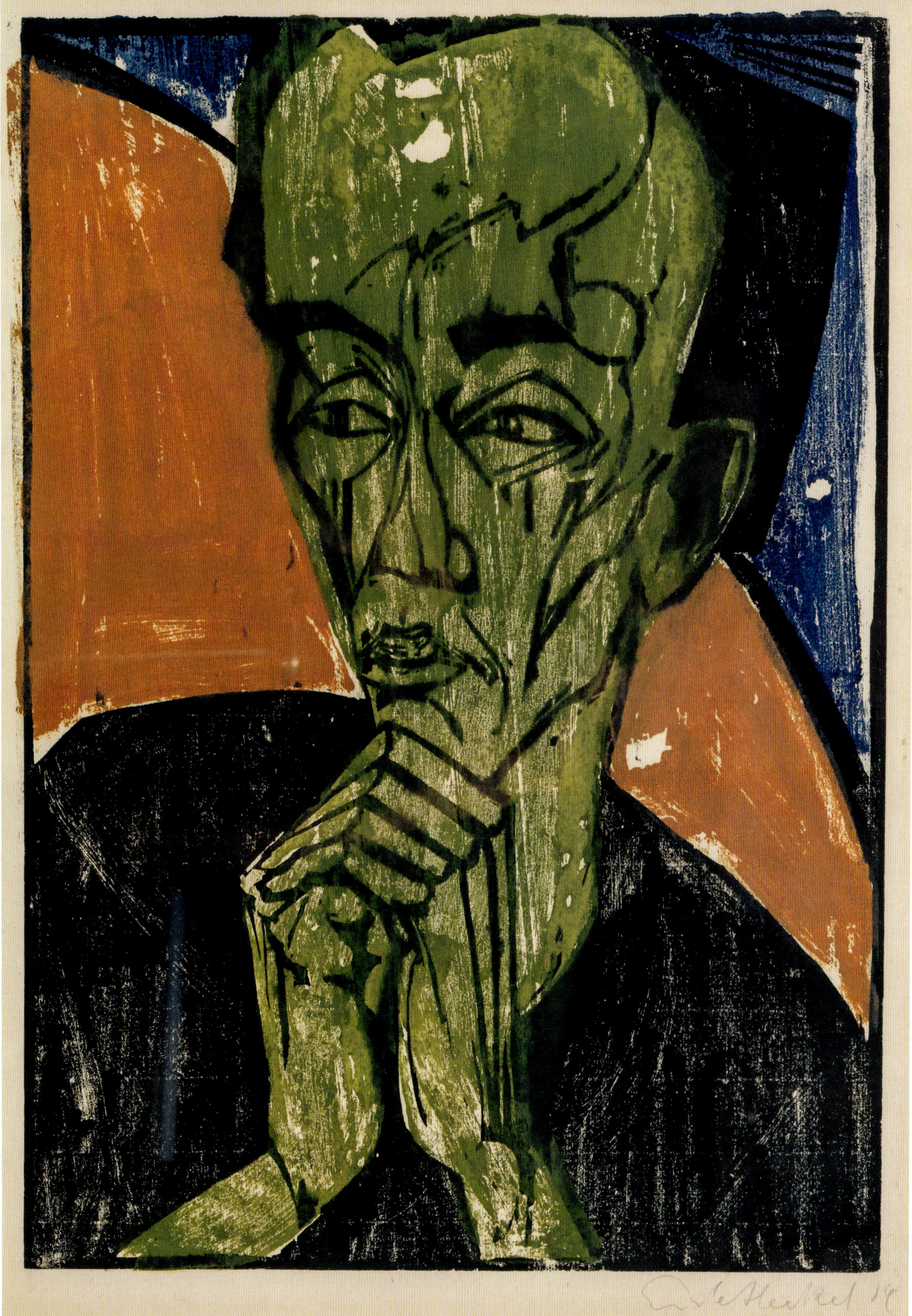

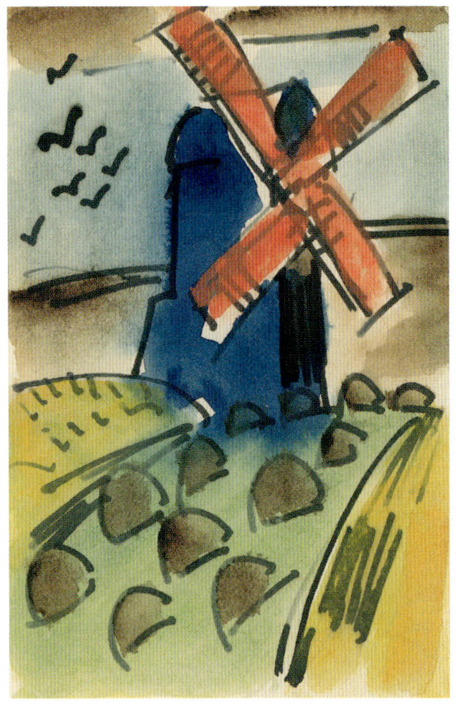

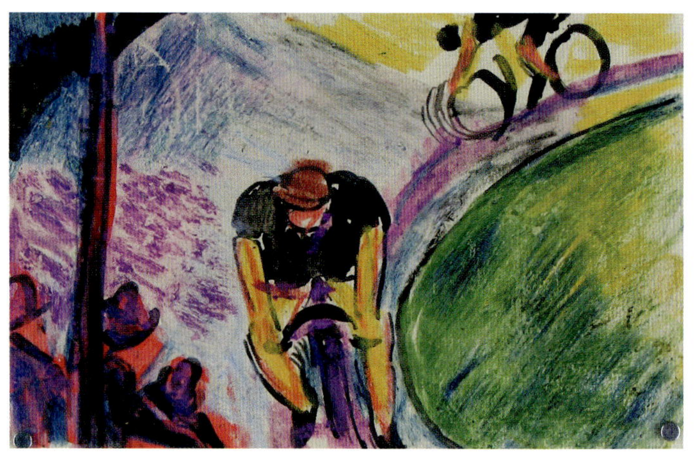

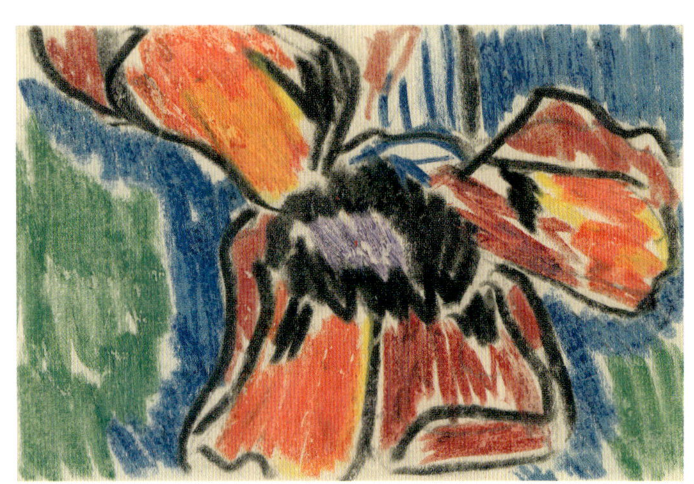

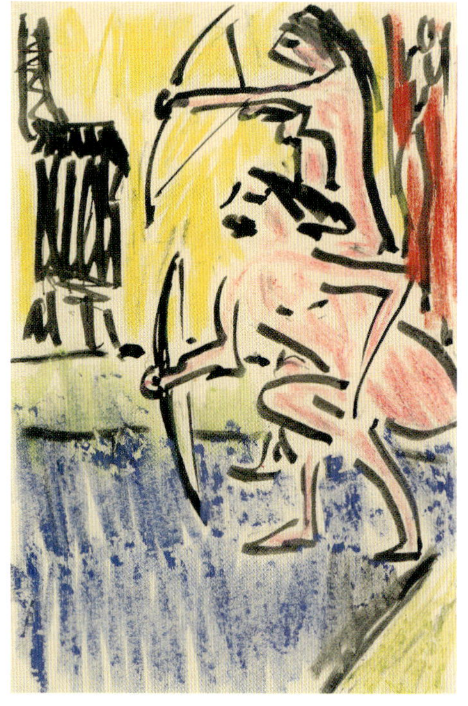

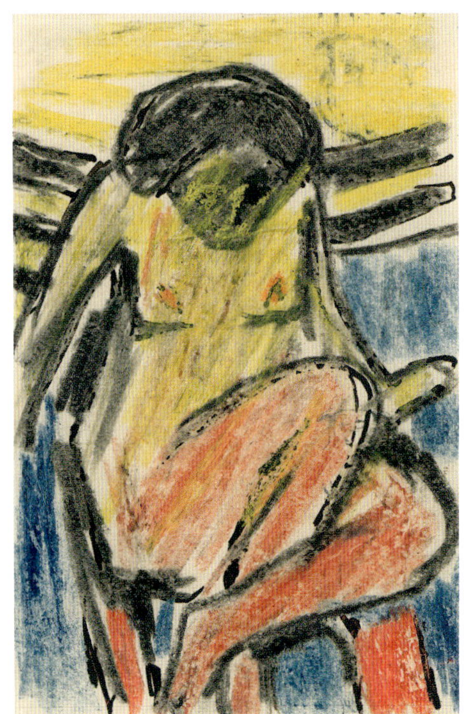

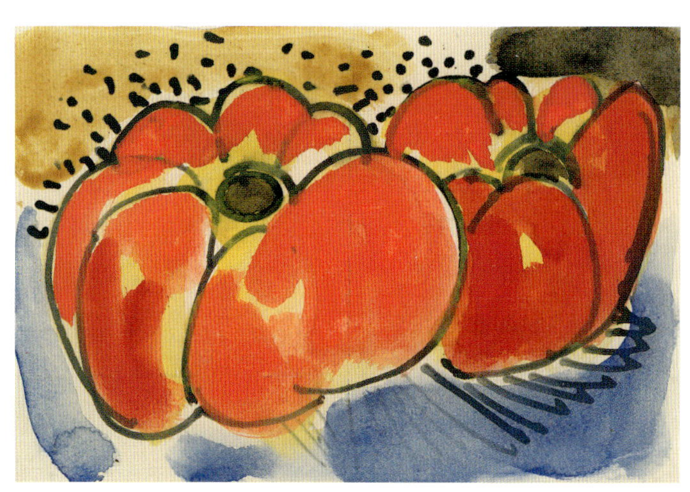

Left to right by row:

Karl Schmidt-Rottluff
1884, Chemnitz, Germany–1976, Berlin, Germany
Untitled [Windmill], c. 1921
Ink and watercolor on postcard, 6.1 × 4 in. (15.5 × 10.2 cm)

Max Pechstein
1881, Zwickau, Germany–1955, Berlin, Germany
Untitled, 1910s–20s
Ink and watercolor on postcard, 3½ × 5½ in. (9 × 14 cm)

Karl Schmidt-Rottluff
1884, Chemnitz, Germany–1976, Berlin, Germany
Untitled [Poppy Flower], 1910
Colored chalk on postcard, 3⅝ × 5½ in. (9.2 × 14 cm)

Erich Heckel
1883, Döbeln, Germany–1970, Radolfzell, Germany
Untitled, c. 1910s–20s
Ink and colored chalk on postcard, 5⅞ × 3⅞ in. (15 × 10 cm)

Karl Schmidt-Rottluff
1884, Chemnitz, Germany–1976, Berlin, Germany
Untitled [Nude], 1911
Charcoal, ink and colored chalk on postcard, 5½ × 3⅝ in. (14 × 9.2 cm)

Karl Schmidt-Rottluff
1884, Chemnitz, Germany–1976, Berlin, Germany
Untitled [Tomatoes], 1910
Ink and watercolor on postcard, 4 × 6 in. (10.2 × 15.4 cm)

Gift of Dr. Rosa Schapire, through the British Friends of the Art Museums of Israel, 1956

Dr. Rosa Schapire, an art historian who specialized in German Expressionism and compiled an impressive collection, donated forty works to the Tel Aviv Museum, including one painting (pp. 166–67) and a selection of woodcuts by her close friend Karl Schmidt-Rottluff, along with fifteen postcards illustrated by members of the artists' group Brücke: Schmidt-Rottluff, Erich Heckel (pp. 114–15), Max Pechstein (pp. 118–19), and Ernst Ludwig Kirchner. Schapire herself chose the works to be donated to the Museum after her death. She passed away in 1954, and the collection arrived at the Tel Aviv Museum two years later.

The postcards, dating between 1909 and 1924, were mailed to Schapire from rural holiday spots in northern Germany, where the artists spent their summers. Uniform in size and spectacular in color, they bear an illustration on one side, and on the other side, in addition to the address, comments often pertaining to the subject of the painting. In the postcard centered on tomatoes, for example, there is a reference to tomatoes grown by the artists themselves, as well as to the design of Schapire's apartment in Hamburg. Due to its fixed, minimalist format, the postcard-turned-artwork posed a challenge to the artists, demanding concentration and discipline. Via standard mail, they offered Schapire rich, colorful, and lively snapshots of their daily lives while vacationing, which included painting outdoors, theatergoing, and cycling.

Apart from a form of communication, these postcards contain traces of what the artists were working on at the time, and also serve as documentation of the relationship between the artists and their dealers, collectors, and art patrons, to whom they were sent. In retrospect, they can be seen as a precedent for mail art, a practice developed by conceptual artists in the 1960s and 1970s as a means to bypass conventional modes of commerce and display.

Alisa Padovano-Friedman

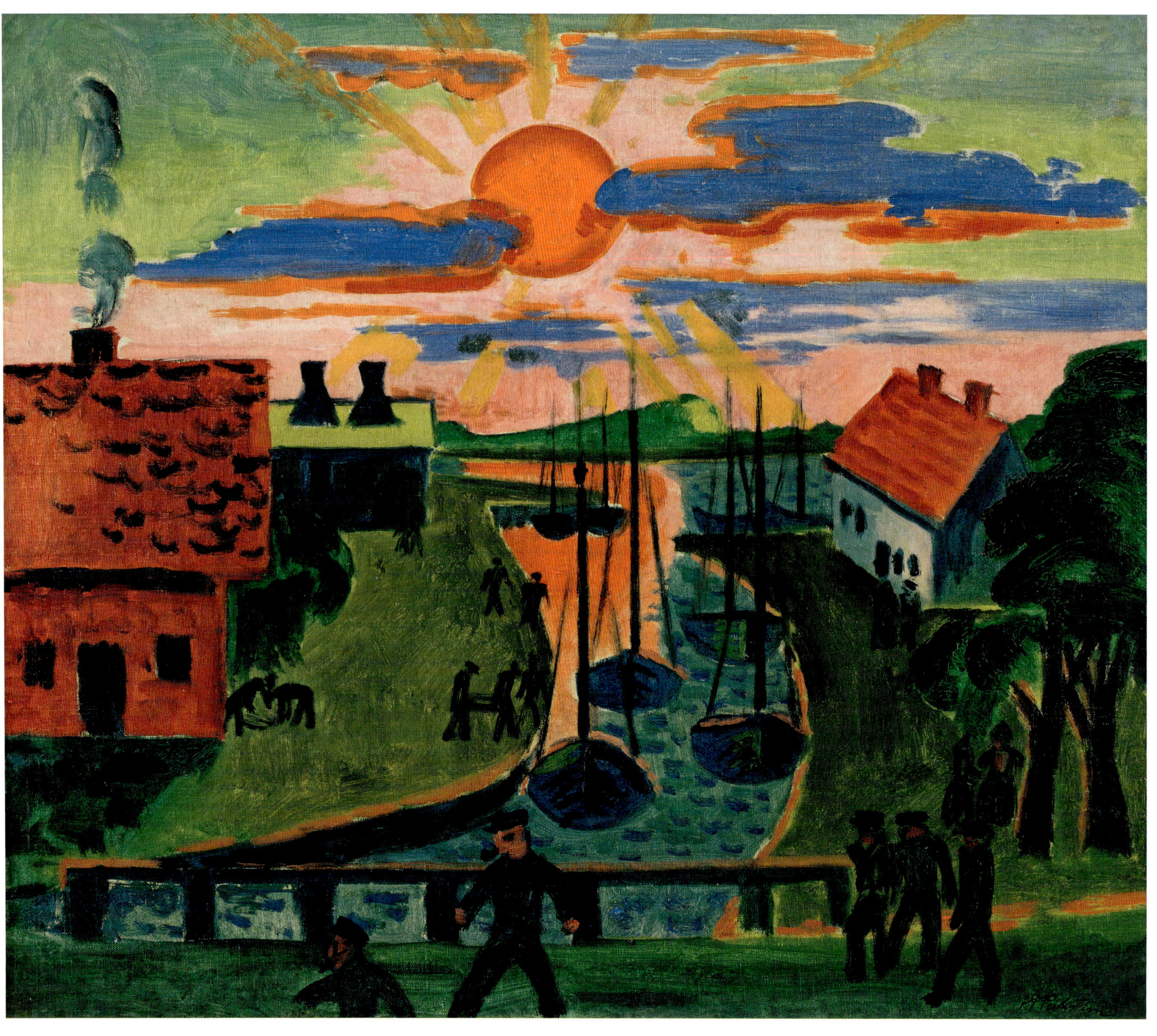

Max Pechstein
1881, Zwickau, Germany–1955, Berlin, Germany
Sunset, 1921–22
Oil on canvas, 18 ⅛ × 21 1/16 in. (46 × 53.5 cm)

Gift of Heinrich Cohen, 1933

In Max Pechstein's *Sunset*, the sky is illuminated with vibrant hues of bright green, red, and blue. The composition's focal point is also the source of light: the sun is simplified, a round orange disc with thick rays that gradually descends towards the water. Its radiant reflection frames the gathering clouds, finding its mirror image in the river. The gentle curve of the water further guides the viewer's gaze to the pedestrian bridge in the foreground of the picture, possibly populated by fishermen as suggested by the figures' hastily sketched caps.

Sunsets take center stage in several of Pechstein's works, particularly during the 1920s and 1930s. Although his earlier fascination with Vincent van Gogh (pp. 36–37) had cooled, his admiration for the Dutch artist's approach is evident in Pechstein's own interpretations of Van Gogh's color, facture, and themes. Pechstein once remarked, "Van Gogh was a father to us all,"[1] emphasizing his profound influence on the artists' group Brücke, of which he was a member. Their engagement with Van Gogh's paintings motivated them to embrace a spontaneous work process, using bold brushstrokes and applying pure contrasting colors directly from the tube onto the canvas. Van Gogh's motifs, particularly his paintings in which the sun shines as a radiant yellow circle, left a lasting impression on the German Expressionists. This departure from the indirect, diffuse portrayal of sunlight commonly seen in Impressionist works further contributed to Van Gogh's appeal.[2]

Pechstein's *Sunset* was created in Leba, a town nestled along the Pomeranian Baltic coast in present-day Poland. Between May and October 1921, Leba became more significant: it was here that he met his second wife, Marta Möller, and two years later they exchanged vows. Pechstein forged deep connections with the local community and discovered abundant inspiration for his artwork. Consequently, the town and its surroundings became recurring motifs in his works, including the prominent outlines of the Große Mühlengrabenbrücke (Great Mill Canal Bridge) featured in this painting.

Elena Schroll

1 Pechstein, quoted in Jill Lloyd, *Vincent van Gogh and Expressionism* (Ostfildern, Germany: Hatje Cantz, 2007), 11.

2 For further reading, see *Making Van Gogh. A German Love Story*, ed. Alexander Eiling and Felix Krämer, with the assistance of Elena Schroll (Frankfurt: Städel Museum, 2019).

Henri Matisse
1869, Le Cateau-Cambrésis, France–1954, Nice, France
Two Women on a Balcony, 1921
Oil on canvas, 27 3/16 × 21 1/4 in. (69 × 54 cm)

Bequest of Boris and Alexandra Pregel, 1986

Page 122

Woman with Gladiola, 1922
Oil on canvas, 19 7/8 × 24 5/8 in. (50.5 × 61.5 cm)

On long-term loan from the Moshe and Sara Mayer Collection

Page 123

The White Dress, Banks of the Loup, 1921
Oil on canvas, 18 1/2 × 55 7/8 in. (47 × 55.9 cm)

Private collection

At the end of the 1910s, Henri Matisse began spending more time in Nice, on the French Riviera. Every autumn, he settled in a different hotel room that would become his studio until the following spring. He completed this painting in the first months of 1921, while staying at the small Hôtel Méditerranée, in a room with a balcony overlooking the Promenade des Anglais and the sea. His daughter Marguerite, then twenty-six, had joined him at the end of January and was slowly recovering from a difficult surgery. She is seated on the left, her elbow resting on the balustrade. The other model is Henriette Darricarrère, a young dancer and violinist whom Matisse had recently hired. The two women got along well and appear together in a number of Matisse's paintings from this period.

The entire painting looks quickly sketched: the models' facial features and hands are just as roughly suggested as the palm tree at left, the black silhouettes on the promenade, and the horse-drawn carriage visible through the balustrade. Matisse's refusal to depict any detail too specifically allows the eye to meander freely across the entire surface of the painting, blurring the distinction between foreground and background. The unity of the work's surface also derives from its vivid, scattered colors: the reds of the pillow on the chair and the umbrella echo the amorphous red stripe paralleling the sea, along with the French flags waving above, as if they were all on the same plane. The blurring of depth is further emphasized by a series of horizontal lines that structure the composition, from the waves on the sea to the balcony's architecture.

On the right, a vertical band runs the length of the canvas, recalling the French doors that open out to the balcony, and signaling the presence of the artist painting from inside the hotel room. Defining a threshold between the inside and the outside, this abstract element frames the composition while emphasizing the artificiality of the scene. Years later, Matisse would remember the Hôtel Méditerranée as a place where "everything was fake, absurd, amazing, delicious."[1] The balcony acts like a theater stage where his favorite models could dress up in sophisticated costumes and accessories. Such a disguise comes with a sense of distance and emptiness: an atmosphere of indifference, solitude, and boredom prevails over the apparent tranquility of the scene. Here, Marguerite and Henriette face each other but do not communicate, each of them waiting in silence while gray clouds accumulate above their heads.

Charlotte Barat-Mabille

1 Jack Cowart, cat. *Henri Matisse: The Early Years in Nice, 1986–87* (Washington, D.C.: National Gallery of Art, 1986), 24.

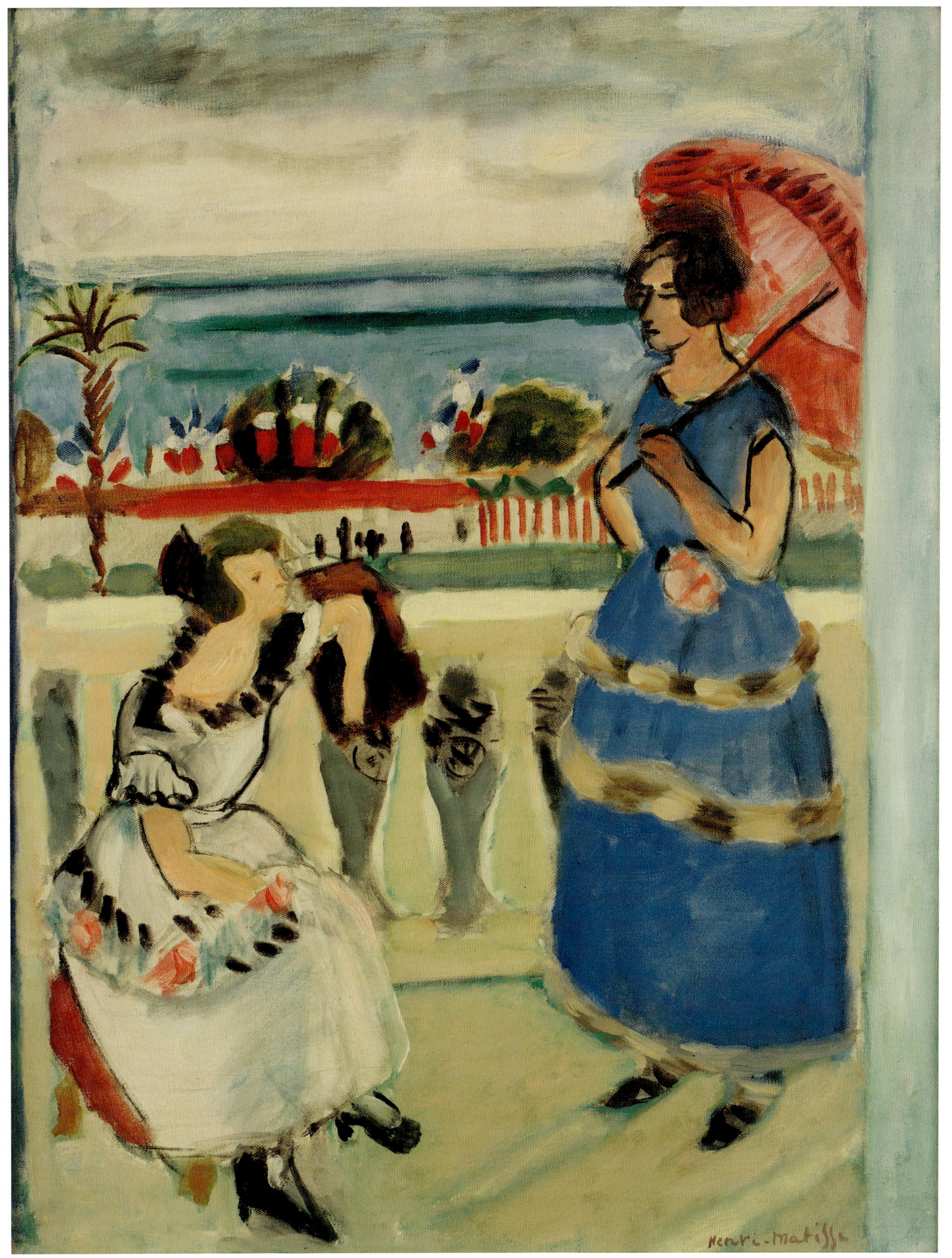
Henri-Matisse

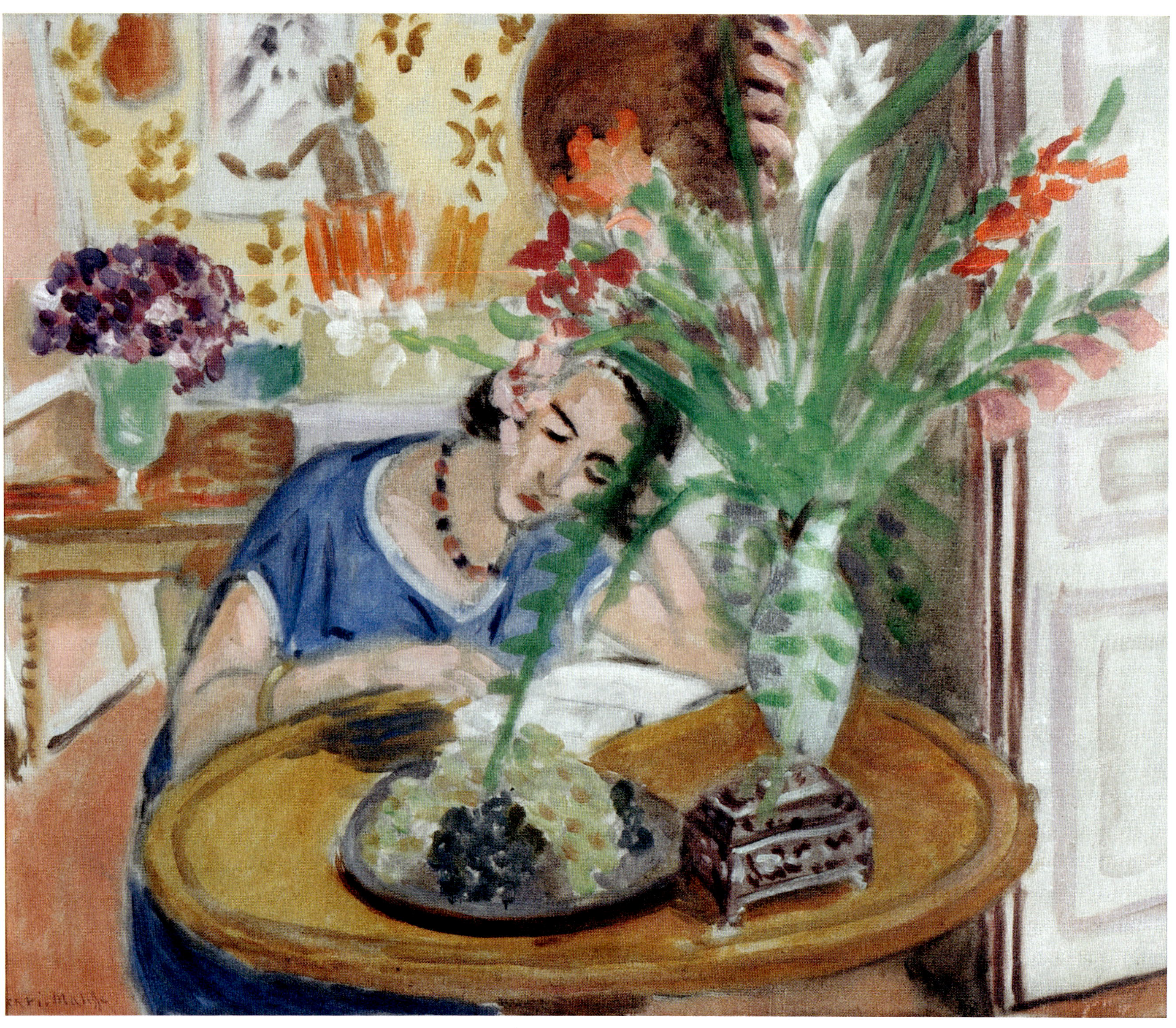

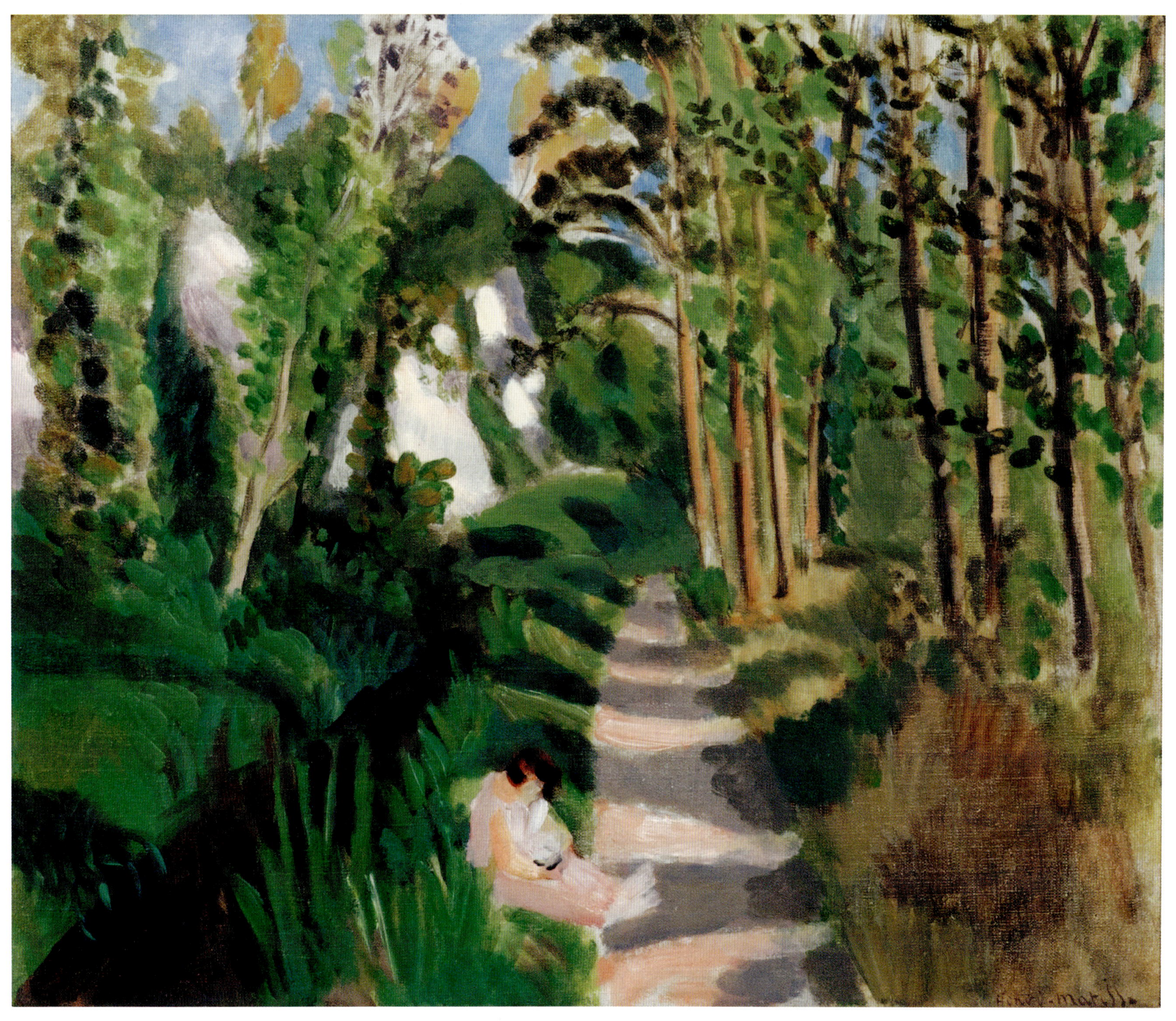

Pablo Picasso
1881, Málaga, Spain–1973, Mougins, France
Woman with a Red Underskirt, 1921
Oil on canvas, 18 ⅛ × 15 1⁄16 in. (46 × 38.3 cm)

On long-term loan from the Moshe and Sara Mayer Collection

Between July 1 and October 1, 1921, Pablo Picasso transformed the garage of a rented villa in Fontainebleau, France, into a temporary studio. During this three-month period, Picasso worked prolifically and simultaneously in two disparate styles seemingly at odds with one another: Cubism, which he had pioneered with Georges Braque (pp. 54–55) a decade earlier, and a classicism associated with the "return to order," which developed as a rejection of the avant-garde in the wake of World War I.

Woman with a Red Underskirt reflects his classical leanings that summer, which culminated in two 6-foot (1.8-meter) versions of *Three Women at the Spring*.[1] The colossal pair and their many preparatory studies feature similarly dressed trios of women at rocky fountains. The azure background, bright white tunic, and titular red skirt of this painting represent the French flag, the *tricolore*—evocative of the politically charged, postwar moment, to which the conservative classicizing movement was responding.

This painting may also be related to two other subjects that Picasso explored at this time. Likely inspired by the nearby Château de Fontainebleau's allegorical *Nymph*, which adorns the château's elaborately decorated Galerie François I, Picasso executed a suite of works featuring a single, seated figure at a fountain or spring.[2] Like the recurring protagonist of this group, the sitter in *Woman with a Red Underskirt* turns in three-quarter profile to the left and gazes serenely into the distance while seated at the natural source. The shallow vessel she cradles in her left hand to catch the flowing water, meanwhile, refers to another motif of Picasso's: the Wallace fountain, the urban counterpart to the mythological spring.[3] Installed across Paris in the nineteenth century, the public fountains—named after the British philanthropist Sir Richard Wallace, who invented them in 1872—offered Parisians potable water and included drinking cups.

Despite its ambition and scope, Picasso's Fontainebleau production initially had an uneven reception. Dealer Paul Rosenberg expressed great curiosity and made repeated inquiries about the artist's progress in the summer of 1921, but did not purchase any paintings from Picasso's summer stockpile until April 1922. *Woman with a Red Underskirt* was one of the first five works that Rosenberg acquired.[4]

A prime example of Picasso's classicizing experiments in Fontainebleau, *Woman with a Red Underskirt* is one of the few single-figure variants from this period and exemplifies how the artist used a single subject as a source of endless recombination.

Alexandra Morrison

1 These two works on canvas are now in the collections of the Musée national Picasso-Paris and the Museum of Modern Art, New York.

2 See Anne Umland, Anny Aviram, and Erika Mosier, "The Spring," in *Picasso in Fontainebleau* (New York: Museum of Modern Art, 2023), 98–101.

3 See Francesca Ferrari and Erika Mosier, "The Wallace Fountain," in *Picasso in Fontainebleau* (New York: Museum of Modern Art, 2023), 176–77.

4 In April 1922, Rosenberg purchased twenty-five paintings from the artist, only five of which may be definitively identified as part of Picasso's Fontainebleau production, including this painting and three small oil studies for *Three Women at the Spring* and the Moderna Museet's *The Spring* (then called *Fontaine à Fontainebleau*). See Rosenberg Collection of Artist Letters, MA 3500.375–76, Department of Literary and Historical Manuscripts, Pierpont Morgan Library, New York.

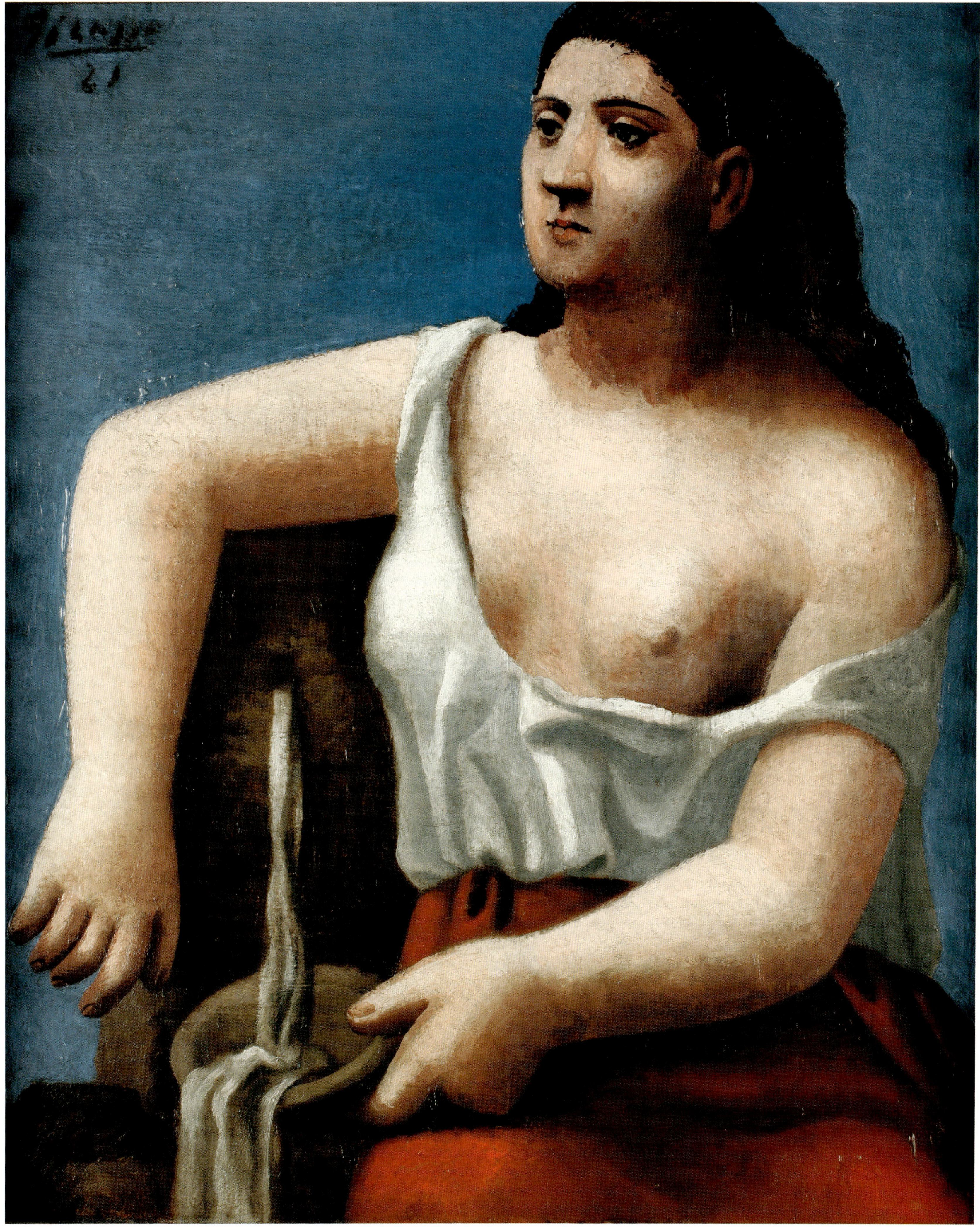

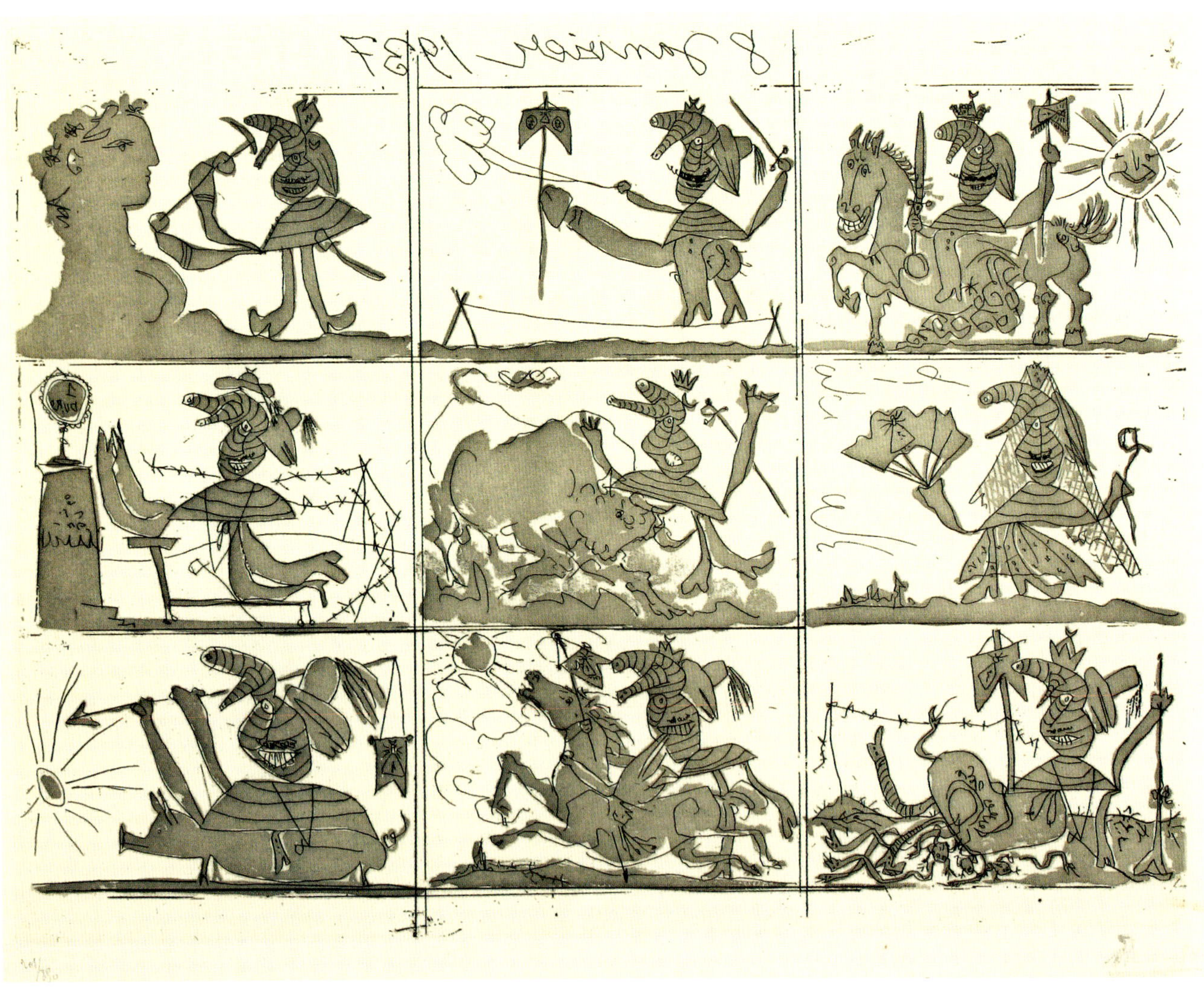

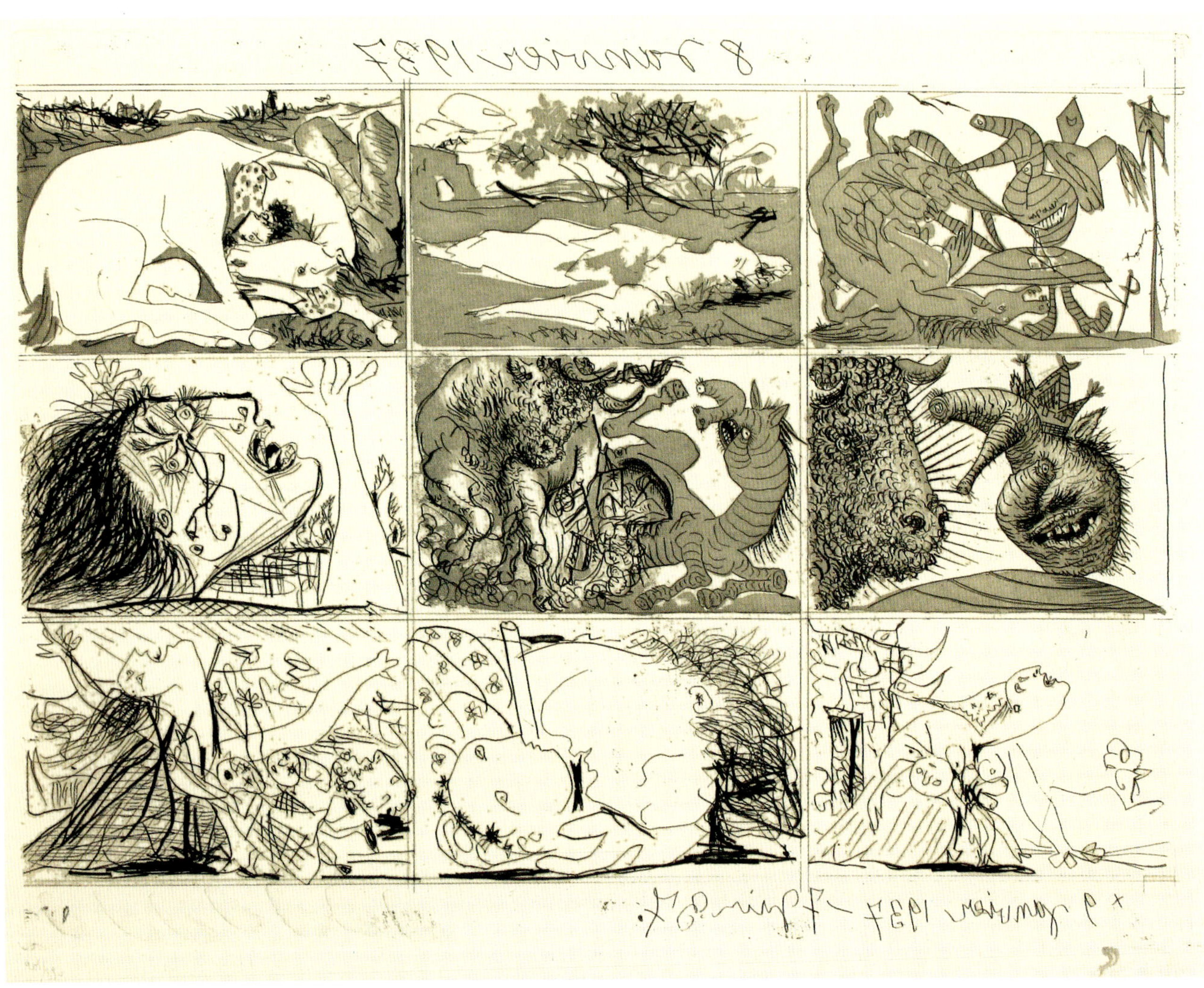

Pablo Picasso
1881, Málaga, Spain–1973, Mougins, France
The Dream and Lie of Franco, 1937
Etching and sugar-lift aquatint, two sheets,
each 15 3⁄16 × 22 7⁄16 in. (38.5 × 57 cm)
Published by the artist, edition of 150

Gift of Charles and Evelyn Kramer, New York, through the American Friends of the Tel Aviv Museum of Art, 1990

With the outbreak of the Spanish Civil War in the summer of 1936, Picasso—who had been living in France for several decades—declared his unequivocal support for Spain's Republican government. One of his outlets of expression in venting his fierce opposition to the fascist regime of General Franco was this pair of highly satirical prints. The two sheets are divided into small compartments in comic-book fashion. Because of the inversion that resulted from the printing process, they are meant to be read from right to left.

Franco is presented as a surreal figure composed of forms with sexual connotations, and as a ferocious, warmongering monster: in one of the scenes, the monster demolishes a classical statue, and in another it kills a horse—images that are fraught with symbolism. Picasso invoked Spanish national mythology through the image of the bull, and references to Don Quixote.

Picasso created fourteen of the eighteen scenes in January 1937. The last four scenes on the second sheet were added later, in June of the same year, after he had completed the monumental painting *Guernica*, his passionate outcry against the bombing and destruction of the Basque town. This work is regarded as modern art's most renowned antiwar statement. The screaming woman with outspread hands, the mother holding her dead child—motifs from *Guernica* that Picasso cited here—have become icons of pain and suffering. The final four scenes differ in content and style from the previous ones; here Picasso avoids parody and satire, and focuses instead on an expression of agony and sorrow.

The two prints served to illustrate a poem written by Picasso himself. The poem and prints were published and sold as an album in a limited edition, and the money raised was used to aid Spanish refugees.

Ruth Feldmann

Pablo Picasso
1881, Málaga, Spain–1973, Mougins, France
Child in a Chair (Maya), 1939
Oil on canvas, 21 5/8 × 14 15/16 in. (55 × 38 cm)

Mizne-Blumental Collection, Bequest of Annette Celine, 2018

Child in a Chair (Maya) is part of a larger series of representations that Pablo Picasso made of his daughter María de la Concepción, nicknamed Maya, from the first drawings he made of Maya with her mother, Marie-Thérèse Walter, just after she was born in 1935, to the spectacular series of fourteen portraits painted between January 1938 and October 1939, including the one here.

This painting is singular in many ways, but particularly in its ambiguous treatment of the subject. Indeed, although it is a portrait of Maya, the child's features are obviously reminiscent of her mother's: one can recognize the oval face and the imposing nose in the extension of the forehead, characteristic of the artist's first representations of Walter, which undoubtedly mark the filiation between mother and daughter. The work also departs from the codes of children's portraiture, such as those found in *Maya in a Sailor Suit* (January 1938), *Maya with a Doll and a Horse* (January 1938), or *Crowned Girl with a Boat* (June 1939), in which the little girl is depicted with a butterfly net, a doll and a horse, or a toy boat, attributes intimately associated with the levity of childhood.

On the contrary, this composition takes up the motif of the woman in the armchair, linked with Picasso's companions (Marie-Thérèse Walter, Dora Maar), which he developed particularly in the late 1930s and 1940s. The artist's sketchbooks made in Royan[1] illustrate the importance of this ambiguous motif, of which Picasso said, "When I paint a woman in an armchair, the armchair implies old age and death, right? [...] Or else the armchair is there to protect her."[2]

The composition is also striking for the difference between the child's head and the rest of the canvas. The head is treated in grisaille, executed entirely in shades of gray, and in an organic style, similar again to the portraits of Marie-Thérèse Walter done a few years earlier. Conversely, the body is broken down into geometric facets whose lines echo those of the chair, but whose bright colors only slightly diminish the impression of solemnity conveyed by the blue background and the child's serious face.

Joanne Snrech

1 Sketchbooks 43 (object number MP1877) and 45 (object number MP1879), Musée national Picasso-Paris.

2 André Malraux, *Picasso's Mask* (New York: Holt, Rinehart & Winston, 1976), 138.

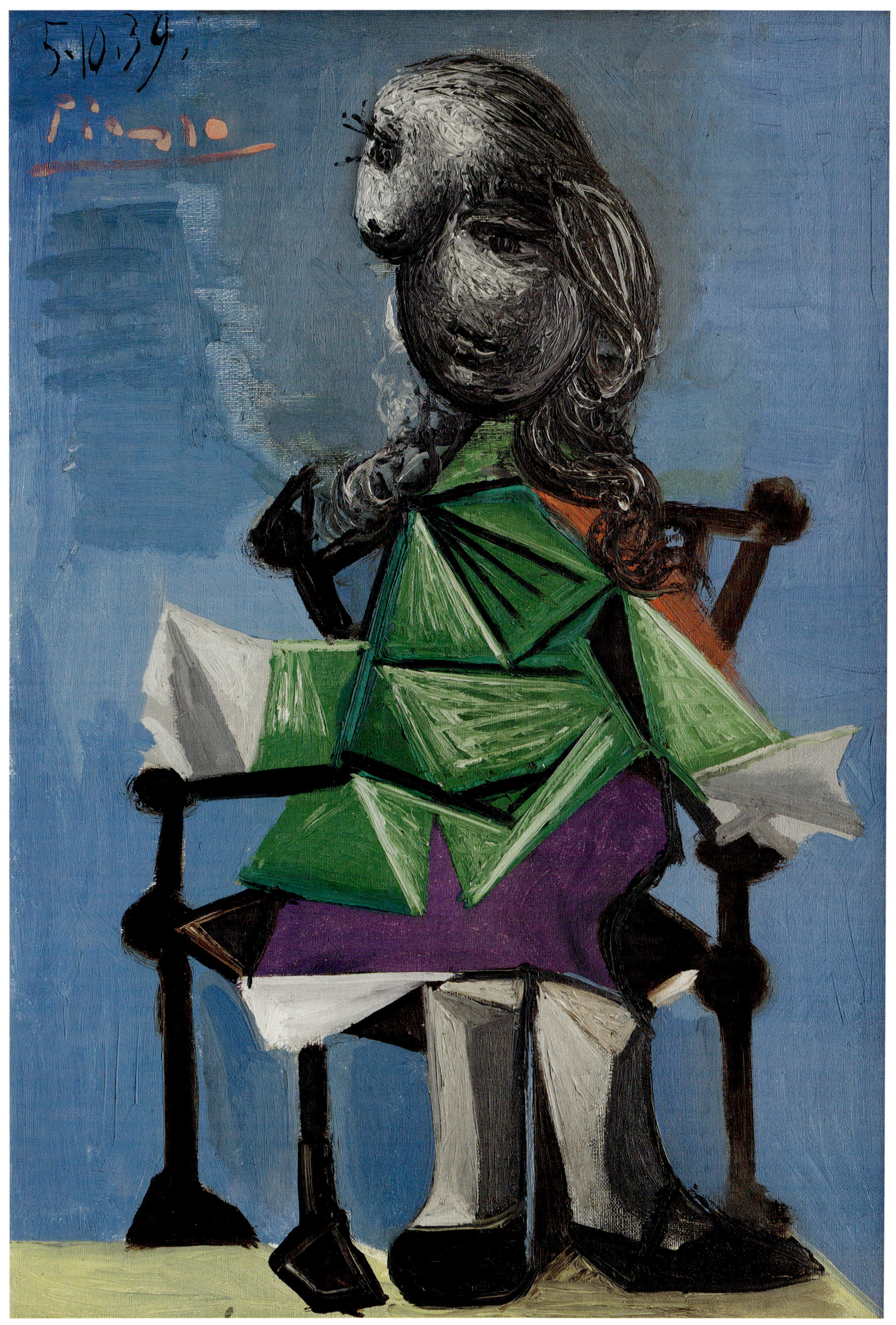
5.10.39.
Picasso

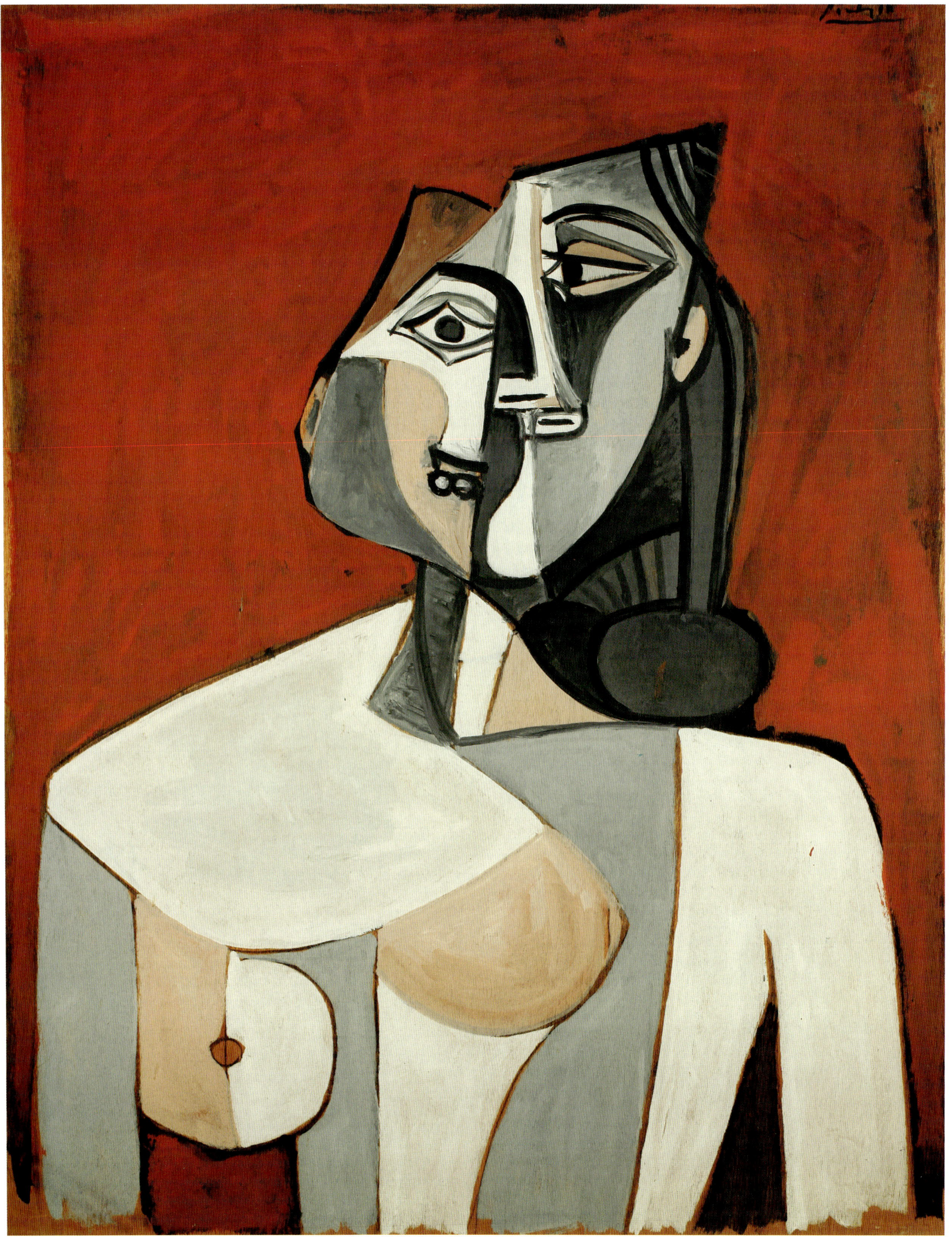

Pablo Picasso
1881, Málaga, Spain–1973, Mougins, France
Bust of a Woman, 1953
Oil on panel, 36 × 28 9⁄16 in. (91.5 × 72.5 cm)

Bequest of Marya Rubinstein Bernard-Adir, New York, in memory of Dr. Bernard Bernard, New York, 1978

Throughout Picasso's career, the women in his life were constantly present in his art—as muses and models, in a spectrum of styles ranging from the realistic to the nearly abstract. Even his most schematic and reductive images feature specific women.

The last in a group of eight works to be executed in the summer of 1953, this female bust represents Françoise Gilot, Picasso's life partner for almost ten years. At the time, Gilot had decided once and for all to leave Picasso and their home in Vallauris on the Côte d'Azur, and to return to Paris with their two children.

The painting is emblematic of Picasso's compositions of the 1930s, in which he positioned a figure against a neutral background and combined clearly defined forms and loose brushwork. It also evinces some of Picasso's countless other modulations of the defining strategies of Cubism: breaking up volumes, faceting forms, and incorporating multiple vantage points—as here, where both the frontal and profile views of Gilot's head are visible. Picasso, who together with Georges Braque (pp. 54–55) pioneered Cubism in the first decade of the twentieth century, employed characteristics of the style in his later works as well, configuring these over time in ever new and startling ways.

In her book *Life with Picasso*, Gilot recounts that when painting her Picasso devoted a great deal of time to the shape of her head, often painting and erasing it many times. Evidence of such a procedure can be seen in the traces of a triangle peering through the layers of paint to the right of her hair, collected in a bun—an identifying feature in many portraits of her.

Ruth Feldmann

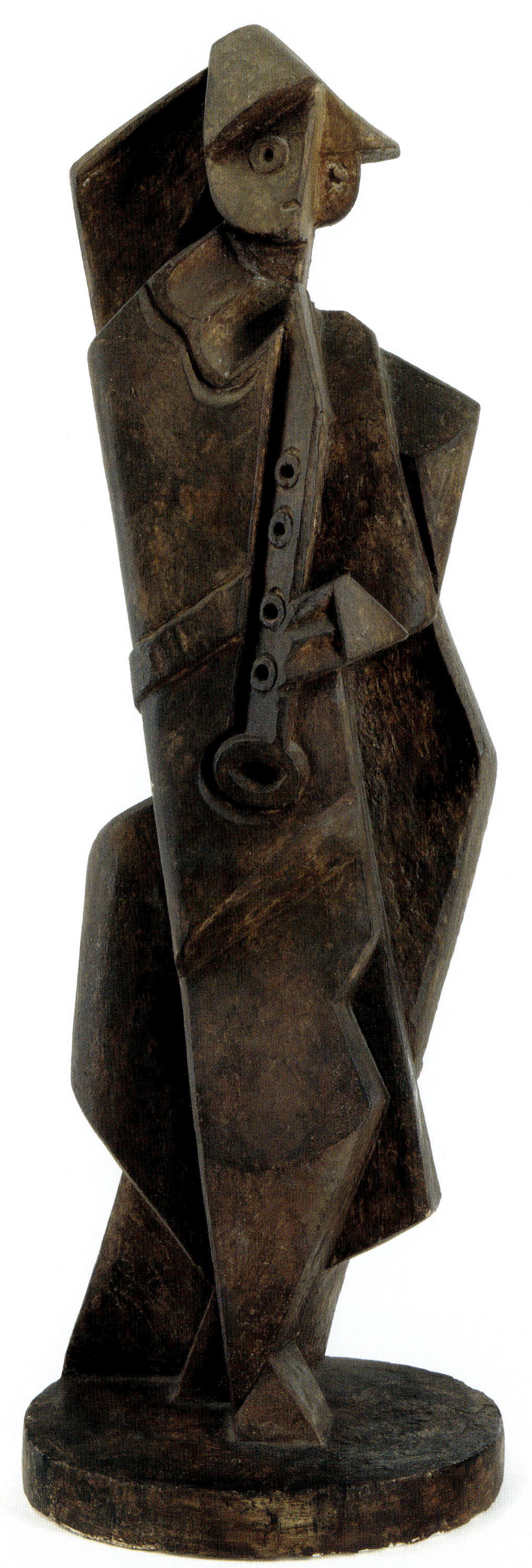

Jacques Lipchitz
1891, Druskeniki, Grodno Governorate, Russian Empire (now Druskininkai, Lithuania)–1973, Capri, Italy
Active Paris, France
Harlequin with Clarinet, 1919
Painted plaster, 29 ½ × 10 ¼ × 10 ¼ in. (75 × 26 × 26 cm)

Gift of the Jacques and Yulla Lipchitz Foundation, New York, through the American Friends of the Tel Aviv Museum of Art, 1988

Jacques Lipchitz was born to a Jewish family in Lithuania, then part of the Russian Empire, and immigrated to Paris in 1909 to study art. In his youth, he received academic training in sculpture but soon adopted the anti-classical posture ubiquitous in Paris at the time. Breaking away from tradition, Lipchitz aspired to create organic sculpture based on Cubist elements. Working in a formal language similar to that of his fellow sculptor and close friend Alexander Archipenko (pp. 82–89), he made innovative use of negative space by orchestrating rhythmic interplays of convex and concave forms. Among the first artists who interpreted the fragmentation of Cubism in three dimensions, Lipchitz created sculptures that contain multiple viewpoints.

The figure of the harlequin is made up of cascading angular planes and geometric shapes. It is essentially constructed from two overlapping surfaces placed atop each other in opposite directions, creating a sense of dynamism. This prompts the viewer, in turn, to move around the sculpture to fully perceive its diverse elements and intersecting forms from different vantages—upending a basic principle of classical sculpture in which there is a single ideal viewing position.

While faceted geometric forms dominate the work, Lipchitz added a number of human touches. There are recognizable eyes and a nose, and fingers that clasp the clarinet—which, along with the stylish collar point to the figure's identity as a harlequin, a trickster figure from the commedia dell'arte, who appears in the works of many Cubists. He seemed to serve as a kind of artistic alter ego, or a symbol of a mysterious outsider. Lipchitz had a simpler explanation: "The Pierrots and harlequins were part of our general vocabulary [...]. We may have been attracted to them originally because of their gay traditional costumes, involving many different varicolored areas."[1]

Sophia Berry-Lifschitz

1 Jacques Lipchitz with H.H. Arnason, *My Life in Sculpture* (London: Thames and Hudson, 1972), 58.

Jean Metzinger
1883, Nantes, France–1956, Paris, France
Figure (Columbine), 1922
Oil on canvas, 36 × 25 9⁄16 in. (91.5 × 65 cm)

Bequest of Marya Rubinstein Bernard-Adir, in memory of Dr. Bernard Bernard, New York, 1978

Beginning in 1922, Jean Metzinger turned away from Cubism and embraced a more realistic style. Like many other European artists in the aftermath of World War I, he adhered to a model of art making that expressed stability and harmony, and that integrated the values of classical art with modern characteristics. Known as the "return to order," this phenomenon opposed the radical experimentation and breakdown of tradition that typified pre-war avant-garde styles.

This painting, which depicts a woman performing a juggling act, belongs to a small group of works from the same period into which Metzinger incorporated motifs from the circus and the commedia dell'arte—two classic art historical subjects that became especially prevalent in European art in the 1920s and 1930s. The figure here is the commedia dell'arte stock character Columbine, an intelligent and comedic maid.

During this period, Metzinger was influenced by the art of Fernand Léger (pp. 92–93), discernible here in the sharp contrast between flat and voluminous forms, the shading that closely follows the outlines of the figure, and the almost geometrical division of the composition into uniform areas of color. Metzinger used these techniques to a create a sleek, nearly mechanized image. Its clearly defined forms—which are at once schematic and realistic—imbue the figure with a doll-like quality, while the smooth surface blurs the presence of individual brushstrokes. These qualities also point to Metzinger's growing interest in Purism, a movement founded by Le Corbusier and Amédée Ozenfant (pp. 100–101) that reached its apogee in the mid-1920s. Seeking to unify the classical and the mechanical, they championed pure and schematic forms over total abstraction.

Ruth Feldmann

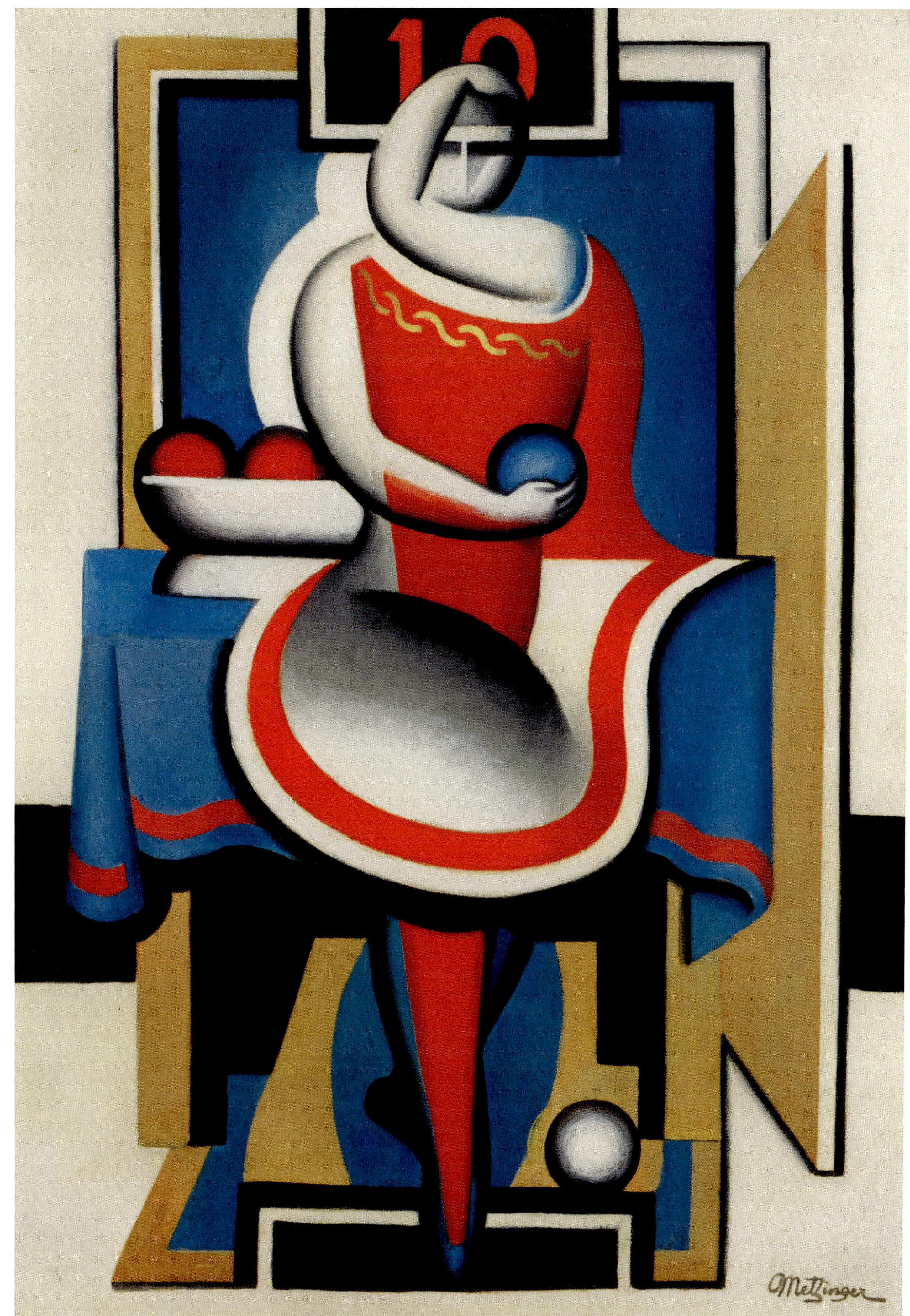
10
Metzinger

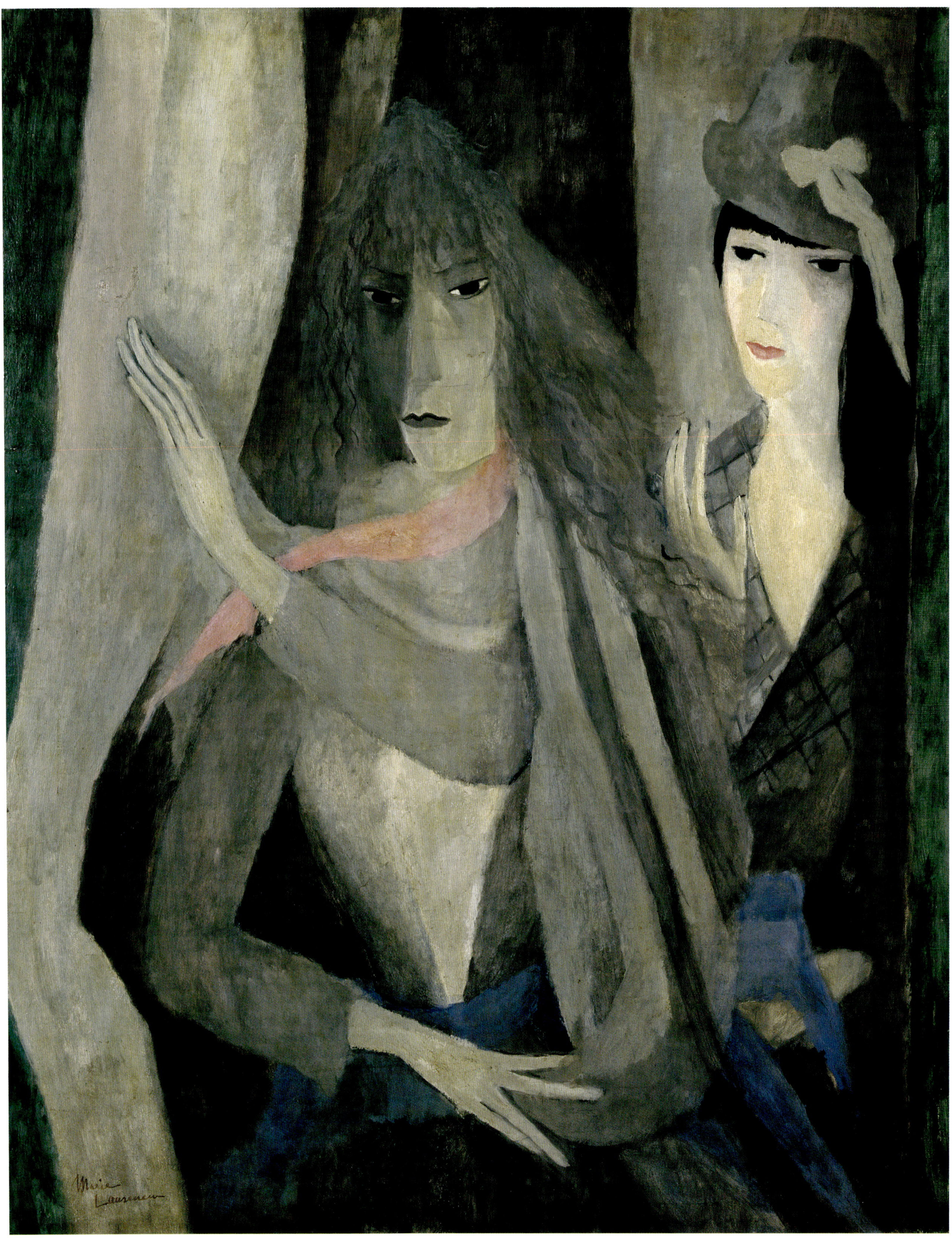

Marie Laurencin
1883–1956, Paris, France
The Zebra, 1917
Oil on canvas, 36 7⁄16 × 28 15⁄16 in. (92.5 × 73.5 cm)

Gift of Oscar Fischer, Antwerp-Tel Aviv, 1933

"One of the things that I like about Marie Laurencin is that she paints like a woman, whereas most women artists seem to want to paint like men and they only succeed in painting like hell," wrote the American collector John Quinn soon after purchasing this painting in 1920.[1] Supportive yet inherently sexist reactions such as this one might partially explain why Laurencin, an artist who in pre-war years was closely associated with the Parisian avant-garde, carved a place for herself in a largely male field by embracing a personal, traditionally feminine aesthetic. "Living in [men's] shadow is possible, when one doesn't intend to imitate them," she would later declare.[2]

At first glance, *The Zebra* exemplifies the unfettered femininity that many valued in Laurencin's portraits. Painted with soft brushstrokes, a palette of pale grays, pastel blue, and pink, it depicts two figures in a lyrical mood. Accessories such as ribbons, scarves, and a fashionable hat serve to place it in the realm of the conventionally bourgeois feminine. However, as with many of Laurencin's works, a closer analysis reveals ambiguities and encoded iconography that challenge a straightforward reading of the work, testifying to the artist's ability to masquerade her topics under the guise of the acceptably feminine.[3]

Based on writings addressed to her confidante and lover, Nicole Groult, the painting began as a portrait of a male dancer.[4] But while the central, androgynous character's commanding gesture could be seen as a dance move, the figure also bears Laurencin's facial features and curly hair, suggesting a self-portrait. The woman on the right appears to be holding her waist, a blue scarf covering this ambiguous gesture and possibly pointing to a silent intimacy. As a result, the painting can be read as a discreet double portrait of the artist and Groult, whose lesbian relationship was never publicly disclosed.[5] In addition, the slender woman wears a crosshatched jacket, a pattern that Laurencin associated with cages and confinement. Subsequently, her melancholic gaze speaks more to a feeling of stifled sorrow than dreamfulness. What is more, the viridian and gray curtains that frame the scene can be doubly interpreted as signifiers of a domestic private space and a theatrical stage—perhaps an allusion to Laurencin's ability to simultaneously conceal and uncover her subject matter on the canvas.

Laura Braverman

1 Letter from John Quinn to Henri-Pierre Roché, September 24, 1920, quoted in *Benjamin Lawrence Reid, The Man from New York: John Quinn and His Friends* (New York: Oxford University Press, 1968), 470. Quinn purchased six other paintings by Laurencin around that time.

2 Marie Laurencin, "Le Génie de l'homme m'intimide," *Arts*, July 24, 1952 [French; author's translation].

3 For further reading about Laurencin's protofeminist approach, see Chika Amano, "Marie Laurencin—Women, Decoration, and Painting," in *Marie Laurencin: A Retrospective* (Tokyo: Tokyo Metropolitan Teien Art Museum and Kyodo News, 2003): 207–16; Elizabeth Louise Kahn, *Marie Laurencin: Une Femme Inadaptée in Feminist Histories of Art* (Hants, UK, and Burlington, VT: Ashgate Publishing, 2003); and Jelena Kristic, *Marie Laurencin*, exh. guide (New York: Galerie Buchholz, 2020).

4 "I am working on another painting that is called the zebra, it is the portrait of the dancer when it will be a bit more decided […] It is your idea that I followed." Letter from Marie Laurencin to Nicole Groult, undated, Barcelona, private archive of Blandine de Caunes, Paris [author's translation]. Also in Barcelona, Laurencin addressed an elusive poem to Nicole: "Do not believe Nicole / That the zebra is an animal / Like the horse / The zebra is a Spanish dancer / Whom I am fond of" [author's translation]; this poem was first published in Marie Laurencin, *Petit bestiaire* (Paris: François Bernouard, 1926).

5 In subsequent works, Laurencin represented their love symbolically with a bluebird. As a result, the blue scarf in *The Zebra* could be read as an abstracted precursor to the bird motif.

Amedeo Modigliani
1884, Livorno, Italy–1920, Paris, France
Gaston Modot with Hat, 1918
Oil on canvas, 17 11/16 × 10 3/4 in. (45 × 27.3 cm)

On long-term loan from the Simon and Marie Jaglom Collection

Amedeo Modigliani arrived in Paris from his native Italy in 1906, at the age of twenty-one. About a quarter of the city's population at that time was composed of immigrants from all over Europe, including artists and poets who gathered in Montmartre and later in Montparnasse, together inventing new, modern modes of expression. Modigliani's dominant personality stood out among the members of these avant-garde movements. Celebrating his Jewishness, he was known for walking the streets of Paris with a Bible in one pocket and Dante's *Divine Comedy* in the other, quoting whole chapters from both by heart. Within a decade of Modigliani's arrival in Paris, 160 cinemas had opened in the city, and moviegoing became a major pastime. The impact of the new medium was also felt in Modigliani's circle of artists, which included the subject of this portrait, actor Gaston Modot (1887–1970), who appeared in numerous films throughout his career, and even studied painting for a short time. This portrait of Modot is one of two Modigliani painted of the actor in 1918.

In Modigliani's signature style, the actor's face and neck are inordinately elongated, filling the entire height of the rectangular canvas. His facial features are exaggerated, and his frozen, blank expression reveals nothing of his personality. Like many early twentieth-century artists, Modigliani was drawn to the simplified forms and graphic power of African art, which he first encountered at the Musée d'ethnographie de Trocadéro, an anthropological museum in Paris. In this painting, Modot's face resembles a mask, with its slitted eyes and long, wooden features, likely influenced by an amalgamation of African sculptural styles. Modigliani also frequented the Louvre, studying ancient Egyptian and classical Greek statuary—in fact, he himself primarily made sculpture between 1909 and 1914, when his failing health forced him to abandon it. He subsequently focused on portraiture for the rest of his short life, developing a body of work—to which this painting belongs—typified by an elegant linearity and stark, stylized figuration that reflects his deep affinity for a diverse range of sculptural forms, as well as his own practical experience working in three dimensions.

Sophia Berry-Lifschitz

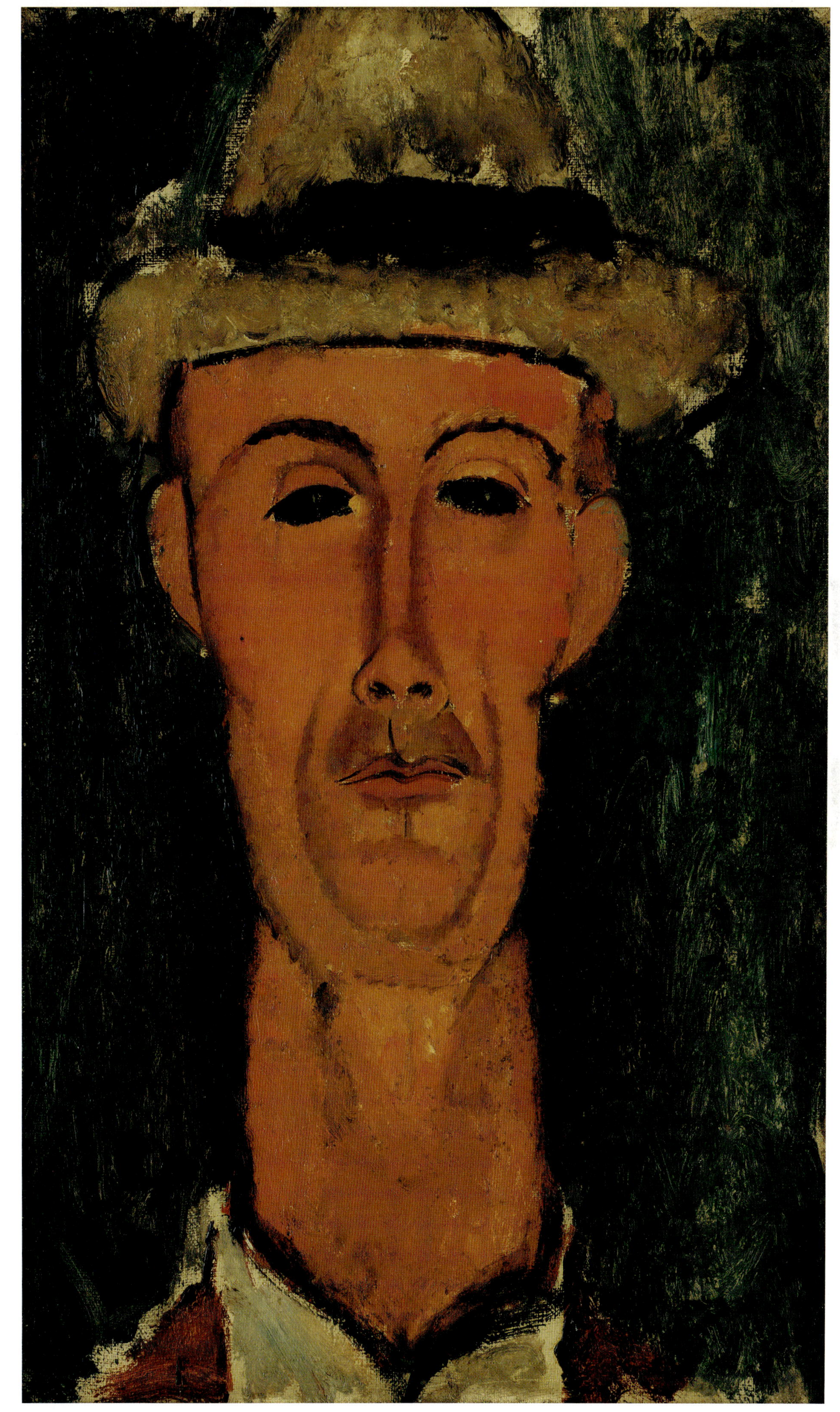

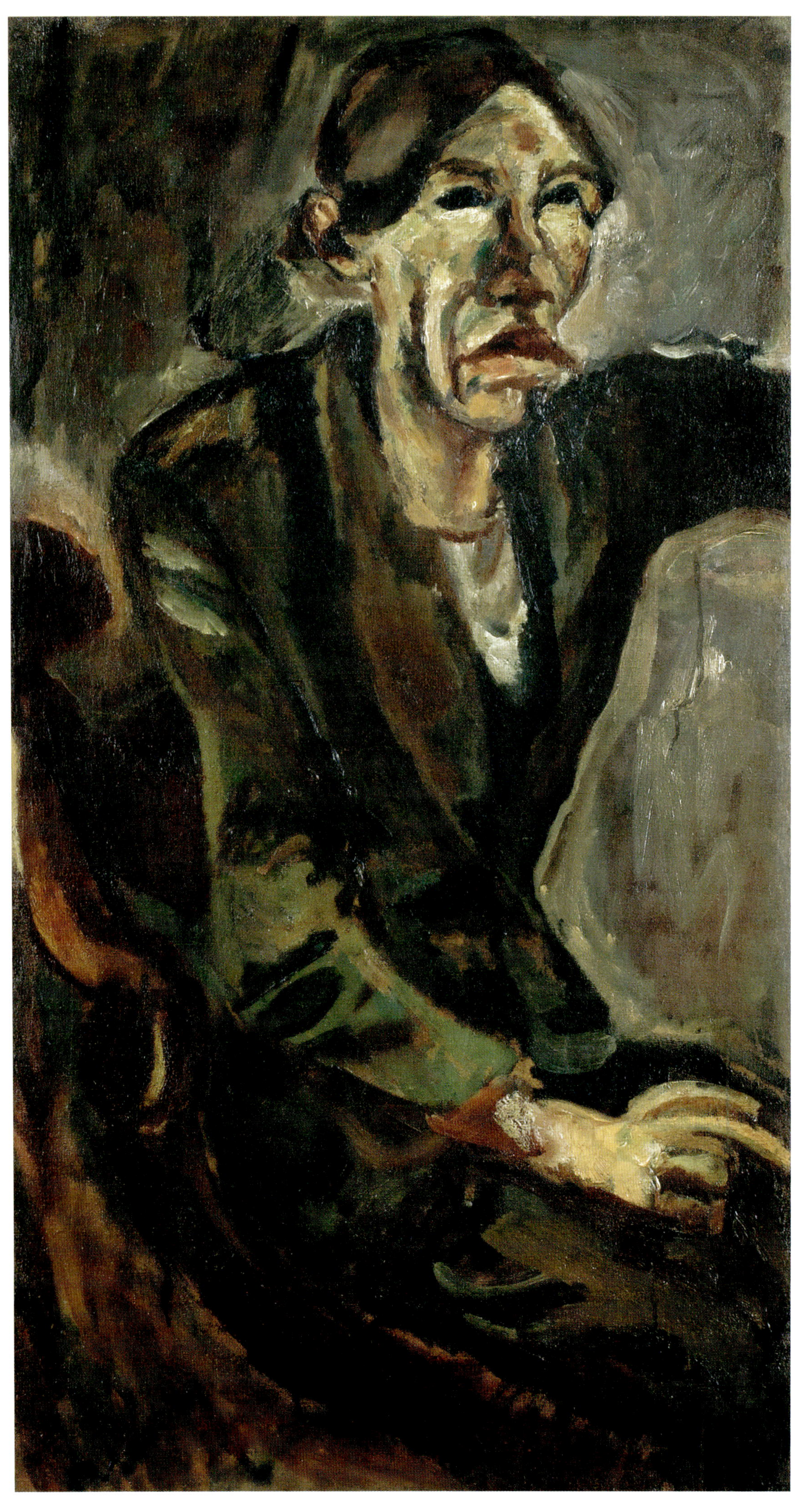

Chaim Soutine
1893, Smilovitchi, Minsky Governorate, Russian Empire (now Belarus)–1943, Paris, France
Self-Portrait, c. 1916
Oil on canvas, 32 × 17 15⁄16 in. (81.3 × 45.5 cm)

Bequest of Mrs. Mala Silson, New York, in memory of her husband Victor Silson, 2000

This painting is likely the earliest example of seven or eight known self-portraits that Chaim Soutine created, primarily early in his career.[1] Although he is among the most prominent artists associated with the School of Paris, surprisingly few studies have focused on these works. Here, Soutine depicts himself somewhat harshly. Seated, his body is turned to the side, his right hand is stretched forward (probably the hand holding the brush), his sausage-like lips are emphasized disproportionately to the rest of the face, his nose is long and bulbous, his eyes are black and opaque, and his left hand rests on his thigh, appearing lifeless. Soutine's expressive painting style, characterized by rough, textured brushstrokes, reinforces the painting's sense of tumult and distress.

Soutine arrived in Paris in 1913 at the age of nineteen, impoverished and with a great hunger for painting. He relied on his old friends from the Vilna School of Fine Arts, artists Pinchus Kremegne and Michel Kikoïne, to find accommodation and a studio, though in general, Soutine was not known for being very sociable and was often somewhat unkempt. Nevertheless, testimonies of acquaintances and portraits of Soutine, including those by Amedeo Modigliani (pp. 138–39), indicate that the artist's appearance was far from the grotesque image of himself he put forth in this work.[2] It appears that the artist consciously sought to create an unflattering, graceless, and distorted image of himself as an other: a foreigner with an Eastern European Jewish countenance, an identity he seems to exaggerate and even ridicule in this self-portrait.[3]

About two years after he made this painting, Soutine painted another self-portrait.[4] In the later portrait, his prominent facial features are much more refined. He is wearing a white-collared shirt, a tie, and a blue jacket, his facial expression is concentrated, and he directs his gaze at the viewer. Soutine includes the canvas itself in the painting—a classic trope in self-portraits by artists from Rembrandt van Rijn to Vincent van Gogh (pp. 36–37)—perhaps indicating a newfound sense of self-possession and confidence as an artist.

Sophia Berry-Lifschitz

1 In the first two volumes of *Soutine Catalogue Raisonné*, only three self-portraits are listed (not including the one in the Tel Aviv Museum of Art). In volume three (forthcoming), this self-portrait, along with a few others, will be included. See Esti Dunow email to Hillary Reder, February 7, 2024, Tel Aviv Museum of Art Archives.

2 See Chana Orloff on Chaim Soutine, in Haim Gamzu, *Chana Orloff* (Tel Aviv: Masada, 1949) [Hebrew].

3 See Avigdor W.G. Poseq, "On Ugliness, Jewishness, and Soutine's Self-Portraits," *Konsthistorisk Tidskrift* 63, no. 1 (1994): 31–52.

4 *Self-Portrait* (c. 1918) is in the collection of the Princeton University Art Museum.

Chaim Soutine
1893, Smilovitchi, Minsky Governorate, Russian Empire (now Belarus)–1943, Paris, France
Landscape of Montmartre, 1919
Oil on canvas, 24 13⁄16 × 35 7⁄16 in. (63 × 90 cm)

Gift from Mr. and Mrs. George Friedland, Merion, Pennsylvania, 1957

From the late nineteenth century, Paris's Montmartre district, with its narrow streets and the turrets of the Basilica of the Sacré-Coeur, was home to the city's leading artists and soon became a major tourist destination. The wave of immigrant-artists in the early twentieth century raised housing prices in the area, and many artists moved to Montparnasse, across the Seine on the Left Bank. When Soutine arrived in Paris in 1913, he first stayed in the artist residence La Ruche in Montparnasse, which provided cheap studio space.[1] Drawn to the legendary allure of Montmartre, he used to cross the Seine to paint its picturesque scenery.

In 1919, Léopold Zborowski, Soutine's art dealer, encouraged him to go to the south of France with Amedeo Modigliani (pp. 138–39) to pursue landscape painting. Soutine settled in the town of Céret and began to paint the countryside in addition to portraits of local townspeople. He lived there until 1922, and while it was a prolific period for him, he longed to return to Paris. He visited occasionally, and it was likely on one of his stays in Paris that he created this painting.

Landscape of Montmartre is centered on a two-story house, with a high roof and windows surrounded by a thick red frame. A long white wall runs down the hill on the left side of the house, and another house with a green roof is visible behind the trees. Considerably smaller houses appear on the right side of the painting. The trees, some boasting red and white inflorescence, enclose the composition in a circle from above on either side. The foreground is left bare, with thick brushstrokes creating red, blue, and white stains. The hill, with its houses and trees, seems to be in motion: the houses "trickle" down, and the trees push inward, towards the house with the blocked windows at the painting's center. As in the landscapes he made in the same years in the south of France, Soutine painted *Landscape of Montmartre* with intensely expressive, vigorous brushstrokes, generating a visceral sense of agitation. With its abundance of trees, bright blue sky, and open areas of green, the scene also suggests a hidden urban oasis.

Sophia Berry-Lifschitz

1 La Ruche housed many important artists of the early twentieth century, including Alexander Archipenko, Marc Chagall, Fernand Léger, Jacques Lipchitz, Amedeo Modigliani, and many others.

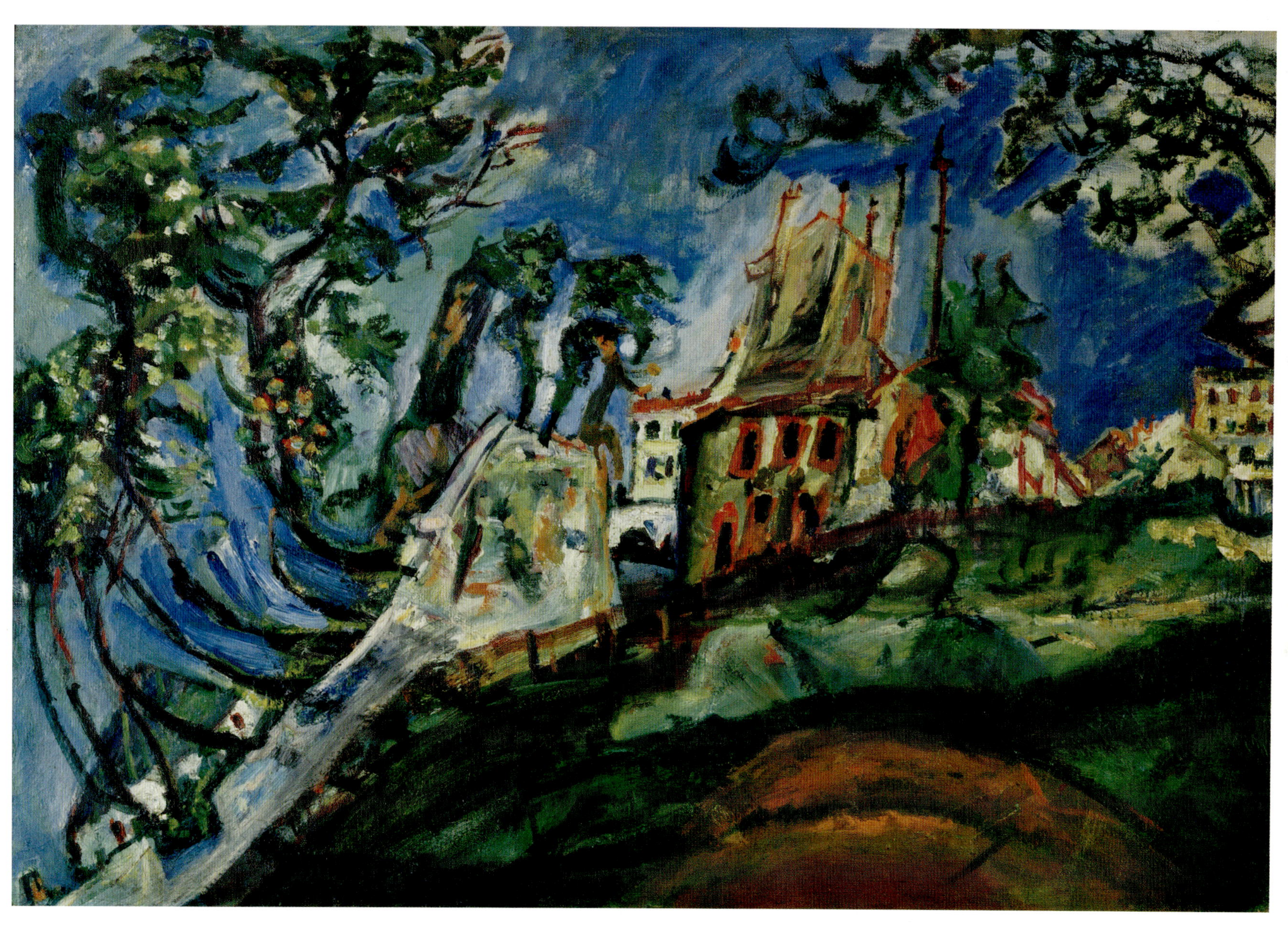

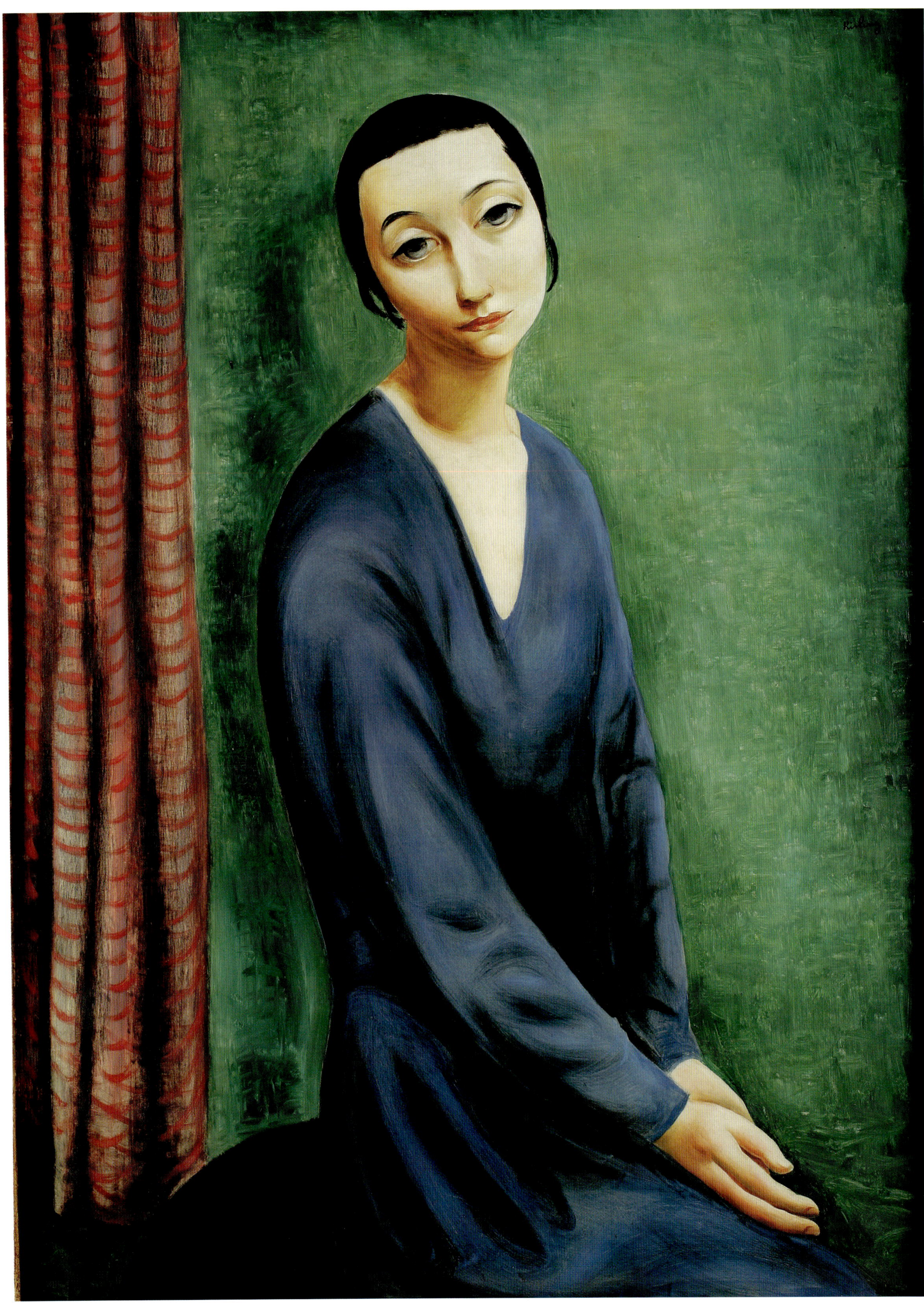

Moïse Kisling
1891, Krakow, Austria-Hungary (now Poland)–
1953, Sanary-sur-Mer, France
Lady in Blue, 1922
Oil on canvas, 39 3/8 × 31 5/16 in. (100 × 79.5 cm)

Gift of Mrs. Fernand Halphen, Paris, 1935

The eye contact between the viewer and the figure in Moïse Kisling's singular portraits is not easily forgotten. In this painting, the woman's heavy gaze and the way her body folds into itself convey a quiet sadness or remoteness, which contrasts with the painting's rich colors. Almost all of Kisling's numerous sitters—from blue-eyed children to famous women from the worlds of theater and literature—are engulfed by his signature melancholic aura.

Kisling grew up in Krakow in a well-off Jewish family and, on the advice of a teacher at the Academy of Art in his hometown, moved to Paris in 1910 to pursue art studies. He initially lived in Montmartre and painted in a style influenced by Paul Cézanne (pp. 30–31) before settling in Montparnasse, where he began to develop his own style. Kisling was part of a group of artists—among them Amedeo Modigliani (pp. 138–39), with whom he had a special affinity—soon to be known as the Circle of Montparnasse or the School of Paris. Many of these artists had immigrated to Paris in the early twentieth century and were of Jewish origin.

In 1922, when he painted *Lady in Blue*, Kisling (or "Kiki" as he was affectionately known) was already an established artist, and had exhibited extensively in Paris. As opposed to a sensuality in some of his nude paintings—which form a prominent part of his oeuvre alongside still-life and landscape paintings—*Lady in Blue* conveys modesty and humility manifested in the hands resting on her knees and the tilt of her head, while the use of saturated jewel tones of green, red, and blue contributes to a sense of harmony and balance.

Nathalie Andrijasevic

Chana Orloff
1888, Tsarekonstantinovka, Kharkov Governorate, Russian Empire (now Starokostiantyniv, Ukraine)–1968, Ramat Gan, Israel
Portrait of Mrs. Harari, c. 1925
Bronze, 51 1/6 × 30 1/4 × 8 3/4 in. (130 × 77 × 25 cm)

Gift of the artist, 1931

Chana Orloff was born in Ukraine, in an area then known as the Pale of Settlement, the only section of the Russian Empire where Jews were granted permanent residency. At sixteen, she and her family immigrated to Ottoman Palestine to escape the ever-growing threat of pogroms. Four years later she went to study art in Paris, where she settled down. Orloff was a member of the School of Paris, alongside other Jewish artists such as Chaim Soutine, Amedeo Modigliani, and Marc Chagall (pp. 140–43, 138–39, 148–53). Following her debut at the Salon d'Automne in Paris in 1913, she consistently made art and exhibited throughout her life. Orloff maintained close ties with Israel, and played a key role in the founding of the Tel Aviv Museum. Her travels back and forth between Paris and Tel Aviv established her as an important link between European modernism and Israeli art during the nascent years of the state.

Marked by a human scale, Orloff's sculptures are remarkable for their formal precision. They are often made of a uniform, closed, and rounded mass that extends upwards, like a tree or a person standing upright. In the sculpture *Portrait of Mrs. Harari*, the figure and the chair seem to have fused into one. The figure's hand, which rises and touches its neck, is kept close to the body rather than creating an opening in the sculpture's solid form. Centered on the female figure, Orloff's oeuvre engages with the basic facts of life: growth, motherhood, movement, and connection. Her portraits reflect a deep observation of human experience and often convey a sense of restraint, tension, and silent clarity.

Adi Dahan

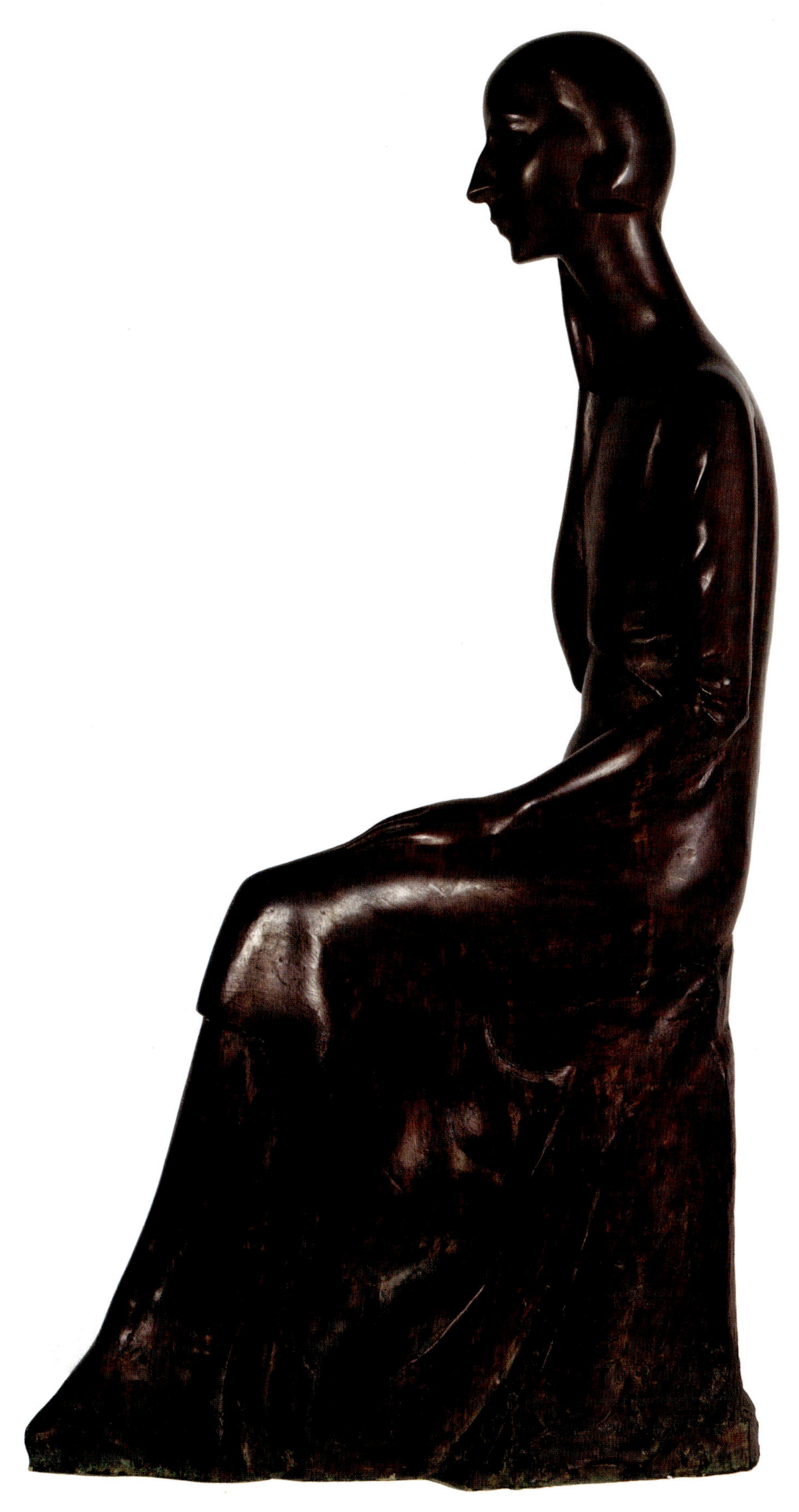

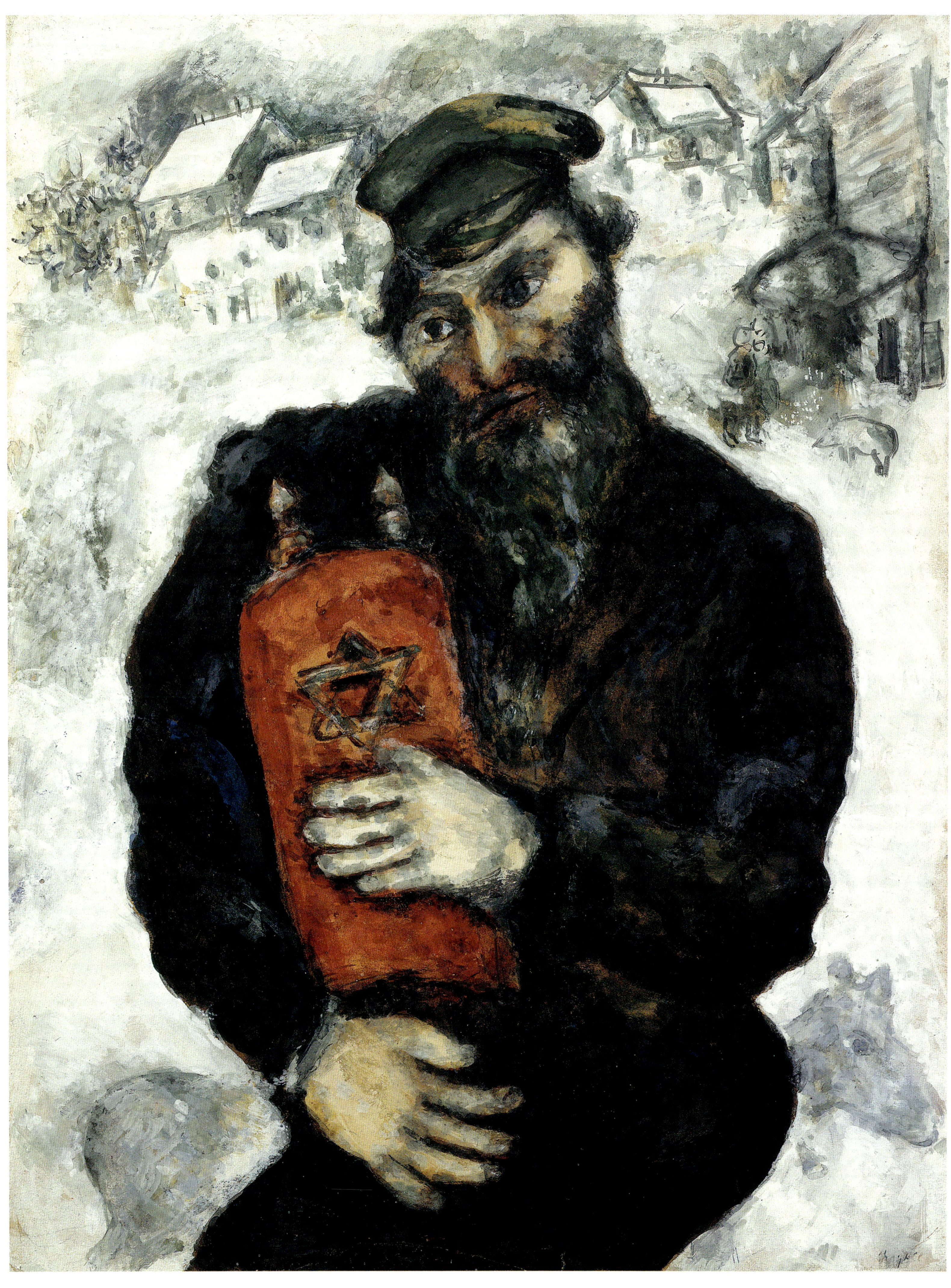

Marc Chagall
1887, Vitebsk, Russian Empire (now Belarus)–
1985, Saint-Paul-de-Vence, France
Jew with Torah, 1925
Gouache on paper, mounted on board,
26 ¾ × 20 1⁄16 in. (68 × 51 cm)

Gift of the artist, 1931

Pages 150–51 *Solitude*, 1933
Oil on canvas, 44 ½ × 66 9⁄16 in. (113 × 169 cm)

Gift of the artist, through the State of Israel, 1953

Even after settling in Paris in 1923, Marc Chagall incorporated into his works motifs taken from the world of his childhood in the village of Vitebsk, where he grew up in a Hasidic family. Among these motifs, which he returned to throughout his career, the Jew holding a Torah scroll is one of the most familiar.

This painting depicts a Jewish man standing in a snowy landscape. The small, simple village houses evoke the atmosphere of the shtetl, which Chagall depicted in many of his paintings. An elongated goat appears behind the figure, rendered in such light colors that it almost merges with the snow.

Even when based on scenes from reality, Chagall's iconography is often associative and symbolic. Holding a Torah scroll—an inherently protective act—can be interpreted more broadly in this work as a representation of the Jewish people's tenacious safeguarding of its faith.

Jew with Torah is the second version of a painting from around 1911, made during the first period Chagall lived in France (1910–14). When he returned to Paris from Russia in 1923 he discovered that a large portion of his works had been scattered and lost, and he began painting new versions of them, for which he relied on photographs and reproductions.

On his first visit to Tel Aviv, in 1931, Chagall gifted this work to Meir Dizengoff, mayor of Tel Aviv and founder of the Tel Aviv Museum. One year later, when the Museum was officially inaugurated, the work was registered as No. 1, and became the first work of its collection.

Ruth Feldmann

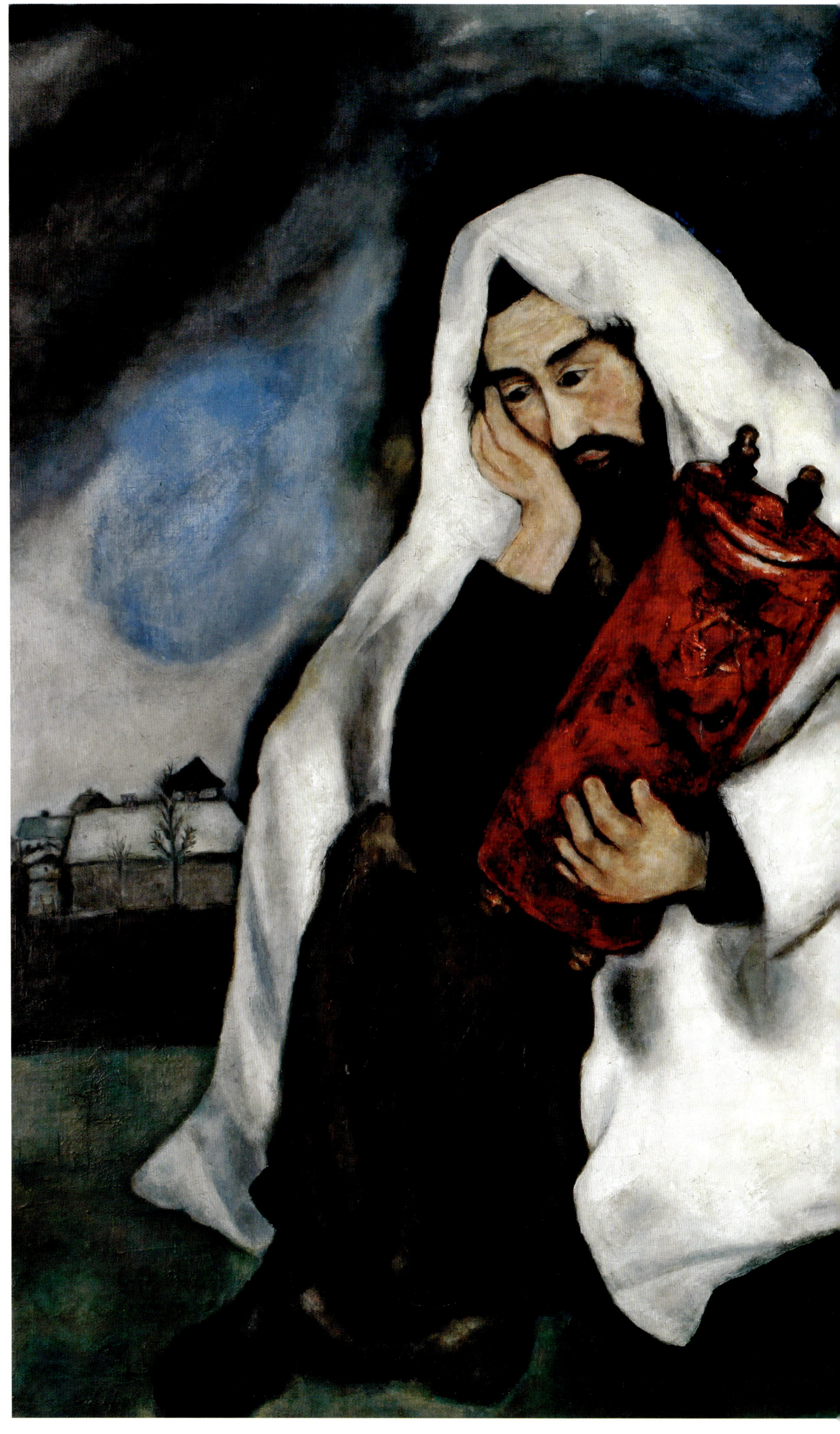

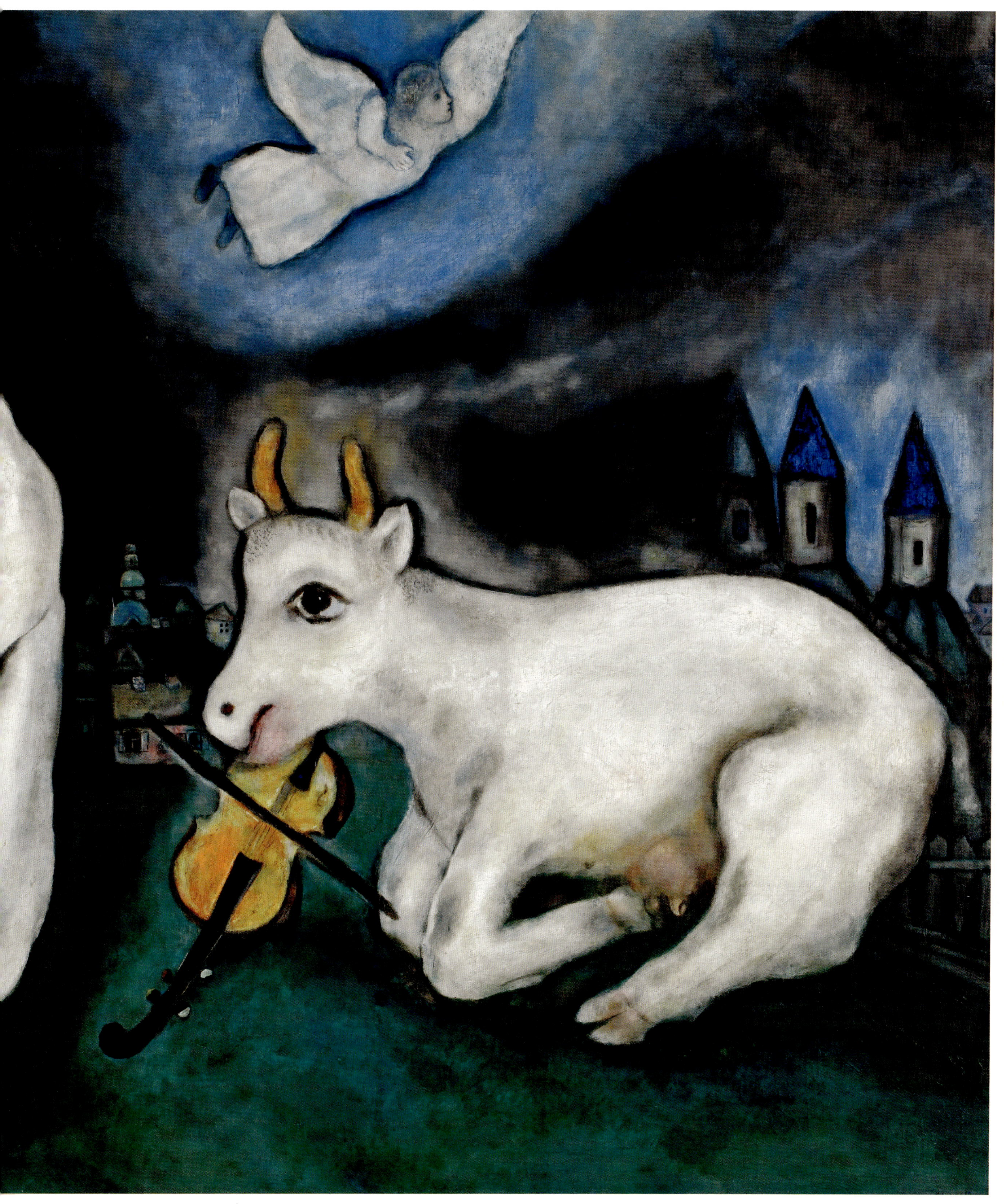

למר מאיר דיזנגוף ידידי היקר מארק שאגאל

1931

תל-אביב

КАБАК

СБИТЕН

Marc Chagall

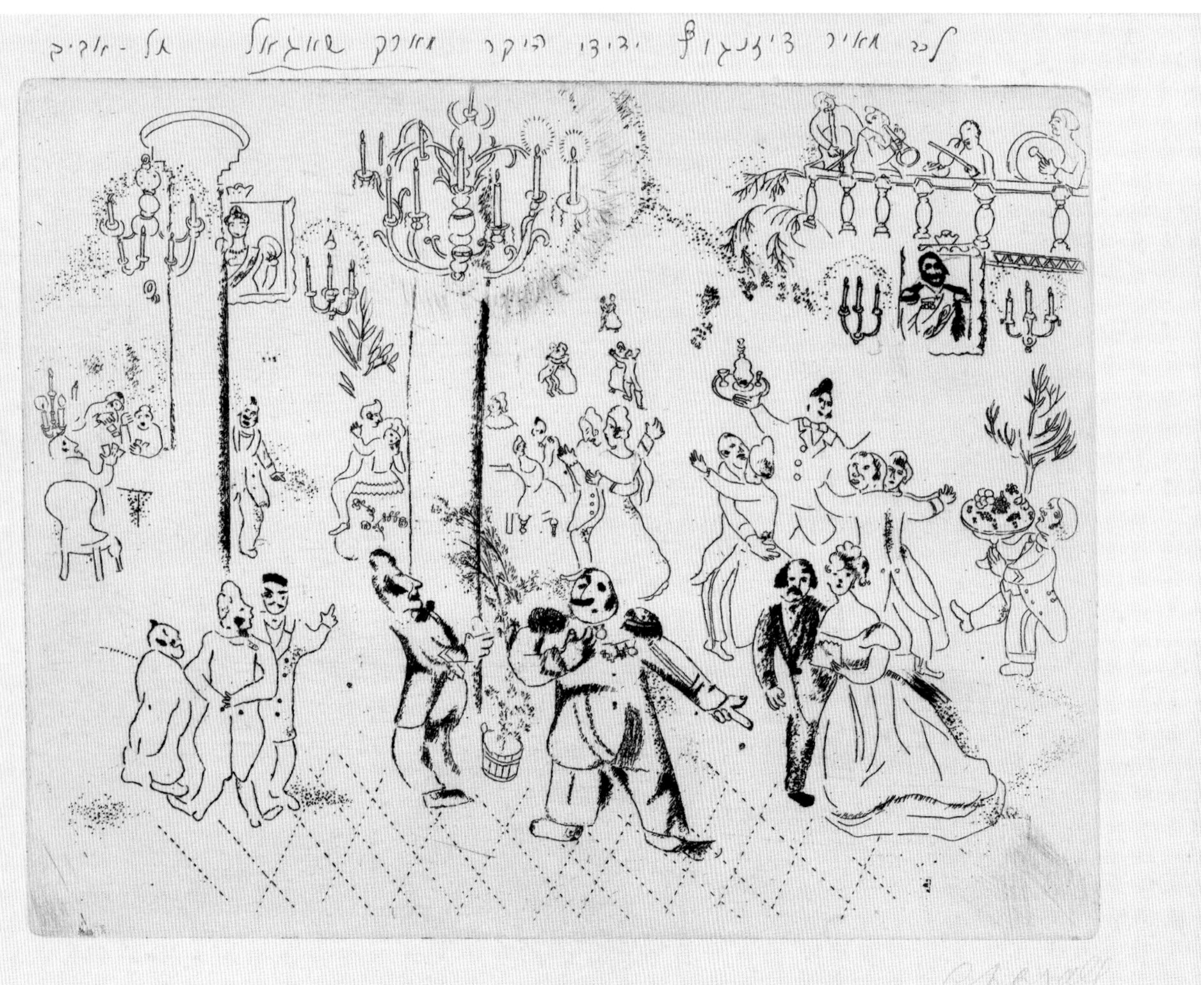

Marc Chagall
1887, Vitebsk, Russian Empire (now Belarus)–
1985, Saint-Paul-de-Vence, France
Deads Souls by Nikolai Gogol (1842), 1924–27
Two from an unpublished version of illustrated book
with 96 etchings

Top *The Soiree at the Governor's House*
8 5⁄8 × 11 5⁄16 in. (21.8 × 28.8 cm)

Bottom *The Arrival of Tchtichikov*
8 11⁄16 × 11 5⁄8 in. (22 × 28.5 cm)

Gift of the artist through Meir Dizengoff, c. 1933

In the spring of 1931, Marc Chagall and his family visited Mandatory Palestine at the invitation of Meir Dizengoff, the first mayor of Tel Aviv. Dizengoff infected Chagall with his enthusiasm for building an art museum for the city, a vision that was realized in 1932. As a gift to his host, Chagall brought the ninety-six etchings of his *Dead Souls* series, illustrations for Nikolai Gogol's eponymous novel, published in 1842.[1]

Chagall, whose works often revolve around memories of the magic of village life from his childhood in Vitebsk, felt great closeness to the world of Gogol's novel, which masterfully unfolds a spectacular panorama of Russian life, humor, and experience. At the heart of the chronicle—a satire of Russian society—is the figure Tchichikov, a cunning, charming con man, who buys dead serfs whose names have not yet been taken off the official census from landowners. His scheme is to enrich himself by presenting these "dead souls" as still-living persons and "deposit" them as collateral against a bank loan. Gogol describes the assortment of individuals Tchichikov encounters—the greedy, lazy landowners, the power-hungry officials, and the serfs who were the property of their masters both in life and after death—with exaggerated, larger-than-life grotesqueness, but not without compassion.

Chagall's compositions are rife with detail and rich in texture, with the bold, twisting contours and the distorted perspective transmitting a sense of motion and instability. He created his illustrations between 1923 and 1927 while living in Paris at the invitation of the legendary art dealer and publisher Ambroise Vollard. The series was printed in 1927, but not published until 1948 in conjunction with the French translation of the novel. Chagall's masterful etchings are a testament to his profound identification with Gogol, reflected in the album's cover illustration, in which the writer and the painter appear back-to-back with heads bowed down, engrossed in their respective work.

Alisa Padovano-Friedman

1 As a personal gift to Dizengoff, Chagall included a dedication in Hebrew on several of the sheets. After receiving the prints in 1931, Dizengoff transferred the gift to the Museum sometime in the early 1930s.

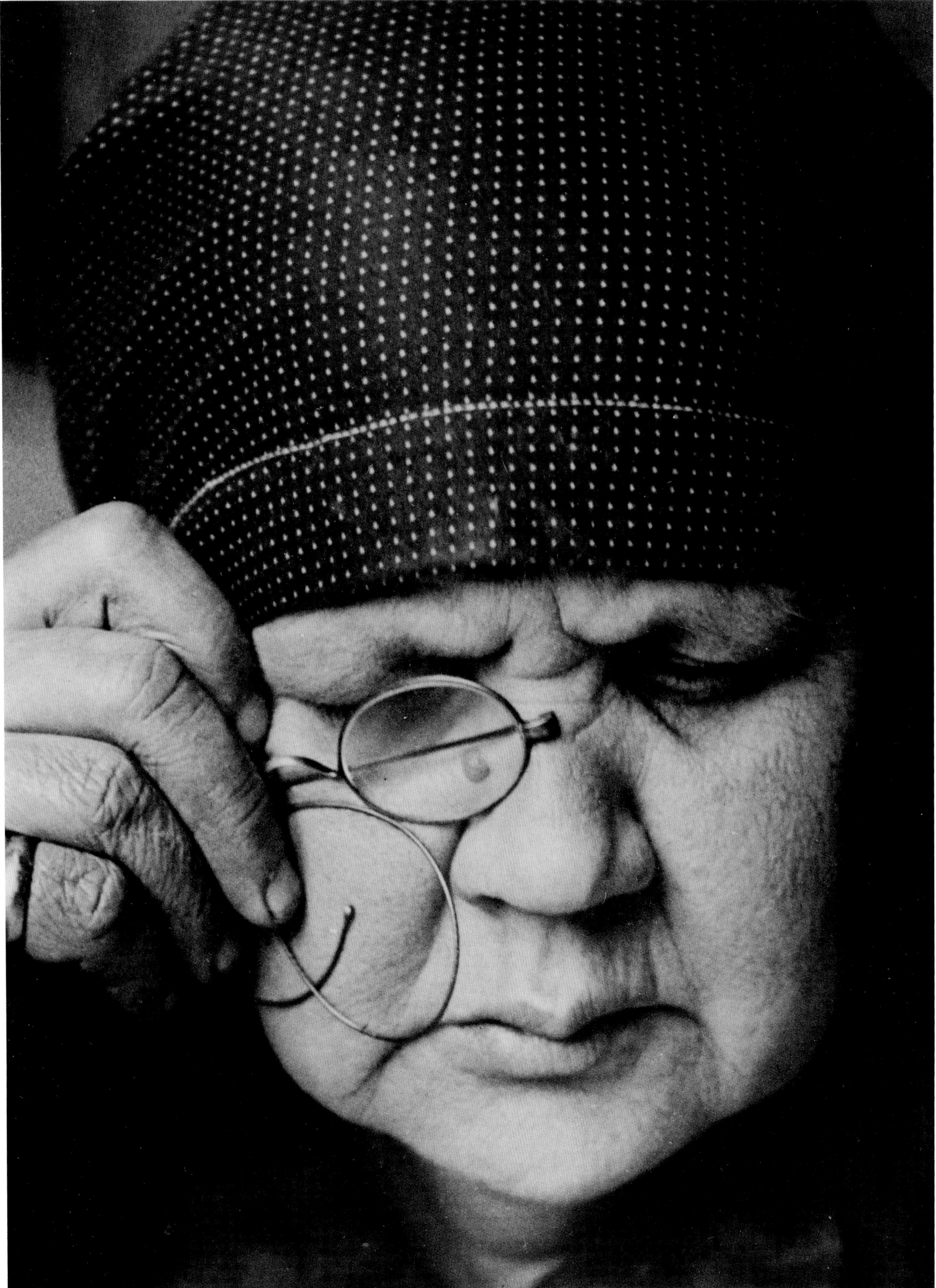

Aleksandr Rodchenko
1891, Saint Petersburg, Russia–1956, Moscow, Russia
Portrait of the Artist's Mother, 1924
Gelatin silver print, 9 5/8 × 7 5/16 in. (24.5 × 18.5 cm)

Anonymous gift, through the American Friends of the Tel Aviv Museum of Art, 2008

In 1921, Aleksandr Rodchenko declared the death of painting with his three monochrome canvases *Pure Red Color*, *Pure Yellow Color*, and *Pure Blue Color*. Jettisoning representation, the artist switched gears entirely, setting out to picture everyday life as a means of communicating with the masses.[1] The medium of photography literalized Rodchenko's wish to see the world from different points of view. During his lifetime, his photographs and photomontages were published widely in both avant-garde periodicals, such as *Lef* and *Novyi Lef*, and in state-run publications, including *Sovetskoe Foto* and *USSR in Construction*.

One of Rodchenko's earliest photographs, *Portrait of the Artist's Mother*, is among his most renowned images. It is an intimate look at his mother, Olga, who worked various jobs—as a nanny and a laundress—to support her family. While very few details of the context are revealed in this tightly cropped, macro-focused version of the portrait, she appears with a modest kerchief on her head and a hardened expression on her face. With pursed lips and a furrowed brow, she clasps her wire-rimmed glasses, holding a single lens—as if a monocle—to her right eye. She squints downward with laser-sharp concentration. The bottom edge of the photograph is shrouded in the darkness of her clothing and the shadow cast by her face. Two wider views, extant in other collections, of this same scene—from the front and the side—show her leaning over a table reading a newspaper. The reference to reading is critical because it ascribes a level of education to his mother, and signals the importance of printed matter as an outlet for Rodchenko's own artistic production.

Although Rodchenko faced criticisms of formalism from the artistic establishment aligned with state-sanctioned Socialist Realism, he continued to exhibit in significant international venues until his death, including at the Städtische Ausstellungshallen in Stuttgart (1929); the Staatliche Kunstbibliothek in Berlin (1931); Manes Exhibition Hall in Prague (1936); and the Museum of Modern Art, New York (1936 and 1941).

Ksenia Nouril

1 Yve-Alain Bois, "Painting: The Task of Mourning," in *Painting as Model* (Cambridge, MA: MIT Press, 1990), 238.

Antoine Pevsner
1886, Klimovichi, Mogilev Governorate, Russian Empire (now Klimavichy, Belarus)–1962, Paris, France
Red Background, 1923
Oil and resin on oxidized plastic (celluloid), treated with acid and scratched, mounted on wood, 15 9/16 × 18 7/8 in. (39.5 × 48 cm)

Mizne-Blumental Collection, Bequest of Annette Celine, 2018

Antoine (Natan) Pevsner is often discussed alongside his older brother Nahum Gabo (born Nahum Nehemiah Pevsner). Both were sculptors and painters, as well as theorists of Constructivism. They spoke out in 1920 against Cubism and Futurism, opposing these movements by advocating for the pursuit of depth and three-dimensionality instead. *Red Background* was created in a period of close interaction between the brothers, who had just left Soviet Russia for political reasons after working for five years—and in Antoine's case, teaching—in the country's most forward-thinking artistic educational institution, Vkhutemas.

Red Background marks the result of a radical experiment: the artist tried to solve the problems set about in his *Realistic Manifesto* (co-written with Gabo and Gustav Klutsis, Moscow, August 5, 1920), using completely unconventional techniques. At first glance, the work resembles an easel painting, but this is a mistaken impression. The strange bubbles on the translucent brick-red surface of this piece are traces of an acid attack on celluloid, one of the earliest forms of plastic. This material support was chosen very intentionally, as a marker of the new and "progressive." Pevsner drew the lines of the composition with a hard object on the soft plastic surface, which he then partially filled with paint. He sought to offer a provocation in terms of both art's composition and its production.

By introducing new elements into a form of easel painting he considered outdated, Pevsner hoped to completely transform what he saw as an obsolete system of art. *Red Background* is a programmatic work in this sense, marking a transition from "archaic" oil painting to what would become known as Kinetic Art.

Kira Dolinina, Roman Grigoryev

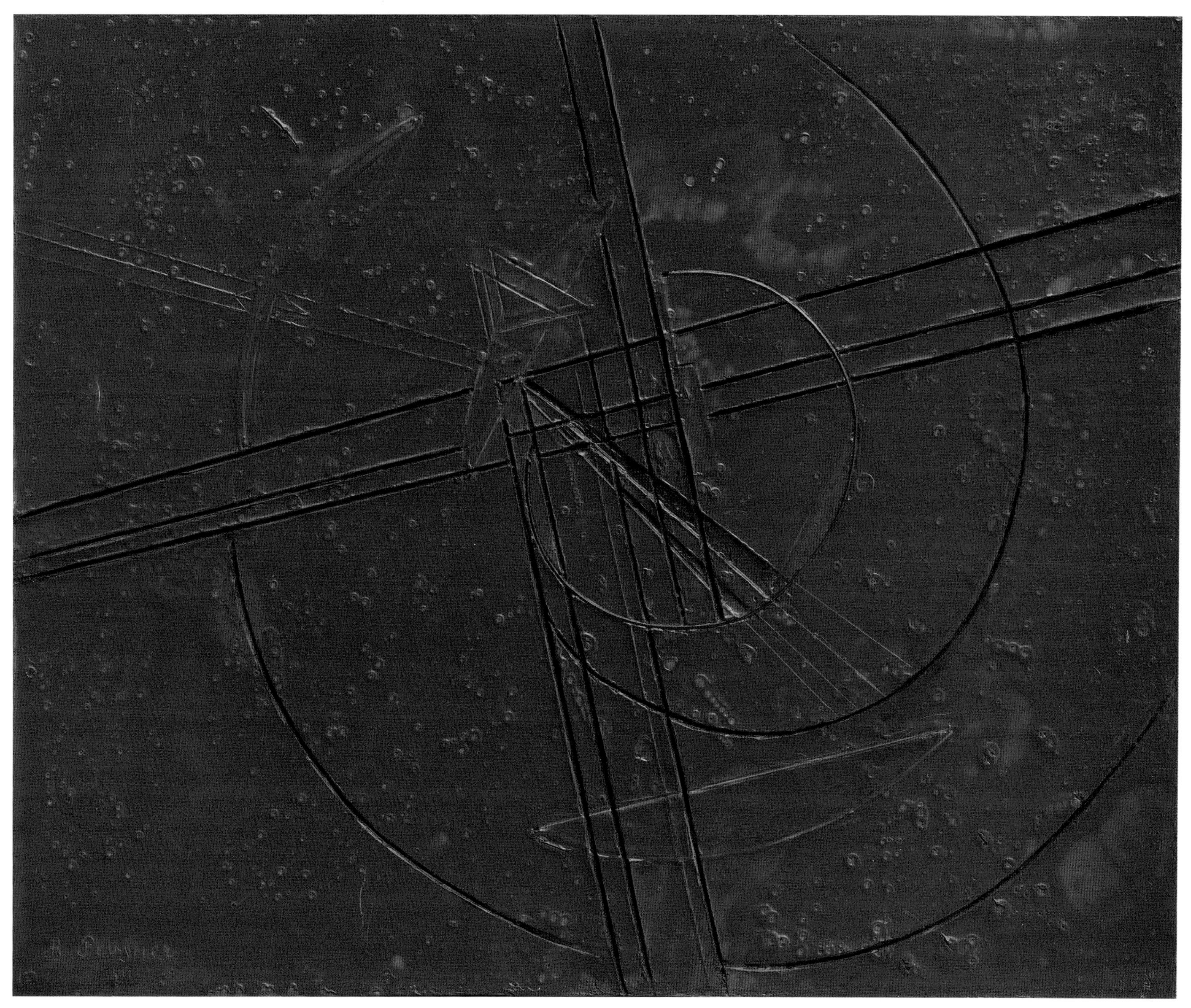

Edward Weston
1886, Highland Park, IL, United States–
1958, Carmel-by-the-Sea, CA, United States
Conch, 1927
Gelatin silver print, 14 15/16 × 13 3/16 in. (38 × 33.5 cm)

Gift of Michael S. Sachs, Westport, Connecticut, through the American Friends of the Tel Aviv Museum of Art, 2008

Edward Weston's *Conch* features a black-and-white close-up of a snail's shell, representing its stark beauty and the wonder of its intricate and delicate details. The conch's curves coalesce into an abstract, geometric form, while maintaining an organic quality. He used a large-format camera and long exposure time to bring the conch's textures and patterns into sharp focus. By isolating the shell in the center of a dark background, he amplified the intensity of the contrast between light and shadow. He also created a broad tonal range, so that the shell, with its pale and dark tones, alternately blends into or shines brightly against the background.

This image is part of a series of twenty-six still-life images of shells Weston took in his Glendale, California, studio in 1927, after his return from an extended stay in Mexico. It is a prime example of his innovative style, known as straight photography, in which the final print gives no sign of manipulation by the photographer. Developed as a counter-reaction to the late nineteenth-century Pictorialist style, with its soft-focus lenses, low tonalities, and myriad surface manipulation techniques, Weston's photography prioritized high contrasts, sharp focus, and an emphasis on the formal and abstract qualities of the subject.

Like other artists of his generation, such as Georgia O'Keeffe (pp. 160–61), who sought to articulate a uniquely American modernism, Weston's broader exploration of nature's forms and textures aimed to capture their beauty and complexity, express their "pure" essence, and underline their rhythms and harmonies.

Ayelet Carmi

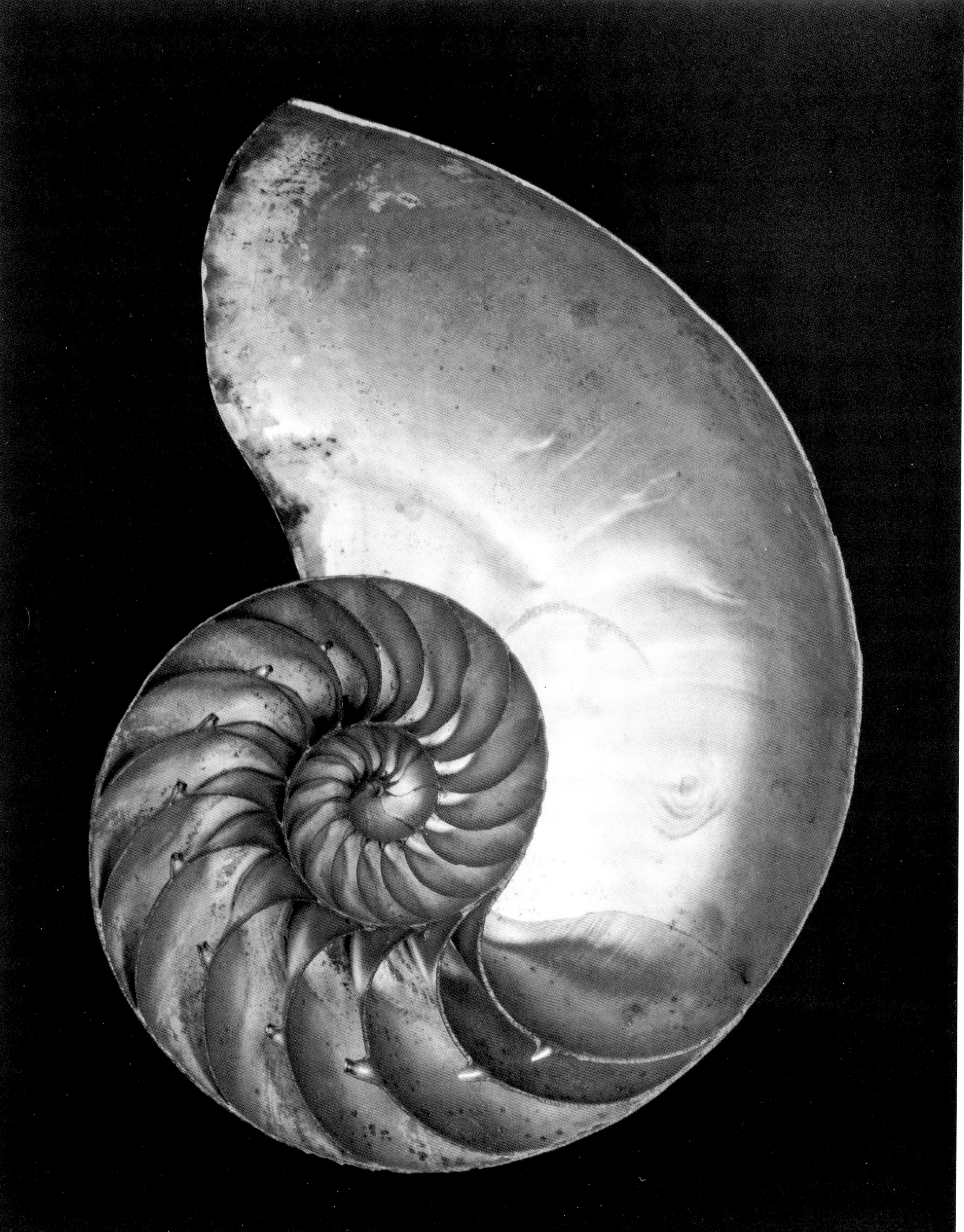

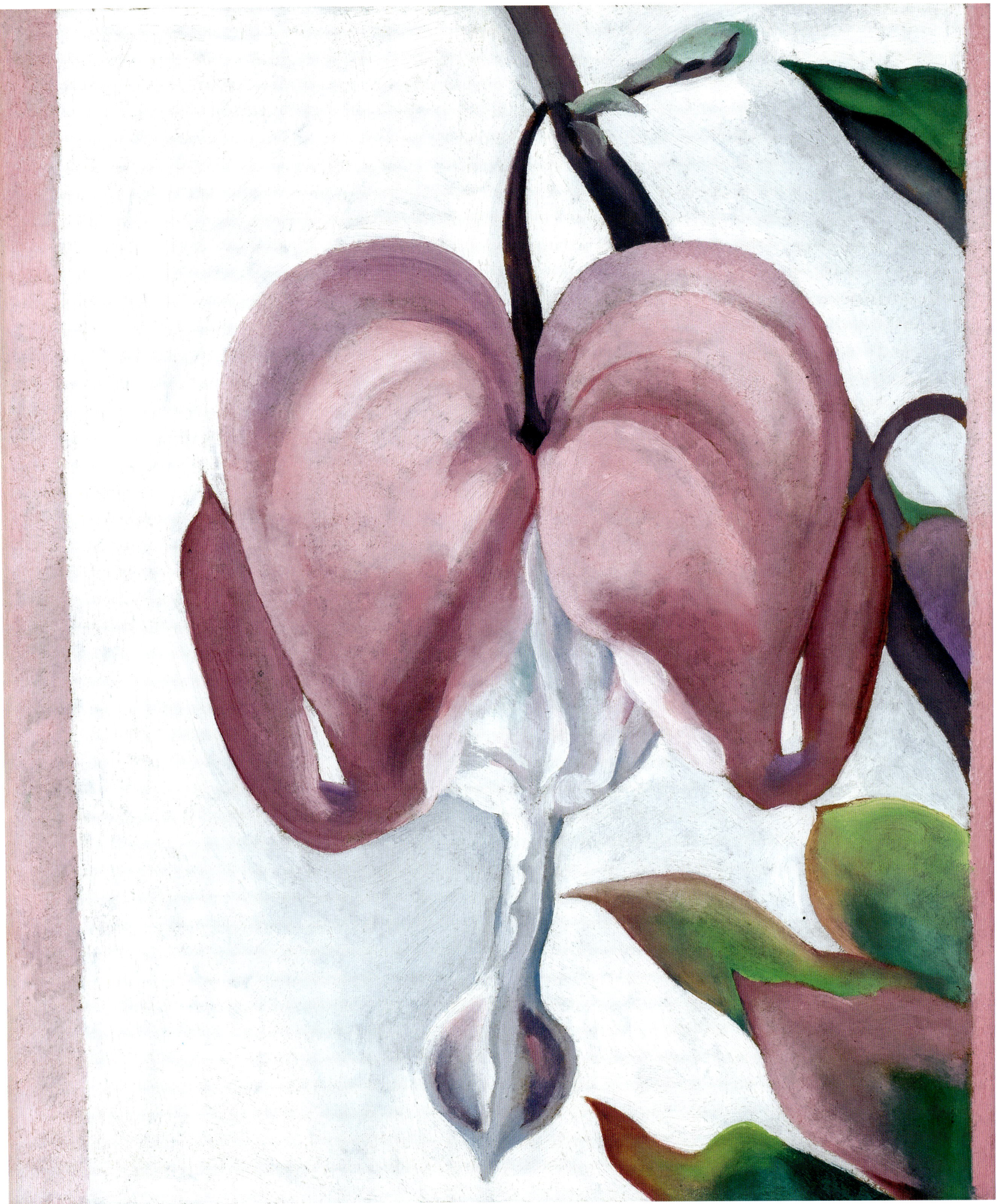

Georgia O'Keeffe
1887, Sun Prairie, WI, United States–
1986, Santa Fe, NM, United States
Bleeding Heart, 1928
Oil on canvas, 13 7⁄16 × 11 7⁄16 in. (34.2 × 29.1 cm)

Gift of Susan and Anton Roland-Rosenberg, Los Angeles, through the American Friends of the Tel Aviv Museum of Art, 1996

This painting depicts a close-up image of a bleeding-heart flower, whose distinctive heart-shaped, drooping petals have symbolic associations with love, affection, and sensitivity. Rendered in shades of pink and red subtly blended together with dramatic contrasts of light and shadow, the flower is elongated, the contours of its undulating shape accentuated, lending the image a sense of movement and dynamism. Building on her close creative connections to photographers, O'Keeffe often drew on photography's capacity for minimalism and abstraction. Here, for example, the composition appears cropped. She centered the flower on the canvas, highlighting its striking shape and intricate construction, zooming in on its form as if to reveal its essence.

In 1928, when O'Keeffe completed *Bleeding Heart*—the first in a series of larger-than-life flower paintings that would extend into the early 1930s—she was already an established figure in the American art world. In the same year, she exhibited some of her most iconic works at the Intimate Gallery (1928), run by her husband Alfred Stieglitz, and the Brooklyn Museum (1927), where she received acclaim for her bold and innovative style.[1] Yet, it was also an extremely difficult period for the artist. O'Keeffe was dealing with a range of personal and professional challenges, including the breakdown of her marriage and major health problems—all of which contributed to her decision in 1929 to leave New York permanently, opting instead for the solitude and natural beauty of New Mexico.

During O'Keeffe's lifetime, critics read the flower paintings as a metaphor for the artist's body, psychology, womanhood, and sexuality. Today, they are understood as part of a wider artistic movement of American artists in the 1920s and 1930s, including Edward Weston (pp. 158–59) and Ansel Adams (pp. 204–05), who found inspiration in the natural world and searched for an abstract-modernist aesthetic that would express the magnitude and wondrousness of the American landscape.[2] O'Keeffe's work, in particular, was deeply influenced by the spiritual theories of her time, and aimed to explore and convey the concepts of renewal, wholeness, infinitude, sublimity, and transcendence.

Ayelet Carmi

1 Works exhibited in these venues included *Red Canna* (1924) and *Radiator Building—Night, New York* (1927).

2 Other prominent examples of O'Keeffe's fascination with the American natural world from this same period include her abstracted and stylized paintings of enlarged objects, such as *Shell No. 1* and *Shell No. 2* (1928).

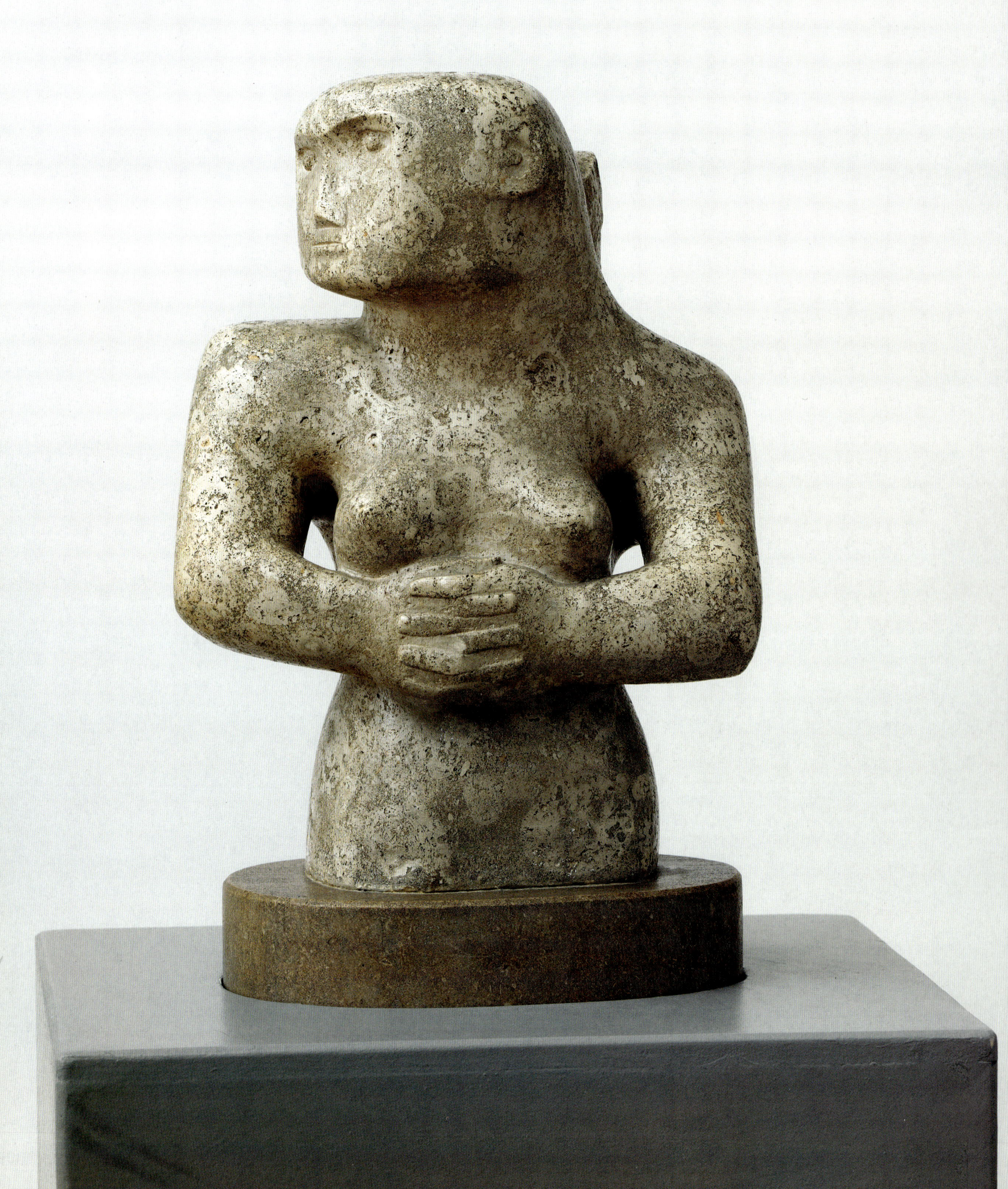

Henry Moore
1898, Castleford, United Kingdom–
1986, Perry Green, United Kingdom
Woman with Clasped Hands, 1929
Travertine stone, 20 1/16 × 13 3/8 × 6 5/16 in. (51 × 34 × 16 cm)

Gift of A. Wix, London, through the British Friends of the Art Museums of Israel, 1947

Henry Moore's sculpture *Woman with Clasped Hands* reimagines the classical female bust as a modern icon of shifting angles and proportions. The figure's oversized head rests on a modestly scaled torso, its broad, bent arms creating unexpected openings in an otherwise solid form. Shallow, incised lines, triangles, and circles create the model's features, including a heraldic, apotropaic face, and clasped hands with delicate, interlocking fingers.

A prominent critic of Moore's work, David Sylvester, singled out the "in-the-round" experience of viewing this work as emblematic of the artist's early career explorations of mass: "Every view expresses a different feeling, ranging from the stolid to the quick. The deeply moving plasticity of the head is tense to breaking point as the protruding stylization of gathered hair at the back struggles to wrench round and touch the face."[1]

The sculpture's stylized forms and iconography are an outgrowth of Moore's decade-long study of the art of Pre-Columbian cultures, reflected here in its visual similarities to Mezcala figures. This pursuit was inspired by influential primitivist texts such as Roger Fry's *Vision and Design*, which encouraged modern British artists to find, in the various cultures of the non-Western world, sources of abstract and emotional inspiration. It is informed, as well, by the British Museum's large and diverse displays of art from Mexico that were prominently exhibited there throughout the 1920s.[2]

The immediacy of *Woman with Clasped Hands* owes much to Moore's direct carving method: a reductive process that relishes the inherent materiality of its stone, in this case, porous Italian travertine.[3] In so fully conveying his sculptures' physical weightiness, an analogue for their emotional gravitas, Moore created representations of the human figure—and of women, in particular—which were heralded for their openness and humanism.

Levi Prombaum

1 David Sylvester, "The Evolution of Henry Moore's Sculpture," *The Burlington Magazine* 90, no. 543 (June 1948): 159.

2 See Alice Correia, "Mask 1929 by Henry Moore OM, CH," catalogue entry, December 2012, in *Henry Moore: Sculptural Process and Public Identity*, Tate Research Publication, 2015, https://www.tate.org.uk/art/research-publications/henry-moore

3 See Judith Zilczer, "The Theory of Direct Carving in Modern Sculpture," *Oxford Art Journal* 4, no. 2 (November 1981): 44–49.

Jankel Adler
1895, Lodz, Russian Empire (now Poland)–
1949, Aldbourne, United Kingdom
Purim Spiel, 1931
Oil and sand on canvas, 48 13⁄16 × 68 7⁄8 in. (124 × 175 cm)

Gift of Jakob Sonnenberg and Aaron Mazur Danzig, 1938

In his works, Jankel Adler combined themes and motifs drawn from Jewish folk art with stylistic aspects of European modernism.[1] He created typological portraits of Jews, depicting scenes from the life of the Hasidic community, as well as monumental figures from the Hebrew Bible in an expressionistic style with mystical overtones. Like the Cubists, Adler was exploring the tension between abstraction and naturalism.

Purim Spiel refers to satiric plays traditionally performed during the festive holiday of Purim in the synagogue courtyard, considered too profane to be performed inside the building. Purim offered occasions for plays featuring songs, jokes, and lighthearted renditions of Jewish history and contemporary life.

Adler grew up a Hasidic Jew. He studied art at the Barmen Kunstgewerbeschule (School of Decorative Arts), and in 1918 he became close to the radical left-wing group *Die Aktion*. He later contributed to the group's literary and political magazine, a leading organ of the Expressionist movement in Berlin. In 1918–19, Adler lived in Poland, where he became a founding member of Yung-yidish, an avant-garde Jewish group of painters and writers. After settling in Germany in 1920, he joined the activities of experimental artist groups in Berlin, Cologne, and Düsseldorf.[2] Between 1922 and 1933, he participated in major German and international art exhibitions while also continuing to play an active role in Poland's artistic life.[3]

During the March 1933 Reichstag election campaign, Adler, together with other left-wing artists and intellectuals, published an "urgent appeal" against the policies of the National Socialists and left Germany. His works were included in the National Socialist exhibition *Kulturbolschewistische Bilder* (Images of Cultural Bolshevism) in 1933, and the notorious *Entartete Kunst* (Degenerate Art) exhibition in 1937. During the "degenerate art" campaigns, the Nazis removed twenty-five of Adler's works from German public collections.

Alla Rosenfeld

1 See Antje Birthalmer and Gerhard Finckh, eds., *Jankel Adler und die Avantgarde: Chagall, Dix, Klee, Picasso*, exh. cat. (Wuppertal: Von der Heydt–Museum, 2018).

2 Jankel Adler was a member of the Novembergruppe, Das Junge Rheinland, and Rheinische Sezession. He became a co-founder of the Gruppe progressive Künstler in Cologne, whose socialist ideas of bettering the world touched upon his own convictions.

3 On Adler's work, see *Jankel Adler: On the 20th Anniversary of the Artist's Death, From Collections in Israel*, exh. cat. (Jerusalem: Israel Museum, 1969); Ulrich Krempel and Karin Thomas, *Jankel Adler, 1895–1949*, exh. cat. (Cologne: DuMont, 1985); and Michael Middleton, *Memorial Exhibition of the Works of Jankel Adler, 1895–1949*, exh. cat. (London: Arts Council of Great Britain, 1951).

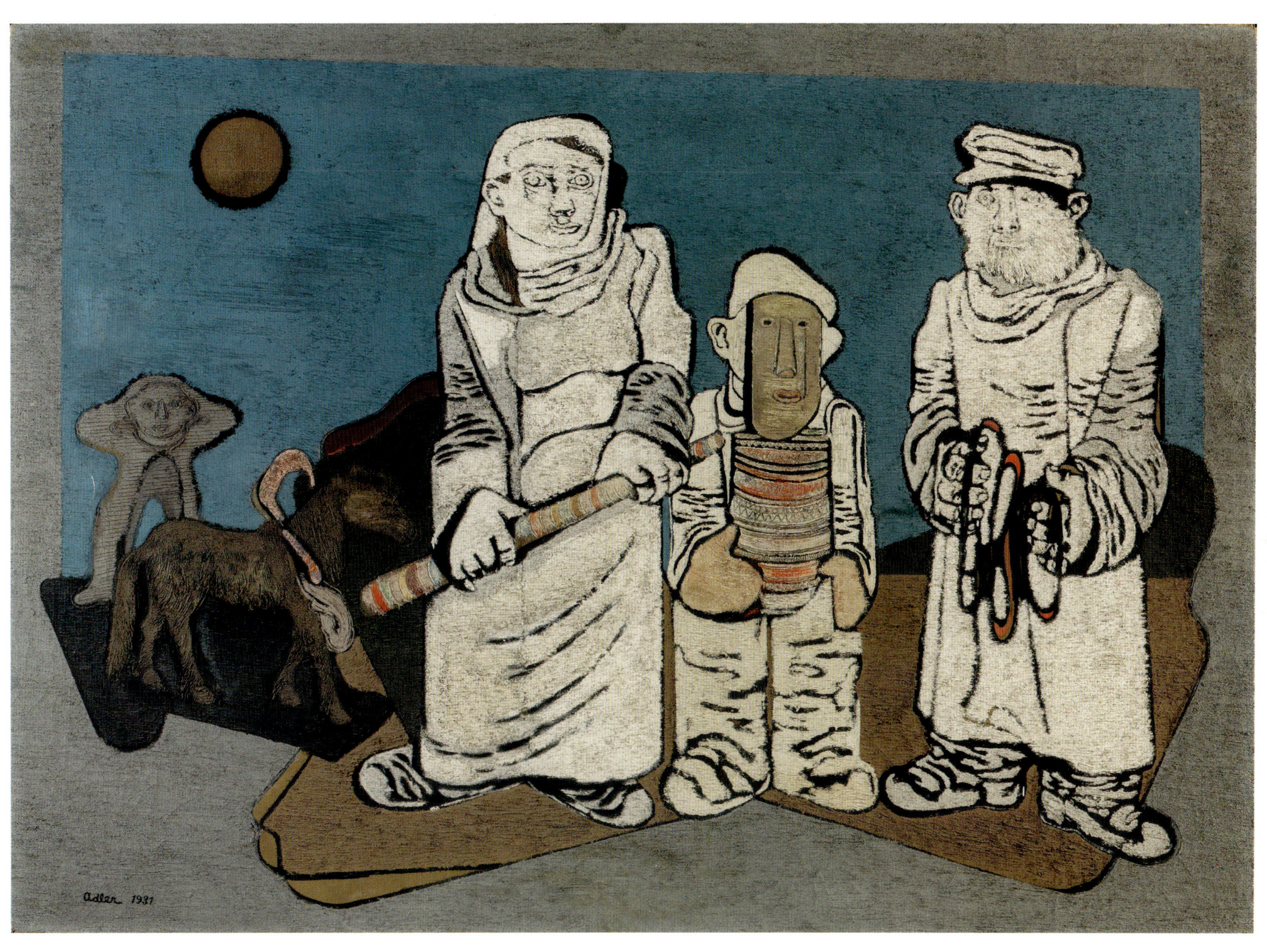
Adler 1931

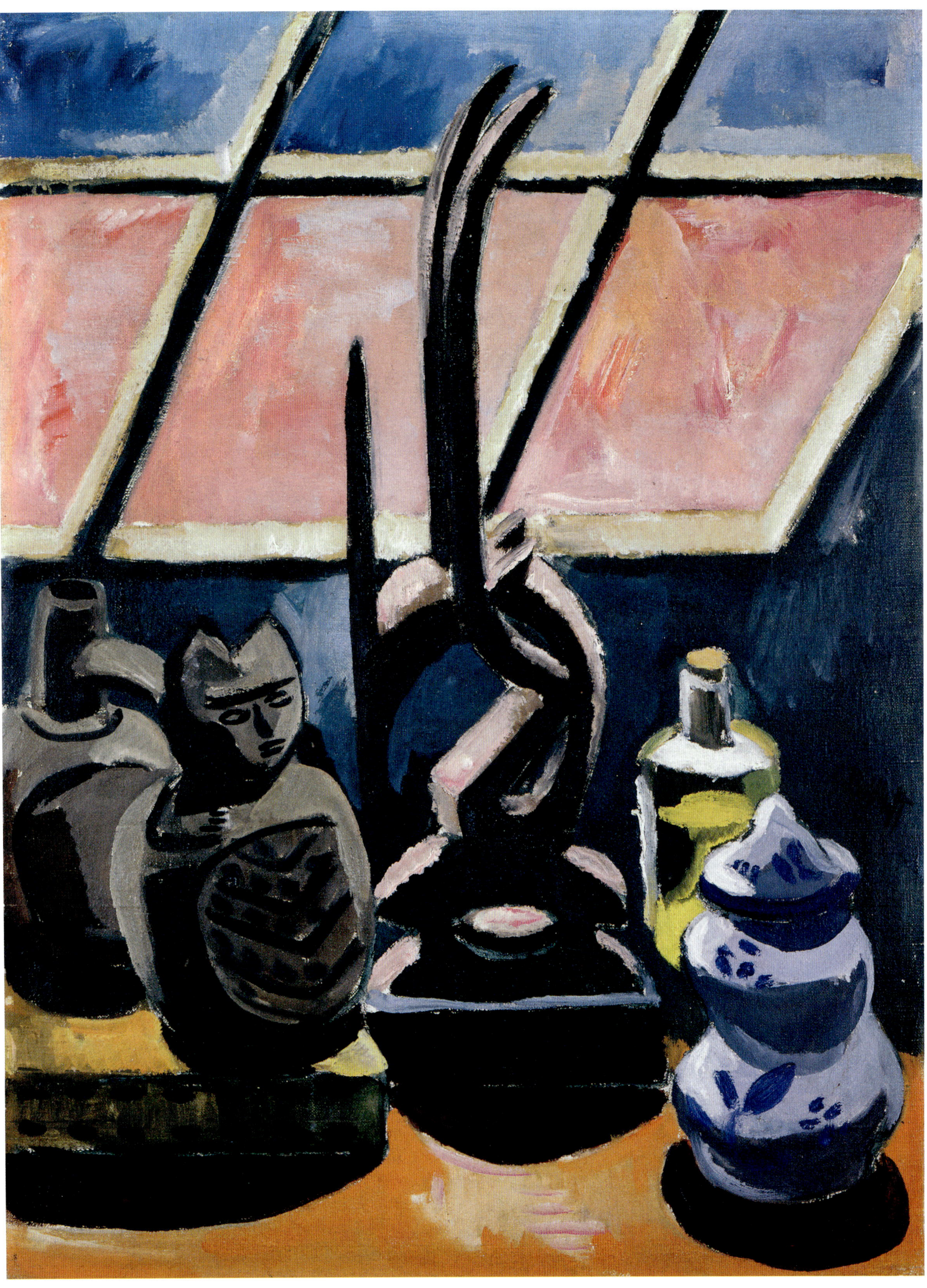

Karl Schmidt-Rottluff
1884, Chemnitz, Germany–1976, Berlin, Germany
Still Life in the Studio, 1932
Oil on canvas, 35 7⁄16 × 25 9⁄16 in. (90 × 65 cm)

Gift of Dr. Rosa Schapire, through the British Friends of the Art Museums of Israel, 1956

In the 1930s, Karl Schmidt-Rottluff painted a number of still lifes in which he positioned objects in the foreground of the composition, in the vicinity of a window. The cramped spaces of these compositions have been interpreted as an expression of the increasing isolation and pressure the artist was experiencing at the time. The work was made during the two-year period in which Schmidt-Rottluff was admitted into, and subsequently expelled from, the conservative Prussian Academy of Arts, which came under Nazi control in 1933.

In this painting, the artist placed two carved sculptures among the domestic objects in the composition: an African figurine and a rather modern, abstract form. When he first encountered African sculpture in 1912, it became a major influence on his work, and he began collecting African art objects and emulating their style in his work.

Still Life in the Studio is an example of the so-called "soft style" that Schmidt-Rottluff developed during this period. His paintings became more realistic; flowing lines and rounded forms replaced the angularity of his early expressionistic work, which dates to his period of membership in the artist's group Brücke. He also moderated his bold colors and adopted a more restrained palette, characterized by earth tones.

Since none of the objects in this painting are part of Schmidt-Rottluff's estate, it is possible that the studio he depicted here was not his own but that of the painter and patron of the arts Hanna Bekker vom Rath, who owned a number of non-Western sculptures. Schmidt-Rottluff was staying with her in the spring of 1932, the year he painted this work.

Ruth Feldmann

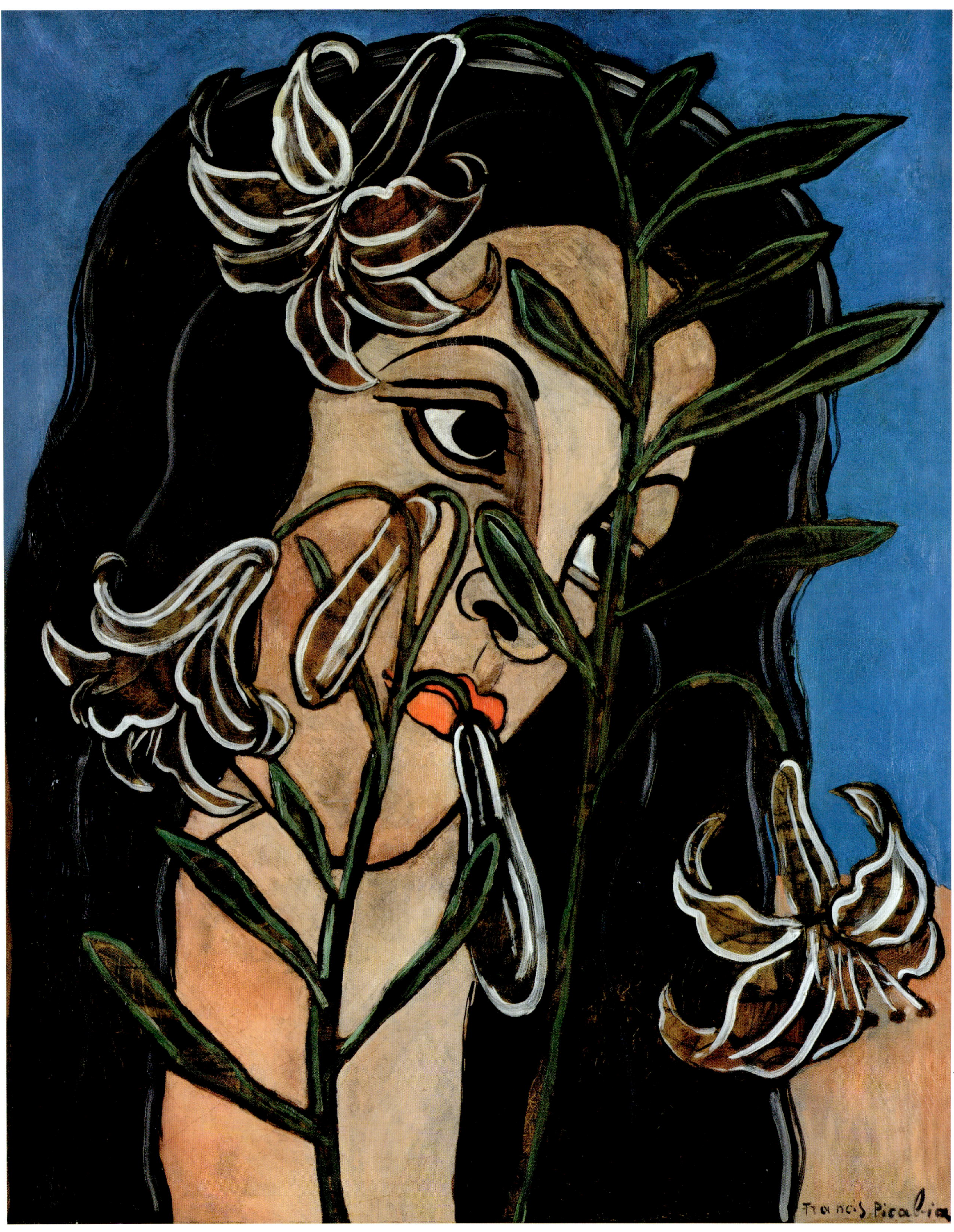
Francis Picabia

Francis Picabia
1879–1953, Paris, France
Untitled, c. 1934
Oil on canvas, 63 × 51 3/16 in. (160 × 130 cm)

Gift of Mr. Alex Maguy, Paris, 1963

"If you don't want dirty ideas," Francis Picabia declared in 1921, "change them like shirts."[1] That is indeed what Picabia did in this work. He made the painting during a transitional moment in his long career, when he shifted his focus from a body of work known as "transparencies"—named for the artist's suspension of foreground and background elements between varnish layers to create intricately overlaid compositions—to a series of portraits and pinups whose subjects were lifted from popular imagery, such as soft-core pornography magazines and photographs of Hollywood stars.[2]

In this painting, the viewer is presented with the profile of a woman whose face is obscured by the leafy branches of large lilies. The shapes of the leaves and the flower petals are delineated with contrasting colors of white, green, and black paint that echo the woman's sharp features. Pentimenti, preparatory sketches from an earlier composition, were discovered when this painting was treated by conservators in the 1980s. Picabia had a penchant for overpainting and remaking earlier works, and it is possible that Untitled is a reworking of a "transparency."

The painting's provenance also provides interesting insight into the milieu in which this work and the artist circulated. Alex Maguy, a fashion designer and art dealer who ran the Galerie de l'Élysée, gave the painting to the Tel Aviv Museum in 1963.[3] Picabia was appreciated by many in the fashion world—renowned couturier Jacques Doucet also collected his works. This work appealed to avant-garde circles that connected the worlds of fine art and fashion, reflecting the intermixing of creative networks in Paris that was pivotal within the history of modernism.

Talia Kwartler

1 Francis Picabia, *Funny-Guy* (1921), reproduced in *I Am a Beautiful Monster: Poetry, Prose, and Provocation*, trans. Marc Lowenthal (Cambridge, MA: MIT Press, 2007), 279.

2 See Michael Duffy, Talia Kwartler, Natalie Dupêcher, and Anne Umland, eds., *Francis Picabia: Materials and Techniques* (New York: Museum of Modern Art, 2017), 47, 62, mo.ma/picabia_conservation.

3 See the entry for the work (no. 1294) in *Francis Picabia Catalogue Raisonné*, vol. 4, *1940–1953*, ed. Candace Clements, Arnaud Pierre, and William A. Camfield (Brussels: Mercatorfonds, 2023), 306.

Giorgio de Chirico
1888, Volos, Greece–1978, Rome, Italy
The Philosopher and the Poet, 1955
Oil on canvas, 15 ¾ × 11 ¾ in. (40 × 30 cm)

Mizne-Blumental Collection, Bequest of Annette Celine, 2018

Giorgio de Chirico founded the movement known as pittura metafisica, or metaphysical painting, together with Futurist artist Carlo Carrà in Ferrara, Italy, in 1917. De Chirico had been developing this style since as early as 1911, when he began painting realistic yet dreamlike scenes, often representing eerily empty city squares, with neoclassical architecture towering above mannequins, ancient statuary, and long shadows. The term "metaphysical painting" was coined by the poet and critic Guillaume Apollinaire, likely after he heard de Chirico use the word in relation to his own work.

The Philosopher and the Poet is a metaphysical painting produced in the 1950s based on an identically titled 1914 painting by the artist that was preceded in 1913 by a preparatory sketch.[1] A comparison between the earlier and later versions reveals that in the 1914 painting, de Chirico did not include precise details such as the drawing on the blackboard or the lines drawn on the floor. The art historian James Thrall Soby described this earlier painting as unfinished, because of its free technique in comparison to de Chirico's other paintings that include mannequins from the same period.[2] De Chirico often created nearly exact replicas of his works from the metaphysical period—which he called *verifalsi*, or "true-fakes," seeing the later work as no less authentic than the earlier, and often embedded new associations or details.

According to the art historian Paolo Baldacci, the mannequin figure in *The Philosopher and the Poet* is derived from Apollinaire's 1913 poem, "The Musician of Saint-Merry," whose protagonist is a flutist with no facial features, except for a mouth, who likely symbolizes Apollinaire himself.[3] De Chirico often integrated faceless mannequins in works, finding in them "ineffable and mysterious poetry."[4] Here, the mannequin is also depicted as a philosopher in the classical sense, as both a thinker and an expert of the sciences—de Chirico portrays him contemplating a blackboard covered with equations and formulas related to geometric inquiry.

Dorit Yifat

1 The 1914 painting is in a private collection, and the 1913 preparatory sketch is in the collection of The Morgan Library & Museum, New York.

2 James Thrall Soby, *Giorgio de Chirico* (New York: Museum of Modern Art, 1955), 109.

3 *Italian Art in the 20th Century* (London: Royal Academy of Arts, 1989), 66–67.

4 Giorgio de Chirico, "The Birth of the Mannequin," *Metafisica*, 1938, https://fondazionedechirico.org/metafisica/n-1-2-2001-2002-2/.

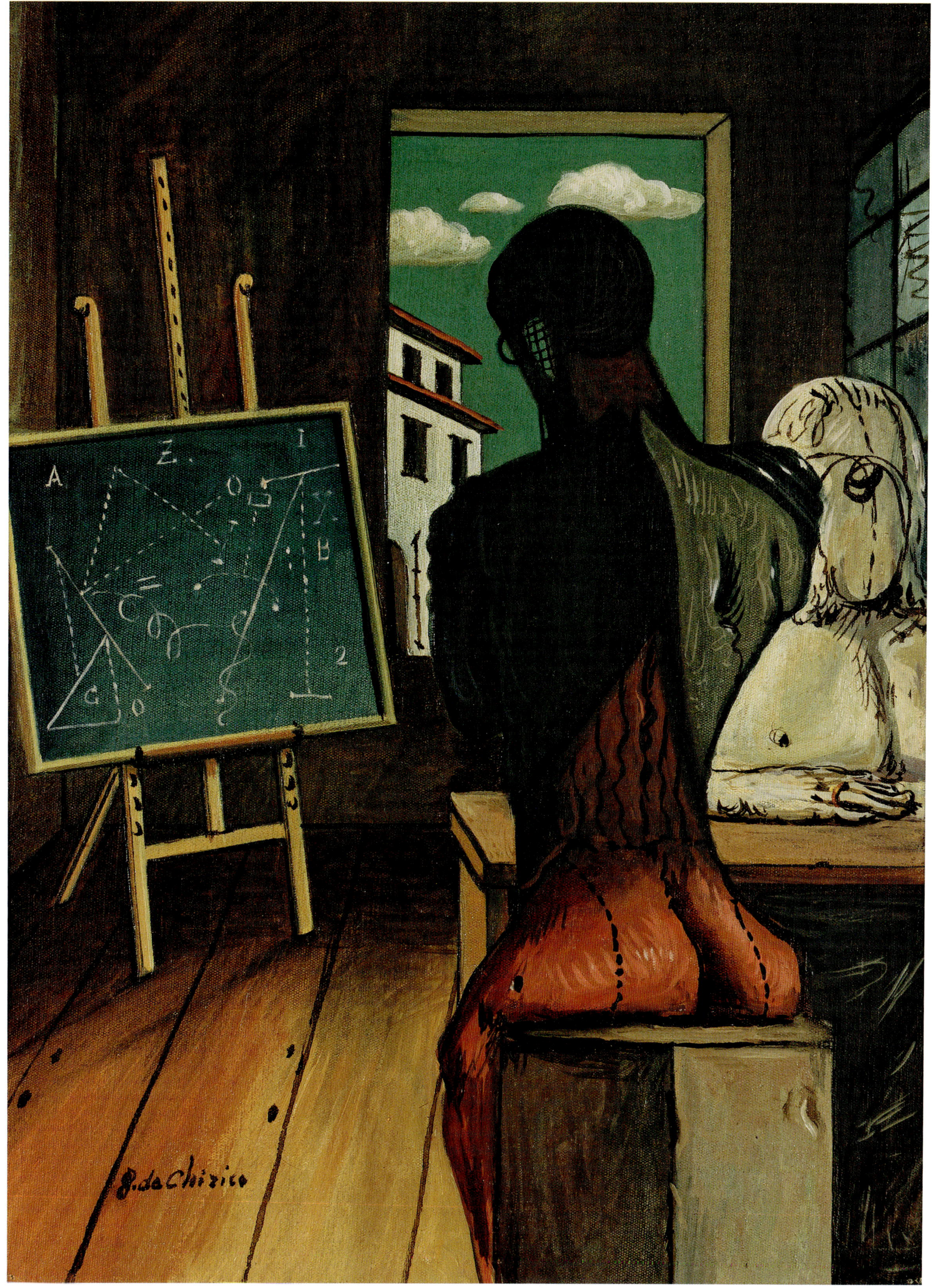
G. de Chirico

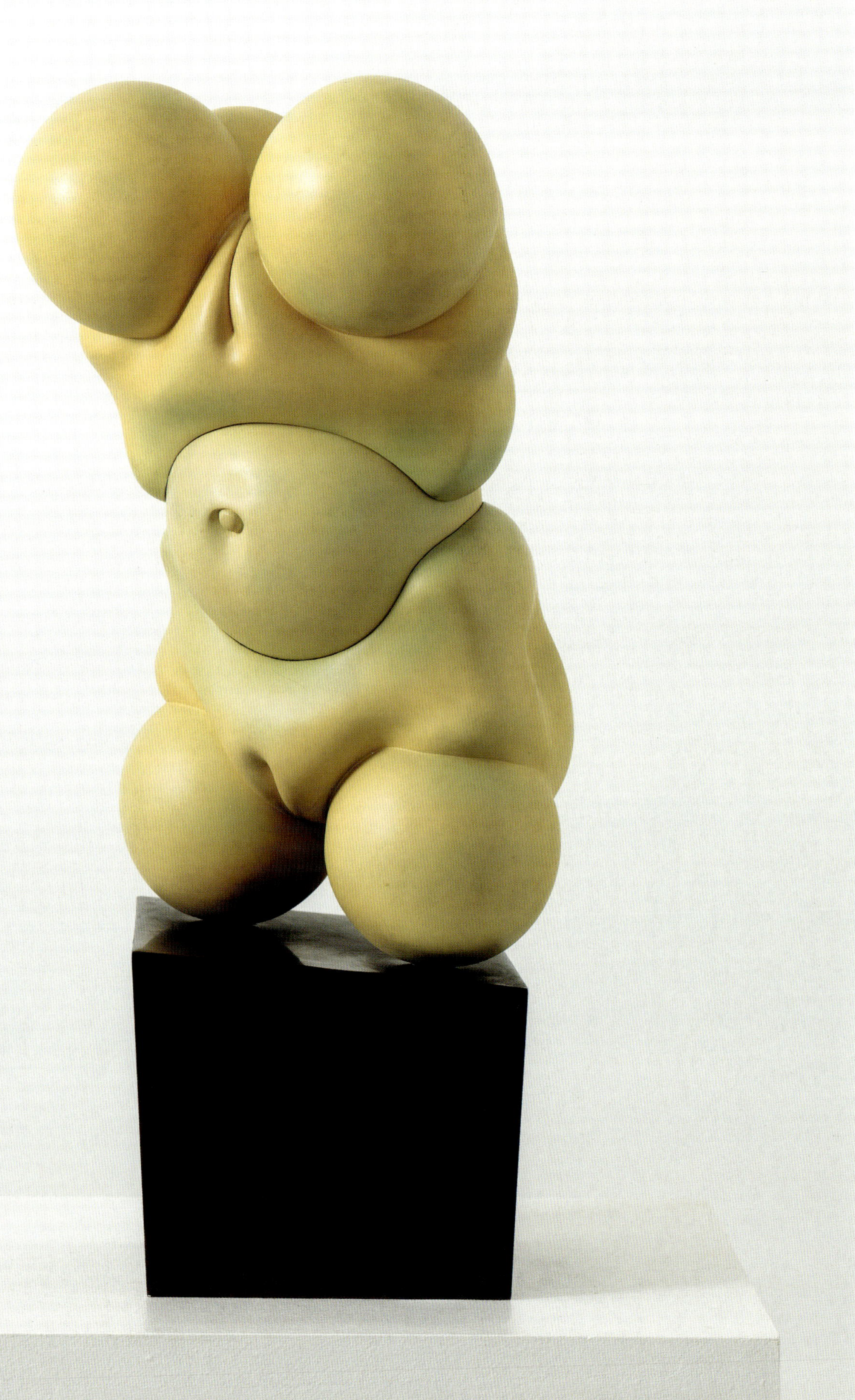

Hans Bellmer
1902, Kattowitz, German Empire (now Katowice, Poland)–1975, Paris, France
Doll, 1936/1965
Painted aluminum on bronze base, 34 ⅝ × 28 15⁄16 × 9 in. (88 × 73.5 × 23 cm)

Promised gift of Virginia and Herbert Lust, Greenwich, Connecticut

When German artist Hans Bellmer created this sculptural object, *Doll*, in 1936, his work was already familiar to a certain coterie of French Surrealists. Two years earlier, he had published the small artist's book for which he remains best known. Titled *Die Puppe* (*The Doll*), it presents photographs of a near-life-size female figurine, built by the artist and photographed around his Berlin home in various stages of construction or disarticulation. The images were republished in the Surrealist journal *Minotaure* in the winter of 1934–35, and Bellmer spent the first weeks of 1935 visiting Paris, where he befriended several artists associated with the group.

In the late spring of 1935, Bellmer began work on this sculpture, the second doll. A persistent origin myth attends its creation—namely, a visit to the Kaiser-Friedrich Museum in Berlin, where a pair of sixteenth-century wooden dolls fascinated the artist. Their appendages were connected by ball joints, yielding a highly manipulable body capable of bending and twisting in ways that approximate the movements of human limbs.

Working through the summer, Bellmer built *Doll* around a similar mechanical device, a belly ball joint, to which he attached two pelvises. Any distinction between upper and lower body was effaced, with the figure's top half transformed into a mirror reflection of the bottom. Enamored with the anti-naturalistic possibilities offered by what was ostensibly a more naturalistic construction, the artist proceeded to wildly reorient the body, capturing its anatomically impossible arrangements in dozens of staged photographs.

Bellmer compiled some of these images into an artist's book. A partial collaboration with the French Surrealist poet Paul Éluard, *Les jeux de la poupée* (*The Games of the Doll*) was published in 1949, after numerous delays related to World War II. In his preface to the book, Bellmer explained the significance of the ball joint: with its incredible mobility, it was a form of "experimental poetry."[1] Aligning his work with the aim of the Surrealist movement, Bellmer wrote that the ball joint allowed for the creation of a "superior reality,"[2] one that unified dream and waking states.

Natalie Dupêcher

1 Hans Bellmer, "Notes on the Subject of the Ball Joint" (1938), translated in Sue Taylor, *Hans Bellmer: The Anatomy of Anxiety* (Cambridge , MA: MIT Press, 2000), 212.

2 Bellmer, in Taylor, "Notes on the Subject of the Ball Joint," 212.

Germaine Krull
1897, Posen, German Empire (now Wilda-Poznań, Poland)–1985, Wetzlar, Germany
Still Life, c. 1938
Gelatin silver print, 8 × 4 ¾ in. (20.3 × 12 cm)

Gift of Michael S. Sachs, through the American Friends of the Tel Aviv Museum of Art, 1992

In one of Germaine Krull's engagements with still-life traditions, she captured a medley of vegetables, unconventionally, from above. A cauliflower head, placed on a bed of red lettuce leaves, is crowned by succulent asparagus spears; an artichoke tightly enclosed by its petals; and daikon radishes and potatoes that spill from a cradle of leeks, whose fibrous roots reach upward towards the camera's lens. Forged from a high contrast of light and shadow, and printed with sepia toning, the image offers an abundance of warm, vivid details.

This visual information takes on additional formal and semiotic dimensions when considered in relation to the dark ground that frames the study: a cut piece of paper that resembles a human head in profile. As an anthropomorphizing study, Krull's *Still Life* evokes both the psychological experiments of such friends and Surrealist peers as Man Ray and André Kertész, as well as the portraiture of Italian Renaissance court painter Giuseppe Arcimboldo, whose witty and fantastical human portraits conglomerated from plants and foods have entertained and discomfited viewers in equal measure.

Krull likely made this work while living in Monte Carlo in the late 1930s, a period in which she opened a photography studio that specialized in portraiture, architectural studies, photojournalism, and studies of daily life. It represents a continuation from her previous decade in Paris, where, driven by her leftist politics, she innovated radical darkroom techniques, combined experiments across photography and text, and crafted newly intimate forms of urban reportage to become a leading name associated with Neues Sehen (New Vision) photography. *Still Life* is a testament to the ceaselessly developing style and spirit of investigation that characterizes the long arc of Krull's career.

Levi Prombaum

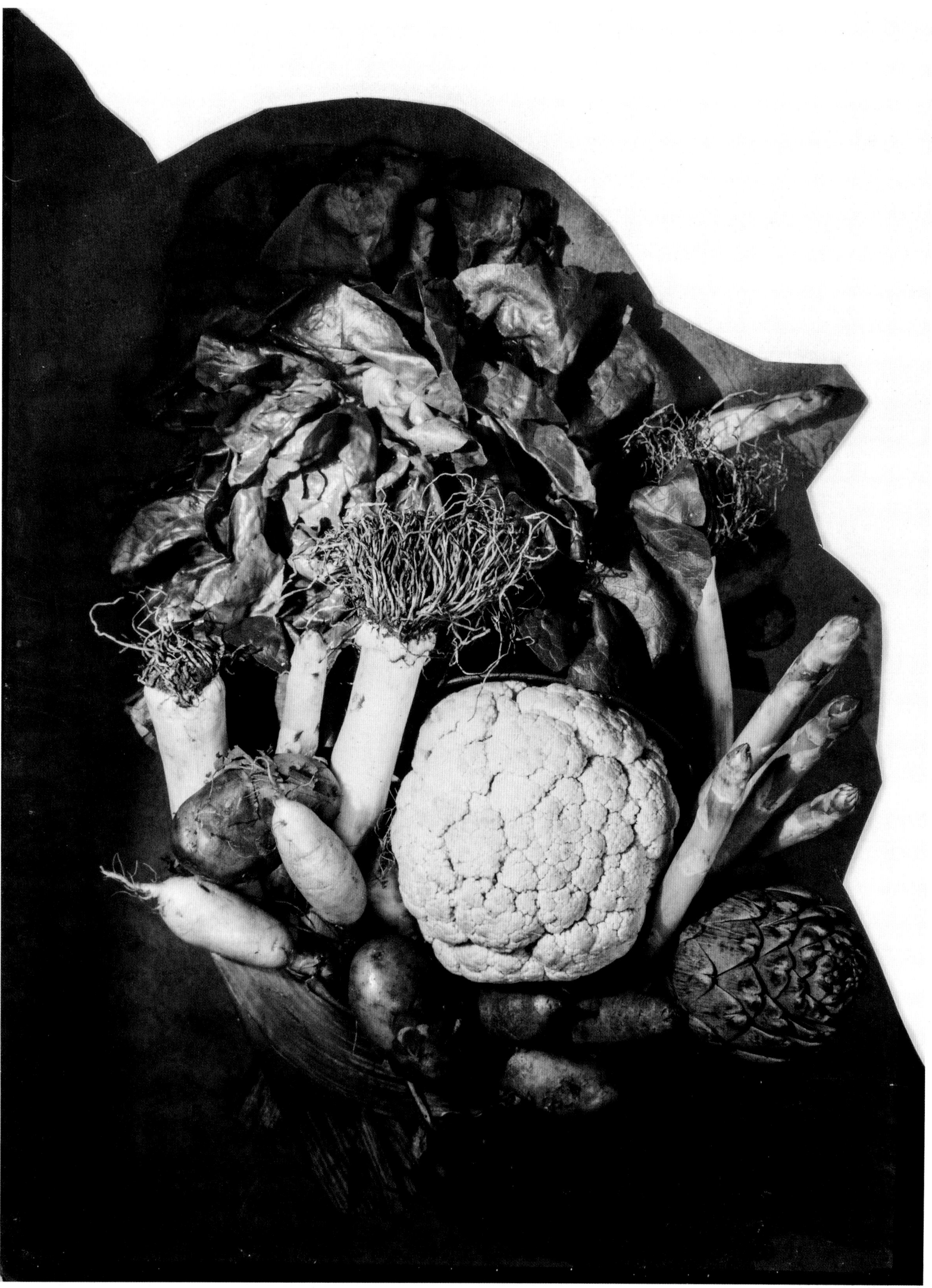

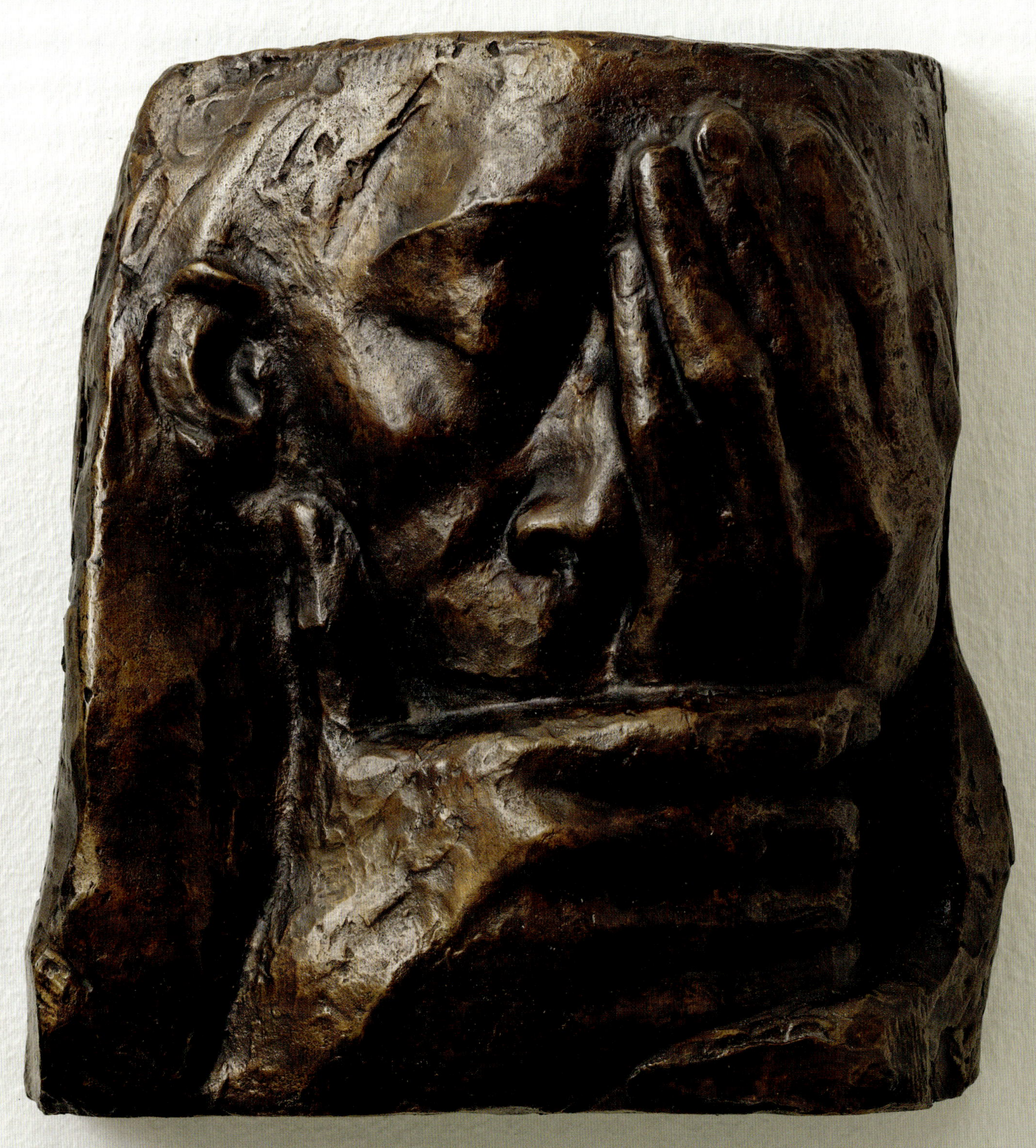

Käthe Kollwitz
1867, Königsberg, Prussia (now Kaliningrad, Russia)–1945, Moritzburg, Germany
Lamentation (*in Memory of Ernst Barlach*), 1938/41 (cast probably 1970)
Bronze, 10 5⁄8 × 9 13⁄16 × 3 15⁄16 in. (27 × 25 × 10 cm)

Gift of Erich Cohn, New York, 1970

Käthe Kollwitz created *Lamentation* after attending the funeral of her friend and fellow artist Ernst Barlach in October 1938. She wanted it, as she wrote, to "give an intimation of my own suffering."[1] The relief sculpture is dominated by two large, expressive hands that frame and also partially obscure a woman's grief-stricken face, covering her mouth and one of her lowered eyes as if to cradle her emotion, to shut out the world, to stifle a cry. Slightly larger than life-size and based on the artist's own features, it is a self-portrait, a homage to Barlach, and a monument to the universality of grief. "When I was making [*Lamentation*] … I was affected by Barlach's death and the terrible injustice that he had suffered," she wrote, referring to the toll that Nazi persecutions exacted on him.[2] Kollwitz, too, was forbidden from selling or exhibiting her work during the Nazi era, and she was forced to resign her teaching position at the Prussian Academy of Arts. She had been the first woman named professor there in 1919.

Though renowned above all for her prints and drawings confronting the hardships of working-class women and children, Kollwitz was also an accomplished sculptor who made at least forty-three sculptures.[3] Only nineteen survived World War II, however, and most of these, including the example in the Tel Aviv Museum of Art's collection, exist primarily as posthumous castings authorized by the artist's heirs. *Lamentation* was donated to the Museum by Erich Cohn, a German-born New Yorker and friend of the artist who was one of her most passionate collectors.[4]

Starr Figura

1 Letter from Kollwitz to Wilhelm Loth, March 30, 1942, in *Briefe der Freundschaft und Begegnungen* (Munich: List, 1966), 46.

2 Letter from Kollwitz to Trude Bernhard, 1941, *Briefe*, 109.

3 Annette Seeler, *Käthe Kollwitz: Die Plastik* (Cologne: Käthe Kollwitz Museum, and Munich: Hirmer Verlag, 2016) https://kollwitz.de/en/catalogue-raisonne-sculptural-works. Seeler's meticulous catalogue raisonné documents forty-three sculptures and, when relevant, their various castings. See no. 38, 354–69, for *The Lament*.

4 See Hildegard Bachert, "Collecting the Art of Käthe Kollwitz: A Survey of Collections, Collectors, and Public Response in Germany and the United States," in Elizabeth Prelinger, *Käthe Kollwitz* (Washington, D.C.: National Gallery of Art, 1992): 120.

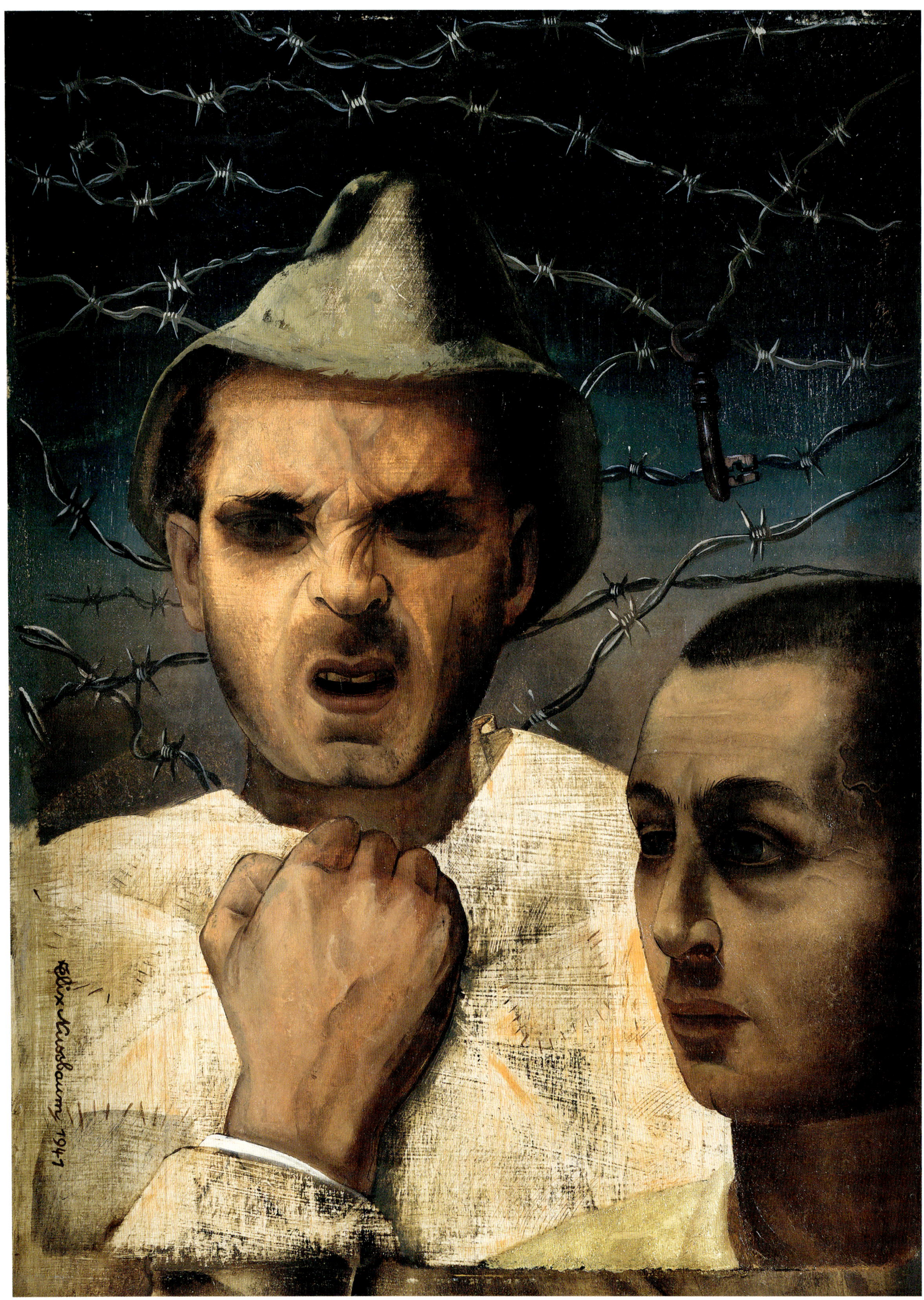
Felix Nussbaum 1941

Felix Nussbaum
1904, Osnabrück, Germany–1944, Auschwitz, Poland
Self-Portrait with Key at St. Cyprien Detention Camp, 1941
Oil on plywood, 18 7/8 × 14 3/4 in. (48 × 37.5 cm)

Gift of Philippe Aisinber and Maurice Tzwern, Brussels, 1991. In memory of Uniyl Tzwern and all the victims of fascism

Felix Nussbaum painted *Self-Portrait with Key* in Brussels in 1940 after his escape from the Saint-Cyprien camp in southern France, to which he had been deported when German troops invaded Belgium in the same year. His imprisonment as an "enemy alien" by the Belgian authorities marked a difficult turning point for the German Jew, who had been relatively safe as an exile in Belgium since 1935. The self-portrait is one of a series of paintings in which the artist addressed the theme of imprisonment as a result of his traumatic experiences in the camp.

In this double portrait, Nussbaum presents himself in front of a symbolically loaded setting: the barbed-wire fence, in which a key is enmeshed as a sign of liberation, signifies the hopelessness of escaping captivity. The staggered color background suggests the Saint-Cyprien coast, with the black and blue of the horizon lending the scene an ominous atmosphere.

Facing forward, in confrontational self-representation, Nussbaum asserts himself against imprisonment: the exaggerated wrinkles of anger and the clenched fist denote an inner struggle between powerlessness and rage. Heightening the sense of pained, inner conflict, Nussbaum juxtaposed this expressive portrait with a second, introverted figure who stares vacantly beyond the picture plane. Further contrasts define the picture: the tattered clothing, under which the fine white of a cuff peeks out, underlines the prisoner's status as an outcast and disenfranchised person. The hat, on the other hand, is an attribute of the wanderer, familiar from other Nussbaum paintings, which can be interpreted as a reference to an unbroken claim to freedom.

The symbolic intensification of external reality through the symbiosis of spatial composition and the artist's personal iconography is characteristic of Nussbaum's work. A means of self-assertion against the circumstances of the time, and evidence of his state of mind, Nussbaum's self-portraits are acts of self-determination against disenfranchisement. They are also acts of resistance.

In 1942, when the artist was in hiding, he entrusted *Self-Portrait with Key* to Josef Grosfils along with more than 100 other works. On August 9, 1944, Nussbaum was murdered after his deportation to Auschwitz.[1] Maurice Tzwern and Philippe Aisinber acquired the painting from Grosfils's heirs in 1987 and donated it to the Tel Aviv Museum of Art in 1991.

Anne Sibylle Schwetter

1 Fifteen years after Nussbaum's death, his estate was recovered by the artist's cousin in Brussels.

Salvador Dalí
1904–1989, Figueres, Spain
Thumb, Beach, Moon and Decaying Bird (The Wounded Bird), 1928
Oil and sand on cardboard, 21 5/8 × 25 13/16 in. (55 × 65.5 cm)

Mizne-Blumental Collection, Bequest of Annette Celine, 2018

Decidedly an outlier in Salvador Dalí's artistic career, this work corresponds with a brief period around 1928 in which the painter experimented with different paths that would lead him to Surrealism. One of these was the anti-artistic movement: an opposition to conventional art, advocating for mechanization, standardization, and objectivity. The painting also suggests the influence of Joan Miró (pp. 196–99), and that of Max Ernst (pp. 190–91), Yves Tanguy (pp. 182–83), and Pablo Picasso (pp. 124–31). In this moment, Dalí took a stand for freedom, for the imagination, for the realm of the subconscious and Freud, and also explored the tangibility of matter and the process of decay and putrefaction.

The composition is centered on a huge thumb, which, as Dalí indicated, could have emerged from a hypnagogic image—hallucinations that occur in the stage before sleep: "A single finger has been the subject of several of my recent paintings and photographic works."[1] The phallic finger, with its evident erotic connotations, stuck onto sand, and more specifically to the sand of the Cadaqués beach, incorporates the artist's perennial indissociable landscape and endows the finger itself with a physical, tangible context, clearly influenced by the work of André Masson.

The wounded, decomposing bird that gives the composition its title demands our attention, and engages in dialogue with the other decomposing animals that Dalí conceived in these years. Another example is the rotten donkey in *Un Chien Andalou* (1929), the provocative Surrealist film that the artist scripted with Luis Buñuel. Interestingly, other references to key scenes in *Un Chien Andalou* appear in this painting as well, such as the cloud cutting across the moon in the upper left corner of the composition.

Montse Aguer Teixidor

1 Salvador Dalí, "The Liberation of the Fingers" (1929), in *The Collected Writings of Salvador Dalí*, ed. and trans. Haim Finkelstein (Cambridge: Cambridge University Press, 1998), 101.

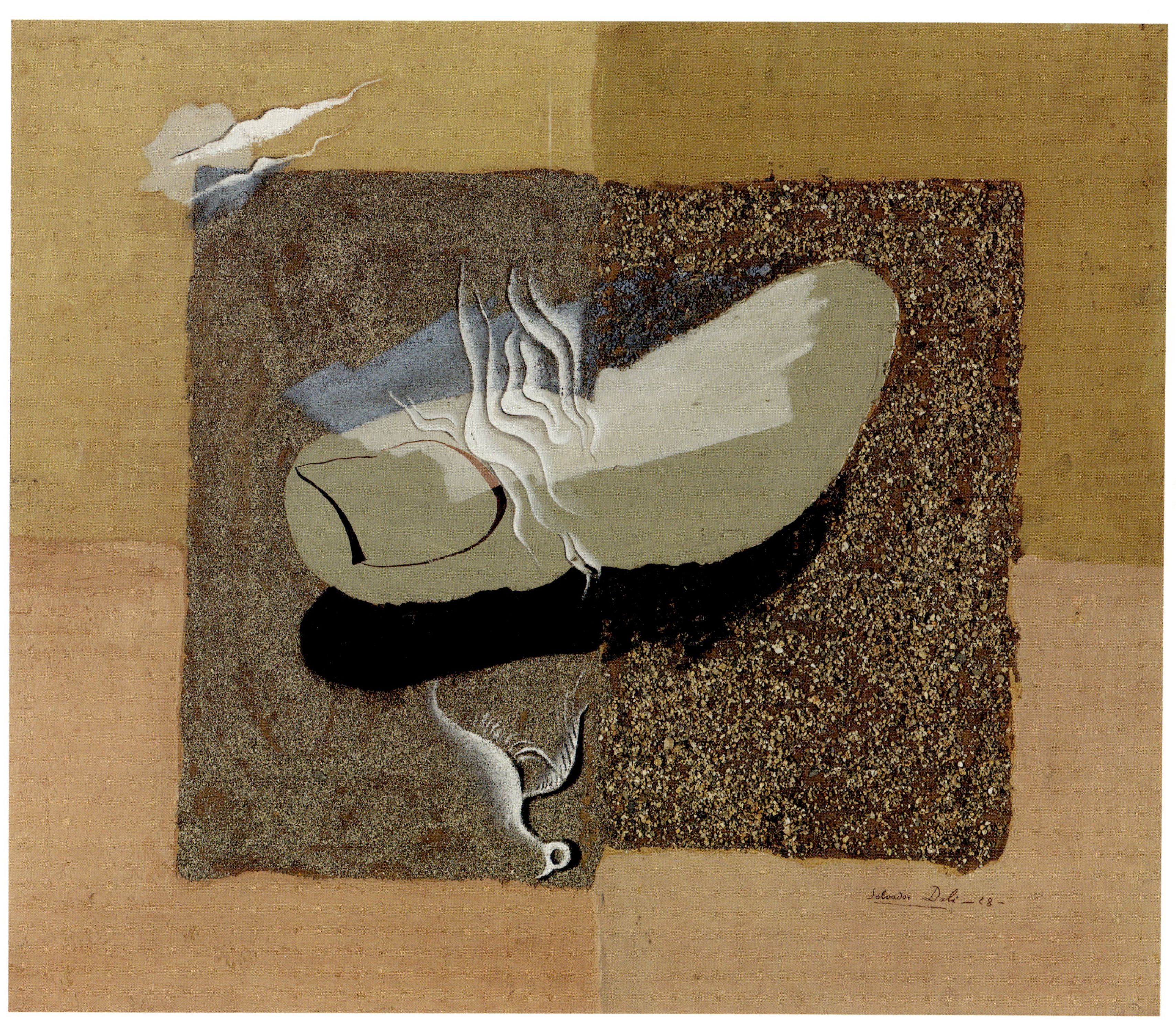
Salvador Dalí -28-

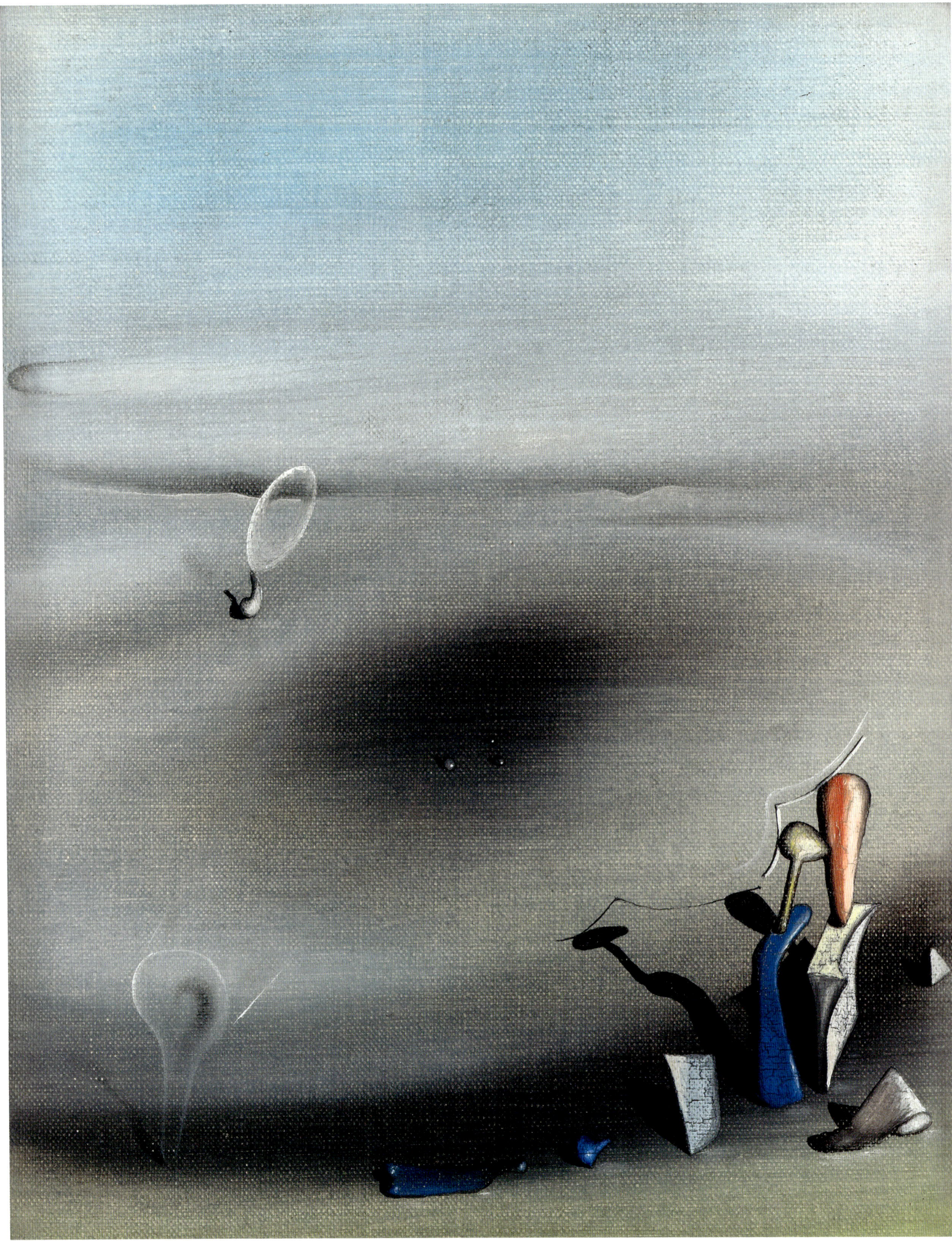

Yves Tanguy
1900, Paris, France–1955, Woodbury, CT, United States
Endless Space, 1938
Oil on canvas, 10 5/8 × 8 11/16 in. (27 × 22 cm)

Gift of Peggy Guggenheim, Venice, through the America-Israel Cultural Foundation, 1954

Endless Space is an emblematic Surrealist scene by the French-born painter Yves Tanguy: an indeterminate, eerie landscape, whose right-hand corner is populated by biomorphic forms. At the age of eight, following his father's death, Tanguy moved with his mother from Paris to the village of Locronan, in Brittany, on France's northern coast. Brittany's foggy skies and rough terrain—inhabited by polished Neolithic boulders and menhirs (upright, monumental stones positioned by prehistoric people in Western Europe)—might have influenced the melancholic mood and the sculpturelike figures painted here. He also drew inspiration from the French region's Celtic legends and folklore about an invisible otherworld.[1] Another possible influence is the geological formations Tanguy encountered in North Africa, which he visited in 1930.

Despite his lack of formal training, Tanguy gained full mastery of oil painting, and in *Endless Space*, he employed a painstakingly veristic technique to create these rock or marine forms against a softly modulated background. As alluded to by the work's title, Tanguy depicted the landscape as a single infinite entity, devoid of a horizon line dividing ground from sky. It appears tangible, but also concurrently mysterious and inexplicable. The poignant emptiness and the subtle variation of tones create a nostalgic yet obscure atmosphere which escapes rational understanding. *Endless Space* presents no evident narrative, and as with other works by Tanguy, the subject matter is less important than the mood it creates.

American art collector and patron Peggy Guggenheim donated *Endless Space* to the Tel Aviv Museum. Having met Tanguy through the filmmaker Humphrey Jennings in Paris, Guggenheim organized a solo exhibition of Tanguy's works at her Guggenheim Jeune gallery in London in 1938.

Gražina Subelytė

1 Susan Nessen, "Yves Tanguy's Otherworld: Reflections on a Celtic Past and a Surrealist Sensibility," *Arts Magazine* 62 (January 1988): 22–28.

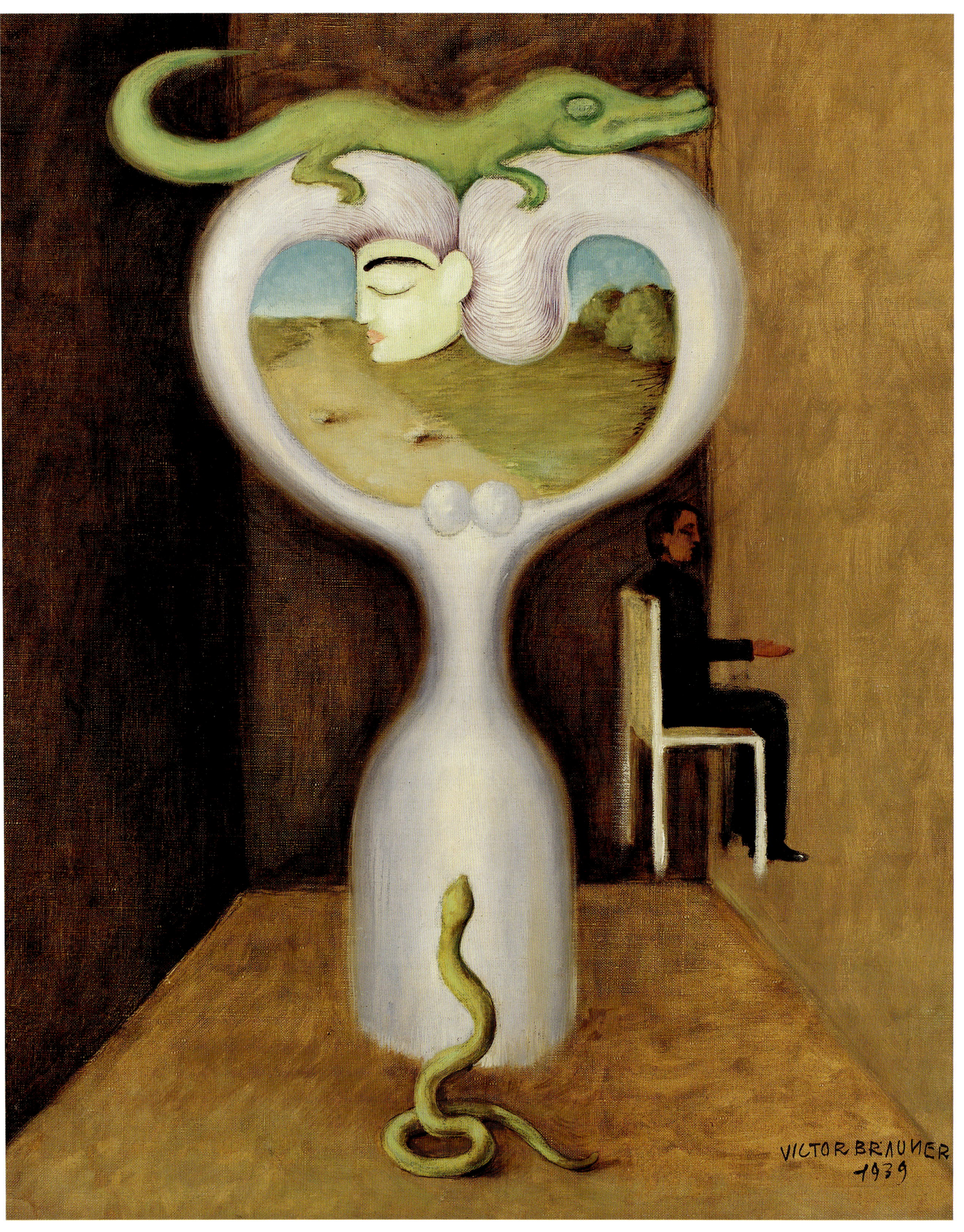
VICTOR BRAUNER
1939

Victor Brauner
1903, Piatra Neamt, Romania–1966, Paris, France
Dream Space, 1939
Oil on canvas, 21 7/16 × 17 15/16 in. (54.5 × 45.5 cm)

Mizne-Blumental Collection, Bequest of Annette Celine, 2018

Victor Brauner was exposed to the realms of the fantastic and the otherworldly through his father, a keen spiritualist. In the 1930s, when he lived between France and Romania, the subject matter of Brauner's works such as *Dream Space* was chiefly inspired by his childhood experiences as well as folklore and occult sources.

Brauner painted *Dream Space* in 1939, a year after a defining violent accident: he lost an eye while attempting to break up a fight between the painters Esteban Francés and Óscar Domínguez. This calamity proved his earlier self-portraits to be premonitory: in several of them, from as early as 1931, he is depicted with a maimed eye. Brauner believed in the incident's symbolic meaning and identified himself as a seer with prophetic vision. Likely referencing this condition in *Dream Space*, he portrayed himself on a levitating chair, with one eye closed, in the room's far right-hand corner.

This representation may also signal the transitory state between dream and reality, two alternate modes that form the basis of Surrealism, a movement that Brauner joined in Paris in 1933. He draws on the tenets that French poet André Breton, Surrealism's founder, posited in *Manifesto of Surrealism* (1924), calling for a "resolution of these two states, dream and reality, which are seemingly so contradictory, into a kind of absolute reality, a surreality."[1]

The towering central object suggests a cross between a human body and an object, possibly a mirror. The snake on the floor may allude to the serpent from the biblical story of Eden, or it might evoke a living Rod of Asclepius, the Greek deity associated with medicine. The eyes of the female face and the crocodile are both shut, reinforcing the allusion to a psychic metamorphosis, and transient states such as sleep, trance, or dream. The bottle neck, formed with hair, opens a portal to a landscape, signifying the revelation of the unconscious, or, on the contrary, a route back to reality from a dreamlike space.

Brauner dedicated the painting's preliminary draft to Jacqueline Abraham, whom he met in 1938, the year of the accident. She was to become his wife and may have been the model for the woman's face in *Dream Space*.

Gražina Subelytė

1 André Breton, *Manifestoes of Surrealism*, trans. Richard Seaver and Helen R. Lane (Ann Arbor: University of Michigan Press, 1972), 14.

Leonora Carrington
1917, Clayton-le-Woods, United Kingdom–2011, Mexico City, Mexico
With the collaboration of Max Ernst (1891, Brühl, Germany–1976, Paris, France), Marcel Duchamp (1886, Blainville-Crevon, France–1968, Neuilly-sur-Seine, France), and Roberto Matta (1911, Santiago, Chile–2002, Civitavecchia, Italy)
Summer, 1941–42
Oil on canvas, 68 ⅞ × 141 ¾ in. (175 × 360 cm)

Gift of Marya Rubinstein Bernard-Adir, New York, through the America-Israel Cultural Foundation, 1968

From the late 1930s, English-born artist Leonora Carrington was a key player in the Surrealist movement. Her work integrated influences from various phases of her life, including Celtic legends and Bible stories she heard as a child, involvement with Surrealist circles in France, artistic exchanges with her former partner, Max Ernst (pp. 190–91), and her personal tragedies. She held to a highly individual style, culled from extensive esoteric knowledge, that combined magical quotations with a fantastic iconography inspired by medieval and Renaissance art.

Having escaped war-torn Europe, Carrington stayed briefly in New York in 1941–42, before departing for Mexico. There, she created *Summer*, assisted by Ernst, Marcel Duchamp, and Roberto Matta.[1] The painting was commissioned by Manka (Marya) Rubinstein Bernard-Adir (sister of cosmetic magnate Helena Rubinstein), who ordered a mural-size painting. Carrington, perhaps as a joke, later reported that because she was short on money at the time, she painted the work on one of André Breton's bed sheets—though recent conservation has shown it is indeed painted on canvas.[2] In *Summer*, like other works, the artist invented a personal visual idiom and numerology, which appear below the date.[3]

Carrington depicted a horizontal, brightly lit landscape that is inscribed with mirror writing. On the left, it is populated by bulls; on the right, half-deer, half-human figures hang on a perch; and in the foreground, two metamorphic amphibian females, recalling mermaids, hover over a blood-red ground.[4] The latter's goddesslike attributes may stem from Carrington's reading of Robert Graves's *The White Goddess* (1948), which she described as the "greatest revelation" of her life. These figures also evoke witches, or enchantresses, which the artist herself adopted as formidable alter egos, and as embodiments of respect for nature's resources. Carrington supported ecology and women's rights—politicized subjects that she understood as inextricably linked to each other.

Ernst added his signature birdlike creature in the top left corner. This beast observes a scene in which the mystical infiltrates reality, reflecting Carrington's interest in the idea of constant magical and spiritual transformation. The animal figures, conceived in her works as superior to humans, serve as guides from earthly reality into otherworldly experience.

Gražina Subelytė

1 See letter from Inés Amor to Ephraim Adir, April 24, 1968, Tel Aviv Museum of Art Archives.
2 Salomon Grimberg, "Traveling Toward the Unknown. Leonora Carrington Stopped in New York," *Woman's Art Journal*, 38, no. 2 (Fall/Winter 2017): 9.
3 See Salomon Grimberg email to Hillary Reder, May 30, 2022, Tel Aviv Museum of Art Archives.
4 There is also a red compass surrounded by four leopard heads that float between the females. Carrington drew a similar leopard head in a sketchbook from 1940, while she was in the Santander sanatorium. See Susan Aberth email to Hillary Reder, May 31, 2022, Tel Aviv Museum of Art Archives.

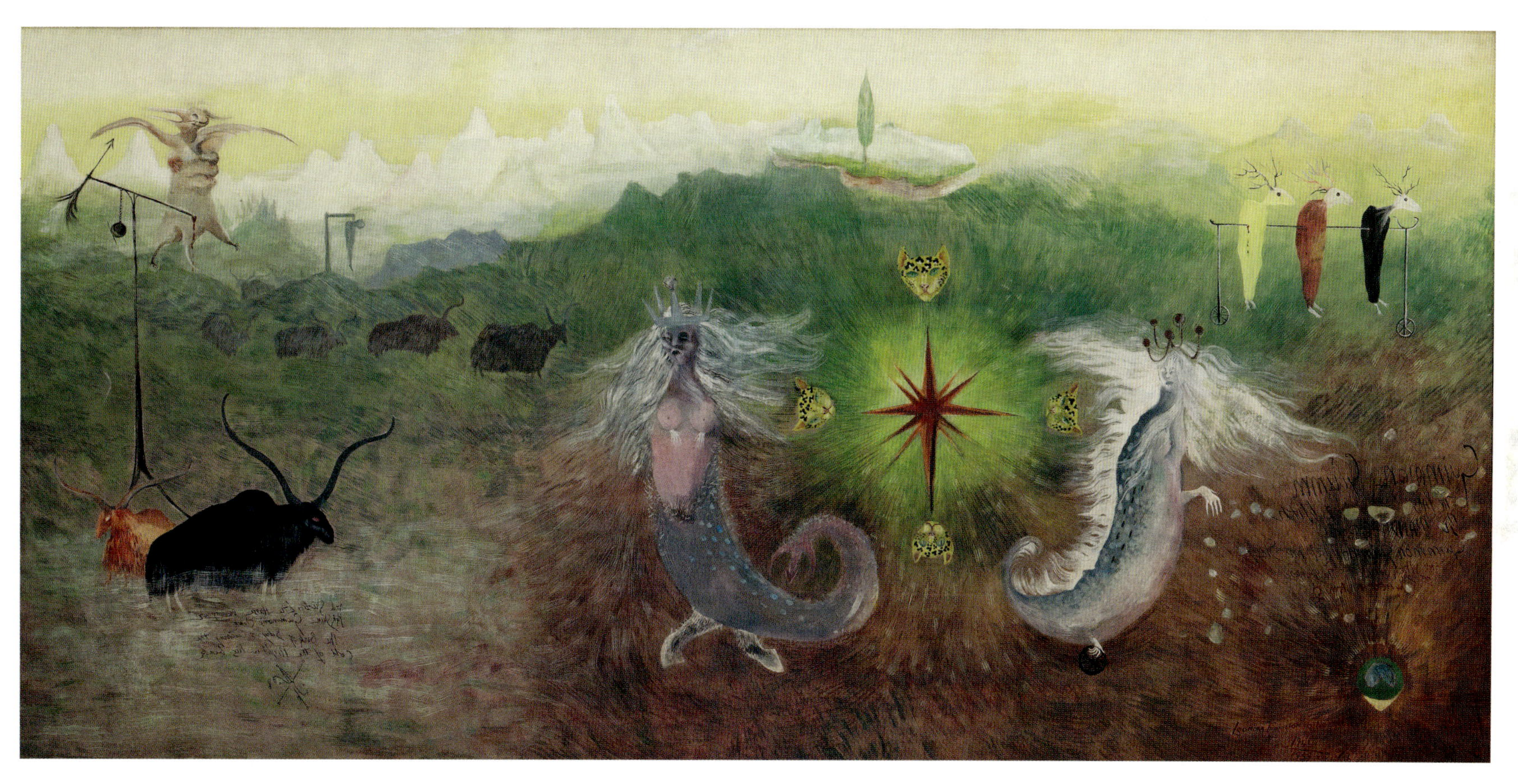

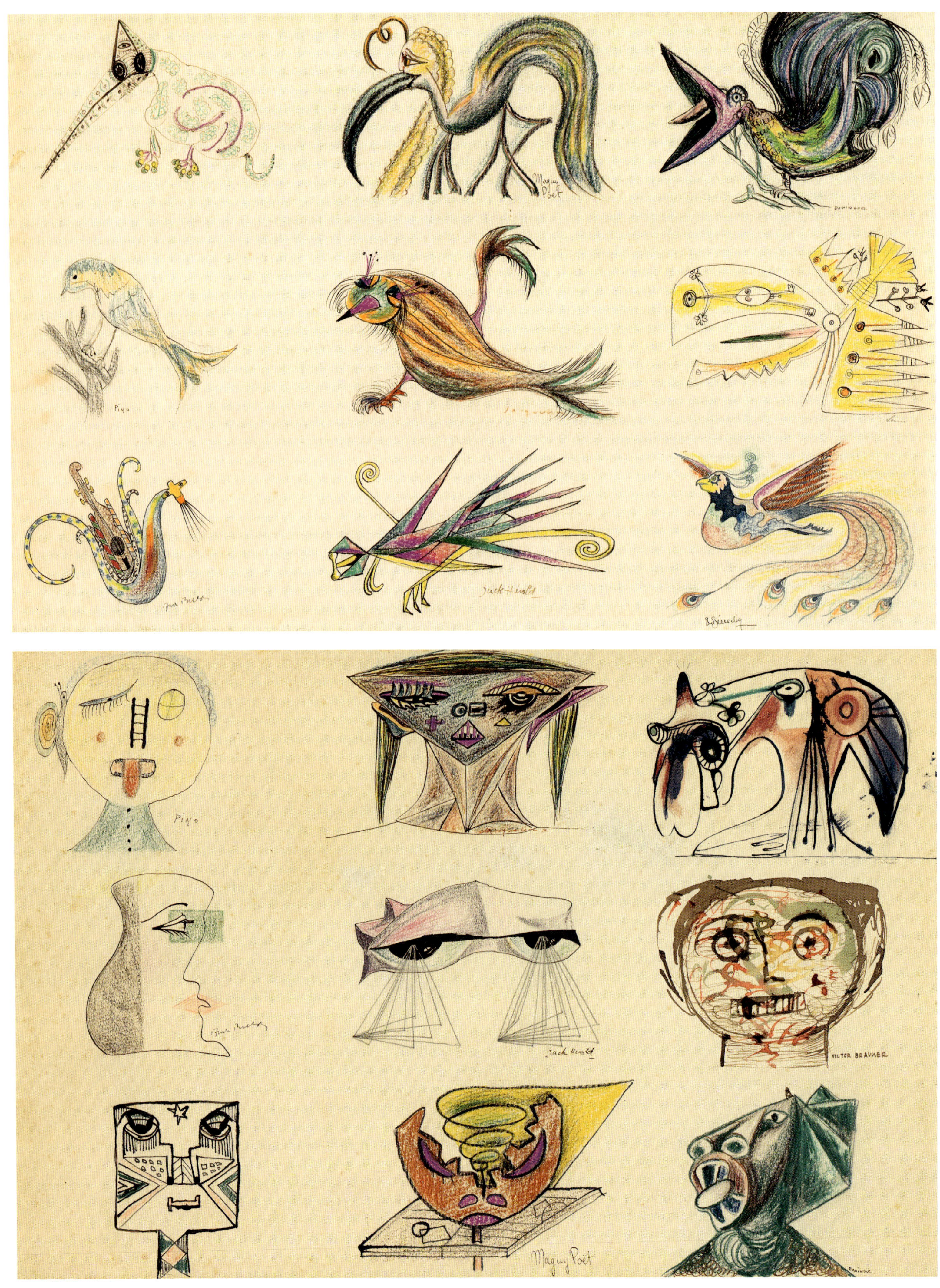
Pino
Jack Herold
Pino
Jack Herold
VICTOR BRAUNER

Surrealist Collective

Top **Untitled, 1940–41**
Ink and colored pencil on cardboard, 12 ½ × 19 1⁄16 in. (31.8 × 48.4 cm)

Bottom **Untitled, 1940–41**
Watercolor, crayon, ink, and pencil on paper, 12 3⁄8 × 19 in. (31.6 × 48.2 cm)

Gift of Peggy Guggenheim, Venice, through the America-Israel Cultural Foundation, 1954

Shortly after the start of World War II, in the winter of 1940–41, a number of Surrealists gathered in the so-called *zone libre* in Marseille, where they waited for the visas and affidavits needed to leave war-torn Europe. The group included Victor Brauner (pp. 184–85), André Breton, Óscar Domínguez, Max Ernst (pp. 190–91), Jacques Hérold, Wifredo Lam, and Jacqueline Lamba, among others.[1] Its headquarters was the Villa Air-Bel, sponsored by the US-backed Emergency Rescue Committee, which had been set up to help German refugees as well as Jewish and Communist artists and intellectuals at risk of persecution.[2] There, at this time of uncertainty and impending exile, the group engaged in collaborative social games, such as creating collective drawings that encapsulated the playful spirit of the Surrealist movement.

American art collector and patron Peggy Guggenheim gifted three Surrealist Collective drawings, two of which are shown here, to the Tel Aviv Museum. She had spent time at Villa Air-Bel and financially backed the passage of some artists and writers to the United States. Two of the drawings represent fantastic animals and birds created by the Surrealists, while the third depicts imaginary heads. The artists—who, in the case of the first two works, included Daniel Bénédite, one of the leaders of the Emergency Rescue Committee—drew inspiration from the fauna and flora in the villa's surroundings as well as its owner's collection of stuffed birds. They unleashed the potential of their imagination, depicting phantasmagorical creatures and promoting startling associations. Rather than producing a work of fine art, the drawings sought to trigger new experiences and discoveries.[3]

The nature of collective activity, going beyond what could be done by the isolated individual, reflected the solidarity of those associated with Surrealism and their wish to embrace a shared response to socio-political concerns. In their collaborative pursuits, the artists adhered to the dictum of nineteenth-century poet Lautréamont (Isidore Ducasse): "Poetry must be made by everyone. Not by one."[4] This quality was manifested not only in art making but also in co-written manifestos, group exhibitions, and public demonstrations.

Gražina Subelyté

1 For a thorough account of this period, see Martica Sawin, *Surrealism in Exile and the Beginning of the New York School* (Cambridge, MA: MIT Press, 1995).

2 The Emergency Rescue Committee was headed by Varian Fry with the assistance of Théo and Daniel Bénédite. For an account of the Surrealist activities at Villa Air-Bel, see Sheila Isenberg, *A Hero of Our Own: The Story of Varian Fry* (New York: Random House, 2001), 126–34.

3 See Christopher Buch, "Collective Identity," in *Surrealism Beyond Borders*, exh. cat., ed. Stephanie D'Alessandro and Matthew Gale (New York: The Metropolitan Museum of Art; New Haven and London: Yale University Press, 2021), 304–07, 352.

4 Isidore Ducasse, "Poésies," 1871, in *Isidore Ducasse, Maldoror and Poems*, trans. Paul Knight (London: Penguin, 1978), 279.

Max Ernst
1891, Brühl, Germany–1976, Paris, France
The Bewildered Planet, 1942
Oil on canvas, 43 5/16 × 55 1/8 in. (110 × 140 cm)

Gift of the artist, 1955

Like many Surrealists, Max Ernst fled to New York after the start of World War II, in 1941, and his uncanny dreamscapes from this time seem to reflect an existential anguish. *The Bewildered Planet* is one of the first works Ernst painted in the United States, a diptych that signals his embrace of new semi-automatic procedures. He created the network of elliptical lines—possibly representing planetary orbits—with an oscillation technique, performed by swinging a punched tin can containing liquid paint, allowing the pigment to drip onto the canvas.[1] While the desolate landscape appears primeval, it is an allegory for the rise of fascism and the ensuing catastrophic events that, as the title suggests, "bewildered" the world.

In this work, Ernst used division and contrast as organizing principles. The painting anticipates his series of works featuring a framework akin to a grid, in which rectilinear geometry clarifies the picture plane's structure. It also highlights the relentless passage of time through the artist's signature technique of decalcomania—appearing here on the ground and poles—in which paint is spread onto the canvas, and, while still wet, covered with glass, paper, or other materials, resulting in abstracted forms.

The greenish "totem" pole (stemming from Ernst's ethnographic interests) in the work's center vertically splits the sky into yellow and blue registers animated by oscillating black lines. While the right side implies a state of imbalance and illness, the left side alludes to order and cosmic harmony. The composition evokes decay and trauma, but also faith in the possibility of renewal and healing. This metaphor for struggle and eventual redemption may reflect Ernst's embrace of alchemy, an ancient branch of natural philosophy, and its core concept of infinite duality.[2] Alchemy is a metaphor for transformation, both physical and spiritual, achieved through the union of opposites, often represented as the sun and the moon, which the colors yellow and blue might respectively reference here. Additionally, these dichotomies may suggest the states of mind that Ernst's work traverses: reality and dream, the conscious and the unconscious.

Gražina Subelytė

1 Ernst's oscillation technique may have been an important influence on the artists that associated with the New York School. It is regarded as a precursor to Jackson Pollock's drip method (pp. 200–203).

2 For an elaboration on Ernst, alchemy, and Surrealism, see M. E. Warlick, *Max Ernst and Alchemy: A Magician in Search of Myth* (Austin: University of Texas Press, 2001); Gražina Subelytė and Daniel Zamani, eds., *Surrealism and Magic: Enchanted Modernity*, exh. cat. (Munich: Prestel, 2022).

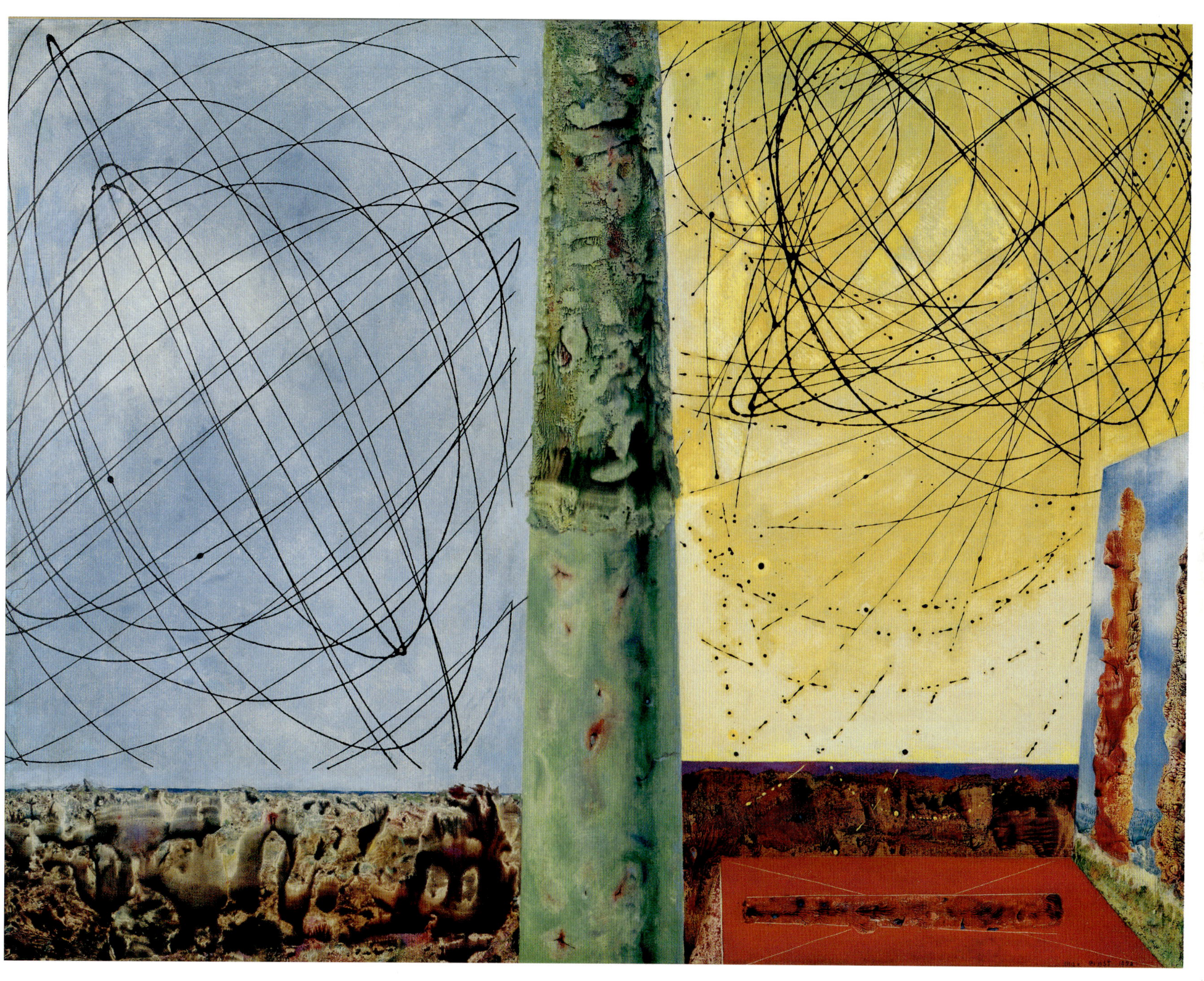

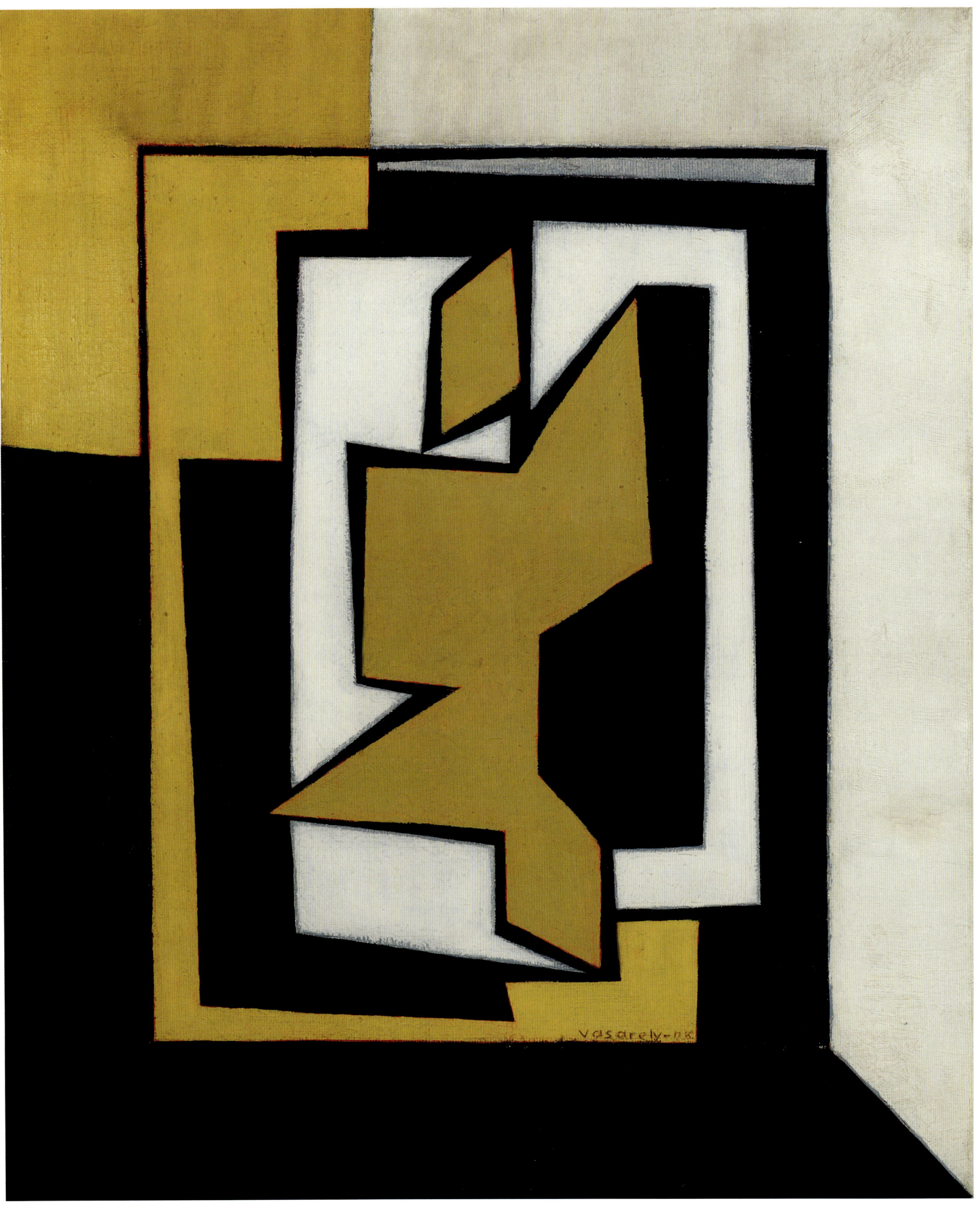
Vasarely

Victor Vasarely
1906, Pécs, Hungary–1997, Paris, France
No. 136–10F (Lombok), 1949
Oil on canvas, 20 ⅞ × 18 11⁄16 in. (53 × 47.5 cm)

Mizne-Blumental Collection, Bequest of Annette Celine, 2018

Victor Vasarely became known in the 1950s as one of the founders and leading representatives of Op Art—a movement concerned with changing optical illusions created through the juxtaposition of colors and forms. Yet Vasarely's early body of work, which includes this painting, did not derive only from his concern with pure abstraction but was also based on natural forms and phenomena. Vasarely recounted that he first became interested in visual illusions and optical deception while staying in Provence in the summer of 1948: "The towns and villages of southern France, parched by an inexorable sun, exposed me to sights that were full of contradiction. My eye never quite managed to identify what belonged to a shadow or a bare wall: filled and empty spaces intermingled, forms and backgrounds alternated."[1]

As a result of this experience, Vasarely began using bold color contrasts to simulate the play of light and shade that had so impressed him; blurring the distinction between subject and background to create an ambiguous perspective; and experimenting with angular forms.[2] He deployed all these techniques to make this painting, which is perhaps most distinguished by its unusual format: the canvas is attached to a stretcher with sloping edges. Its volume is revealed only when seen from the side—it appears completely flat when viewed frontally. The sophisticated coloring of the surfaces on the composition's margins enhances this illusion.

During this period, Vasarely titled his abstract works after places—such as cities, mountains, and rivers. Lombok, in this painting's title, is the name of an Indonesian island. Speaking of his choice of titles for his paintings, Vasarely said, "At first I used to name them for places that impressed me ... Later, I took the names of mountains, bays, or island groups from the atlas. For a rigid, dry painting, I chose a name in which consonants predominated, such as *Karst*, and for a lighter work I looked for a name with more vowels such as *Nivine*."[3] The balance between light and dark hues in *Lombok* is thus reflected in the choice of title, in which the hard consonants are softened by the vowels. In Hungarian, Vasarely's mother tongue, the meaning of the word *lombok* is "foliage"—an allusion to nature, or perhaps a mere coincidence.

Ruth Feldmann

1 Marcel Joray, *Vasarely* (Neuchâtel, Switzerland: Editions du Griffon, 1969), 29.
2 This chapter in his work is known as the Crystal-Gordes period, named for Gordes, the Provençal town where Vasarely stayed in 1948.
3 Jean-Louis Ferrier, "Interview with Vasarely," 1969, in *Vasarely*, exh. cat., ed. Helmut Leppien (Cologne: Kunsthalle Köln, 1971), 13.

Joaquín Torres-García
1874–1949, Montevideo, Uruguay
Composition in Red and Black, 1943
Oil on cardboard, 21¼ × 27 9⁄16 in. (54 × 70 cm)

Mizne-Blumental Collection, Bequest of Annette Celine, 2018

One of the most influential figures in Latin American modernism, Joaquín Torres-García was a migrant artist and theoretician who lived abroad for more than four decades (across Spain, France, Italy, and the United States) before returning to his native country in 1934, at the age of sixty. His repatriation coincided with a combative period in Latin American art discourse during which divergent idiosyncrasies ignited heated debates over the role of art, both nationally and transnationally. Torres-García played a central role in this arena of public deliberation, with significant contributions delivered through publications, lectures, and teaching. As part of this mission, he systematized his mentorship of younger Uruguayan artists through the establishment of the Association of Constructive Art, and then the Torres-García Workshop. Founded in 1943, the latter served as a collective studio and art school based on the principles of what Torres-García coined "Constructive Universalism": a compositional method in which gridlike structures contain graphic symbols of humanitarian connotations, bridging the aesthetic and metaphysical realms.

This painting on cardboard dates from 1943—a foundational year for the widespread dissemination of Torres-García's doctrine—and is a prime example of the artist's late production. The orthogonal spaces filled in pure primary colors, as well as black and white, are examples of Torres-García's embrace of Neoplasticist values. Two distinguishable circular motifs in the bottom right area suggest the presence of a locomotive and imbue the work with dynamism.[1] A symbol of modernity and progress, the locomotive appeared in Torres-García's work as early as 1916 and became a leitmotif in the paintings, drawings, and wooden toys he designed throughout his four-decade career.

The year he completed this painting, Torres-García wrote a collection of thoughts calling for artists to "feel the measurement," to "feel the geometry."[2] According to his own students' accounts, Torres-García would frequently take the compass out of their hands, and appeal to the irrational mechanisms through which he aimed to undermine mathematical methods. Indeed, Torres-García's constructivist doctrine relied on restrictive, intuitive compositional strategies while also seeking spiritual redemption through art.

Karen Grimson

1 The title of this work in the artist's catalogue raisonné, *Locomotora estructurada a cinco tonos* (Structured Locomotive in Five Tones), confirms the painting's representational nature. See "*Locomotora estructurada a cinco tonos*, 1943 (1943.80)," in *Joaquín Torres-García Catalogue Raisonné* (2015), https://www.torresgarcia.com/catalogue/entry.php.

2 Joaquín Torres-García, "Reflexiones," *Círculo y Cuadrado* (Montevideo), no. 8–10 (December 1943): 20 [Spanish, author's translation].

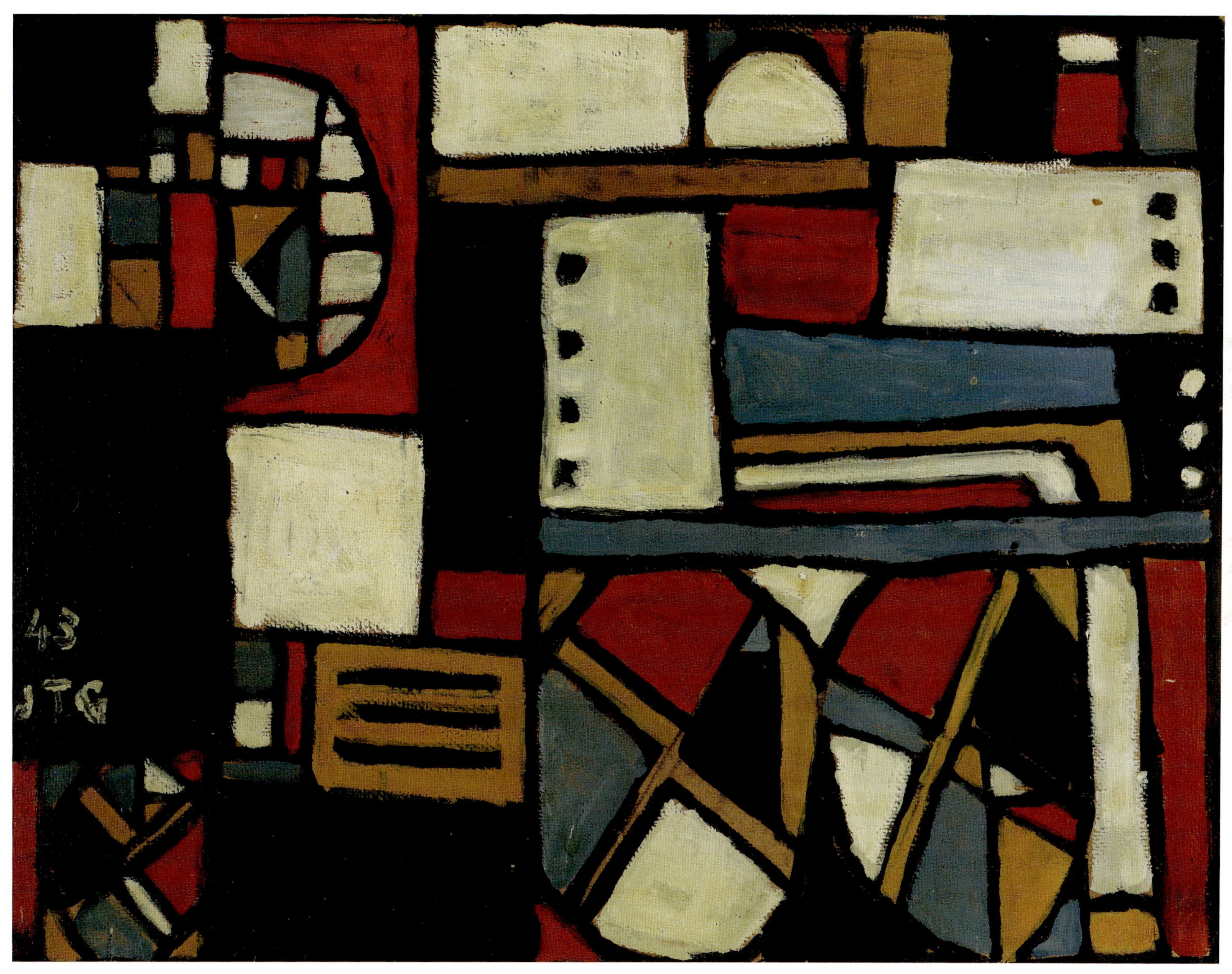
43
JTG

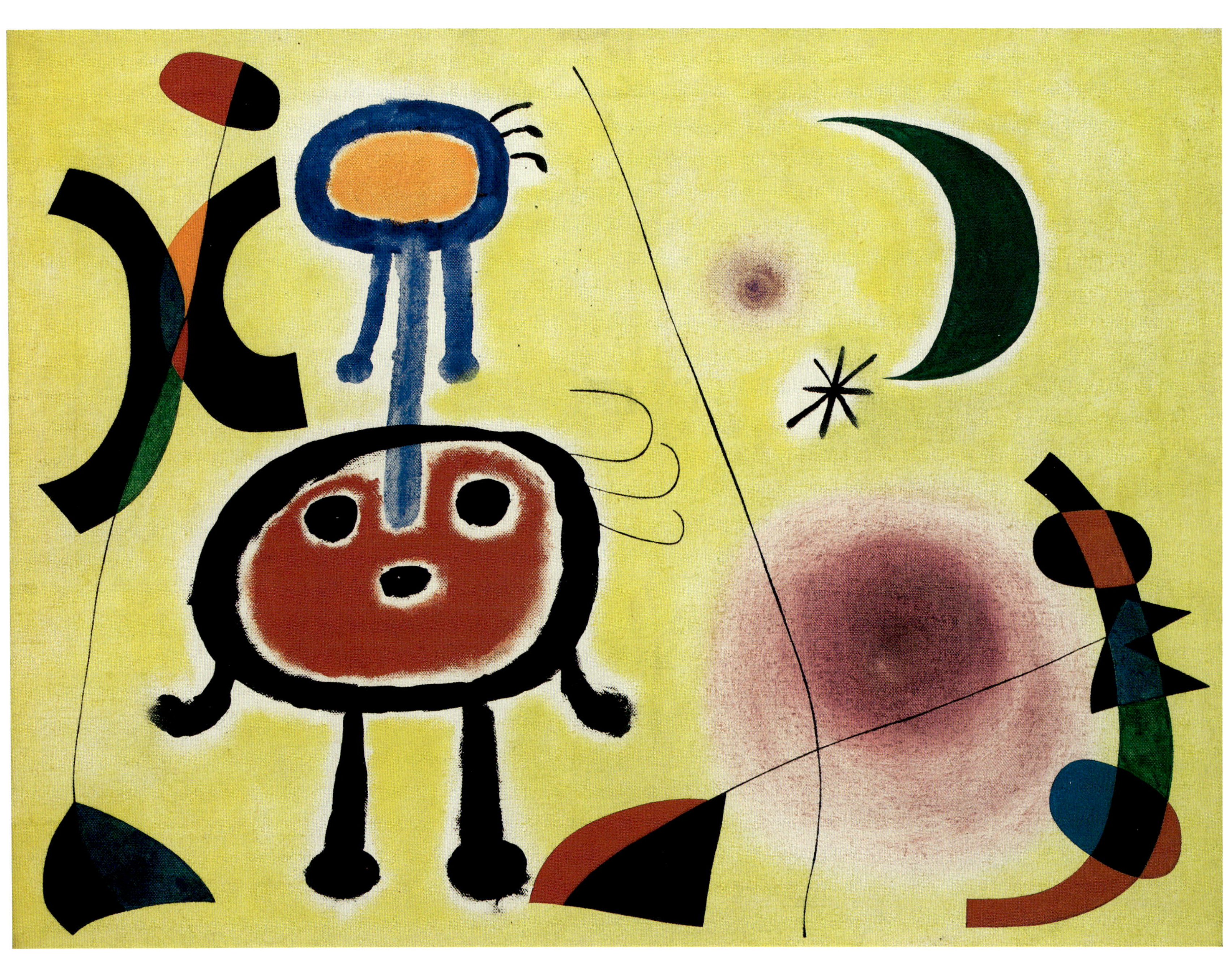

Joan Miró
1893, Barcelona, Spain–1983, Palma de Mallorca, Spain
At the Bottom of the Shell, 1948
Oil on canvas, 29 15⁄16 × 37 13⁄16 in. (76 × 96 cm)

On long-term loan from the Moshe and Sara Mayer Collection

For this painting, Joan Miró prepared a washy luminous ground on which he placed schematic figures, tailed creatures, and cosmic symbols. The elements appear held in suspension in a non-gravitational ambiguous space, an impression emphasized by the white halo surrounding several of them. Executed with a reduced palette and simplified shapes that are typical of the artist's imagery, the motifs are purposefully abstracted so as to suggest multiple readings. Miró wanted his iconography to have a universal value, once declaring that "when a viewer recognizes himself in one of my figures, he does not think about what separates him from other men, he thinks about what unites him with everyone else."[1] The central character—whose ochre-red face and graffitied appearance recall prehistoric cave paintings or children's art—can be seen, in that sense, as a symbol of elemental humanity.

Miró painted *At the Bottom of the Shell* at a moment when material and gestural improvisation began to play a larger role in his creative process. "I now felt the need to work more freely, more gaily," he explained, "the slightest thing served me as a jumping off place."[2] Miró would usually provoke "accidents, a form, a spot of color" from which he derived a more conscious organization of his motifs.[3] A sense of spontaneity and movement is thus palpable in this painting: the large plum-colored circle seems to be painted from the center outward in one decisive spiraling gesture, and the two stick figures appear to emerge from a few rapid brushstrokes. Around these dynamically sketched elements, the artist added more apparently intentional motifs, which he then carefully filled with color. This coexistence of impulsive, expressive effects and controlled forms would come to characterize much of Miró's postwar oeuvre.

Laura Braverman

1 Joan Miró, interview by Yvon Taillandier, *XXème siècle* (Paris), February 15, 1959, in Margit Rowell, *Joan Miró: Selected Writings and Interviews* (Boston: G.K. Hall & Co, 1986), 252.
2 Miró, interview by James Johnson Sweeney, *Partisan Review* 15, no. 2 (February, 1948), in Rowell, *Joan Míro*, 210.
3 Miró, interview by Georges Charbonnier, French National Radio, 1951, in Rowell, 219.

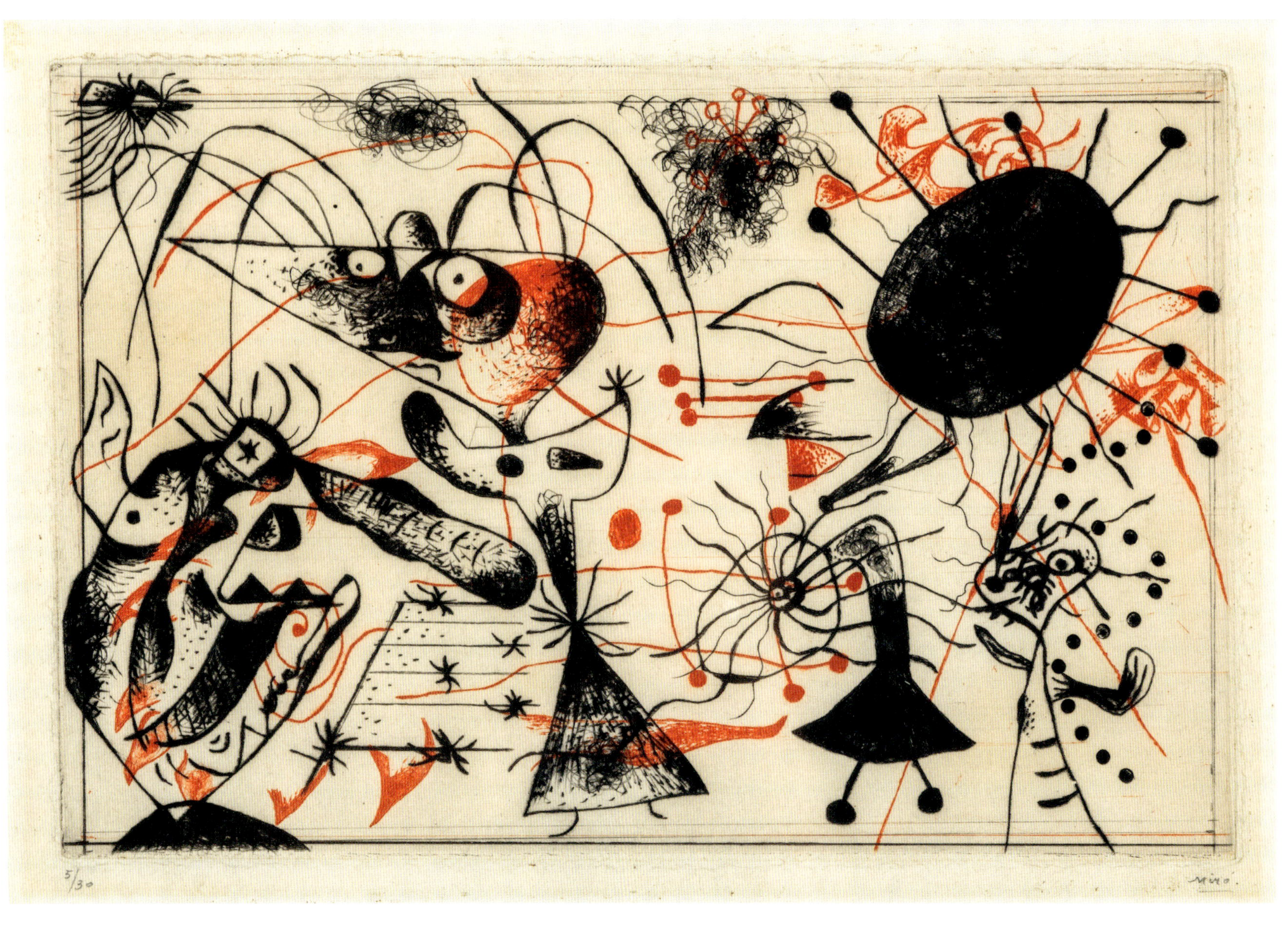
5/30
miró.

Joan Miró
1893, Barcelona, Spain–1983, Palma de Mallorca, Spain
Untitled from *Black and Red Series*, 1938
Etching, 12 13/16 × 17 3/8 in. (32.6 × 44.1 cm)
Published by Pierre Matisse, New York, and Pierre Loeb, Paris, edition of 30

Gift of Charles and Evelyn Kramer, New York, through the American Friends of the Tel Aviv Museum of Art, 1990

Joan Miró produced this print—the sixth in a group of eight titled the *Black and Red Series*—while studying etching, a technique whose experimental potential he believed would "open up new possibilities" for his practice.[1] He began this series by etching two equally sized copper plates. Alternately inking the plates in red or black, and superimposing them in different positions, Miró created eight distinct prints.

Here, the combination of both plates results in a dense and visually complex composition. Printed in black, one set of imagery appears clearly: a large blazing sun shines over four figures in various states of anguish atop what could be interpreted as a tilled field. The tallest figure raises its arms, as if to protect the two smaller characters from the monstrous, long-nosed creature on the left. Conceived at the height of the Spanish Civil War, when the artist was living in exile with his wife and daughter, the three figures have often been read as a symbolic family—and a possible allusion to Miró's own—facing the threat of violence and fascism, itself embodied by the ferocious creature.

In contrast to the figural imagery of the scene printed in black, the plate printed in red features biomorphic elements floating in an undefined space. The seemingly haphazard placement of its motifs in relation to the black figures generates new meanings. The bestial figure, for instance, is now submerged in red flames, shifting the reading of its gaping fanged mouth from threat to agony. And the tallest figure's face is here covered with a "sun-spider," whose blood-red color suggests a wound. Other celestial and birdlike motifs printed in red—pictorial elements often associated with Miró's absorption of free, Surrealist automatism—are less legible here, shrouded by the more prominent black motifs. It is as if the figural, violent reality depicted in black ink is hindering a full expression of the poetic imagination represented by the signlike motifs in red. As Miró stated at the time: "We are living through a hideous drama that will leave deep marks in our mind."[2]

Laura Braverman

1 Letter from Miró to Pierre Matisse, February 5, 1938, in Margit Rowell, *Joan Miró: Selected Writings and Interviews* (Boston: G.K. Hall & Co., 1986), 158. For more information about Miró's growing fascination with printmaking and contextual details about the *Black and Red Series* as a whole, see Deborah Wye, *Joan Miró, Black and Red Series: A New Acquisition in Context* (New York: Museum of Modern Art, 1998).

2 Letter from Miró to Pierre Matisse, February 12, 1937, in Rowell, 146.

Jackson Pollock
1912, Cody, WY, United States–
1956, Springs, NY, United States
Prism, 1947
Oil on canvas, 16 ⅛ × 18 ⅛ in. (41 × 46 cm)

Page 202 *Dancers*, 1946
Oil on canvas, 22 1⁄16 × 18 ⅛ in. (56 × 46 cm)

Page 203 *Earth Worms*, 1946
Oil on canvas, 38 3⁄16 × 26 ¾ in. (97 × 68 cm)

Gifts of Peggy Guggenheim, Venice, through the America-Israel Cultural Foundation, 1954

These three paintings by Jackson Pollock are part of the gift of thirty-six works Peggy Guggenheim made to the Tel Aviv Museum from 1954 to 1956. Guggenheim was Pollock's first dealer, and between 1943 and 1947, she paid him a monthly stipend and organized his first four solo exhibitions at her gallery, Art of this Century, significantly contributing to his ascendance. Pollock, who struggled with alcohol addiction and depression, found his sudden fame difficult, and he and his wife, the artist Lee Krasner, left New York in 1945 for the natural beauty and quiet of Springs, Long Island.

Pollock made *Dancers* and *Earth Worms* soon after they moved, a period of rare contentment for the artist. Part of a series of seven called *Sounds in the Grass*, completed in 1946, these works reflect his newfound optimism.[1] His palette became lighter and brighter, and he introduced forms inspired by his natural surroundings. The two paintings display Pollock's practice at a juncture, as he transitioned from a symbolic, Surrealist-inflected style to the purely abstract drip paintings for which he is most known. With its rhythmic, textured picture plane, *Dancers* approaches abstraction, yet the black lines cohere into stick figures wildly swinging and kicking up their feet. *Earth Worms* is made up of interlocking swirls of paint that form an all-over pattern. The only hint of figuration can be found in the title, a playful suggestion that the paint marks resemble wriggling worms.

While making the *Sounds in the Grass* paintings, Pollock began to work in his barn studio, where he dripped and poured paint onto canvas laid on the floor. *Prism*, among the earliest of the drip paintings, exemplifies this radical new approach. Skeins of thin black and white paint form a pulsating spiral, accentuated by thicker splashes of yellow, crimson, and gray. Flinging paint from a hardened brush, or perhaps spilling paint from a can in an elliptical motion, Pollock partnered with gravity, creating an image that evokes the chaos and order of a swirling cosmos.

This breakthrough abstraction, soon to be known as action painting—in which the physical act of creation is intrinsic to the final work—is considered among the most innovative of the twentieth century. Yet, Pollock was exposed to certain precedents, including Max Ernst's technique of swinging paint from a perforated can held from a string. Pollock learned about this method, which Ernst called oscillation, when he saw *The Bewildered Planet* (pp. 190–191) at Art of this Century in 1942, an encounter replayed in the Tel Aviv Museum of Art's galleries, where the Ernst painting is often hung adjacent to Pollock's works.

Hillary Reder

1 In addition to the two in the Tel Aviv Museum of Art's collection, the other five works in this series, all made in 1946, include *Shimmering Substance* at the Museum of Modern Art, New York; *Eyes in the Heat* at the Solomon R. Guggenheim Museum, New York; *Croaking Movement* at the Peggy Guggenheim Collection, Venice; *Something of the Past* at Glenstone, Potomoc, MD; and *The Blue Unconscious* in a private collection.

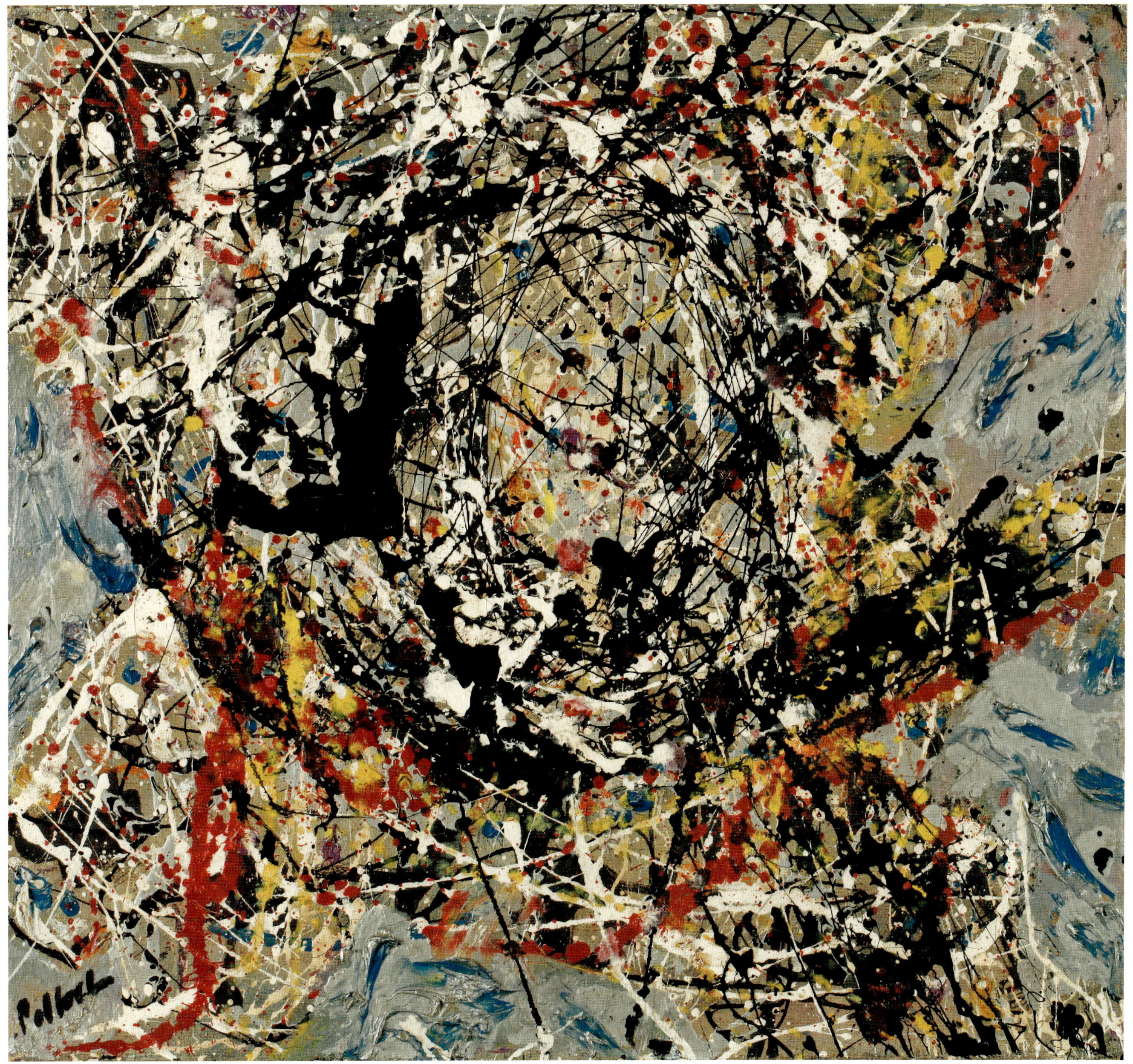

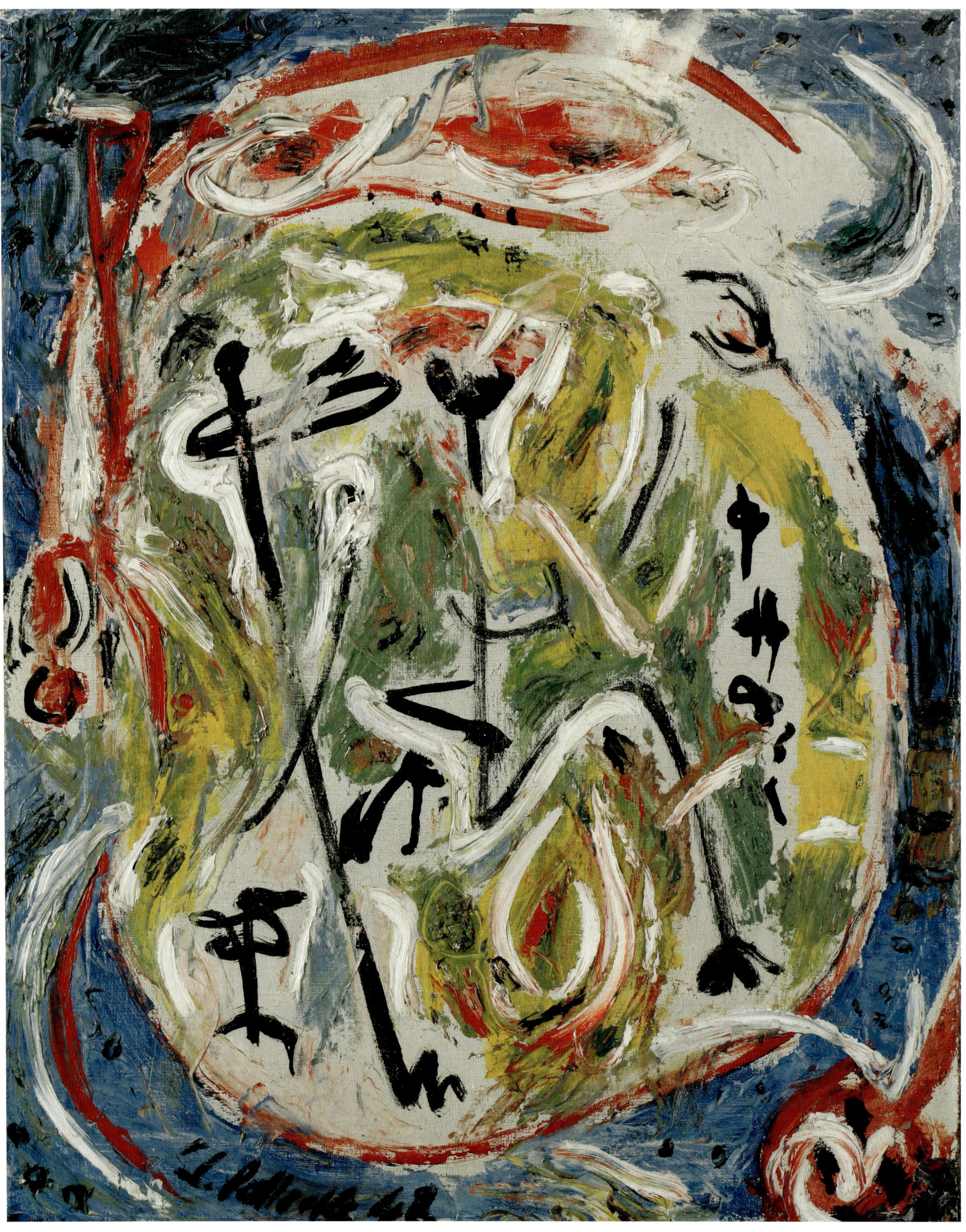

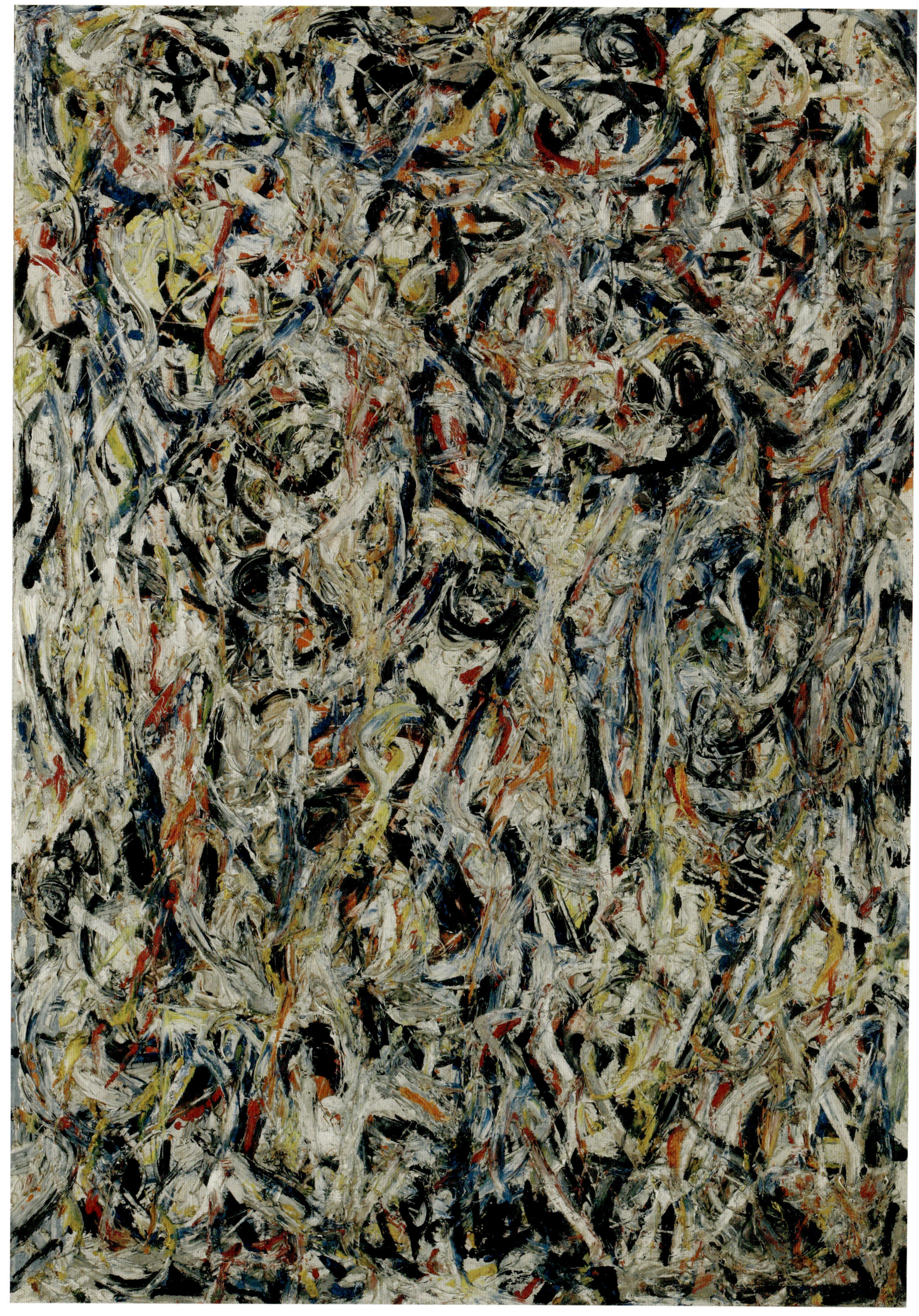

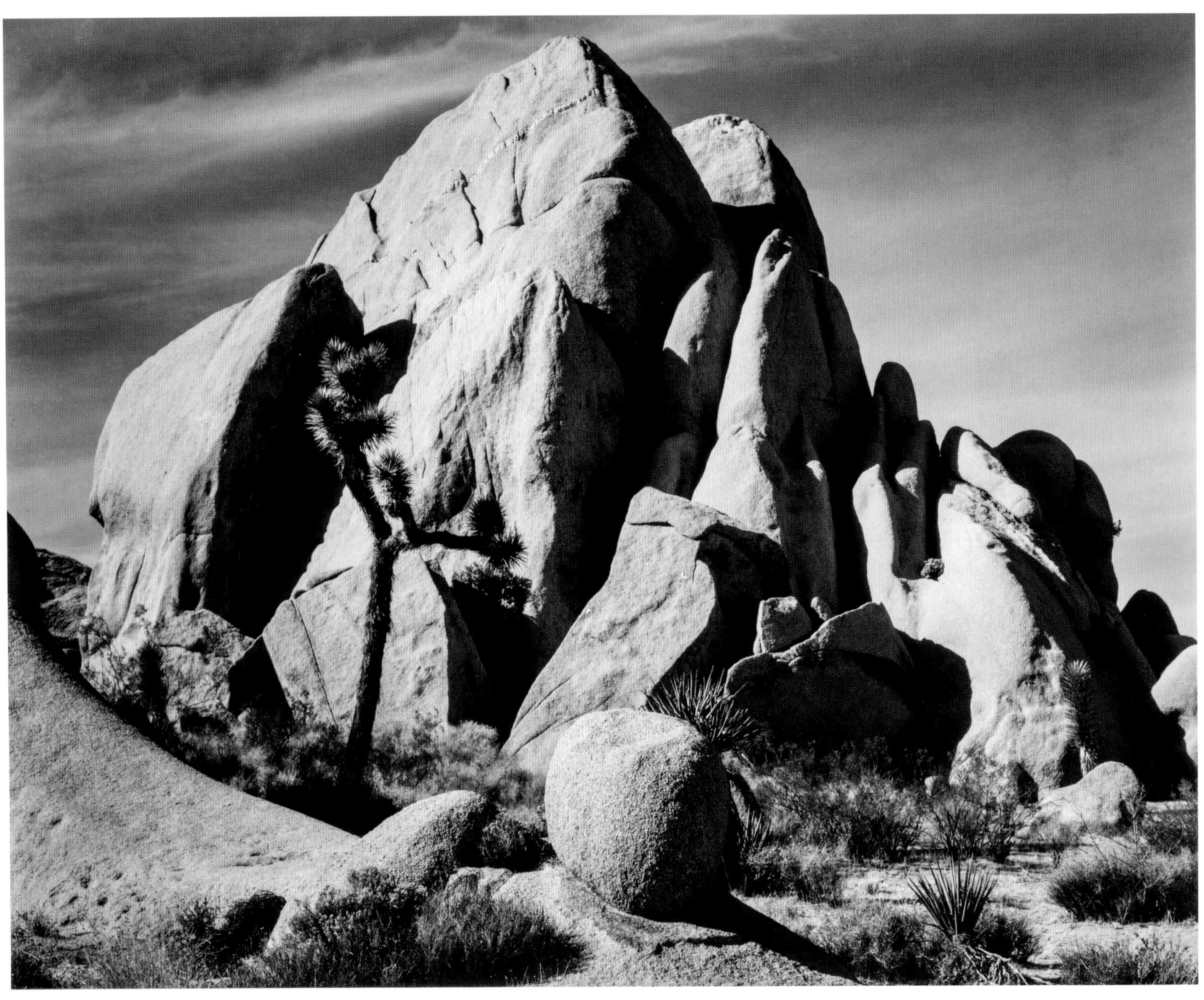

Ansel Adams
1902, San Francisco, CA, United States–
1984, Monterey, CA, United States
In Joshua Tree National Monument, California, from *Portfolio Two: The National Parks and Monuments*, 1942
Gelatin silver print, 7 ½ × 9 7⁄16 in. (19 × 24 cm)

Gift of the British Friends of the Art Museums of Israel, 1997

Ansel Adams's iconic photograph is a black-and-white panoramic view of the Joshua Tree National Park in California, and a prominent example of his unique aesthetic, techniques, and goals. From the 1940s to the 1980s, he examined the wild landscapes of the nature reserves in the American North and West through an elevated and enchanted gaze. His photographs attempt to decipher the qualities of the landscape at large and to capture its quintessentially American spirit.

Adams's quest for the intensification and spiritual experience of beauty—which he hoped would provoke in viewers an emotional response to nature's sublime magnificence—was part of his political struggle to protect and preserve America's natural environment and raise public awareness about its vital role in human life and culture. His photography, and his work with the Sierra Club, a pioneering environmental organization, played an important role in the founding of the US National Park System and in raising awareness around environmental conservation.

Designated as a national monument in 1936, Joshua Tree National Park is known for its unique geological features, including its distinctive rock formations that have been eroded by wind and water over millions of years, and the Joshua tree—a hardy, desert-dwelling species that is able to survive in harsh conditions. Adams's photograph is characterized by its clarity, sharp focus, and wide depth of field, creating a representation of a place that is both symbolic and realistic, abstract and specific. The Joshua tree has been considered a symbol of strength and resilience in American culture, of flourishing borne through perseverance. It also has played an important role in the cultural and spiritual traditions of the indigenous peoples of the region for thousands of years.

Using a large-format view camera, Adams's image features a dark Joshua tree with twisted branches and a textured trunk, positioned off-center to the left of the frame, set against the desert mountains and rocks. The contrast between the dark tree and the bright background, and the rich tonal range of shades of gray in the sky and clouds, create a dramatic, dynamic scene that conveys the rugged beauty of the desert landscape.

Ayelet Carmi

Alice Neel
1900, Merion Square, PA, Unites States–
1984, New York City, NY, United States
Tony Mattei, 1940
Oil on canvas, 30 ½ × 24 in. (77.5 × 61 cm)

Gift of Dr. Alvin I. and Edith Orlian, New York, through the Tel Aviv Museum of Art American Friends, 2021

Alice Neel invited friends, family, lovers, artists, left-wing politicians, and neighbors into her studio, painting them with humor and warmth to create some of the most singular portraits of the twentieth century. Here, she depicts a man named Tony Mattei with a resigned expression, his lips tightly pursed and his left eyebrow raised quizzically. His right leg is hiked up at a surprising angle, lending this frontal portrait an air of spontaneity. Mattei wears a crumpled brown suit with a crimson necktie, which along with the sienna background amplifies the yellowish browns, tans, and oranges of his complexion. These tones project a muted autumnal harmony that is pierced by his extraordinary aquamarine eyes. Like many of Neel's paintings, a lack of finish imbues the work with a lifelike, slightly jarring quality.

While nothing of his demeanor or clothing strongly suggests Mattei's profession, he was a fellow painter. Like Neel, Mattei was employed by the WPA Federal Art Project, a Depression-era New Deal program that guaranteed artists a monthly income, as well as a supply of 24 × 30-inch canvases, such as the one used here. While little is known about their relationship, both artists shared a commitment to representational art at a time when abstraction was ascendant. As a realist painter who resisted prevailing styles and normative renderings of the body in her work, and as a woman who navigated the macho mid-century New York art world, Neel struggled early in her career. She worked in near obscurity from the 1920s to the 1950s, gaining renown only late in her life.

Neel would have painted Mattei in her studio. A skilled conversationalist, she used this talent to put her models at ease, allowing their authentic body language to emerge. Neel sought, above all, to represent her models for who they were: embracing all that was peculiar, honest, and real. She infused her works with her belief that "you can't leave humanity out. If you don't have humanity, you don't have anything."[1]

Hillary Reder

1 Neel, quoted in Cindy Nemser, "Alice Neel: Portraits of Four Decades," *Ms. Magazine*, April 1973, 53.

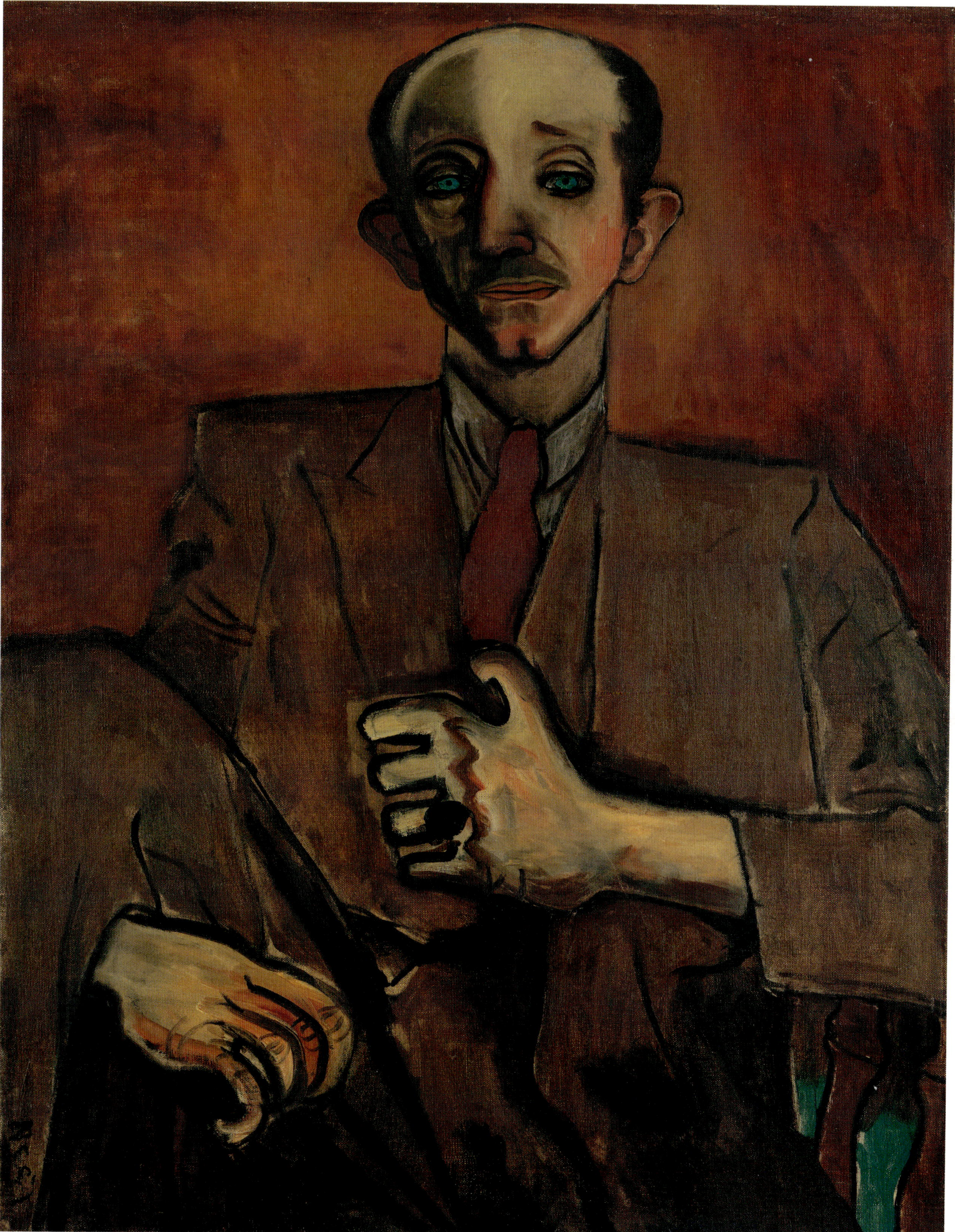

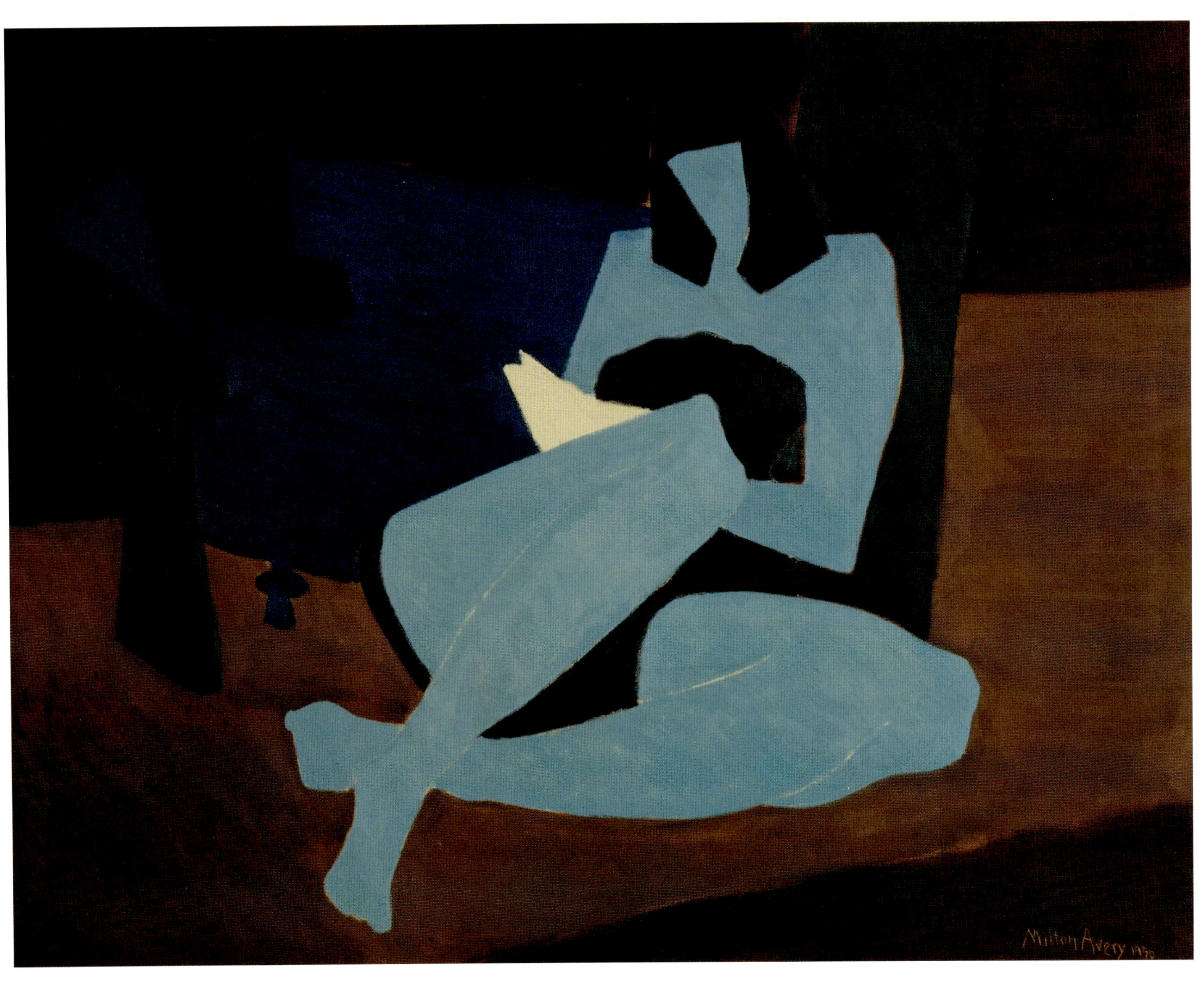
Milton Avery

Milton Avery
1885, Altmar, NY, United States–
1965, New York, NY, United States
Summer Reader, 1950
Oil on canvas, 34 × 44 in. (86.3 × 111.7 cm)

Gift of Susan and Anton Roland-Rosenberg, Los Angeles, 1996

Something of an uncategorizable artist, Milton Avery had no interest in helping others place his work. As he once famously asked, "Why talk when you can paint?" Above all, Avery sought to depict the essence of form and color in painting, creating a reflection of his experience of reality through formal means. An idealist who remained faithful to his values and independent vision throughout his career, Avery combined pure aesthetics with fidelity to the depicted subject. He formed a crucial bridge between early twentieth-century American realism and Abstract Expressionism.

While Avery's early works were anchored in the daily life of New York, his focus soon shifted to landscapes, ocean views, still lifes, and figure studies. By the 1940s, influenced by European artists such as Henri Matisse (pp. 120–23) and Pablo Picasso (pp. 124–31), he began to explore the possibilities of abstraction. Avery's simplified, harmonious forms, along with his innovative approach to composition—his scenes, with thin paint application and subtle, matte colors, appear flattened out—demonstrate his sophisticated knowledge of European modernism at a time when it was far from mainstream in American art. His emphasis on surface and use of color juxtapositions made his work an essential reference for the Abstract Expressionists. In particular, color field painters such as Mark Rothko (pp. 210–11) and Barnett Newman regarded him as a mentor and drew on his work as a source for their own attempts to capture the sublime.

Although his work grew increasingly abstract over the years, it always maintained a discernible link to realism and figuration. In *Summer Reader*, Avery depicted his daughter, March. A few months earlier, he had suffered a heart attack and was advised to restrict his physical activities. He spent the summer with his wife and March at an artists' colony in Woodstock, New York, where he made this painting. The dramatic reduction of elements in the composition and the use of diluted paint accentuate the blue figure with her bright white book against the background, but also fuse her with it, conveying the calm, inner world of reading. Avery's ability to explore the language of abstraction, while still representing human experience and reality, distinguishes his work as pivotal in the history of American modernism.

Tal Lanir

Mark Rothko
1903, Dvinsk, Russian Empire (now Daugavpils, Latvia)–1970, New York, NY, United States
Number 24 (Untitled), 1951
Oil on canvas, 93 ¼ × 47 ½ in. (236.9 × 120.7 cm)

Gift of the Mark Rothko Foundation, Inc., New York, through the American Friends of the Tel Aviv Museum of Art, 1986

Mark Rothko was one of the foremost exponents of color field painting, a manifestation of Abstract Expressionism that is distinct from gestural abstraction or action painting. Searching for a way to express a yearning for transcendence and the infinite, these artists focused on the contemplative power of color and deployed it in large fields that would engulf the viewer when seen at close range.

This work is a prime example of the compositional structure that Rothko began exploring in 1947. Narrowly separated rectangular color blocks with soft and irregular edges hover, one over the other, against a colored ground. They appear to vibrate, creating an optical flicker. In fact, the canvas is full of gentle movement, as color areas seem to emerge and recede, and surfaces breathe. Just as edges tend to fade and blur, the faint unevenness in the colors' intensity introduces ambiguity, a shifting between solidity and impalpable depth. These subtle effects do not diminish the contemplative stillness exuded by the work in its totality.

The sense of boundlessness in Rothko's paintings has been associated with the aesthetics of the sublime, an implicit or explicit concern of several of his fellow painters in the New York School. In fact, color was for him only a means to a greater end—or, as he put it, a vehicle designed to express "basic human emotions."[1] He regarded the light that appears to emanate from the painting as an embodiment of inner light, a key to emotion and spirituality.

Ruth Feldmann

1 Rothko, quoted in "Notes from a Conversation with Selden Rodman, 1956," in Mark Rothko, *Writings on Art*, ed. Miguel López-Remiro (New Haven and London: Yale University Press, 2006), 119.

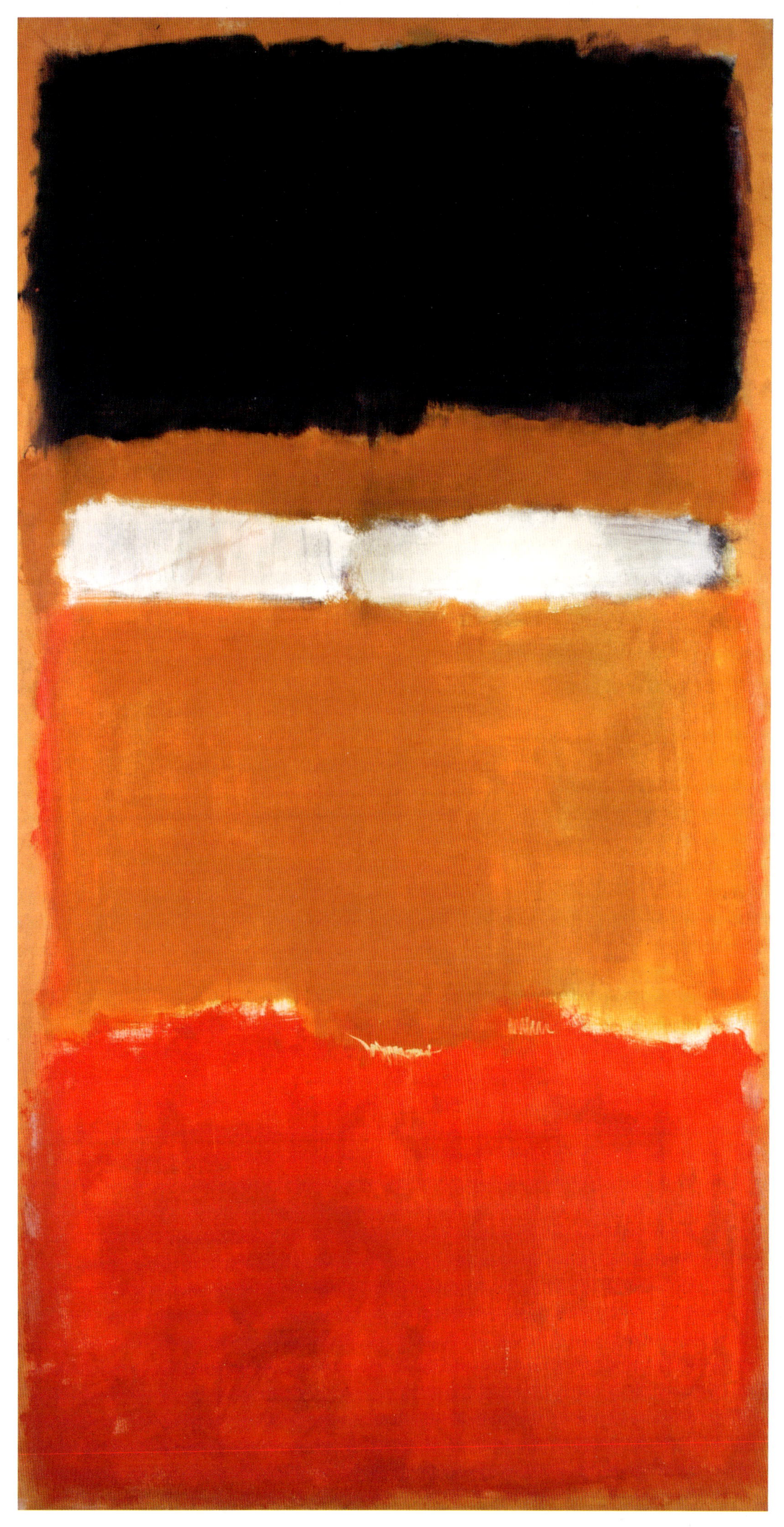

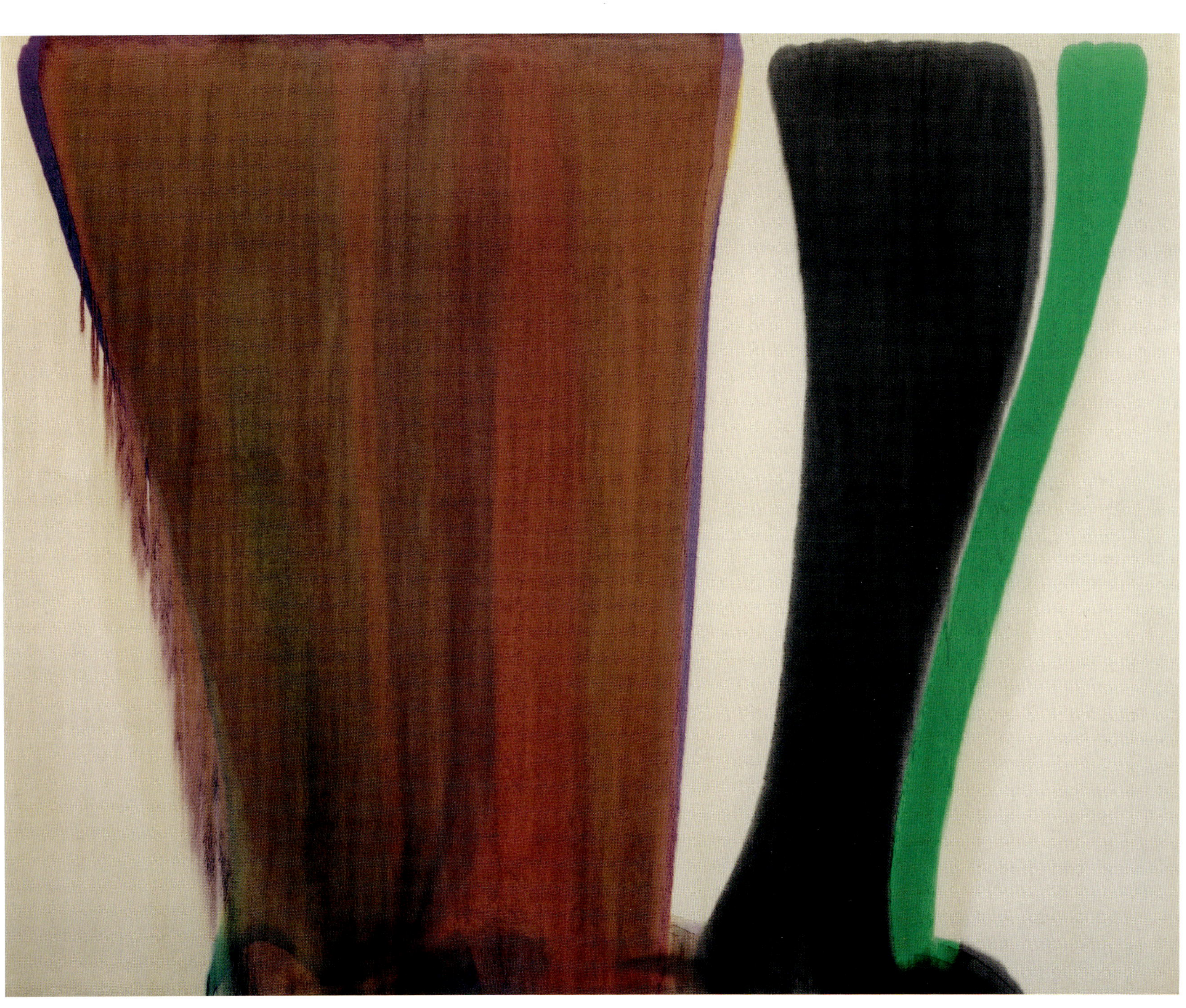

Morris Louis
1912, Baltimore, MD, United States–1962, Washington, D.C., United States
Dalet Tzadi, 1958
Acrylic on canvas, 97 5⁄8 × 142 1⁄8 in. (248 × 361 cm)

Gift of Susan and Anton Roland-Rosenberg, Los Angeles, through the American Friends of the Tel Aviv Museum of Art, 1996

Morris Louis made *Dalet Tzadi*[1] by pouring streams of thinned-out, fluid acrylic paint onto canvas, using the pull of gravity to create luminous washes of color that pool together at the painting's bottom edge. The shapes resemble billowing, translucent swaths of fabric, an effect emphasized by the title of this painting's series, *Veils* (1954, 1958–59). Although Louis never allowed anyone to observe him working, nor detailed his techniques in writing, certain aspects of his process are known. He started by loosely affixing canvas to a stretcher, which he tilted as he worked. He poured bright colors first, which he then often obscured with darker pours, lending the veil paintings a mystical quality, a sense that they glow from within.

It is unusual, then, that Louis preserved the brilliance of the forest-green pour here, rather than veiling it in darker tones. Just a sliver of bare canvas separates it from the middle pour, a rich near-black that likewise seems to be constituted of a single color. The crimson pour comprises purples, pinks, oranges, and even some green. Unlike most of his veils, whose pours stretch over the expanse of the canvas, large portions of the canvas are left visible in *Dalet Tzadi*. Despite the strong contrast between the painted and unpainted sections, they possess the same matte, velvety appearance—Louis used unprimed canvas, allowing the paint to be absorbed deep into its fibers.

The optical and physical flatness of the veil paintings was a significant breakthrough. A leading proponent of color field painting, Louis moved away from the gestural work of the Abstract Expressionists, instead creating uninterrupted, smooth expanses of color that limit traces of the artist's hand. Art critic Clement Greenberg recognized the quietly radical nature of Louis's brushless technique, which upended the conventional relationship of paint to canvas and figure to ground:

> *Louis spills his paint on unsized and unprimed cotton duck canvas, leaving the pigment almost everywhere thin enough, no matter how many different veils of it are superimposed, for the eye to sense the threadedness and wovenness of the fabric underneath. But "underneath" is the wrong word. The fabric, being soaked in paint rather than merely covered by it, becomes paint in itself, color in itself. . .*[2]

Hillary Reder

1 While Louis left many of his paintings untitled, after his death, his widow, Marcella Louis Brenner, titled the veil paintings with letters from the Hebrew alphabet, including this work, *Dalet Tzadi*.

2 Clement Greenberg, "Louis and Noland," *Art International* 4 (May 1960): 28.

Helen Frankenthaler
1928, New York, NY, United States–
2011, Darien, CT, United States
Cinerama, 1957
Oil on canvas, 11 13⁄16 × 61 13⁄16 in. (30 × 157 cm)

Gift of the artist, through the America-Israel Cultural Foundation, 1960

Cinerama's dramatically wide format is filled with unexpected compositional weights and counterweights. The canvas, soaked in azure and amber, is divided into two abutting fields of color. Yet the work reads as a triptych, too: a prominent vertical brushstroke divides the larger, amber color field, suggesting three distinct, unfolding "scenes." Instead of narrative moments, however, viewers are presented with gestural experiments. On the left, impasto dabs of white are placed atop subtly accrued layers of blue. In the center, a red, circular, calligraphic form radiates beside a nearly transparent, ethereal wash, produced by a thinning agent like kerosene or turpentine. On the right, different monochrome forms, placed side by side, toy with our perception of perspectival depth.

In its dimension and form, *Cinerama* exemplifies how Frankenthaler, like other Abstract Expressionists, looked to European landscape traditions, transforming their character to newly sublime effects. Yet the motive for such immersive views is equally located in the cultural zeitgeist of the 1950s, as suggested by the title: Cinerama was a new, wide-format theater design with a curved screen, consisting of three projectors, and seven speakers, that produced an engrossing image and surround-sound experience for its audience.[1] For the artist, this technology's effects would remain a metaphor and reference for her painting in the coming decades when conceiving of the possibilities of horizontal formats.[2]

Frankenthaler's painting techniques in the 1950s reflect her engagement with contemporaneous discourses around abstraction and gesture. Marking her presence before the canvas, Frankenthaler also strove to evoke imminently interior worlds—qualities that would carry through to her signature, monumental works defined by lush fields of pigment.[3]

Levi Prombaum

1 See John Belton, "Glorious Color, Breathtaking Cinemascope and Stereophonic Sound," in *The Classic Hollywood Reader*, ed. Steve Neal (London: Routledge, 2012), 359.

2 See, for example, E.A. Carmean, Jr., exh. cat., *Helen Frankenthaler: A Paintings Retrospective* (New York: Museum of Modern Art, 1989), 60.

3 See Christa Noel Robbins, *Artist as Author: Action and Intent in Late-Modernist American Painting* (Chicago: University of Chicago Press, 2021), 76.

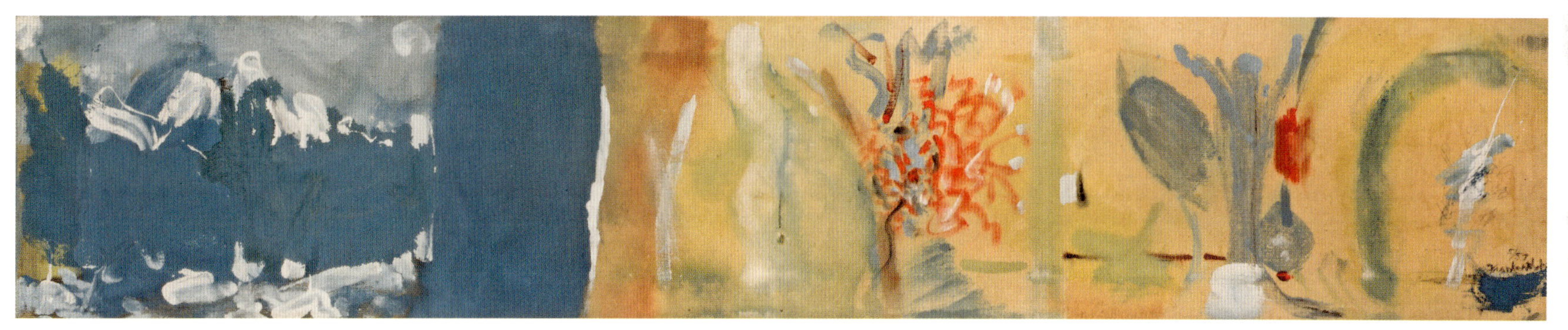

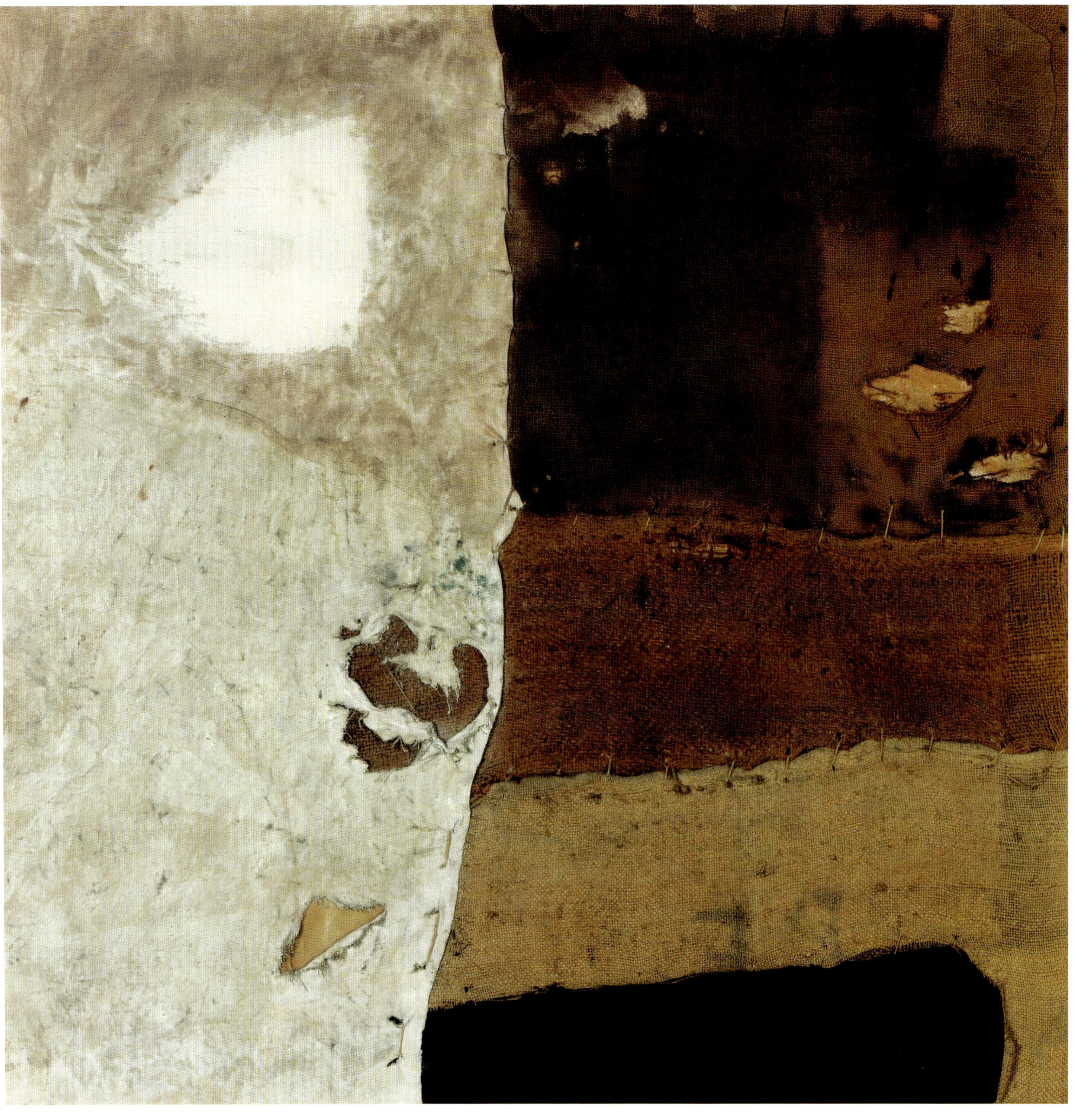

Alberto Burri
1915, Città di Castello, Italy–1995, Nice, France
Sack, 1951
Burlap, fabric, and oil on canvas, 35 7/16 × 35 7/16 in. (90 × 90 cm)

Bequest of Richard S. Zeisler, New York, through the American Friends of the Tel Aviv Museum of Art, 2008

Alberto Burri, a physician by training, served in the Italian army during World War II. He was captured by the Allies and interned for eighteen months in a prisoner-of-war camp in Texas, where he began painting, without prior training. Upon his release and return to Italy in 1946, he settled in Rome and became involved in the city's blossoming postwar cultural scene. He initiated a practice characterized by creative autonomy and innovation, and a poetic, sensuous approach to materials. In 1949 he traveled to Paris for the first time and became acquainted with Art Informel—with which Burri's work is now associated—a diverse style that spanned various trends in European abstraction in the 1940s and 1950s, and rejected logic in favor of intuition and expression.

This work is part of Burri's best-known series, *Sacchi* (Sacks), which was initiated in 1949 with the work *SZ1*, initials for *sacco di zucherro*, or "sack of sugar." When Burri returned from captivity, he brought a bundle of sacks from the POW camp kitchen—while interned, he used them as makeshift canvases. Back in Rome, he began to deconstruct them, stretching and tearing them and then gluing or stitching the pieces to his canvases, interspersed with planes of monochromatic paint, usually browns, whites, and blacks. Combining paint and found materials in this way, he created hybrid collage-paintings that defy traditional art historical categories.

Burri sought to emphasize the materiality and the physical presence of his works. Calling himself a "polymaterialist," he intermixed diverse mediums in an alchemical process that resulted in dynamically alive objects, particularly resonant in the postwar era. The damaged surfaces and rough seams in the sack series perhaps can be seen as the reflection of a wounded soul seeking renewal or redemption. The stitches holding the pieces of burlap together convey a dual sense of fragility and strength, while the intentionally accentuated tears in the painting reveal its underlayer, recalling an open wound. And yet, for Burri, his work was not meant to transmit messages—the materiality of the work represents only itself, and is not a metaphor for anything else. As he once explained, "The words don't mean anything to me; they talk around the picture. What I have to express appears in the picture."[1]

Alisa Padovano-Friedman

1 Burri, quoted in Milton Gendel, "Burri Makes a Picture," *Art News* 53, no. 8 (Dec. 1954): 67.

Giorgio Morandi
1890–1964, Bologna, Italy

Top *Still Life*, 1946
Oil on canvas, 10 ½ × 23 ⅛ in. (26.7 × 58.8 cm)

Gift of Susan and Anton Roland-Rosenberg, Los Angeles, through the American Friends of the Tel Aviv Museum of Art, 1996

Bottom *Still Life with Bottles and Vase*, 1951
Oil on canvas, 13 × 16 15/16 in. (33 × 43 cm)

Bequest of Alma Morgenthau, New York, through the America-Israel Cultural Foundation, 1955

Giorgio Morandi was known as "il monaco," or "the monk," for his quiet lifestyle and total commitment to his work. His studio—which doubled as his bedroom—was full of various objects that also became the subjects of his paintings, including bottles, receptacles, jugs, vases, boxes, and kitchen utensils. He arranged these objects to form a given composition, contemplated them, moved them around, drew preliminary sketches for days on end—and then painted the work rapidly, confidently, and with absolute control in one session, without pentimenti. No hint of pathos or emotion ever penetrated his paintings, which are devoid of allusions to the ephemeral, the fleeting, or the variable.

Morandi drew his inspiration from various sources, and took special interest in Renaissance artists and Paul Cézanne (pp. 30–31). Like them, what he sought in objects was their stability, their solidity, and the geometrical forms hidden within them.

From 1940 on, Morandi painted a series of works in which he repeated the same composition over and over again with a restless obsession and only slight variations. In the two paintings here, which are part of this body of work, objects stand upright on a smooth, bare surface, in a narrow space that can be encompassed in a single glance. The palette, muted, restrained, and non-sensual, is characterized by hues of brown, off-white, and beige. The everyday objects, which were painted inside the artist's most intimate living space, have been taken out of context so that we may concentrate on their shapes. They have been stripped of any superfluous elements and abstracted in a manner that preserves only their basic contours, as if only the idea of the object remained.

Morandi sought to raise the concrete object to the level of an enigmatic, metaphysical expression, which would reveal a new and more profound meaning in it. His works compel us to pause, observe, and contemplate.

Alisa Padovano-Friedman

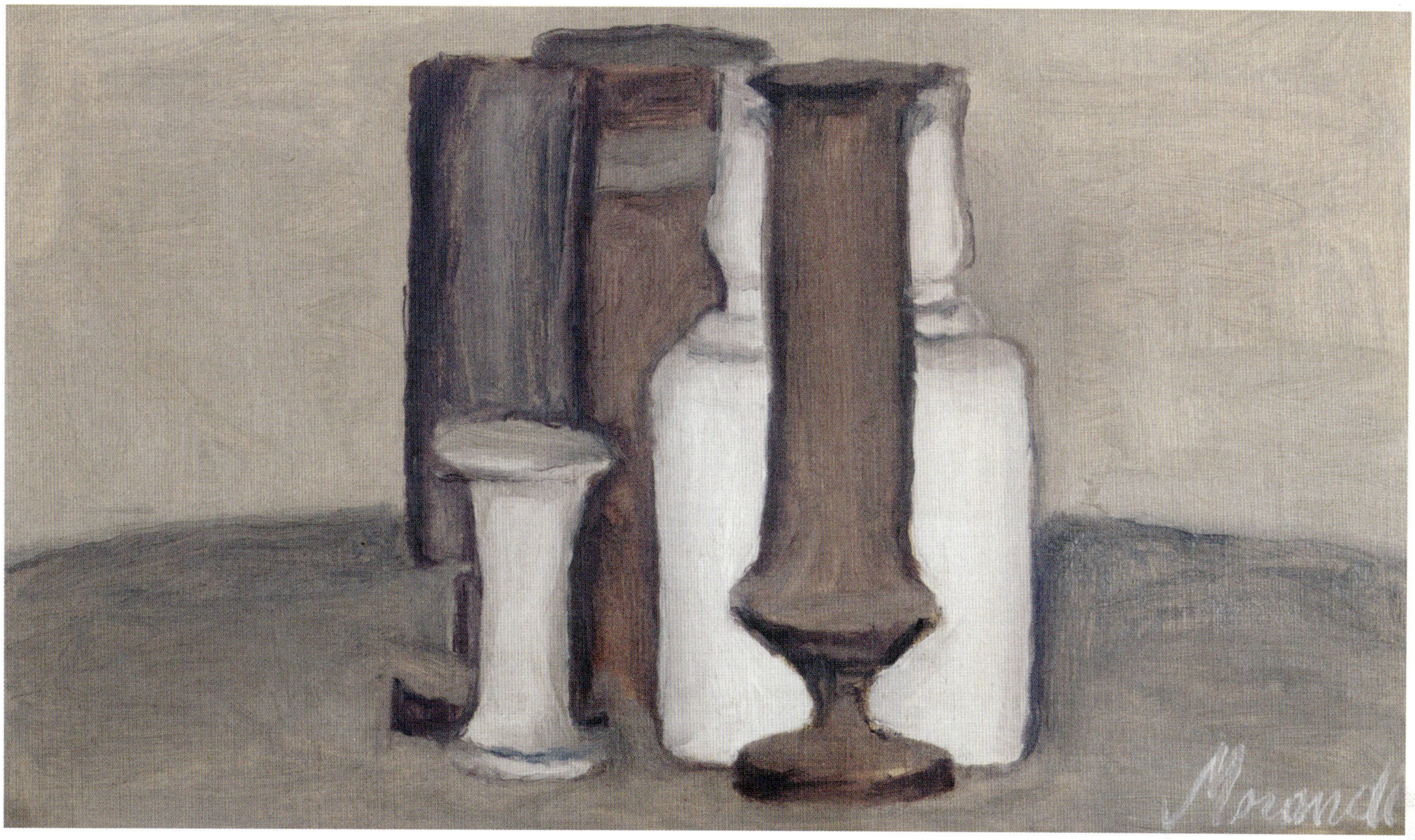

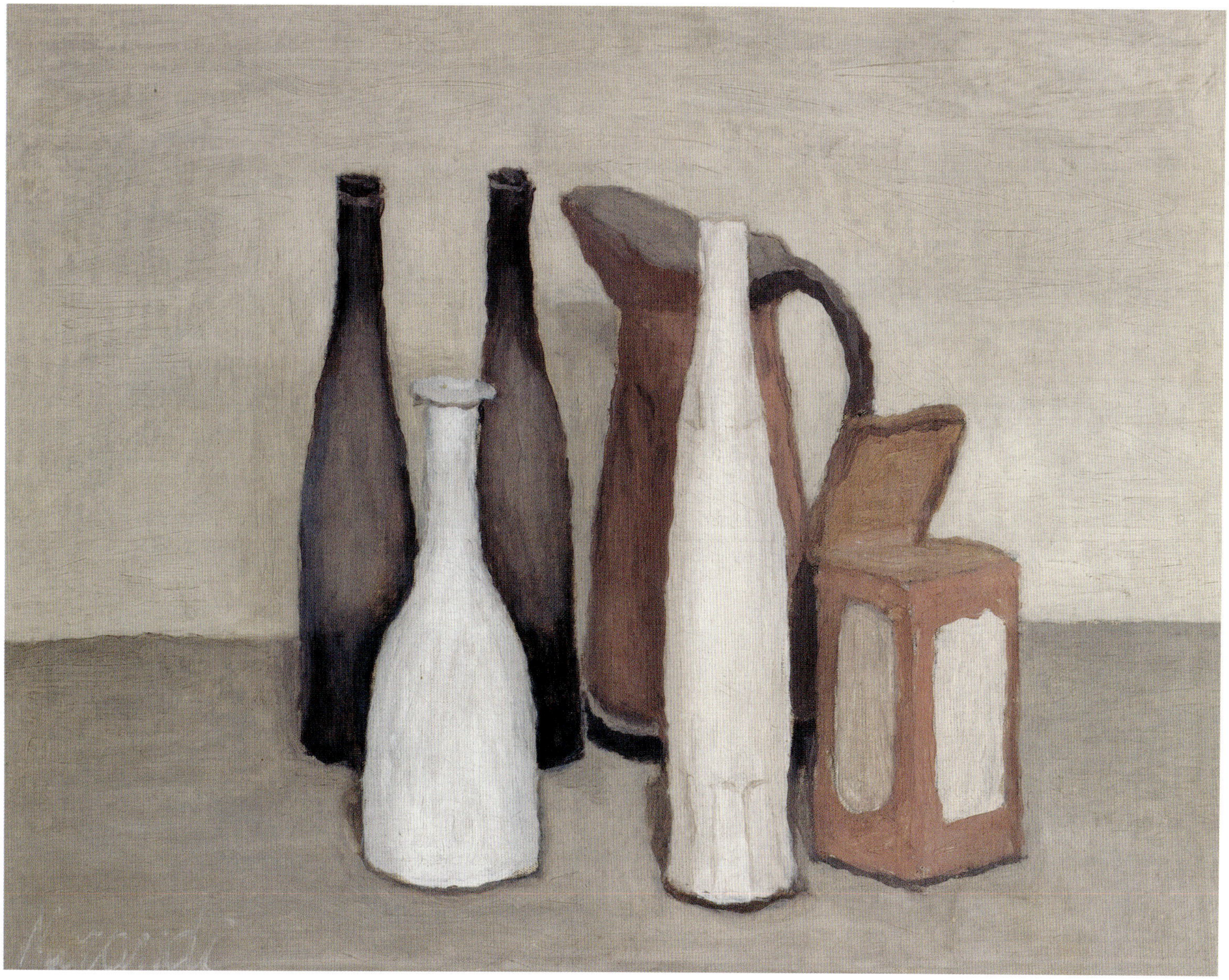

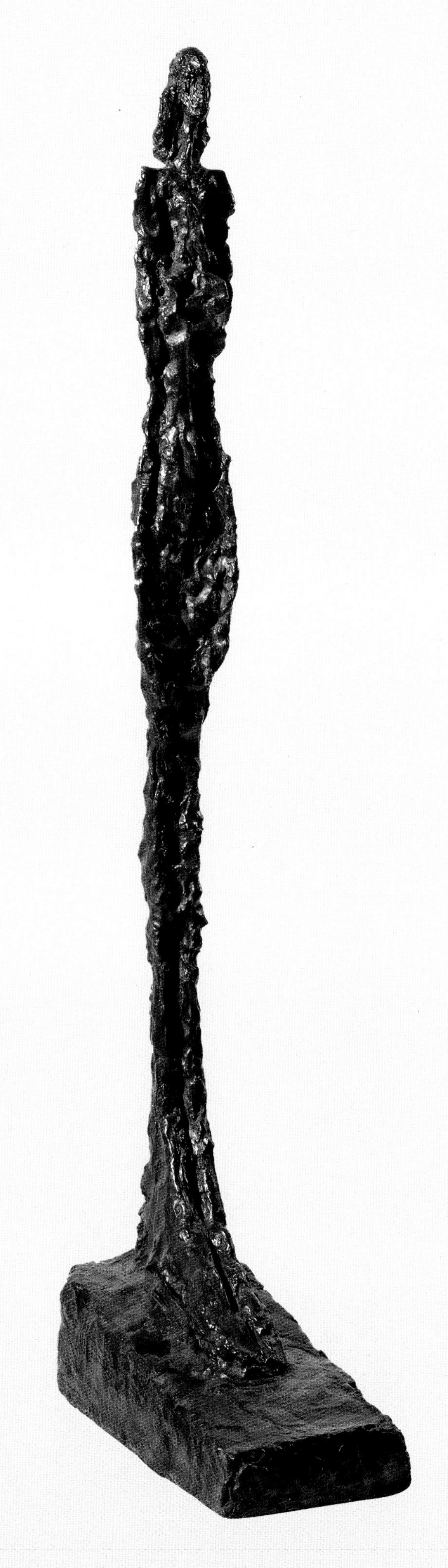

Alberto Giacometti
1901, Borgonovo, Switzerland–1966, Chur, Switzerland
Active in Paris, France
Woman of Venice IX, 1956
Bronze, 44 ¾ × 6 5⁄16 × 13 ⅜ in. (113.7 × 16 × 34 cm)

Gifts of Peggy Guggenheim, Venice, through the America-Israel Cultural Foundation, 1954

Page 222(r) *Figure in the Studio*, 1954
Lithograph, 25 ⅝ × 19 11⁄16 in. (65 x 50 cm)
Published by Maeght Editeur, Paris, edition of 30

Gift from Virginia and Herbert Lust, Greenwich, Connecticut, through the American Friends of the Tel Aviv Museum of Art in the United States, 2003

Page 223 *The Cage (First Version)*, 1949–50 (cast in 1990)
Bronze, 35 ⅝ × 14 3⁄16 × 13 ⅜ in. (90.5 × 36 × 34 cm)

Gift of Rivka Saker and Uzi Zucker, through the Tel Aviv Museum of Art American Friends, 2020

Page 222(l) Henri Cartier-Bresson
1908, Chanteloup-en-Brie, France—2004, Céreste, France
Alberto Giacometti Places Sculptures at Galerie Maeght,
Paris, 1961
Gelatin silver print, 11 ⅞ × 12 3⁄6 in. (30.3 × 31 cm)

Gift from Virginia and Herbert Lust, Greenwich, Connecticut, through the American Friends of the Tel Aviv Museum of Art in the United States, 2004

In the mid-1950s, Alberto Giacometti created *Woman of Venice IX*, part of a group of sculptures of standing women that was first exhibited at the 1956 Venice Bienniale. The figures in this ensemble stare blankly into space, their bodies dramatically elongated and narrow, with concave pelvises, heavy feet, and hands resting along their sides.

Woman of Venice IX generates notable visual tension. The rich surface texture enhances a sense of proximity, yet it also resembles a line in space—taut as a vibrating string—so that the sculpture simultaneously conveys an illusion of great distance. Like an amalgam of views from the zoom lens of a camera, which can move between a narrow focal point and a wide field of vision, *Woman of Venice IX* vacillates between impressions of near and far, presence and absence. At its most isolated, a self-enclosed object on the verge of disappearing, the sculpture also invokes associations with the then-recent traumas of World War II.

Giacometti's work became an important touchstone in the Existentialist philosophy of Jean-Paul Sartre, who was a close friend of the artist. Across two essays, Sartre's writings inspired subsequent generations of viewers and critics to identify in Giacometti's sculptures the power of the creative will in the face of existential threat and anxiety. "With each of his paintings," Sartre wrote in 1954, "Giacometti takes us back to the moment of creation *ex nihilo*. Every one of them raises anew the old metaphysical question: Why is there something rather than nothing? And yet there is something—this stubborn, unjustifiable, and superfluous apparition."[1]

Mordechai Omer

1 Jean-Paul Sartre, "The Paintings of Giacometti," *Situations*, trans. Benita Eisler (Greenwich, CT: Fawcett, 1969), 129.

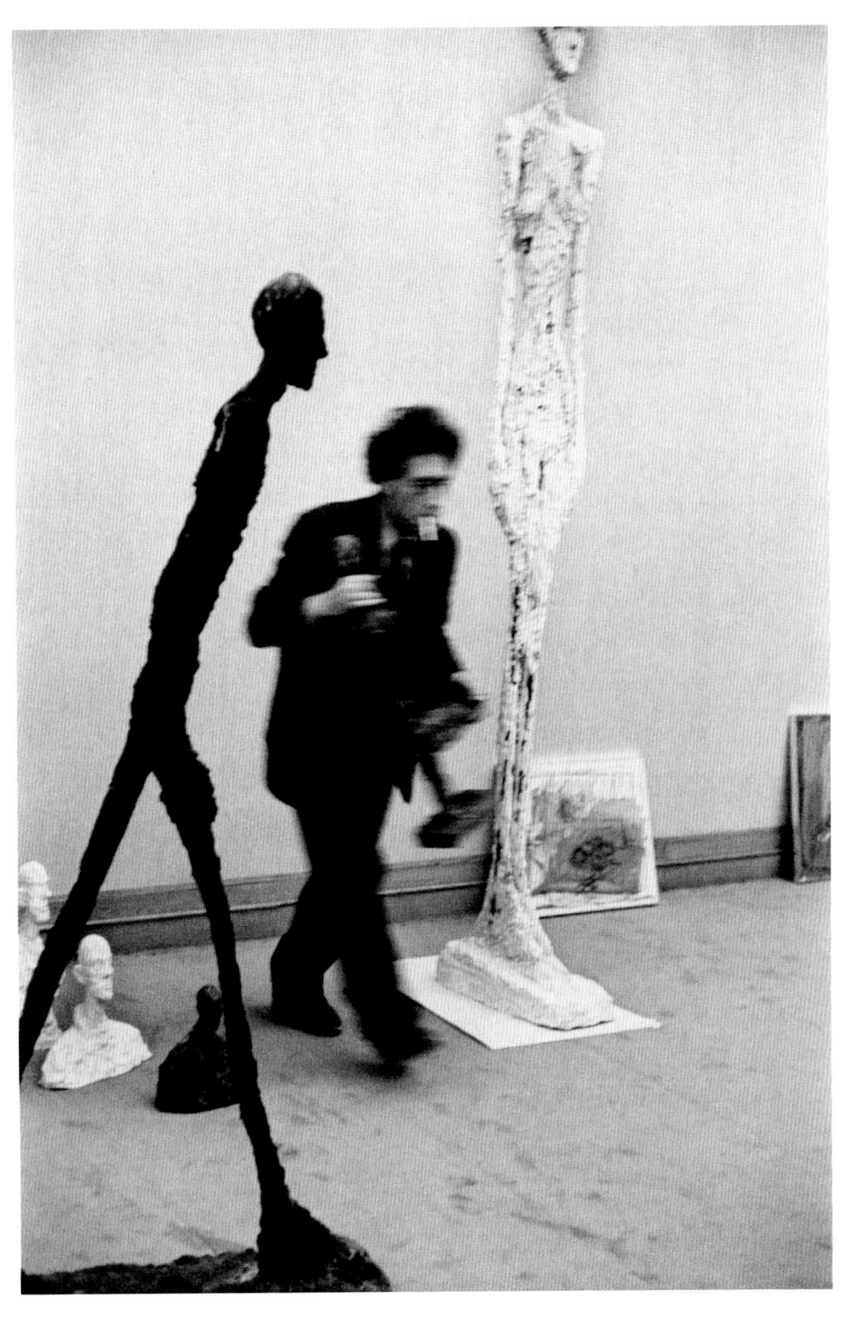

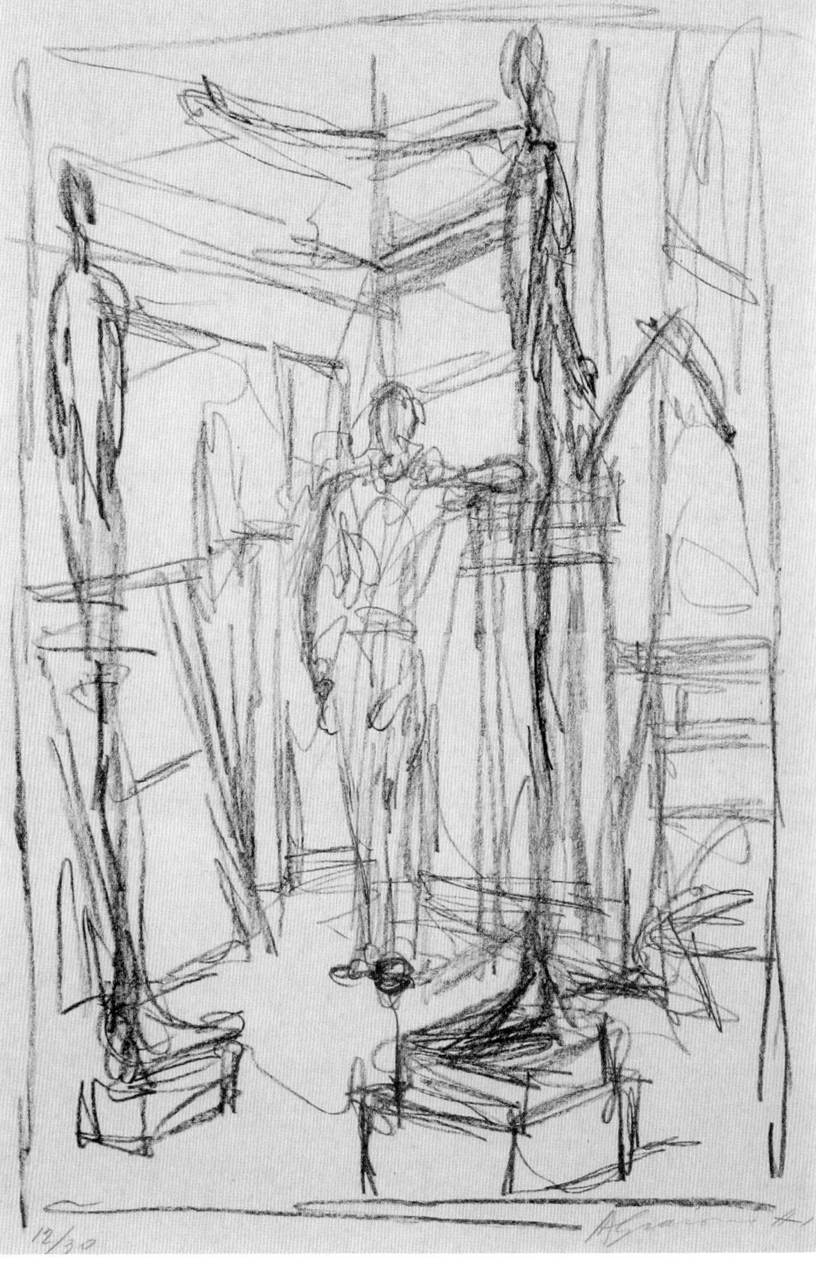

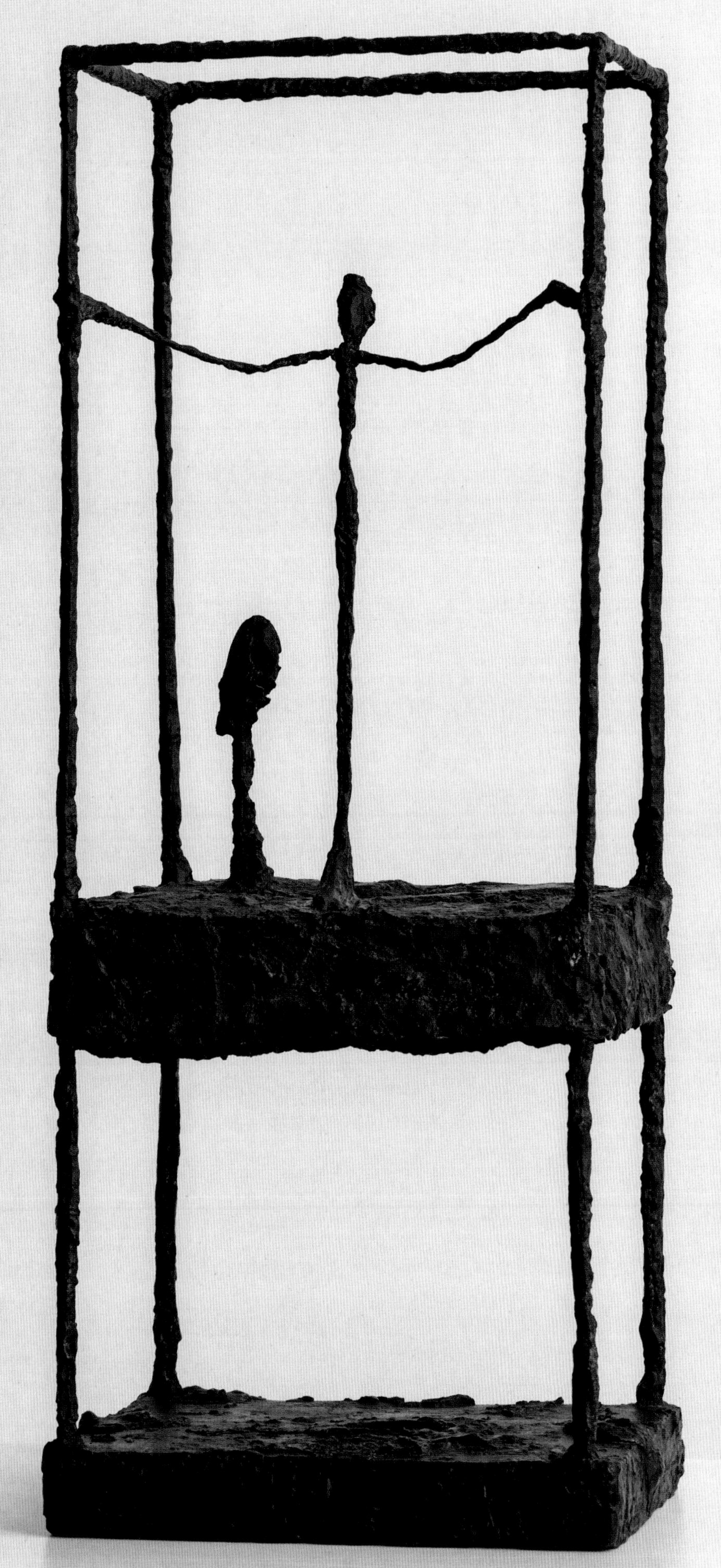

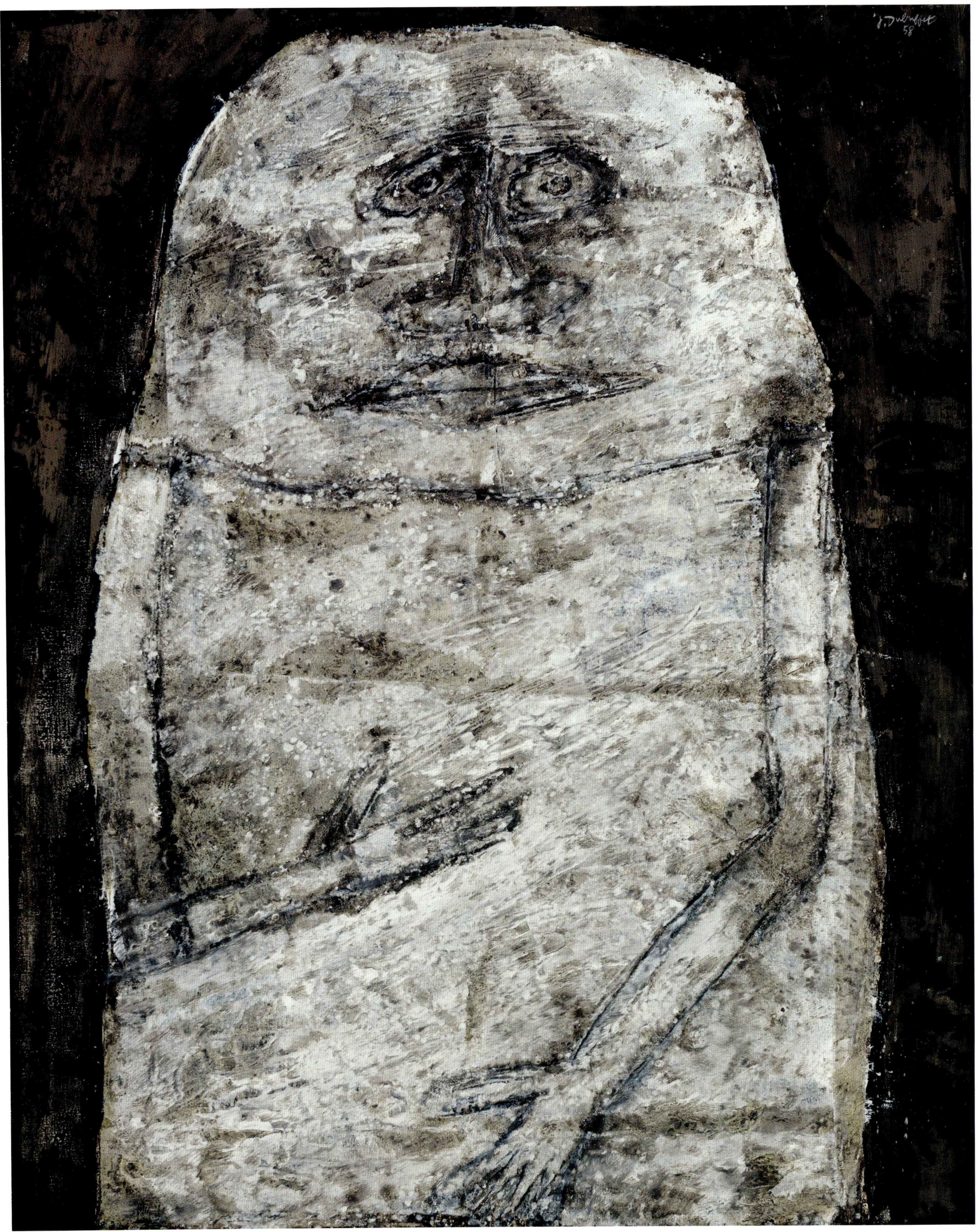

Jean Dubuffet
1901, Le Havre, France–1985, Paris, France
Appearance in Court, 1958
Oil on canvas, 39 3/8 × 31 7/8 in. (100 × 81 cm)

Mizne-Blumental Collection, Bequest of Annette Celine, 2018

Appearance in Court features a nearly formless figure placing a spindly hand on its chest as if testifying under oath in court, its alarming proportions almost completely filling the canvas. With the composition's raw, unrefined quality that breaks from convention in its compositional structure and rejection of classical beauty, Jean Dubuffet introduces a sense of the ridiculous into an ordinarily dignified occasion. Humor and satire are characteristic of the series to which this painting belongs, *Figures augures* (*Soothsayers)*, which also includes works that mock social conventions, such as *The Frivolous Patient*, *The Wealthy Rogue*, and *The Heights of Marriage.*

To make this painting, Dubuffet first covered the canvas with several thick layers of dark oil paint thinned with turpentine. He then applied a very light layer of paint, and covered it with another dark layer. Later, he crumpled and folded newspaper clippings, dipped them in ink, and dabbed them on the canvas, thus exposing underlying layers of paint and creating dots and stains across the surface. An amorphous black area frames the figure, creating a contrasting background, while also restricting or even entombing the figure, ostensibly freezing it in place. Chance occurrences and associative processes are an integral part of Dubuffet's work, and he welcomed seemingly unintended painterly elements, such as drips, stains, incisions, and rivulets of paint that coalesce to form the figure's facial features.

Dubuffet's process and formal language reflect his great interest in the art of non-Western cultures, untrained artists, children, and the mentally ill, all of which he grouped under the term *art brut*, or "raw art." Finding expressive power in these art forms, which he found lacking in traditional fine art, Dubuffet sought to infuse his own work with a similar unmediated, primal authenticity and emotional intensity.

Olga Cohen

Eva Hesse
1936, Hamburg, Germany–
1970, New York, NY, United States
Untitled, 1964
Gouache, ink, and collage on paper, 19 ½ × 25 ½ in. (49.5 × 64.8 cm)

Gift of Helen Charash, New York, through the American Friends of the Tel Aviv Museum of Art, 1984

Eva Hesse became one of the most significant artists in postwar America during a short career that ended with her premature death in 1970. She is best known for her Post-Minimalist sculptures, which deploy unexpected industrial materials to suggest the tactile fragility of the human body. In Hesse's sculptures, the seriality of Minimalism gives way to something that appears disorderly and organic, sometimes on the verge of decay.

Throughout her career, Hesse also produced a significant number of drawings. The artist's drawing practice ranged from delicate investigations of primary forms such as circles and squares to loose abstractions that rest ambiguously between biomorphic and technological forms. *Untitled* is an example of the latter strand of Hesse's drawings. Although the forms appear distant and disconnected, Hesse incorporated a series of arrows in the drawing as if to imply unseen relationships among the composition's elements. The arrows are sometimes hard-edged and precise, as in the top left corner, sometimes curved and sketchy. Close to the center, another arrow appears to have been cobbled together from disparate elements in the composition.

These arrows give the drawing a hint of the diagrammatic, which plays against the abstraction of its other forms. Some of these resemble tanks or teapots, others suggest more natural, bodily structures. Yet they remain resolutely unresolved, giving the drawing an air of something familiar that cannot quite be placed, or a machine on the verge of falling apart.

Hesse's abstraction on paper echoes the interplay between systems and their disintegration that characterizes much of the artist's sculptural work, yet also pushes our understanding of her production into uncharted territory. The drawing links Hesse's style to precedents in modern abstraction and, crucially, experiments in Surrealism, recalling works by artists like Max Ernst (pp. 190–91). Both traditions are well-represented in the collection of the Tel Aviv Museum of Art. *Untitled* was a gift from Hesse's sister, Helen Charash, and is the only work by Hesse in the Museum's collection.

Giampaolo Bianconi

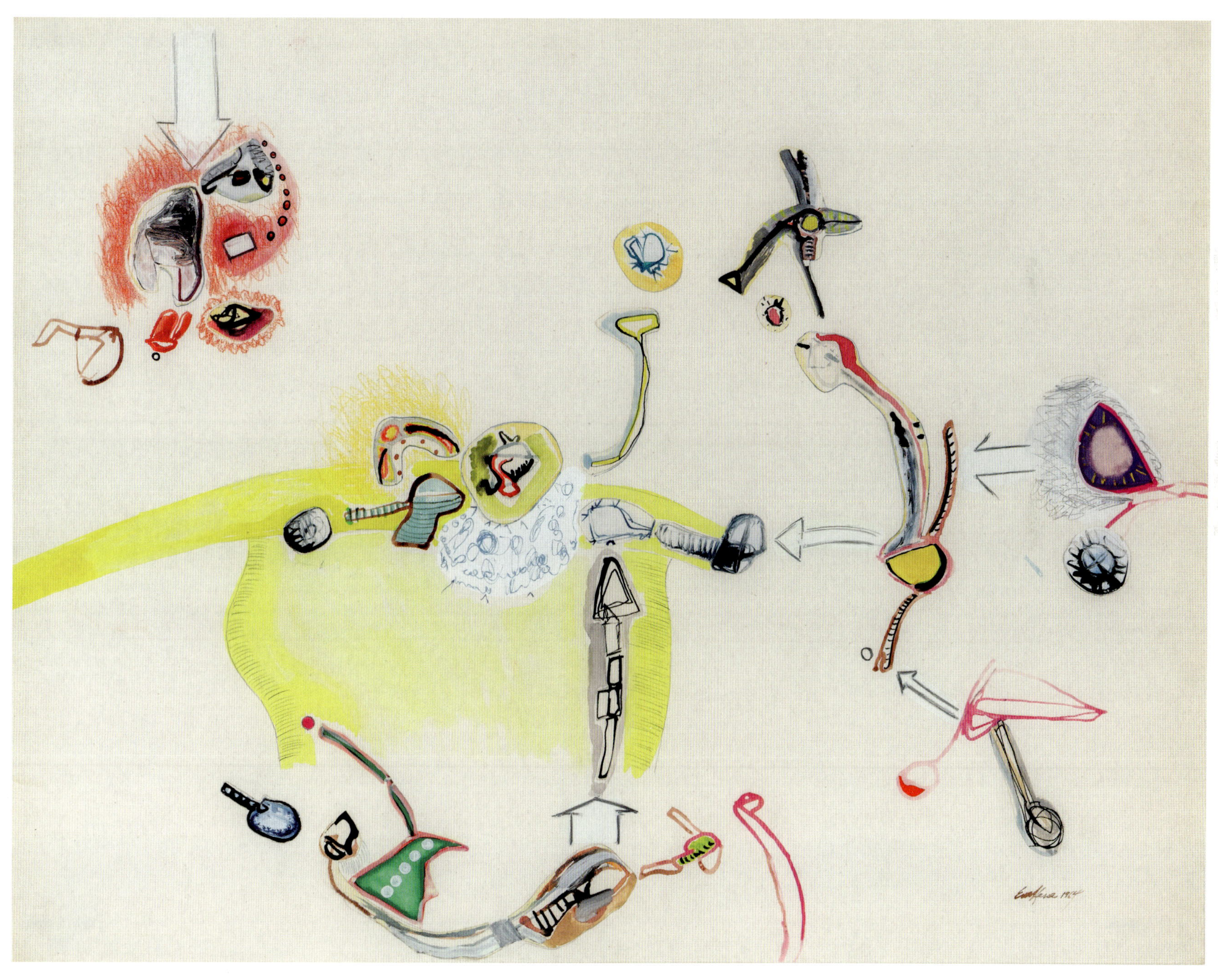

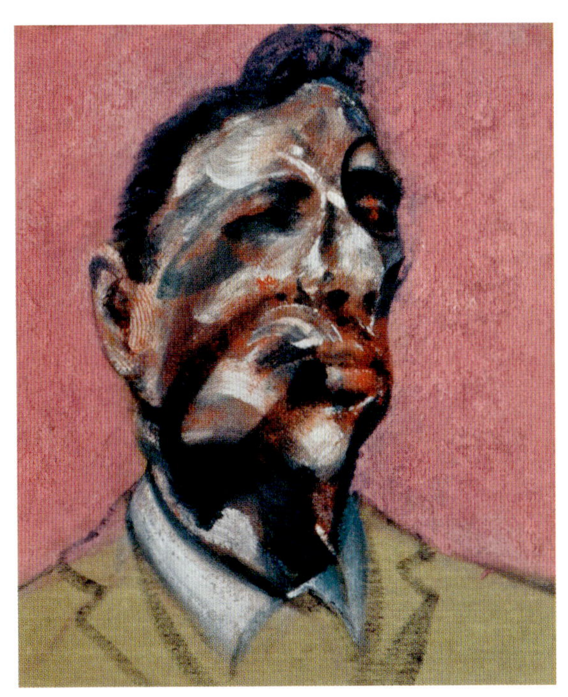
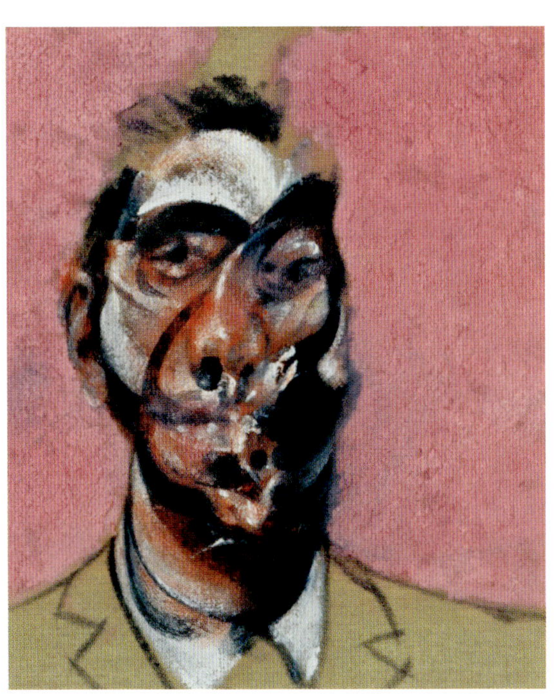
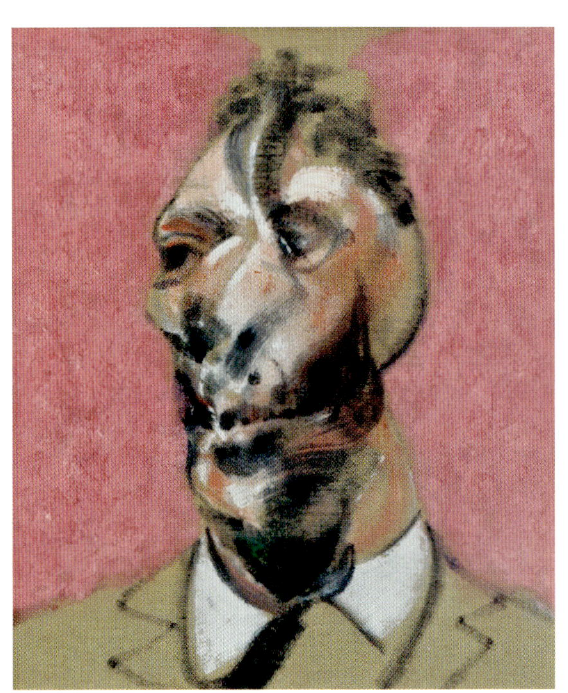

Francis Bacon
1909, Dublin, Ireland–1992, Madrid, Spain
Active London, United Kingdom
Three Studies for Portrait of George Dyer (on pink ground), 1964
Oil on canvas, three panels, each 14 × 12 in. (35.5 × 30.5 cm)

Gift of Susan and Anton Roland-Rosenberg, Los Angeles, through the American Friends of the Tel Aviv Museum of Art, 1996

The figure of George Dyer appears frequently in the works of Francis Bacon. Some of the portraits date from the period when the two were lovers, while others were painted after Dyer committed suicide in 1971. Despite their close relationship, it seems most of the portraits were likely made from photographs. As Bacon explained:

> *Even in the case of friends who will come and pose . . . I find it easier to work from the photographs than actually having their presence in the room. I think that, if I have the presence of the image there, I am not able to drift as freely as I am able to through the photographic image.*[1]

He also emphasized his artistic need for distortion; only through distortion could he capture the image. As he saw it, the image could only be presented in an injured state, and this type of violent act seems to have enabled him to create devastating yet authentic and intimate images. By distorting the figure of Dyer, Bacon forces the picture to throb with intensity, emotion, and poignancy.

In light of the violent nature of the portraits, it is notable that in all his various representations of Dyer, Bacon depicts, almost obsessively, the white collar and tie—essential elements of the Western male dress code. The symmetry of the collar, and the contrast between the white shirt and the black tie—features that Bacon retains even in those paintings where he seems to rip and squash Dyer's face—accord these symbols a status almost equivalent to the face itself. To an equal extent, there is great tension in the stark contrast between the richly painted monochrome backgrounds and the expressiveness of the open brushstrokes making up the figure. The aggressively depicted facial features are particularly hard to distinguish; through their materiality, the brushstrokes and jarring color patterns evoke profound distress.

Mordechai Omer

1 David Sylvester, *The Brutality of Fact: Interviews with Francis Bacon* (London: Thames and Hudson, 1993), 38.

Maryan
1927, Nowy Sącz, Poland–1977, New York, NY, United States
Personnage, 1970
Watercolor and ink on paper, 23 15/16 × 18 1/16 in. (60.8 × 45.9 cm)

Gift of Alex Maguy, 1979

Pinkas Bursztyn, the artist who came to be known as Maryan, grew up in a traditional, working-class Jewish home in Poland. In 1939, he and his family were captured by the Nazis. He endured imprisonment at various forced labor camps and finally at the Auschwitz and Birkenau concentration camps. He was the sole survivor of his family. After the war, he lived in Jerusalem for three years and enrolled at the Bezalel School of Arts and Crafts, where he began his formal art education; he then moved to Paris in 1950, where he changed his name to Maryan. Ultimately, Maryan immigrated to New York in the early 1960s, where he spent the most vibrant years of his career. He died prematurely of a heart attack at the age of fifty in 1977 at the Chelsea Hotel, where he lived and worked.

Drawing was central to Maryan's artistic process. At the Académie des Beaux-Arts in Paris, he studied lithography, learning to create images by making exacting drawings on stone or metal plates. This rigorous training left an imprint on his practice; for example, he often treated the same subject matter in various permutations.

Personnage is emblematic of Maryan's works on paper from his American period. A watercolor and ink drawing, it features a single faceless and genderless "personnage"—the generic term for the characters Maryan developed from the late 1950s on—crowned with a jumble of unruly hair and extruding strange bodily emissions. The figure wears a baker's cap, a charged reference to the artist's own father, which was revealed in a later series of autobiographical drawings Maryan made while in psychotherapy. The frenetic energy of the slender lines that compose *Personnage* is a hallmark of this tumultuous yet highly productive period from 1970 to 1977, in which Maryan's traumatic memories and unresolved emotional torment dominated the iconography of his work. The corporeal abjection suggested by the visceral details of *Personnage* evokes one of the key themes of his oeuvre: the struggle to maintain one's humanity in the face of unspeakable horrors.

Alison M. Gingeras

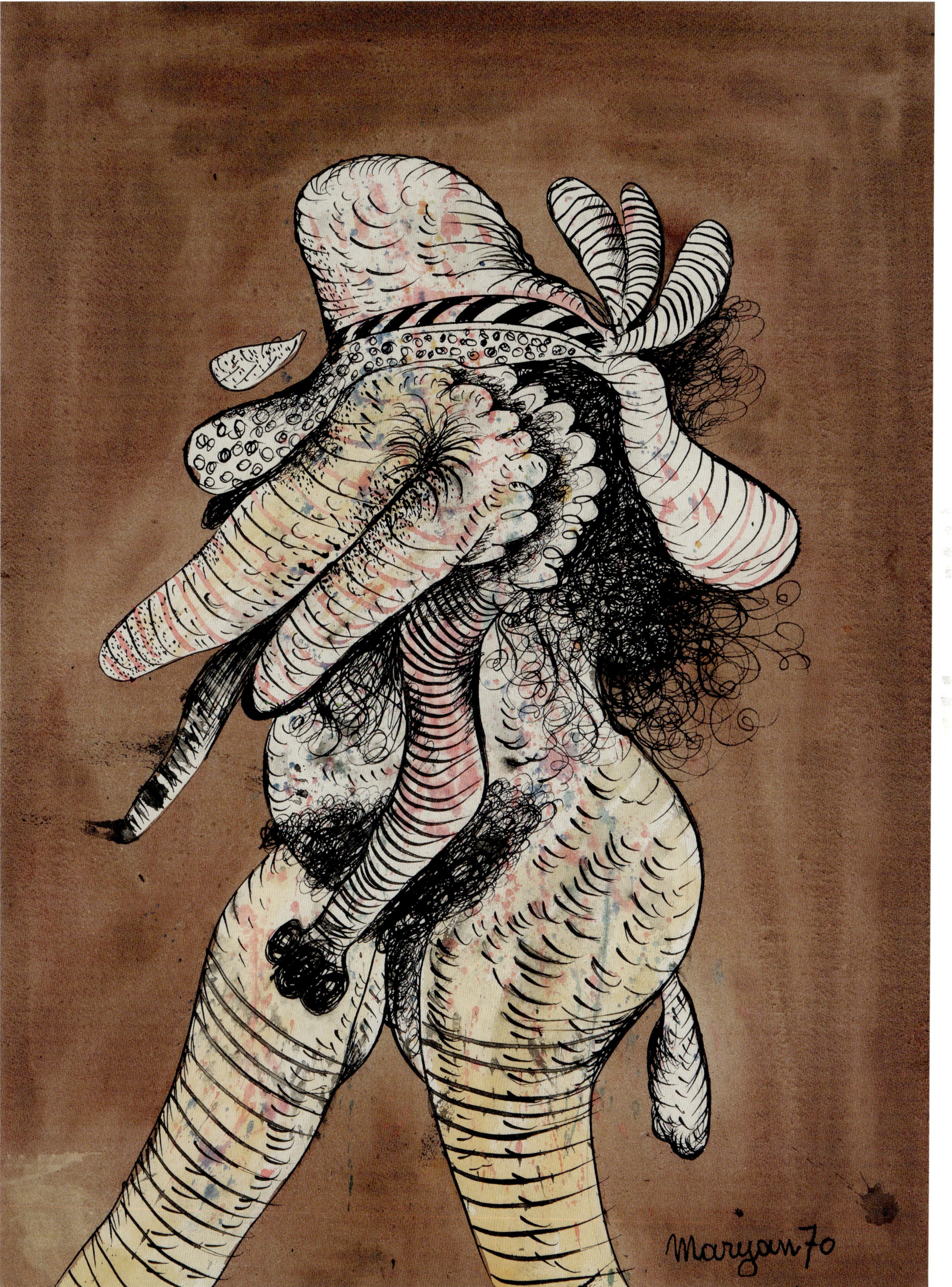
Maryan 70

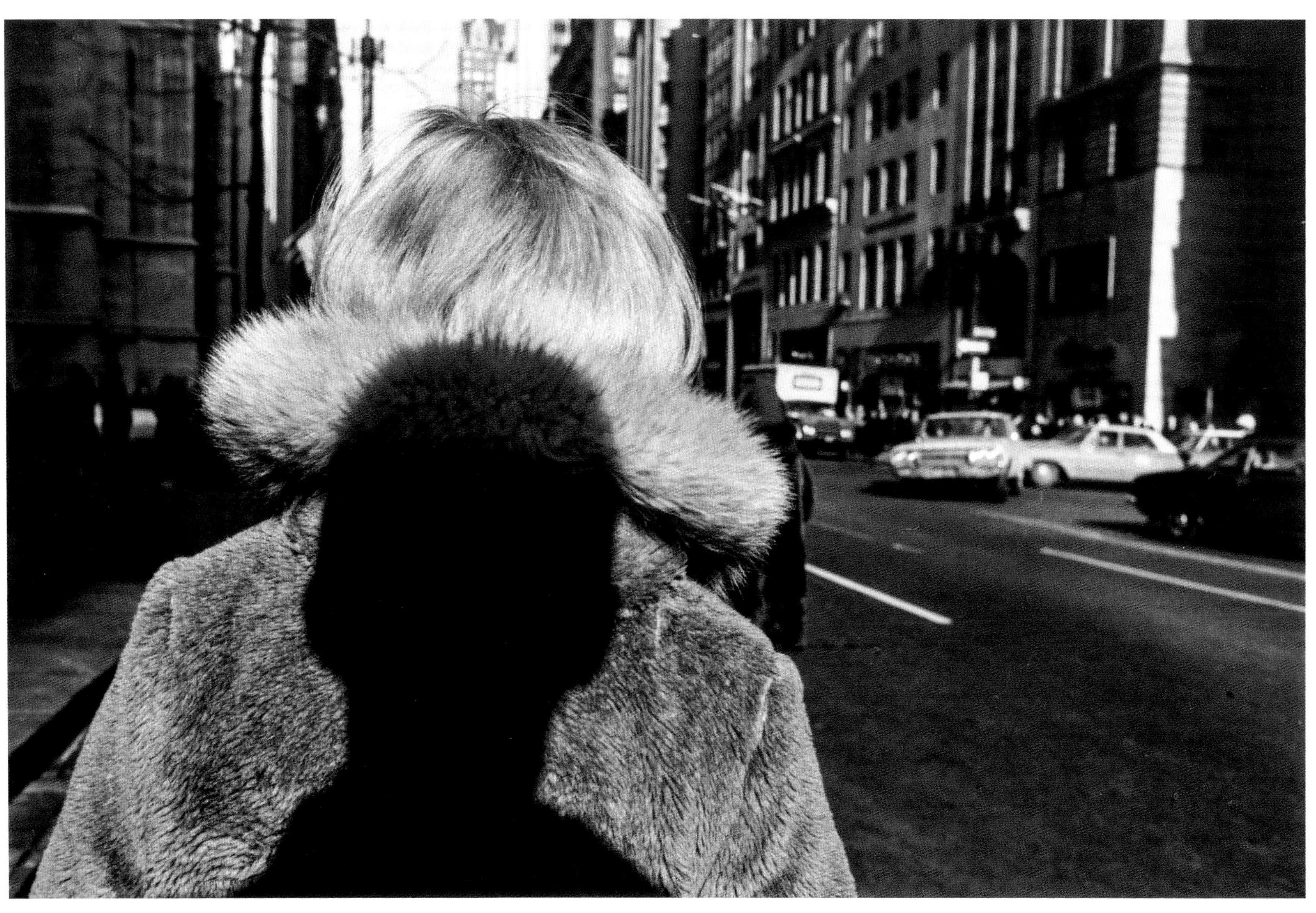

Lee Friedlander
b. 1934, Aberdeen, WA, United States
New York City, 1966
Gelatin silver print, 11 × 13 ⅞ in. (28 × 35.3 cm)

Purchase, 1991

While developing his informal, understated photographic aesthetic, steeped in a study of the fleeting qualities of urban life, Lee Friedlander began using his own shadow—which, at first, inadvertently crept into his images—as a photographic device that could cultivate formal and psychological gravity.[1] These shadows alternately function as his images' substrate, subject, or veil. A signature means of inserting commentary or tension into the scene, they merge with aspects of architecture, interrupt the space held by other bodies, and act as protagonists or antagonists in the quotidian worlds that the photographer captures.

In *New York City*, one such everyday moment is infused with dramatic undertones. Friedlander's projected shadow is captured, from a very close distance, on the back of a blonde woman's fur coat. The fur's texture gives the top of his shadow's head an uncanny sense of bodily substance. It lends tactility, too, to the dynamics of voyeurism underpinning the camera's gaze, and frames the city as a site of both desire and foreboding.

Friedlander took this image in 1966 as he walked alongside Saint Thomas Church on the Manhattan block of Fifth Avenue and East 53rd Street, next to the Museum of Modern Art. It was at MoMA, a year later, that Friedlander would be launched to prominence, when this photograph was part of a selection of his work to appear in the groundbreaking exhibition *New Documents*, alongside Garry Winogrand and Diane Arbus, helping to inaugurate a new sensibility characterized by a self-conscious deployment of the interpersonal registers of photography.[2] So, too, would this photograph be reproduced in Friedlander's first publication, fittingly titled *Self Portrait*.

Levi Prombaum

1 Peter Galassi, *Friedlander* (New York: Museum of Modern Art, 2005), 41.

2 See installation images from *New Documents*, Feb. 28–May 7, 1967, Museum of Modern Art Archives, New York.

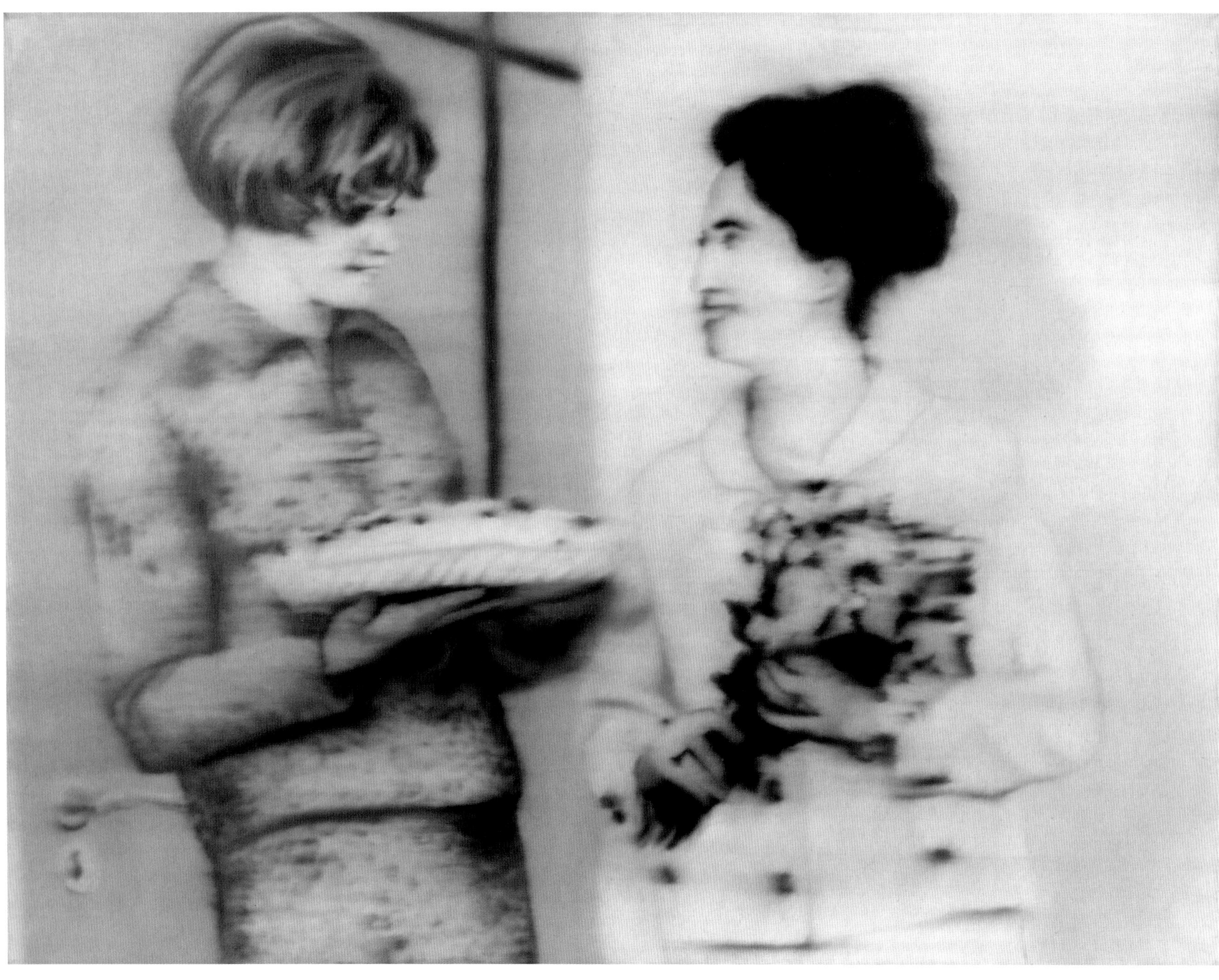

Gerhard Richter
b. 1932, Dresden, Germany
Two Women with a Cream Cake, 1965
Oil on canvas, 29 15/16 × 39 3/8 in. (76 × 100 cm)

Acquisition through the Lucien Baszanger Estate, Geneva, and the Maurice Lewin Estate, Antwerp, 1995

Two Women with a Cream Cake is a quintessential example of a group of paintings Gerhard Richter began in 1962, which later became known as photo paintings. They are based on hundreds of random, amateur, and anonymous photographs, which Richter has been collecting since the mid-1960s, gathered from newspapers, magazines, or family albums, assembled, and meticulously catalogued. These images are also the basis for the evolving and ever-expanding project *Atlas*, which comprises gridded arrangements of the collection, ostensibly disparate visual materials that shaped his world and served as a point of departure for his realistic paintings.

Two Women with a Cream Cake is a painted reproduction of a photographic original, depicting a casual everyday scene: two anonymous smiling women, dressed in tweed suits, stand facing each other. One holds a bouquet of flowers and the other a cream cake dotted with cherries. The slightly streaked, out-of-focus appearance, so characteristic of Richter, is the result of brushwork that seems to almost dissolve the original image, neutralizing its built-in illusory quality. Richter reconstructs the photographic act in black, white, and gray paint, challenging the viewer's perception of the depicted pictorial reality, and thus introducing a visual discourse that literally blurs the boundaries between photography and painting. Since both mediums are concerned with creating images of and about the world, he sees no significant difference between them, and each medium uses the characteristics of the other as a springboard for the realization of the artwork. For six decades, Richter has been painting with oil on canvas, constantly shifting between the figurative and the abstract, while introducing photography itself as a central subject.

Amit Shemma

Günther Uecker
b. 1930, Wendorf, Germany
Spiral 4, 1968
Nails on canvas mounted on wood, 39 3/8 × 39 3/8 in.
(100 × 100 cm)

Gift of the Riklis Collection of McCrory Corporation, New York, through the American Friends of the Tel Aviv Museum of Art, 1987

In an interview with a German newspaper, Günther Uecker recalled the first time he "worked" with nails: as a child he witnessed the arrival of the Soviet army in his village upon the unconditional surrender of the Nazi regime. While feeling sorry for what the Soviet army had endured, he also saw them raping and abusing the women and children in the neighborhood. Uecker, the only male left in the family, nailed wooden planks behind doors and windows, in order to protect his mother and his sisters.[1]

This traumatic experience remained atavistic in his subconscious mind, but it was not until he began studying at the Kunstakademie in Düsseldorf twelve years later that nails reappeared as an artistic material. When drawing nude portraits—a regular course at the academy—he perforated the paper surface with his pencil, a process that led him to the use of nails. When explaining this method, Uecker often paraphrases a famous saying by the Russian artist and poet Vladimir Mayakovsky: "poetry is made with a hammer," consciously adapting this phrase: for Uecker, each nail is tantamount to a drawn line, one that changes during the course of the day as the shadow it casts transforms with the shifting angle of light. The nails accrue into codes, metaphors, or emotions, part of an existential process that represents a seismograph of the artist's inner state.

In the late 1950s, Uecker joined the Zero group, founded by Heinz Mack and Otto Piene, to explore his growing interest in Kinetic Art and the impact of light. For Uecker, the group was an "open space of possibilities, in which we speculated about purity, beauty and silence."[2] By the 1960s, his experiments with light encouraged him to transcend planar, two-dimensional painting and incorporate everyday objects in his work to create moveable kinetic discs. Uecker's *Spiral 4* is a culmination of all these developments. The nails convey a sense of planar shapes in motion that seem to interpenetrate and drift apart from one another, creating a dynamic—and even painterly—composition.

Dorothea Schöne

1 Cornelius Tittel, "Günther Uecker-mit Nägel gegen die Russen," *Die Welt* (Berlin), May 31, 2012 [German, author's translation].

2 For Uecker's adaptation of Mayakovsky, see Dávid Fehér, "'Poetry is Made with a Hammer:' A Conversation with Günther Uecker," *Balkon Yearbook 2013–2015* (Budapest: Akinobooks, 2016), 2016, 23–33.

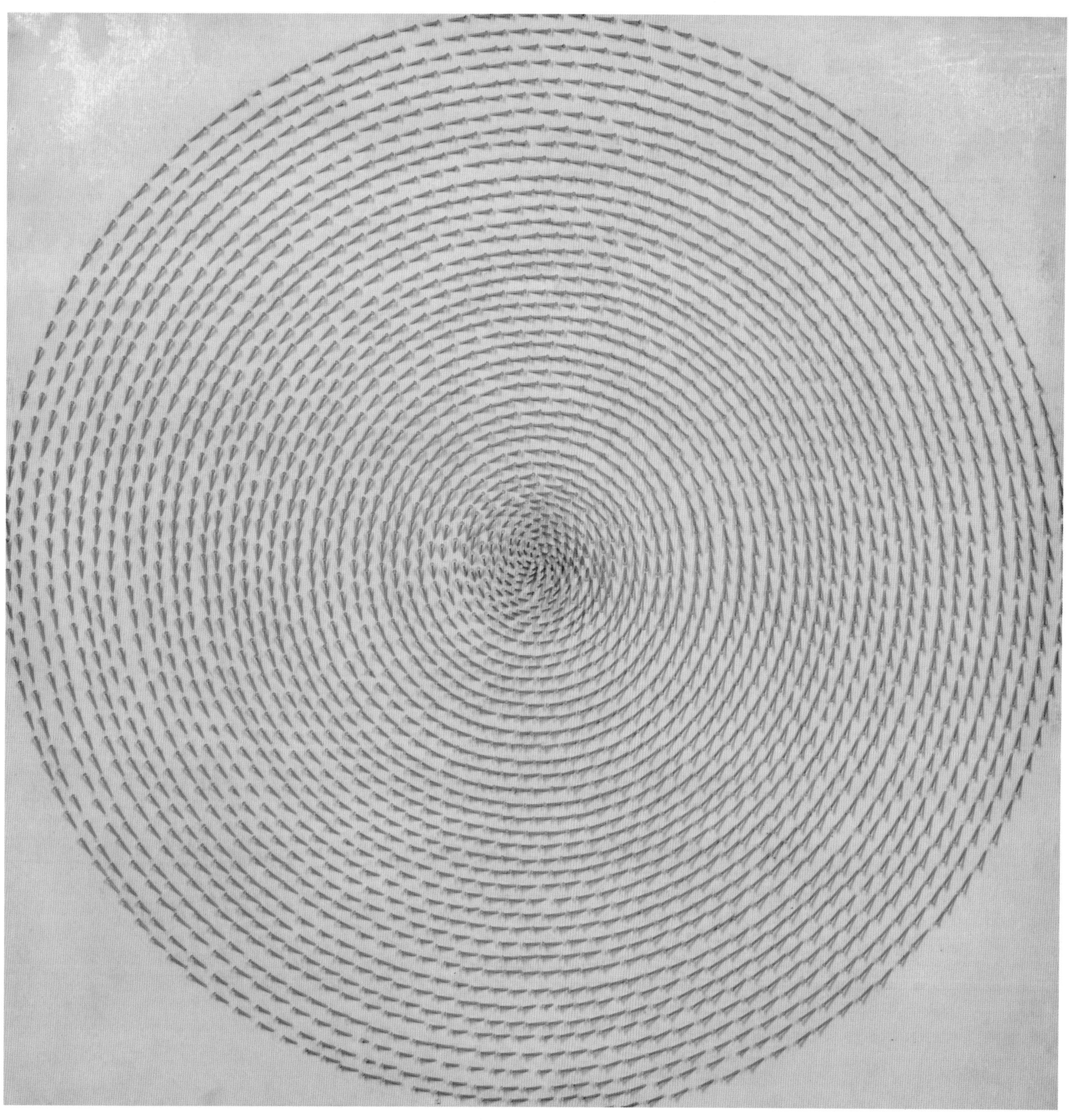

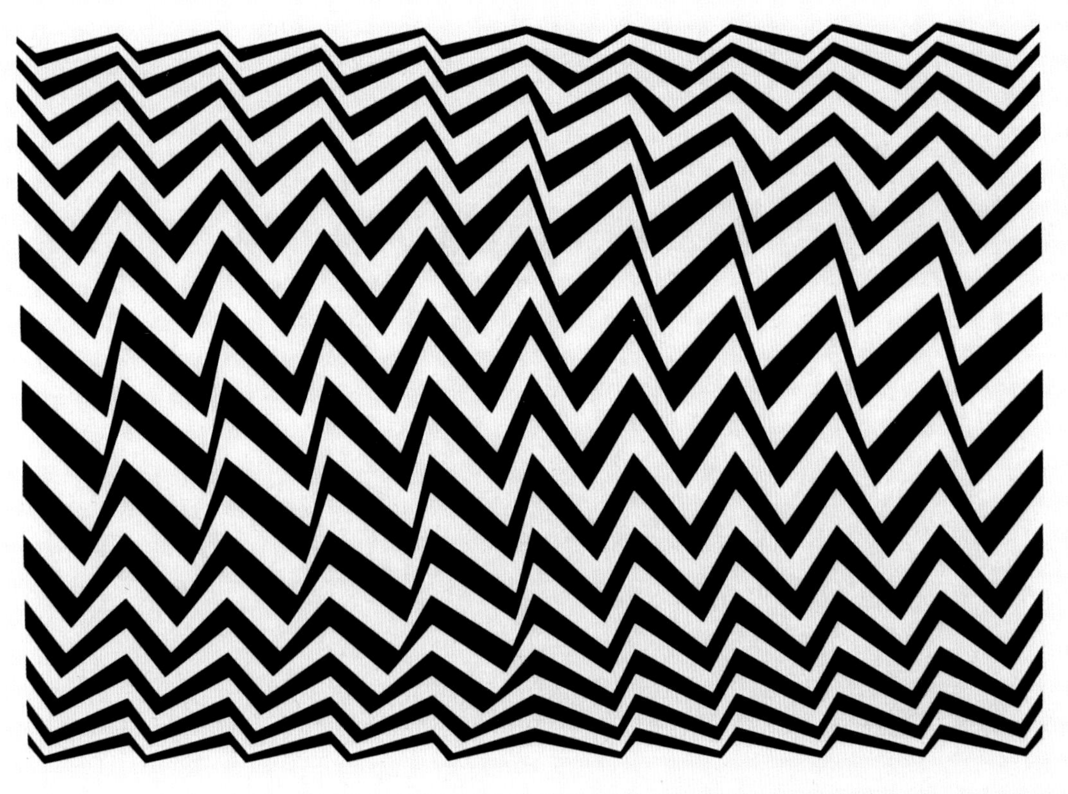

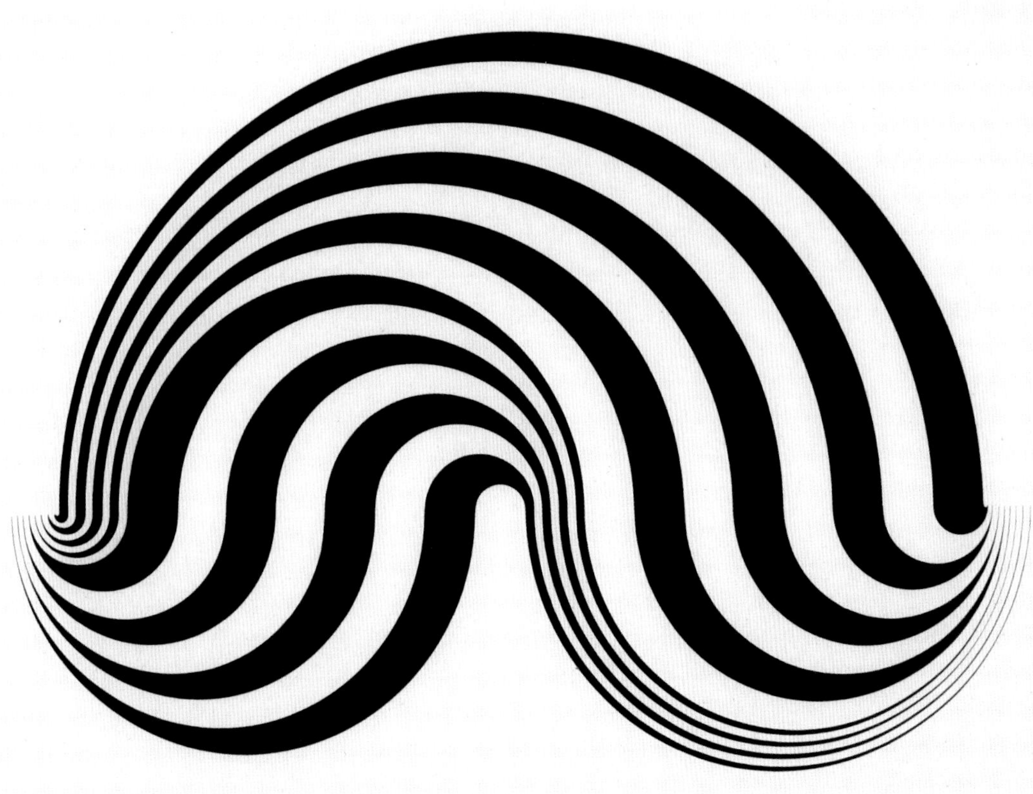

Bridget Riley
b. 1931, London, United Kingdom
Top *Untitled (Fragment 3)* from *Fragments*, 1965
Bottom *Untitled (Fragment 5)* from *Fragments*, 1965
Screenprints on Plexiglas, each 25½ × 32½ in. (64.8 × 82.5 cm)
Published by Robert Fraser Gallery, London, edition of 75

Gifts of the Riklis Collection of McCrory Corporation, New York, through the American Friends of the Tel Aviv Museum of Art, 1987

After her early years working in a figurative style, Bridget Riley experienced a defining moment while visiting the 1960 Venice Biennale. As she watched rain pour down on black-and-white paving stones, light fell for a moment on the water, which seemed to dissolve the stones' pattern. When the rain stopped, the stones dried and the clarity of the pattern returned. The realization that a structure's equilibrium can be disturbed, altered, and then restored had a transformative impact on Riley's work.

Riley reduced her means of expression to black and white and to a restricted number of simple, hard-edge geometric shapes: squares, stripes, ovals. Through the careful juxtaposition of forms focusing on the interplay of large and small, wide and narrow, she created an illusion of volume and space, and most significantly, of movement. Her compositions often resemble undulating waves that produce a dizzying, often disorienting effect. These works would soon become known as Op Art—a form of abstraction that focuses on vision itself, exploring how the brain interprets the signals received by the eye. This trend stood at the core of the exhibition *The Responsive Eye*, which opened at the Museum of Modern Art, New York, in 1965 and featured Riley's work prominently. The exhibition catapulted Riley to international renown, and her works were quickly adopted into the realms of fashion, design, and advertising.

These two works are part of Riley's 1965 series *Fragments*—which started off as studies or "fragments" of larger compositions for paintings—a pioneering body of black-and-white screenprints produced directly on Plexiglas. A new type of plastic invented in the 1930s, Plexiglas was embraced by many artists in the postwar period who were interested in exploring unconventional, industrial materials. For Riley, it provided a mechanically smooth surface that complemented her works' geometric precision. She also chose it for its transparent surface—when hit by light, the images appear to float in space, amplifying the illusion of motion generated by the graphic intensity of her forms.

Emanuela Calò

Alexander Calder
1898, Lawnton, PA, United States–
1976, New York, NY, United States
Machine Gun Traces, 1969
Sheet metal, wire, 19 11⁄16 × 51 3⁄16 in. (50 × 130 cm)

Gift of Helene and Zygfryd Wolloch, Scarsdale, New York, through the American Friends of the Tel Aviv Museum of Art, 1997

Alexander Calder's mobiles fill space—not by volume, but by spatial branching of their flat shapes. His "sculpture in motion" explores the interrelationships among the sculptural object, the space surrounding it, and movement. Calder not only redefined the principles of traditional sculpture but created a completely new perception of the medium: solidity and permanence gave way to new possibilities of dynamism. In the 1950s, he began working with industrial manufacturers, allowing him to expand the scale of his work and to incorporate bold colors alongside black and white.

The mobile *Machine Gun Traces* is a relatively late work. With the exception of one perfect circle, the shapes are variations of a polygon, and the sculpture's formal simplicity is emphasized by its black coloration. The shapes sketch a linear drawing in space, and the movement itself becomes a formal sculptural element. Calder welcomed free and spontaneous movement in his works, initiated by air currents, but at the same time, he sought some control through manipulating weight and balance. The perforations in the outer element, for example, enabled him to achieve a precise balance in the mobile by reducing material and weight. These perforations—"machine-gun traces"—infuse this abstract sculpture with political overtones, suggesting bullet holes. The work was created in 1969, at the height of the Vietnam War and the antiwar movement, with which Calder was identified.

The mobile debuted at the Tel Aviv Museum of Art as part of the Wolloch Collection of Modern Sculpture, which was donated in the 1990s. Featuring various impulses in modern sculpture, from Auguste Rodin to Arnaldo Pomodoro, the works in the collection demonstrate sculpture's liberation from the need to represent reality, and the use of space, time, and movement as formal elements.

Shahar Molcho

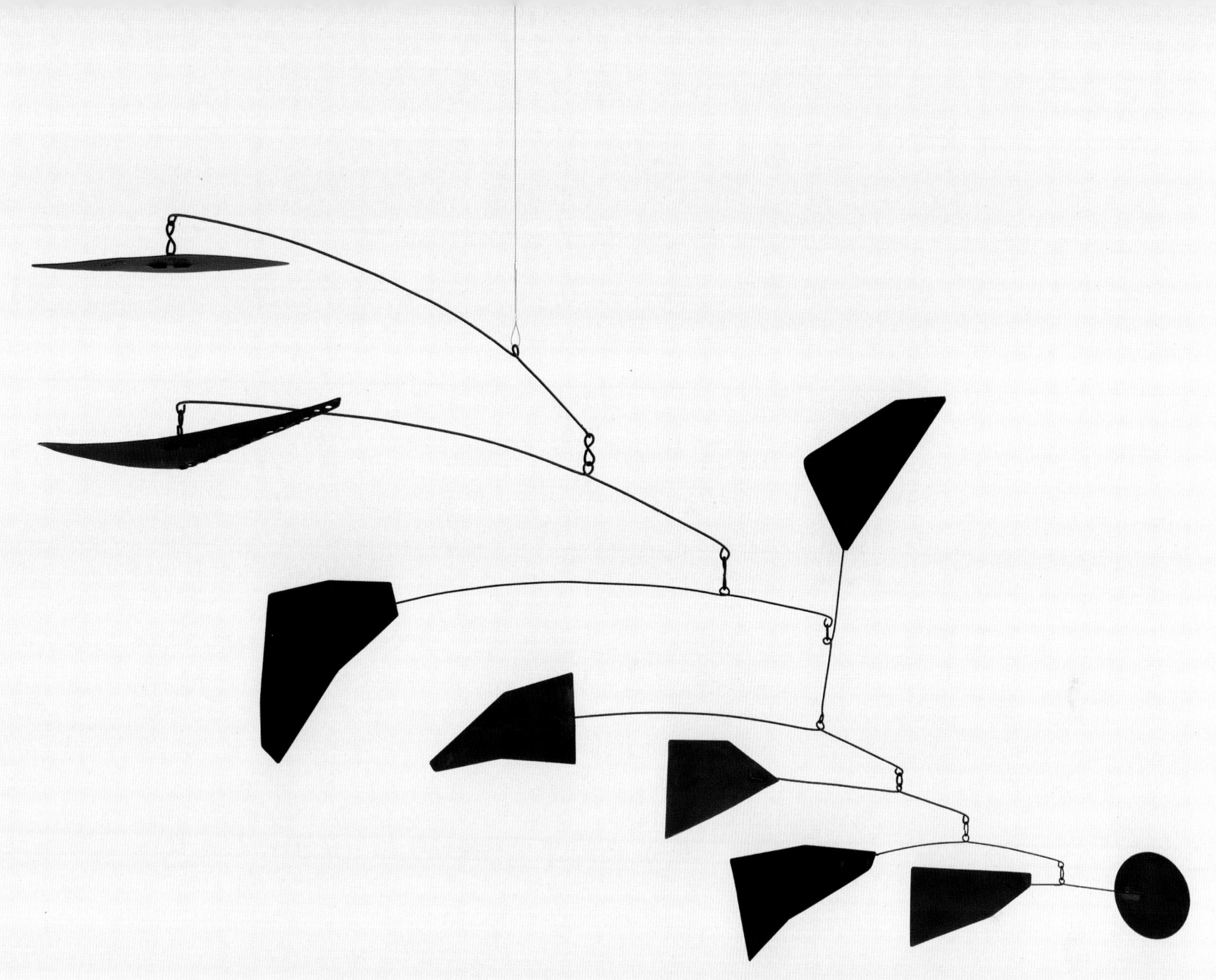

Josef Albers
1888, Bottrop, Germany–1976, New Haven, CT, United States
Homage to the Square (#688), 1970
Oil on canvas, 31 7/8 × 31 7/8 in. (81 × 81 cm)

Gift of Josef Albers Foundation, 1979

Josef Albers, a Bauhaus-trained artist, left Nazi Germany for the United States in 1933, leading the painting department at Black Mountain College in North Carolina before joining the art and design faculty at Yale University in 1950.[1] He pioneered a modern aesthetic based on rigorous explorations of form, material, and color that was reflected in his art practice and teaching.

Although he mastered various mediums, Albers is best known as an abstract painter. At the age of sixty-two, he began what would become his signature series, *Homage to the Square* (1950–76). Over the next two and a half decades, he methodically created more than 2,000 *Homage* paintings that share a set of formal parameters: three or four concentric squares of different colors positioned at varying distances from the bottom edge of a Masonite panel. Albers began each composition in this series with the center square and worked his way out, never painting one square on top of another, and rarely mixing paint. Instead, he used a palette knife to lay in pigments directly from the tube onto the panel. Mexican vernacular architecture may have inspired the genesis of the series, and some historians connect the works to the facades of adobe buildings characteristic of central Mexico, which Albers visited regularly.[2]

Through these strictly ordered compositions, Albers explored an illusion whereby the central square would subtly take on the hue of its neighbors. The value and effect of individual colors change from work to work, depending on their proximity to—and interaction with—adjacent colors. He named this phenomenon the "interaction of color." In *Homage to the Square (#688)*, the optical effects of the color contrasts between the vibrant yellows and umber at the center create an illusion of receding and advancing planes. Albers understood this work and others from the series as dynamic and polymorphous. "I want my inventions to act," he wrote, "to lose their identity. What I expect from my colors and forms is that they do something they don't want to do themselves."[3]

Lauren Hinkson

1 His 1963 book *Interaction of Color*, developed from his courses, remains a touchstone for artists and designers.
2 See Lauren Hinkson, *Josef Albers in Mexico*, exh. cat. (New York: Guggenheim Publications, 2017).
3 Albers, quoted in "Nothing Definite," *Time*, January 31, 1949, 39.

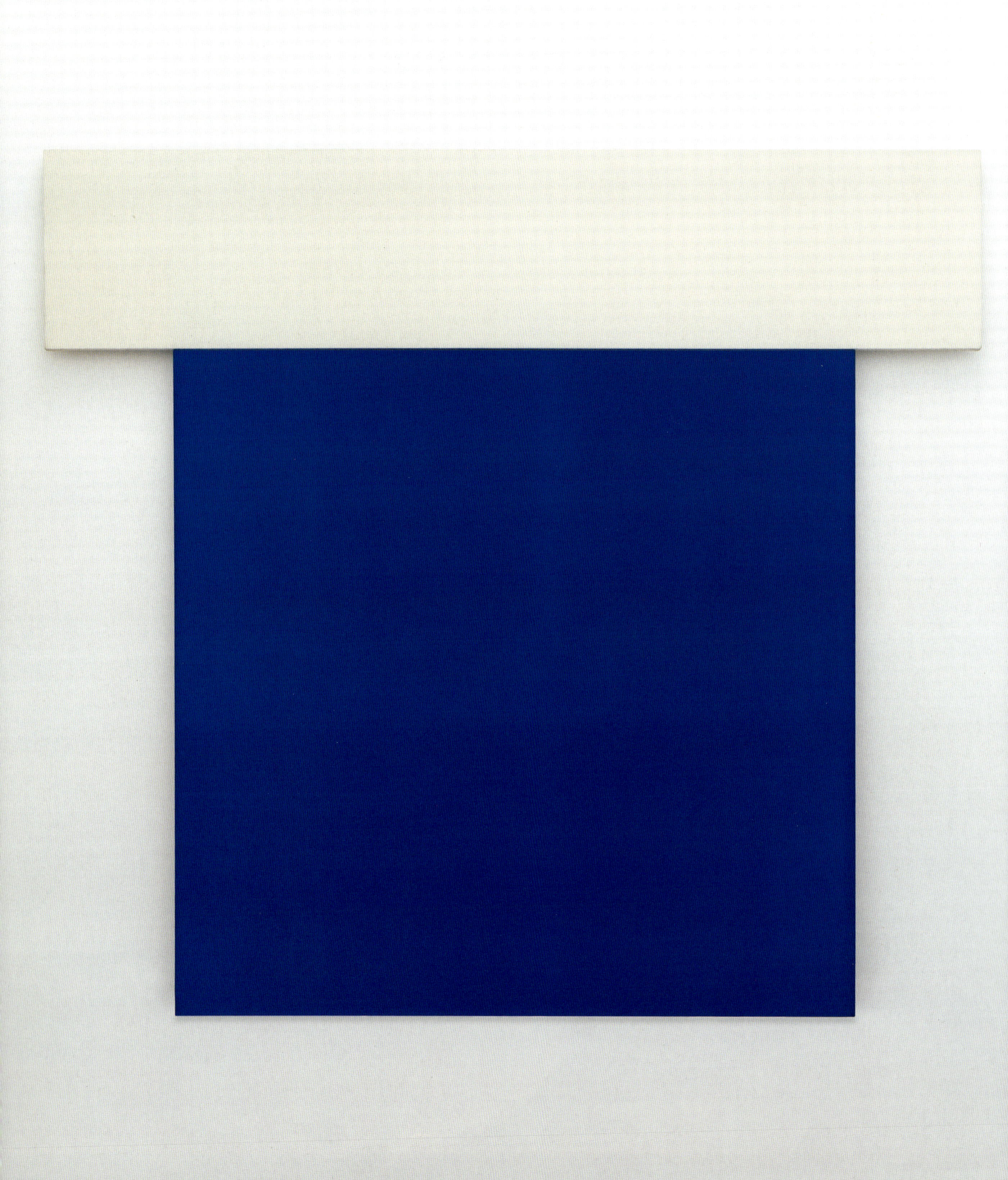

Ellsworth Kelly
1923, Newburgh, NY, United States–
2015, Spencertown, NY, United States
Blue with White Bar, 1970
Oil on canvas, two panels, overall 108 ½ × 97 7⁄16 in.
(275.6 × 247.5 cm)

Gift of the Riklis Collection of McCrory Corporation, New York, through the American Friends of the Tel Aviv Museum of Art, 1987

Among the pioneers of American abstraction, Ellsworth Kelly worked in diverse mediums, including painting, sculpture, drawing, printmaking, and photography—and often blurred the boundaries between them. Beginning in the early 1960s, he was a leading exponent associated with hard-edge painting. This style was characterized by geometric forms, bright colors, and almost no perceptible sign of the artist's hand, and was in part developed in opposition to the emotionally charged, gestural work of Abstract Expressionism, the dominant style in the New York art scene at the time.

Kelly studied art in New York and Boston, and spent six years in Paris in the early 1950s, where he began to experiment with combining two separate panels—often painted in different, monochromatic colors—into one work. The canvases, affixed adjacently so that they form a continuous, smooth surface, possess a sculptural quality: assembled in this way, they become an object in space, or a kind of painting-object. Upon his return to New York, Kelly began to focus intensely on pure form and color, and their interrelation in space. His abstract paintings were inspired by architectural elements, including windows, altarpieces, and building facades.

Blue with White Bar is one of several works, created in 1970–71, comprising two panels joined in a T-shape. The two parts of the work are presented as separate, flat color units, which nevertheless maintain a balance: they exist as both a single work and as two independent entities. Kelly insisted that his work did not *contain* an object, but was *itself* an object:

> *I have worked to free shape from its ground, and then to work the shape so that it has a definite relationship to the space around it; so that it has a clarity and a measure within itself of its parts (angles, curves, edges, and mass); and so that, with color and tonality, the shape finds its own space and always demands its freedom and separateness.*[1]

Galit Landau-Epstein

1 Ellsworth Kelly, *Fragmentation and the Single Form*, exh. brochure (New York: Museum of Modern Art, 1990), n.p.

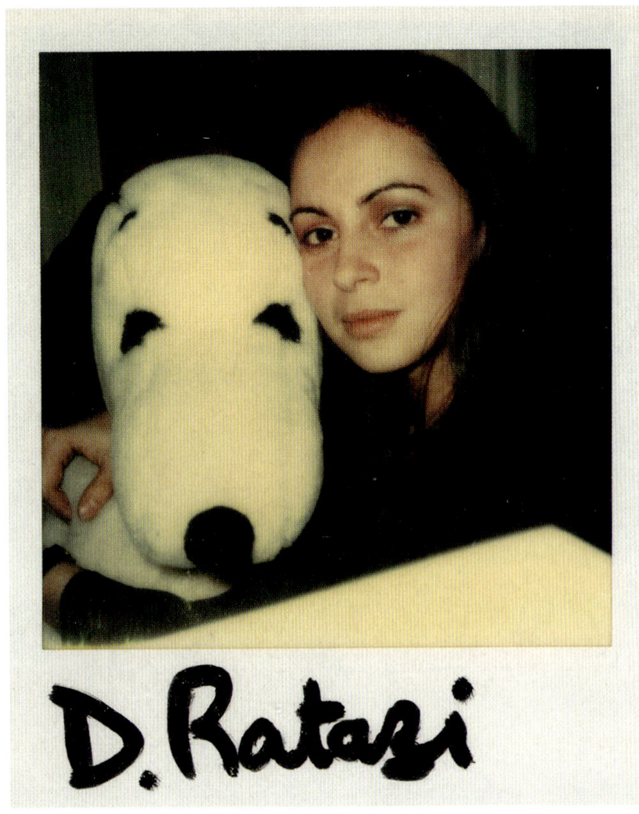
D. Ratazi

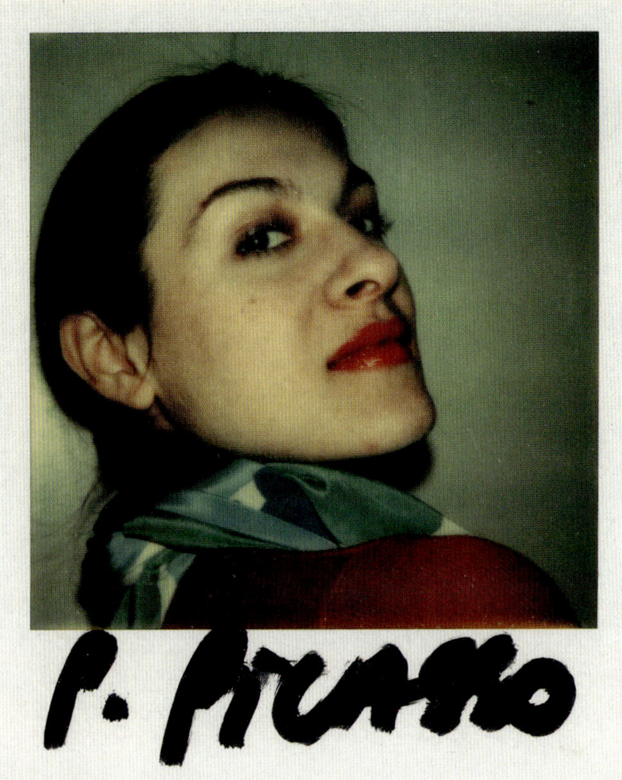
P. Picasso

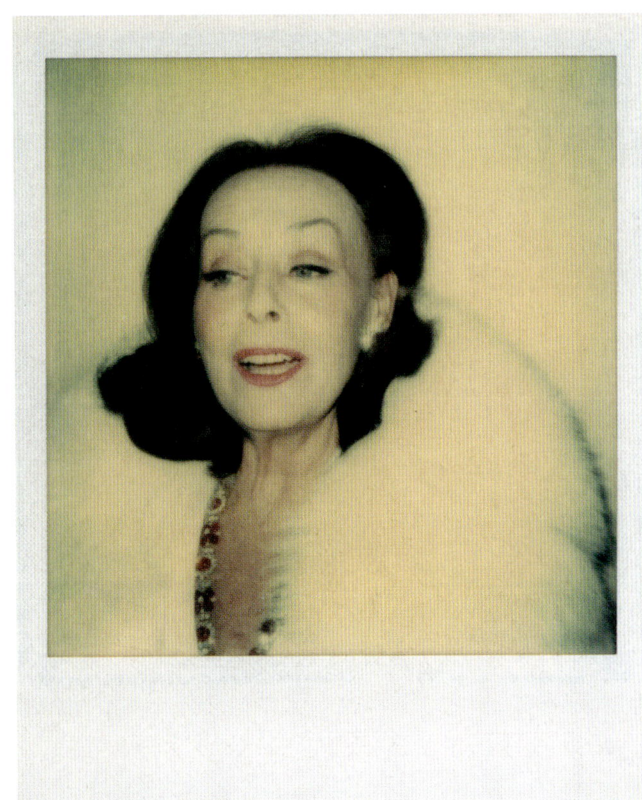

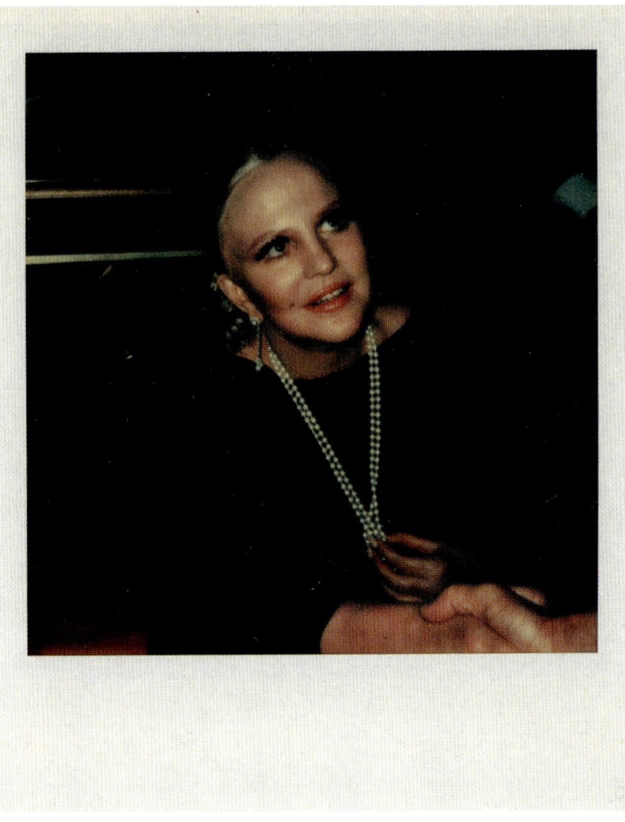

Andy Warhol
1928, Pittsburgh, PA, United States–1987, New York, NY, United States

Left to right by row:

Untitled [Delfina Rattazzi], 1972–73
Untitled [Paloma Picasso], 1972–73
Untitled [Paulette Goddard], 1972–73
Untitled [Peggy Lee], 1972–73
Polaroids, 4 5⁄16 × 3 3⁄8 in. (11 × 8.6 cm)

Gift of the Andy Warhol Foundation for the Visual Arts, New York, 2015

In the early 1970s, Andy Warhol revived his practice of using Polaroids in his work, which had lain dormant for almost a decade. The Polaroids inspired his creative process, served as aids for his screenprints, and, most of all, documented his ever-expanding milieu. Gravitating to the Polaroid Big Shot camera for the rest of his career—a decidedly clunky instrument with a built-in flash, whose focal length of about a meter was designed especially for taking portraits—Warhol made thousands of Polaroid studies.

Instantaneous, and therefore valuable as conversation pieces as well as artworks, Polaroids were a crucial element of the elaborate theater of Warhol's scene-making, both in his studio (called the Factory) and in public. When portrait sitters came to pose for Warhol, they could be captured, with the help of several studio assistants, simultaneously on tape recorder, moving film, and traditional analog photographic film. Polaroids, added to the mix, became part and parcel of the dizzyingly productive excess of Warhol's process, while also helping to impart a memorable experience of being pictured.[1]

The Tel Aviv Museum of Art's selection of Polaroids captures a wide range of Warhol's subjects, exemplifying how different generations and concepts of fame have been flattened by the workings of the artist's instant camera.[2] Among the notable sitters: heiress and socialite Delfina Rattazzi, with an oversized, Snoopy plush toy; Pablo Picasso's daughter Paloma, sporting her trademark red lipstick; silent-film star Paulette Goddard, awash in the white makeup that Warhol often used on his subjects to simplify their features for the transfer from photograph to screenprint; and jazz singer Peggy Lee, captured in the lounge of the Waldorf Astoria following a performance there. In the latter case, multiple other photographers were photographing Warhol as he was taking pictures of Lee—one of many examples in which the artist, throughout his career, actively generated, rather than merely reflected, America's conditions of celebrity and spectacle.

Levi Prombaum

1 Peggy Phelan, "Andy Warhol: Contact Sheets, Photography Without End," in *Contact Warhol: Photography Without End*, ed. Peggy Phelan and Richard Meyer (Cambridge, MA: MIT Press, 2018), 29–30.

2 Andy Grundberg, "Andy Warhol's Polaroid Pantheon," in *Andy Warhol: Polaroids, 1971–1986*, ed. Vincent Fremont (London: Art Data, 1991), 49.

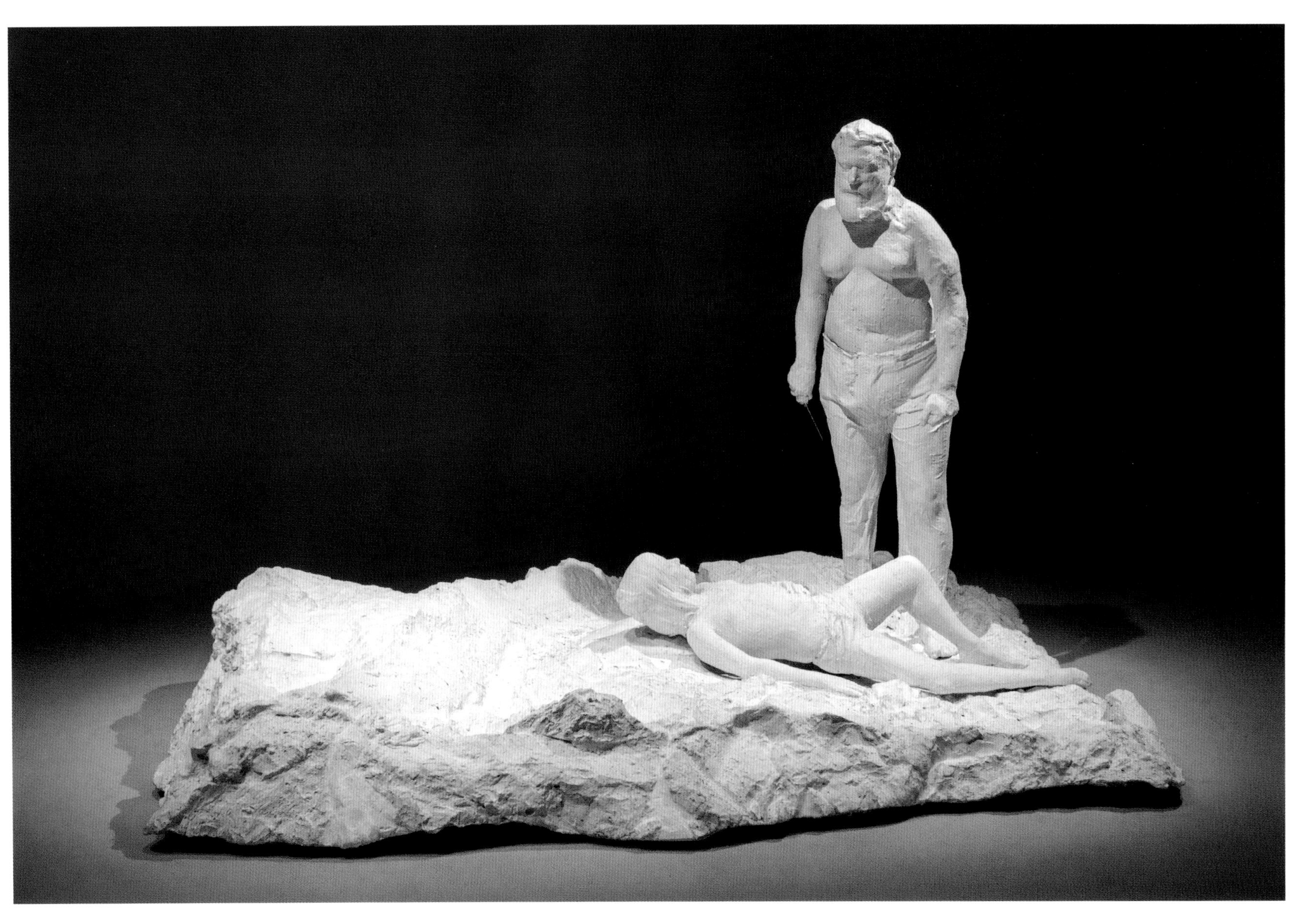

George Segal
1924, New York, NY, United States–
2000, South Brunswick, NJ, United States
The Sacrifice of Isaac, 1973
Plaster, 74 13⁄16 × 104 5⁄16 × 126 in. (190 × 265 × 320 cm)

Gift of the Tel Aviv Literature and Art Foundation, 1977

George Segal's sculpture *The Sacrifice of Isaac* depicts the figures of Abraham and Isaac at the climactic moment. Installed on a rocklike plaster base, Abraham's figure is alert, his arms outstretched, with the right hand holding a kitchen knife in place of the biblical slaughtering knife, and the left hand balled into a fist. He gazes down at Isaac, who lies prone at his feet. The sculpture freezes the moment, anticipating the decisive act.

The work, originally commissioned by the Tel Aviv Literature and Art Foundation for a project to install public sculpture throughout the city, was made in homage to Segal's father, who was fond of Bible stories. In May 1973, the sculpture was exhibited for the first time in the plaza of Tel Aviv's Mann Auditorium.

Segal, an American artist associated with the Pop movement, became known for his life-size white plaster sculptures, and in particular for his multifigured compositions that concurrently capture a contemporary moment and engage the tradition of classical sculpture. The decision to create sculptures from plaster—a material generally used for molds rather than the final work—exposes them to the ravages of time, indicating their physical and metaphorical fragility.

Five months after the sculpture's installation, the Yom Kippur War (1973) broke out, inevitably charging the work with political and social significance. The image of the Binding of Isaac came to signify the wounds of war. The sight of the father about to sacrifice his son was likened to families sacrificing their sons in battle, an analogy that struck a raw nerve. In 1978, Segal made an additional version of this plaster sculpture—which he cast in bronze—as part of his mission to commemorate the violent responses of the US government to the anti-Vietnam War protests that swept college campuses. In both versions, Segal's *The Sacrifice of Isaac* inflected intergenerational struggles around war's constancy in the twentieth century.

Segal's models for the sculpture were his friend, the prominent Israeli artist Menashe Kadishman, and his son, Ben Kadishman, who later made a sculpture of the same scene, installed in the Museum's entrance plaza. Created in the context of the 1982 Lebanon War, Kadishman's sculpture presents a reversal between Isaac and the ram (which in the Bible story was sacrificed instead of him): in his version, the sons are soldiers who are killed in battle, with no ram to save them.

Tal Broitman

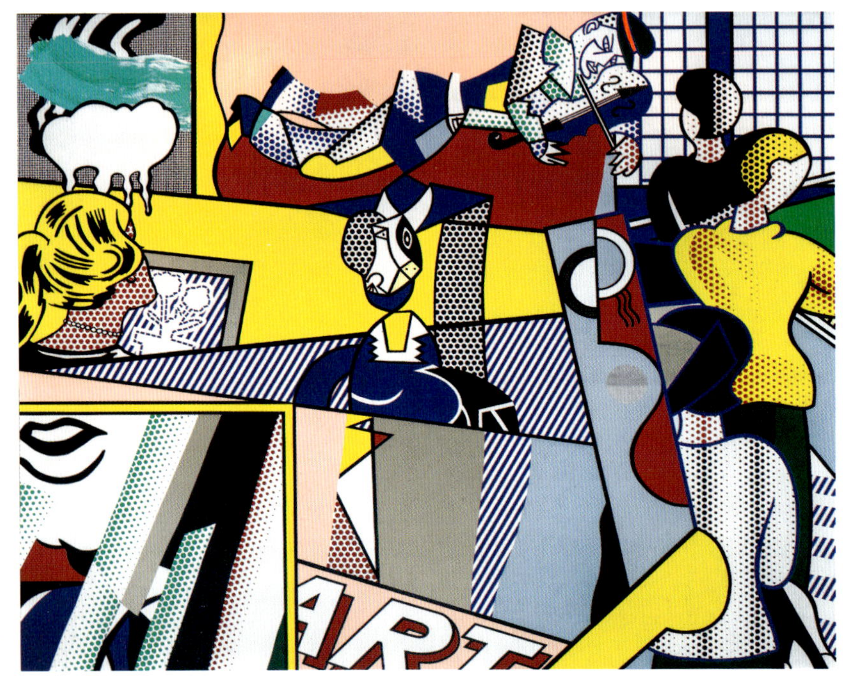
ART

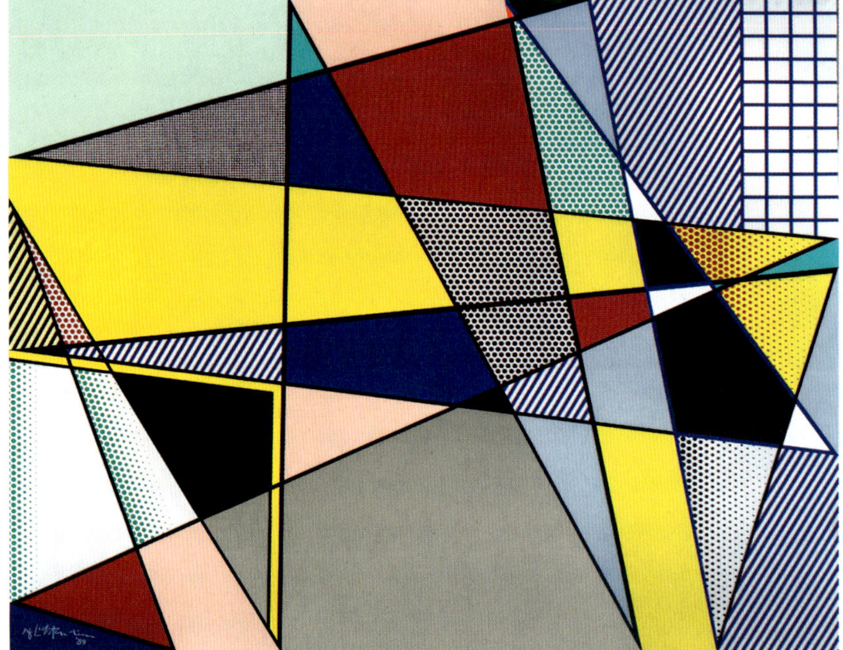

Roy Lichtenstein
1923–1997, New York, NY, United States
Tel Aviv Museum, Mural, 1989
Oil-based acrylic (Magna) on canvas, two panels, each 275 9⁄16 × 330 11⁄16 in. (700 × 840 cm)

Gift of the artist, realization sponsored by McCrory Corporation, an affiliate of Riklis Family Corporation, New York, 1989

American Pop artist Roy Lichtenstein visited the Tel Aviv Museum for the first time in 1987, for the opening of an exhibition dedicated to his drawings. The Museum's director at the time, Marc Scheps, took the opportunity to invite him to create a mural for the main lobby, to which Lichtenstein responded enthusiastically. In April 1989, the artist and several assistants arrived in Tel Aviv and completed the painting over the course of a month.

Tel Aviv Museum, Mural is a diptych, whose two parts are separated by an exposed concrete column—a Brutalist element that characterizes the interior of the Museum's main building. The mural is made in the artist's signature style that he developed in the 1960s—prominent black contours, Benday dots, and stripes in saturated colors—influenced by mid-century print media, including comic strips and advertisements. The right side of the diptych is an abstract composition based on the architectural layout of the Museum's interior, manifested in diagonals that represent the ramp located opposite the mural, and squares that reference the ceiling. In addition, Lichtenstein quotes from his series of paintings *Perfect/Imperfect* begun in 1985—abstract compositions made of lines that form intersecting polygons and triangles, filled with color, lines, and dots.

The diagonals and squares reappear in the figurative part of the diptych, at left, alongside images drawn from art history, which Lichtenstein appropriated and translated into his personal style. In the upper part hovers Marc Chagall's (pp. 148–53) iconic fiddler, while the figures rising up with their backs to the viewer are based on a work Lichtenstein made the year before as a tribute to a 1932 painting by Bauhaus artist Oskar Schlemmer. The central figure was extracted from a 1962 painting by Lichtenstein based on a 1942 painting by Pablo Picasso (pp. 124–31), and the geometric element surmounting one of the figures to the right references a work by Alexander Archipenko in the Museum's collection: *Kneeling Woman* (1916–17). Additional quotations from his own works include a female figure facing a painting, an empty speech bubble, a turquoise brushstroke, and the single word in the mural: "ART."[1]

Nathalie Andrijasevic

1 Lichtenstein planned to add the word *ciao* in Hebrew letters (צ'או) to the speech bubble but ultimately decided to leave it blank to make it more universally comprehensible.

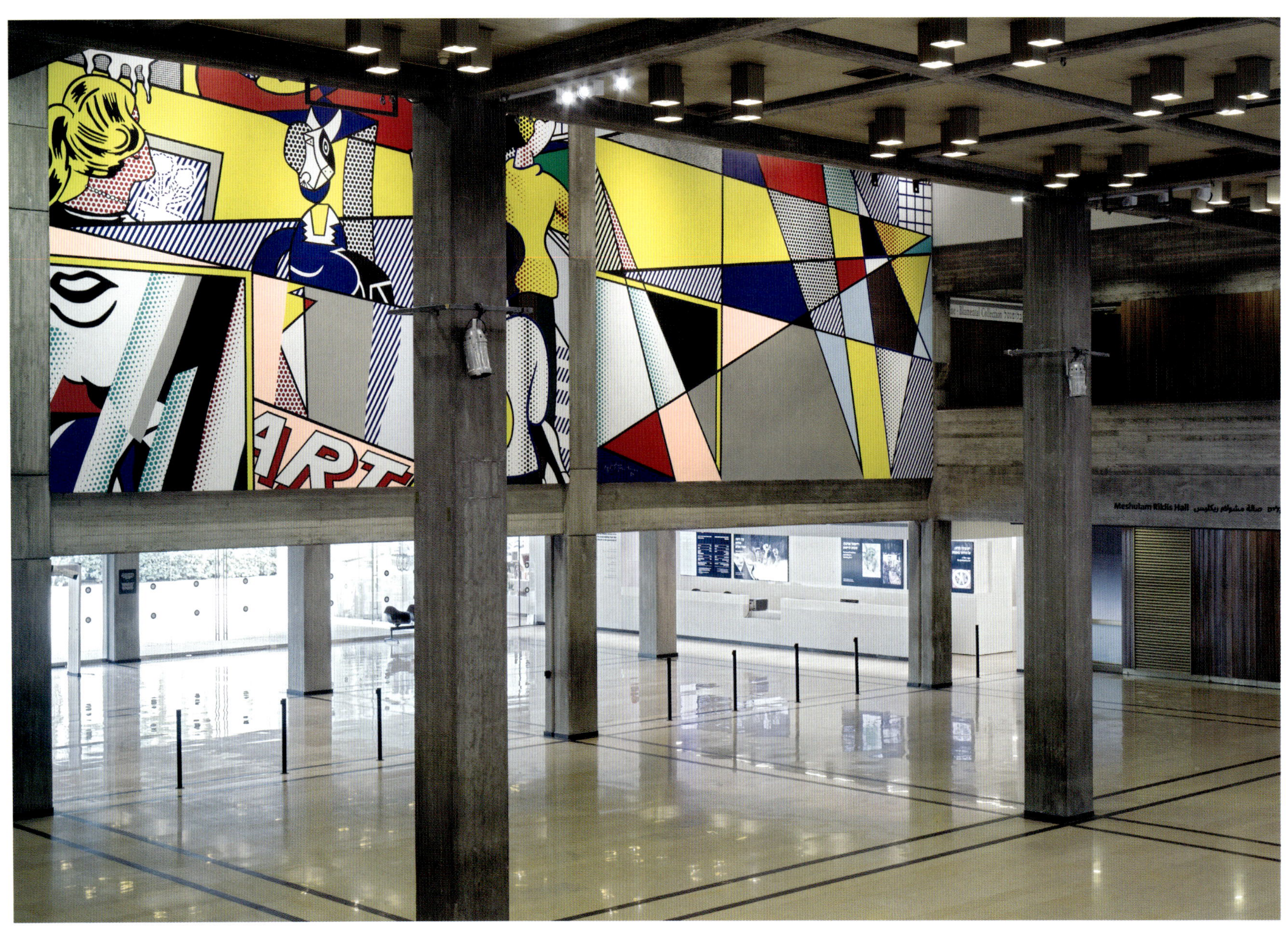

View of Lichtenstein's *Tel Aviv Museum, Mural* in the Paulson Family Foundation Building, Entrance Hall

Author Bios

Montse Aguer Teixidor is the Director of the Dalí Museums. She recently curated the exhibition *Dalí: The Christ of Portlligat* (2023–24). Additionally, she contributed to the book *Why Dalí?: Enigma as Provocation in Art*.

Nathalie Andrijasevic is Assistant Curator of Modern Art at the Tel Aviv Museum of Art. She curated *To Catch a Fleeting Moment: 150 Years of Impressionism* and contributed to the organization of *Alberto Giacometti: Beginning, Again* (2023); *My Name is Maryan* (2022); *The Building: 50 Years* (2021); and *Hey! Did you know that Art does not exist… The Sylvio Perlstein Collection: From Dada to Now* (2021).

Charlotte Barat-Mabille is Curator at the Musée d'Art Moderne de Paris. She recently curated the Nicolas de Staël retrospective at the MAM Paris, and contributed to the organization of the exhibition *Henri Matisse: The Red Studio* at the Museum of Modern Art, New York.

Naama Bar-Or is Assistant Curator of Prints and Drawings at the Tel Aviv Museum of Art. She recently curated the exhibition *Shalom Shebba: As a Matter of Fact* (2023–24) and wrote an essay for the accompanying exhibition catalogue, *Mehr Licht!* She also contributed to the organization of *The Last Photograph: Ran Tal After Micha Bar-Am* (2022).

Sophia Berry-Lifschitz is Assistant Curator of Photography at the Tel Aviv Museum of Art. She is currently working on an exhibition of the photographer Moi-Ver. She has also curated several displays from the TAMA collection, including *Amedeo Modigliani, Among Friends* (2021) and *A History of Beauty: Helena Rubinstein's Miniature Rooms* (2022).

Shua Ben-Ari is Curator and Head of the Younes & Soraya Nazarian Family Experiential Center at the Tel Aviv Museum of Art. She recently curated *So Moving. On Body Movement and Self-Expression* (2023) and *Rock, Textile, Scissors: Erela, Shemuel Katz, Ruth Zarfati* (Herzliya Museum of Contemporary Art, 2023).

Giampaolo Bianconi is Associate Curator of Modern and Contemporary Art at the Art Institute of Chicago.

Laura Braverman is Associate Curator at the Fondation Giacometti in Paris. She previously worked as a Curatorial Assistant at the Museum of Modern Art in New York, where she was part of the curatorial teams for the exhibitions *Sophie Taeuber-Arp: Living Abstraction* and *Joan Miró: Birth of the World*.

Tal Broitman is Coordinator of the Israeli Art Department at the Tel Aviv Museum of Art. He recently directed the George Segal conservation project and contributed to the exhibitions *Shmini Azeret* and *Material Imagination*, the new display of the Israeli art collection.

Emanuela Calò is Curator of Prints and Drawings and Curator of the Haim Shiff Prize for Figurative-Realist Art at the Tel Aviv Museum of Art. She is currently curating the forthcoming exhibition *War & Peace—50 Years of the Jerusalem Print Workshop.*

Dr. Ayelet Carmi is the Head of the Education Department at Beit Uri and Rami Nehoshtan Museum, Kibbutz Ashdot Yaakov Meuhad, Israel. Recent publications include "Sally Mann's Men: Thoughts about Photography, Black Masculinity and Ethics of Representation," in *Southern Studies: An Interdisciplinary Journal of the South* (forthcoming 2026), and "Wounded Men: Sally Mann's Photographs of Black Masculinity," in *Art, Masculinities, and Queerness since 1970* (2024).

Elizabeth C. Childs is the Etta and Mark Steinberg Professor of Art History at Washington University in Saint Louis, Missouri. Her major publications on Gauguin include *Vanishing Paradise: Art and Exoticism in Colonial Tahiti* (2013) and an online transcription and commentary on Gauguin's manuscript "L'Esprit Moderne et Le Catholicisme" (1902) in the collection of the Saint Louis Art Museum.

Masha Chlenova, Ph.D. is an independent curator and part-time Assistant Professor at Eugene Lang College, the New School, New York. She recently organized the exhibition *Encounters: Russian and Soviet Art Across the Borders, 1910–1990* for the Munchmuseet in Oslo. Scheduled to open in February 2023, its presentation became unthinkable following Russia's invasion of Ukraine.

Olga Cohen was Associate Curator of Israeli Art at the Tel Aviv Museum of Art.

Hila Cohen-Schneiderman is Chief Curator of MoBY—Museums of Bat Yam, Israel. She recently curated *World Chants*, a solo show of Eitan Ben Moshe, and her article "'Want of Matter:' the Whole Heart" was published in *Erev Rav 06 Magazine*.

Adi Dahan is Assistant Curator of Israeli Art at the Tel Aviv Museum of Art. She recently curated the group exhibition *Mouthful* (2023) and contributed to *Guy Ben Ner: Go Back Where U Came From* (2022).

Anat Danon-Sivan is Curator and Head of Prints and Drawings at the Tel Aviv Museum of Art. She recently curated *Ruth Schloss: Protests on the Horizon* (2022) and *David Ginton: The Name of the Painting* (2021).

Kira Dolinina is an art historian and art critic focusing on contemporary and modern art. She is currently pursuing a doctorate in the Department of Russian and Slavic Studies at the Hebrew University, Jerusalem.

Natalie Dupêcher is Associate Curator of Modern Art at the Menil Collection in Houston, Texas. She recently curated *Janet Sobel: All-Over* (2024) and *Meret Oppenheim: My Exhibition* (2021–23).

Ruth Feldmann is former Associate Curator of Modern Art at the Tel Aviv Museum of Art.

Starr Figura is Curator in the Department of Drawings and Prints at the Museum of Modern Art, New York. She recently curated *Käthe Kollwitz* (2024) and *Félix Fénéon: The Anarchist and the Avant-Garde* (2020).

Megan Fontanella is Curator, Modern Art and Provenance, at the Solomon R. Guggenheim Museum, New York. She co-edited *Vasily Kandinsky: Around the Circle* (2021) and organized the corresponding exhibition tour (2020–24), as well as the major tour and publication of the Guggenheim's Thannhauser Collection (2018–20).

Bregje Gerritse is a Researcher at the Van Gogh Museum. She curated the exhibitions *The Potato Eaters: Mistake or Masterpiece?* (Amsterdam, 2021–22) and *Van Gogh and the Avant-Garde: Along the Seine* (Chicago and Amsterdam, 2023–24), and edited both exhibition catalogues. She is currently a PhD candidate at the University of Amsterdam.

Alison M. Gingeras is an independent curator and art historian. She recently curated *My Name is Maryan* at the Tel Aviv Museum of Art (2022) and *Pictures Girls Make: Portraitures* at Blum Gallery in Los Angeles (2023).

Roman Grigoryev is former Curator of Netherlandish Prints (1992–2022) and Head of the Western Print Room (1998–2022) at the State Hermitage Museum, Saint Petersburg, Russia. He recently contributed the essay "Rembrandt Seen Through Jewish Eyes" to *Rembrandt Seen Through Jewish Eyes: The Artist's Meaning to Jews from His Time to Ours* (2024). This publication is all that remains of an exhibition planned for the Moscow Jewish Museum in 2023, which was never realized due to the outbreak of the war.

Karen Grimson is Curator and Director of Cultural Programming at the Miami Design District, where she recently curated the exhibitions *Pedro Perez: Back the Same Day* (2023) and *Still There Are Seeds to Be Gathered* (2023).

Irith Hadar is the former Head Curator of Prints and Drawings at the Tel Aviv Museum of Art (2006–20). She recently curated *More than One: The Eighth Biennale for Drawing in Israel* (2022–23).

Lauren Hinkson is Associate Curator for Collections at the Solomon R. Guggenheim Museum, New York. She recently curated the exhibitions *Jenny Holzer* (2023) and *Etel Adnan: Light's New Measure* (2021–22).

Tobias Hoffmann is Director of the Bröhan Museum, Berlin State Museum for Art Nouveau, Art Deco and Functionalism. He is the curator of several recent exhibitions and author of their respective exhibition catalogues: *Hej Rup. The Czech Avant-Garde* (2023–24), *Lucia Moholy. Das Bild der Moderne* (2022–23), and *Braun 100: Design Gestaltung Kunst Haltung* (2021).

Jacobé Huet is Assistant Professor of Modern Architectural History at the University of Chicago. Her writing has appeared in the *Journal of the Society of Architectural Historians* and *Muqarnas: An Annual on the Visual Cultures of the Islamic World*, among other publications.

Ya'ara Keydar is a fashion historian and curator. She recently curated *Alber Elbaz: The Dream Factory* (2023) and *The Ball: Fashion & Escapism* (2022) at Design Museum Holon, and edited the accompanying exhibition catalogues. She is currently a PhD candidate at Hebrew University.

Talia Kwartler, PhD, is a curator and art historian based in Berlin. Her first book, *Suzanne Duchamp par elle-même* (2023), was recently published by the Fondation Giacometti and Fage Éditions.

Galit Landau-Epstein is Associate Curator of Contemporary Art at the Tel Aviv Museum of Art. She recently curated *Roni Taharlev: Not this Light, the Other Light* (2023–24) and *A History of Beauty: Helena Rubinstein's Miniature Rooms* (on permanent view), and co-curated *Annette Messager Desires, Disorders* (2022).

Tal Lanir is Curator of Special Exhibitions at the Tel Aviv Museum of Art. She recently curated the exhibition *Illustrations: David Polonksy* and authored the first monograph on Polonsky. She also organized *24 Frames per Second*, a survey exhibition on Israeli animation.

Dr. Jill Lloyd is an independent art historian and curator. She recently curated *Munch Lebenslandschaft* (Museum Barberini Potsdam, 2023–24) and *Paula Modersohn-Becker* (Neue Galerie New York and the Art Institute of Chicago, 2024).

Shahar Molcho is Associate Curator at the Tel Aviv Museum of Art. She recently curated *Ilya & Emilia Kabakov: Tomorrow We Fly* (2023), and co-curated *Calder: Great Yellow Sun* (2021). Molcho contributed to the organization of *Yayoi Kusama: A Retrospective* (2021) and *Jeff Koons: Absolute Value* (2020).

Eliad Moreh-Rosenberg is Chief Curator, Museums Division, Yad Vashem in Jerusalem. She recently co-curated the exhibition *Responsibility for Memory: The Role of Art in Holocaust Remembrance* at the UN Headquarters, New York. She is currently curating the exhibition *Faith and Defiance: Creating Art during the Holocaust* (forthcoming 2026, Detroit Institute of Arts).

Alexandra Morrison is Curatorial Assistant in the Department of Painting and Sculpture at the Museum of Modern Art, New York. She recently contributed to the organization of *Picasso in Fontainebleau*.

Ksenia Nouril, a scholar of modern and contemporary Eastern European art, is the Gallery Director and Curator at the Art Students League of New York. Her recent exhibition and book projects include *A Brand New End: Survival and Its Pictures* with the artist Carmen Winant and *Ilya Kabakov and Viktor Pivovarov: Stories About Ourselves.*

Mordechai Omer was Director and Chief Curator of the Tel Aviv Museum of Art (1995–2011).

Alisa Padovano-Friedman is Provenance Researcher in the Modern Art Department at the Tel Aviv Museum of Art. She was formerly Head of the Registration Department.

Levi Prombaum, PhD, is currently working as a Fulbright Postdoctoral Researcher at Hebrew University on a project about the demography of Israel's art collections. As a curator, Prombaum has worked for the Solomon R. Guggenheim Museum, MASS MoCA, and the Colby College Museum of Art.

Hillary Reder is Assistant Curator of Modern Art at the Tel Aviv Museum of Art. She curated *To Catch a Fleeting Moment: 150 Years of Impressionism* (2024) and contributed to the organization of *Alberto Giacometti: Beginning, Again* (2023).

Alla Rosenfeld, PhD, is Research Consultant for Russian and Eastern European Art, Merrill C. Berman Collection of the 20th Century Avant-Garde. Recent publications include *Brilliantly Eclectic: Natan Altman between Tradition and Modernity, 1910–1935* and *From the "Pale of Settlement" to Broadway: The Work of Boris Aronson from the Mid-1920s to the Early 1930s*, both published by the Merrill C. Berman Collection in 2022.

Raz Samira is Deputy Director and Chief Curator of the Eretz Israel Museum, Tel Aviv. She is former Head Curator of Photography at the Tel Aviv Museum of Art.

Dorothea Schöne is a Berlin-based art historian and curator, currently heading Kunsthaus Dahlem as Director and CEO. Notable recent exhibitions include *Hans Uhlmann* (2022), *Henrike Naumann* (2021), and *Unknown Political Prisoner* (2021). In 2023, she was guest curator for the Experimental Humanities Collaborative Network's traveling exhibition *To Be Named*.

Elena Schroll is an art historian and independent curator. Her recent projects include *Whose Expression? The Brücke Artists and Colonialism* (Brücke-Museum, Berlin, 2021–22) and *Making van Gogh. A German Love Story* (Städel Museum, Frankfurt, 2019–20).

Dr. Chana Schütz is former Curator and Director of Research at New Synagogue Berlin—Centrum Judaicum Foundation (1995–2022). She recently organized *Robert Capa: Berlin Summer 1945* in cooperation with the Robert Capa Archive at the International Center of Photography, New York (New Synagogue Berlin, 2020).

Amit Shemma is the Assistant to Chief Curator at the Tel Aviv Museum of Art. He recently curated *Into the Unknown* (2024), a screening project with works by Israeli video artists, and contributed to the exhibitions *Erwin Wurm: Away at Home* (2023) and *Urs Fischer: PLAY* (2022).

Anne Sibylle Schwetter is an art historian and curator at the Felix-Nussbaum-Haus/Museumsquartier Osnabrück, Germany. Currently, she is compiling the catalogue raisonné of Felix Nussbaum (forthcoming online 2024). Her recent exhibitions include *#nichtmuedewerden. Felix Nussbaum and Artistic Resistance Today* (2023–24), and *Nussbaum Unexpected—New Perspectives on the Felix Nussbaum Collection* (2020).

Joanne Snrech is Curator in Charge of Paintings at the Musée national Picasso-Paris. She recently curated the exhibitions *Jackson Pollock: The Early years* (Paris, 2024), *Picasso Celebration: The Collection in a New Light* (Paris, 2023), and *Picasso and Abstraction* (Royal Museums of Fine Arts of Belgium, Brussels, 2022).

Janis Staggs is Director of Curatorial and Manager of Publications at Neue Galerie New York. Staggs is curator of the exhibition *Klimt Landscapes* (2024) and is a contributing author to *Tracing Wiener Werkstätte Textiles: Viennese Textiles from the Cotsen Textile Traces Study Collection* (2023).

Gražina Subelytė is Associate Curator at the Peggy Guggenheim Collection in Venice. She recently curated the exhibitions *Surrealism and Magic: Enchanted Modernity* (2022) and *Rita Kernn-Larsen: Surrealist Paintings* (2017).

Herwig Todts is Senior Curator of Modern Art at the Royal Museum of Fine Arts in Antwerp. He directs the Ensor Research Project and is co-editor of the Brepols Publishers series *XIX: Studies in the Art and Visual Culture of the Nineteenth Century*. He recently co-curated *Fantastisch real: Belgische Moderne von Ensor bis Magritte* (2021, Kunsthalle München).

Dorit Yifat is former Curator of Modern and Contemporary Art at the Tel Aviv Museum of Art. She curated the exhibition *Asylum*, featuring the work of Julian Rosefeldt (Herzilya Museum of Art, 2016).

Artist Index

Photo Credits

Every effort has been made to trace the rights holders and to obtain their permission for the use of copyrighted material in this publication. The Museum apologizes for any errors or omissions and would be grateful to be notified of any corrections that should be incorporated in future reprints.

Copyright management: Yaffa Goldfinger, Visual Resources and Copyrights, Tel Aviv Museum of Art

Artists' Copyrights

© Adagp, Paris, 2024: 51, 52, 54, 90, 93, 94, 101, 135, 147, 148, 150–51, 152, 157, 172, 184, 191, 192, 224
© The Ansel Adams Publishing Rights Trust: 204
© The Josef and Anni Albers Foundation / Artists Rights Society (ARS), New York, 2024: 243
© 2024 Estate of Alexander Archipenko / Artists Rights Society (ARS), New York: 82, 85–89
© 2024 Artists Rights Society (ARS), New York / UPRAVIS, Moscow: 106, 109–11
© 2024 The Milton Avery Trust / Artists Rights Society (ARS), New York: 208
© The Estate of Francis Bacon. All rights reserved. DACS, 2024: 228
© Fondazione Palazzo Albizzini Collezione Burri, Città di Castello (Italy): 216
© 2024 Calder Foundation, New York / Artists Rights Society (ARS), New York: 241
© 2024 Estate of Leonora Carrington / Artists Rights Society (ARS), New York: 187
© Fondation Henri Cartier-Bresson / Magnum Photos: 222 (left)
© Fondazione Giorgio e Isa de Chirico: 171
© 2024 Center for Creative Photography, Arizona Board of Regents / Artists Rights Society (ARS), New York: 159
© Salvador Dalí, Fundació Gala-Salvador Dalí, VEGAP, Tel-Aviv, 2024: 181
© Fondation Foujita / Adagp, Paris, 2024: 136
© 2024 Helen Frankenthaler Foundation, Inc. / Artists Rights Society (ARS), New York: 215
© Lee Friedlander, courtesy Fraenkel Gallery, San Francisco and Luhring Augustine, New York: 232
© Succession Alberto Giacometti / Adagp, Paris, 2025: 220, 222 (right), 223
© The Estate of Eva Hesse. Courtesy Hauser & Wirth: 227
© Ellsworth Kelly Foundation: 244
© Estate Germaine Krull, Museum Folkwang, Essen: 175
© Estate of Roy Lichtenstein: 250, 252, and cover
© All rights reserved, Estate of Jacques Lipchitz: 132
© The Estate of Maryan: 231
© 2024 Maryland Institute College of Art (MICA), Rights Administered by Artist Rights Society (ARS), New York, All Rights Reserved: 212
© Ludwig Meidner-Archiv, Jüdisches Museum der Stadt Frankfurt: 66
© Successió Miró / Adagp, Paris, 2024: 196, 198
© The Henry Moore Foundation. All Rights Reserved, DACS: 162
© Giorgio Morandi, 2024: 219
© The Estate of Alice Neel: 207
© Stiftung Seebull Ada und Emile Nolde: 69
© 2024 Georgia O'Keeffe Museum / Artists Rights Society (ARS), New York: 160
© Pechstein Berlin / VG Bild-Kunst, Bonn, 2024: 116, 118
© Succession Picasso, 2024: 125, 126, 129, 130
© 2024 The Pollock-Krasner Foundation / Artists Rights Society (ARS), New York: 201–203
© Gerhard Richter, 2023 (17042023): 234
© Bridget Riley, 2024. All rights reserved: 238 (both)
© A. Rodchenko & V. Stepanova Archive: 154
© 1998 Kate Rothko Prizel & Christopher Rothko / Artists Rights Society (ARS), New York: 211
© 2024 The George and Helen Segal Foundation / Licensed by VAGA at Artists Rights Society (ARS), New York: 248
© 2024 Estate of Yves Tanguy / Artists Rights Society (ARS), New York: 182
© VG Bild-Kunst, Bonn, 2024: 98, 115, 116 (all), 166, 237
© 2024 The Andy Warhol Foundation for the Visual Arts, Inc. / Licensed by Artists Rights Society (ARS), New York: 246 (all)

Photography Credits

Avi Amsalem: 63
Keren Goldsmith, Tel Aviv Museum of Art: 47
Avraham Hai, Tel Aviv Museum of Art: 148, 250
Yigal Pardo: Cover, 41, 43, 58, 61, 66, 69, 110, 115, 159, 160, 165, 175, 182, 198, 204, 227, 232
Margarita Perlin, Tel Aviv Museum of Art: 23, 25, 31, 52, 57, 90, 122, 123, 135, 140, 143, 144, 147, 166, 168, 178, 187, 191, 207, 211, 212, 215, 216, 219 (both), 220, 228, 231, 234, 237, 244
Elad Sarig: 15, 18, 21, 24, 27, 29, 32, 34, 44, 51, 54, 65, 74, 77, 79 (both), 81, 82, 85, 86 (both), 87 (both), 88, 89, 93, 94, 97, 101, 104, 106, 111, 118, 121, 125, 129, 130, 132, 139, 152 (both), 157, 162, 171, 172, 176, 181, 184, 188 (both), 192, 195, 196, 208, 223, 224, 241, 243, 248, 252
Courtesy of the Tel Aviv Museum of Art: 6–7, 17, 26, 37, 38, 48, 71, 73, 98, 102, 112, 116 (all), 126, 136, 150–51, 154, 201, 202, 203, 222 (both), 238 (both), 246 (all)

First published in the United States of America
in 2025 by

Rizzoli Electa
A Division of Rizzoli International Publications, Inc.
49 West 27th Street
New York, NY 10001
www.rizzoliusa.com

In association with
Tel Aviv Museum of Art
27 Shaul HaMelech Boulevard
Tel Aviv
www.tamuseum.org.il

For Rizzoli Electa
Publisher: Charles Miers
Associate Publisher: Margaret Rennolds Chace
Senior Editor: Ellen R. Cohen
Production Manager: Alyn Evans
Managing Editor: Lynn Scrabis

For Tel Aviv Museum of Art
Editor: Hillary Reder

Design by Jesse Kidwell

ISBN: 978-0-8478-4322-0
Library of Congress Control Number: 2024944584

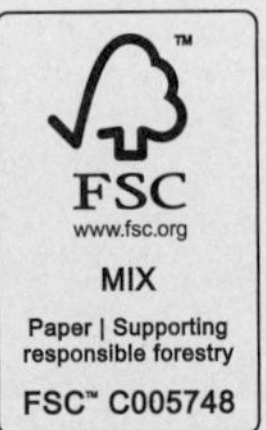

Printed in China

2025 2026 2027 2028 / 10 9 8 7 6 5 4 3 2 1

This publication is made possible by the Paulson Family Foundation

PAULSON
FAMILY
FOUNDATION